VIETNAM VERDICT

JOSEPH A. AMTER

VIETNAM VERDICT

A CITIZEN'S HISTORY

CONTINUUM · NEW YORK

1982

The Continuum Publishing Company
575 Lexington Avenue, New York, N.Y. 10022

Printed in the United States of America

Library of Congress Cataloging in Publication Data

Amter, Joseph A.
  Vietnam verdict.

  Bibliography: p. 385
  Includes index.
  1. Vietnamese Conflict, 1961–1975—United
States. 2. United States—History—1961–1975.
3. United States—History—1969–   . I. Title.
DS558.A48   1982   959.704'33'73   82-8274
ISBN 0-8264-0193-7

The maps on pp. xxii–xxiii are reproduced, with permission, from *The Ten Thousand Day War: Vietnam 1945–1975* by Michael Maclear, copyright © 1981 by Michael Maclear, St. Martin's Press, Inc., New York.

To Vietnam Veterans of America
and so many others whose lives
were shattered by a needless war.

CONTENTS

Part Four: The Vietnam Disaster

FOREWORD

One must recall one of the great traditions of American life. That is the tradition of informed, dedicated, and independently minded men and women, who are not satisfied with the government and its workings, and are not willing to see the future of their country monopolized and controlled purely by politicians and bureaucrats. In the international sphere these men and women feel that peace is far too serious a business to be left to diplomats and presidential advisers; independent emissaries for peace are needed.

The roots of this tradition go deeper than perhaps we realize. The gentleman is not a gentleman because he is gentle or a man of manners, but because he is a *gentis homo,* a man who is dedicated to the people and the polity because he wishes to serve them. The essence here is the concept of service, as opposed to the concept of status and privilege through hereditary right. To the extent that this tradition flourishes, the United States avoids the burden of a permanent elite; to the extent that men and women of concern, commitment, and service question the elite of the day, they live in and honor the tradition.

This tradition lives side by side and flourishes with the basic freedom of speech and enquiry, the right to seek out information at home and abroad and to question, and the right to dissent. So long as these freedoms and rights flourish, the United States is a healthy and sturdy society; when they languish, the nation suffers. When her political leaders seek to undermine and trivialize dissent, when they have so little regard for the American people that they assault them with misrepresentation, when they treat the truth with contempt, when they defy the law, they undermine the very health of the nation. They also undermine the idea of the United States as a sanctuary, a haven from persecution, and as a great and responsible power committed to the values of Western civilization.

Unfortunately, and tragically, the story of the U.S. involvement in Vietnam addresses these concerns. They must be set alongside the seemingly legitimate pursuit of what some saw as a vital national interest and the horror of war, alongside the initial, modest involvement and the ultimate massive cost in lives and resources, alongside the defensible intentions and the actual waste and failure. The Vietnam conflict became one in the long history of assaults on the people of Southeast Asia, and to some it seemed like an assault on the people of the United States. The long U.S. involvement in Vietnam challenged some of the most fundamental bonds which unite America.

Some participants and historians will inevitably seek prescriptions to gloss over the Vietnam imperfections. The author of *Vietnam Verdict* has written "A Citizen's History" so that his readers may become aware of the facts and to assist them in their efforts to avoid a repetition of the errors of Vietnam.

The story bears retelling, therefore, in its entirety, to educate, and, perhaps above all else, to alert and to warn. In the broader sense, it appears that the author of *Vietnam Verdict* warns against the view that there is no possibility of accomodation and accord with the Soviet Union, against Cold War mentalities, against those doctrinaires who seek a crusade against Communism and other alien ideologies, believing, as he does, that such crusades merely strengthen what we fear. The author is concerned about the absence of a sense of the limits of United States power, and is against the use of military power as the only way to solve international problems, while neglecting negotiation and compromise. He is against another Vietnam.

These are the elements, he believes, that may create the possibility of a nuclear war. In the final analysis, we must recognize that if we fear to let the people of the world choose in freedom their own economic and political systems, we are, in the most telling way, declaring our loss of faith in ourselves.

The author is a citizen who believes that the United States has "a grandeur of spirit and a morality of purpose." His confidence in her is undimmed and he remains committed to the values she exemplifies. He has written this book from the best motives as an act of public service. He asks a similarly concerned public to weigh the evidence on Vietnam, to ponder the lessons of the war, and to think about present policies and future dangers.

Michael Fry
University of Southern California

AUTHOR'S NOTE

Our world faces a crisis as yet unperceived by those
possessing the power to make great decisions for good
or evil. The unleashed power of the atom has changed
everything save our modes of thinking, and thus we
drift toward unparalleled catastrophe.

—*Albert Einstein*

Most Americans today realize that the Vietnam War *was* a mistake
and that it *was* immoral. Few of them, however, have been furnished
with enough facts to understand the foreign policy that led to our
involvement in the war. Few are aware of what really happened both
here and in Southeast Asia, and few know who was responsible for
the decisions that were made.

Some historians tend to gloss over the imperfections of U.S.
actions in Vietnam. Books written by the actors—government officials and military men who were personally involved in the decisions—tend to present only facts that justify their own behavior.
Fortunately, we now have access to an enormous amount of material
on the Vietnam War, some of it recently declassified. Many writers
and research analysts have delved into this material, and with no axe
to grind, they tell it like it was.

In order to understand the true significance of Vietnam, we need
to look at the full picture rather than at pieces of the jigsaw. Yet in
surveying all the literature on our twenty-eight-year Vietnam involvement, I have found no document or book that tells what really
happened there, analyzes who was responsible for each action, and
traces how that act affected subsequent events. Seeing that this kind
of overviewing was lacking, I set out to supply it. Years of concentrated effort and research have gone into the narrative now presented
in *Vietnam Verdict*.

Almost twenty years ago I became concerned about the fact that one man, the President of the United States, had been given the power to "press the nuclear button." Thus the fate of my children and grandchildren, the country, and perhaps the world might be in the hands of a recently installed politician. Other safeguards now exist, yet the danger of a nuclear holocaust has increased. The Federation of American Scientists sums up the problem we face: "For the 1980s and beyond, the question will not be how much of the country is destroyed in nuclear war, but how much is left and even whether a functioning country will emerge."[1]

In the early 1960s, although I was at the height of my career as a lawyer and banker, I decided that it was my responsibility as a citizen to help find a way to prevent World War III. I became one of the founders of the Peace Research Organization Fund (PROF), whose membership consisted of educators, foreign policy specialists, scientists, and others who had the same interest in preventing nuclear war. PROF's purpose was to support scientific research into the conditions needed to create and preserve world peace. For years I served as executive director of this organization.

I participated in many foreign policy symposiums and in a conference sponsored by the Industrial College of the Armed Forces. I traveled widely, visited the capitals of most major nations, and discussed foreign policy with political leaders and academics both abroad and in the United States. I found that there was increasing concern about the consequences of covert U.S./CIA Cold War containment activities.

In the spring of 1964, I decided to try and gather firsthand information from the Soviet Union. The State Department encouraged me to go there, on the chance that the Soviets might talk more freely to a private citizen. In Russia I discussed foreign policy with prominent citizens and officials to whom I had access. I was presented to Nikita Khrushchev, the Russian premier, and his wife, who was head of the Soviet-American Friendship Committee. Madame Khrushchev asked me to talk with the editors of *Pravda*, the official government newspaper.

On the following day I was directed to *Pravda* headquarters, where I met with many of its senior editors. It seemed to them, said the men around the conference table, that President Johnson was preparing for open military intervention in Vietnam. An editor explained that the Soviet Union had a mutual assistance treaty with North Vietnam, as did the Chinese. If the United States sent military forces into Vietnam, both the Russians and the Chinese could be drawn into the conflict, which could lead to World War III. The Russians were not eager to be caught up in a war with the Chinese as their allies. In fact, they had an identical interest with the United States in preventing China from expanding into all of Asia.

The *Pravda* group said that the Kremlin had attempted to arrange a summit conference through official channels. This move had failed, as had the efforts of the United Nations, France, and other interested countries. The editors suggested that perhaps I, as a private citizen, might get this message to President Johnson on a personal basis and thereby obtain his consent.

I did deliver their message when I returned to Washington, but I was told that the President had no interest in a summit meeting. Apparently the steamroller pushing toward war in Vietnam had gone too far to stop.

Later that year I accepted the President's invitation to become co-chairman of the White House Conference on International Cooperation. It was "the assignment of the century," as Johnson told the citizens whom he asked to participate. I began to commute regularly from my home in Denver to Washington. There I shared an office in the State Department with Adlai Stevenson, who was then ambassador to the United Nations. I also had access to the White House.

As heads of the conference, Vice President Hubert Humphrey was named the government's chairman, and Robert S. Benjamin (then president of the United Nations Association of the U.S.A.) was appointed chairman for the private sector. Since their time was limited, it was my task to assist in establishing the operational structure. I also chaired one of the national citizens' committees that did the work of the conference.

Over 150 Americans, leaders of almost every important part of the private sector, agreed to participate. The President urged them to "search, explore, examine and discuss every conceivable approach and avenue of cooperation that could lead to peace."

Since this was the theme, it appeared that the most important function of the conference should be to "search, explore, examine and discuss" every avenue that could lead to peace in Vietnam. Although the Vietnam War seemed inevitable, there was little high-

xiv : Author's Note

level debate as to whether it was justified or how it could be stopped. I proposed to Robert Benjamin that my committee focus on the issue of Vietnam. He agreed to present my proposal to the powers that be. In response, he told me later, he received a directive from the White House that the subject of Vietnam was not to be discussed in the conference at any time or in any manner.

Puzzled and disturbed, I went to see Vice President Humphrey. "Joe," he said, "the President has made up his mind. Anyone on his team who disagrees will be put on the bench." I replied that I still felt strongly about it and wanted to talk to the President. The next evening I received a message to meet Humphrey at the White House at ten o'clock in the morning. The Vice President escorted me to a conference room, where the President joined me in the foyer. There the following monologue took place:

> Joe [with a slap on the back], mighty glad to see you again. Hubert tells me that you still want me to talk to the Russians, or at least to discuss Vietnam at our White House Conference. Joe, there is nothing to talk about at this time. My generals, who are entrusted with the defense of this country, tell me that if we don't stop the Commies in Vietnam, they will take over all of Asia, and next time it will be us. I intend to teach those slant-eyed yellow bastards a lesson, and then those Russians and Chinese Commies will know they can't get away with it. Then I'll talk to them.

After this meeting I had no alternative but to give up my desire to have the Vietnam problem discussed at the White House conference. Instead, I and my committee of forty members prepared a report on the assigned topic of "Research on the Development of International Institutions."

The other national citizens' committees that made up the conference were chaired by leaders in a wide range of professions, academic disciplines, and sectors of American business. For example, Isidor I. Rabi, the distinguished atomic scientist, headed the Committee on Peaceful Uses of Atomic Energy; Charles S. Rhyne, president of the World Peace Through Law Center, chaired the Committee on Development of International Law; Andrew W. Cordier, dean of the Graduate School of International Affairs at Columbia University, led the Committee on Peacekeeping Operations; Jerome Wiesner, dean of the School of Science at M.I.T., the Committee on Arms Control and Disarmament; Norman Cousins, the noted editor and writer, the Committee on Culture and Intellectual Exchange; James F. Collins, president of the National Red Cross, the Committee on Disaster Relief; and Louis B. Sohn, professor of international law at Harvard, the Committee on Human Rights.

All the committees labored mightily to prepare reports that could be useful in the cause of international cooperation. The White House Conference, held November 28 to December 1, 1965, was widely publicized and attended by citizens who came from all over America. But in obedience to the President's orders, Vietnam was never mentioned. My address for my own committee came as close to the subject as I felt I could:

> There is a critical need to proceed not inch by inch but by barracuda bites if we are to make meaningful progress in the important areas of international affairs before it is too late. . . . We cannot lessen our efforts to resolve the great political conflicts which dominate the headlines. . . .
>
> Our report documents the fact that our government is not adequately attempting to find a solution for these critical foreign policy practical problems. If we are to find a cure for that malignant disease—international conflict—we must mobilize our intellectual resources in an effort to solve the problems that lead to war.
>
> Of necessity, we spend hundreds of billions of dollars in an ever-increasing amount to buy military hardware for defense, and billions more for research and development on how best to destroy an enemy who refuses to cooperate. But we don't even spend pennies to "search, explore, canvass and thoroughly discuss every conceivable approach and avenue of cooperation that can lead to peace." Besides, searching for peace doesn't gain any headlines, get you elected, or keep you in office.

I left the conference sick at heart, since far from ending, the Vietnam War continued to escalate. News from Washington consisted mainly of misinformation and half-truths. There was a breath of hope when Richard Nixon went to China seeking assistance in ending the war and found that Chinese Communists, at least, were not so bad. Thus the man who had been in the forefront of the long Cold War against the People's Republic now engineered a rapprochement. Few people seemed to wonder why peace with the Chinese could not have been achieved many years earlier, when it would have saved millions of lives in Southeast Asia and billions of dollars for the United States.

Later I too visited China and found a united people struggling to develop their nation. Chinese officials expressed great satisfaction with our country's new attitude, for China had everything to lose and nothing to gain from the Cold War. They had always wanted friendship with the United States, they told me, but it had not been possible while our government was encouraging Chiang Kai-shek's ambitions to reconquer the Chinese mainland.

In spite of his reconciliation with Communist China, however, it became clear that President Nixon remained an unrepentant Cold Warrior and still needed a Communist enemy. This enemy now became the Soviet Union, even though Nixon had participated in a summit conference in Moscow shortly after the Peking summit. During the Moscow conference the Russians had shown themselves even more anxious than the United States to develop friendly relations and coexistence. They explained that they too had nothing to gain from a continuing Cold War and had no designs on any U.S. territories. The President, however, turned a deaf ear. As for Vietnam, it was soon evident that Nixon regarded this small country as only the first battleground of World War III.[2]

Under Richard Nixon's successors too, the Cold War continues unabated and the hate campaign is still directed at Russian Communists rather than Chinese ones. Containment policies that triggered the war in Vietnam are now being considered for other areas of the world. Ronald Reagan has characterized Vietnam as "a noble war," yet he demonstrates only a faint recollection of what really happened there.[3] Other defenders of our role in Vietnam, such as Norman Podhoretz, editor of *Commentary*, continue to castigate the war's critics:

> Nothing is easier to refute than the *moral* case against the American intervention in Vietnam. Indeed, so preposterous was the diabolization of the American role in Vietnam—it was exceeded only by the beatification of the Communists—that Johnson and his people might well have been contemptuous of it simply on the merits. Why dignify such charges with a Presidential reply? Surely it was self-evident that the United States was doing the right thing in trying to save South Vietnam from Communism.[4]

It is easy to understand why the proponents of Cold War policy would like the American people to forget Vietnam, or to feel as good about it as possible. What they ignore is the fact that Vietnam, if repeated, might lead to a nuclear confrontation with the Soviets.

Throughout the book I have attempted to state facts and interpret them without giving my personal opinion, expressing only conclusions derived from legitimate research and consultation. In the Epilogue, however, I will take off my gloves and state my own opinions. I will then ask you, the reader, to give your final judgment as to how the lessons we have learned in Vietnam should influence subsequent U.S. foreign policy.

Acknowledgments

Many individuals assisted me during the long years of research and writing. I could not do justice to all of them in this brief space, but they know how much I appreciate the inspiration and assistance they gave me.

I will give special mention, then, to some who rendered invaluable services over a period of time: Jack C. Steele, my chief research assistant, whose painstaking research and documentation of facts was truly remarkable; Jack K. Jamison, whose twenty years previous background as a member of the U.S. Air Force provided insight into the military action and air war; Phoebe Lawrence, who for years patiently weathered my dictation and with superb expertise typed, retyped, and copyedited the "tons" of material that was finally edited into its present dimensions; James Peck, who not only was a superb final editor but had a profound knowledge of the subject; Michael Fry, who while Dean of the Graduate School of International Studies at the University of Denver, with the assistance of colleagues and graduate students, rechecked and authenticated all of the material in the notes; and last but not least, my darling wife, Donna, who permitted me to spend the long hours and years that were required to complete this work.

CAST OF PRINCIPAL CHARACTERS

The following are some of the principals who had leading roles in the events occurring from the beginning of the U.S. involvement in 1945 through the Johnson administration. Some names were also principals thereafter but we do not repeat their names in the list that follows which covers the Nixon administration until the final defeat in 1975.

Lyndon Johnson and Before

Abrams, General Creighton. Commander, U.S. Forces, Vietnam, 1968–72.

Acheson, Dean. Secretary of State, 1949–53.

Ball, George. Under Secretary of State under President Johnson.

Bundy, McGeorge. Special Assistant for National Security Affairs, 1961–66.

Bundy, William. Assistant Secretary of Defense, 1961–64; Assistant Secretary of State, 1964–69.

Bunker, Ellsworth. U.S. Ambassador to South Vietnam, 1967–73.

Chiang Kai-shek. Ousted as ruler of Nationalist China by Mao Tse-tung in 1949, fled to Taiwan.

Chou En-Lai. Communist Chinese representative to Geneva Conference, 1954.

Clifford, Clark. Secretary of Defense, 1968–69.

Diem, Ngo Dinh. President, South Vietnam, 1955–63.

Dulles, Allen. Director of the CIA, 1953–62.

Dulles, John Foster. Secretary of State, 1953–59.

Eisenhower, Dwight David. President, United States, 1953–61.

Fulbright, J. William. U.S. Senator; Chairman, Senate Foreign Relations Committee during 1966 hearings.

Gruening, Ernest. U.S. Senator; critic of the Tonkin Gulf Resolution, 1964.

Ho Chi Minh. President, North Vietnam, 1945–69.

Humphrey, Hubert. Vice President, 1965–69.

Johnson, Lyndon Baines. President, United States, 1963–69.

Kennan, George. Former Ambassador to Soviet Union; testified at Fulbright Committee Hearings, 1966.

Kennedy, John Fitzgerald. President, United States, 1961–63.

Kennedy, Robert. Presidential candidate, 1968.

Khanh, General Nguyen. Premier, South Vietnam, 1964–65.

King, Rev. Martin Luther. Black leader; critic of Johnson's war in Vietnam, 1960s.

Kosygin, Alexei. Premier, Soviet Union during the U.S. buildup, 1965.

Ky, Marshall Nguyen Cao. Premier, South Vietnam, 1965–67.

Lansdale, Colonel Edward. Political advisor, South Vietnam, 1954–56; Special Assistant to U.S. Ambassador, South Vietnam, 1965–68.

Lodge, Henry Cabot. U.S. Ambassador to South Vietnam, 1963–64, 1965–67.

Mao Tse-tung. Leader of Communist forces that overthrew Chiang Kai-shek, 1949.

McCarthy, Eugene. U.S. Senator; presidential candidate, 1968.

McCarthy, Joseph. Architect of the McCarthy Era, 1940s–1950s.

McNamara, Robert. Secretary of Defense, 1961–68.

Morse, Wayne. U.S. Senator; critic of Tonkin Gulf Resolution, 1964.

Nixon, Richard Milhous. Vice President, 1953–61.

Roosevelt, Franklin Delano. President, United States, 1933–45.

Rostow, Walt. Special advisor to Kennedy and Johnson, 1961–69.

Rusk, Dean. Secretary of State, 1961–69.

Stevenson, Adlai. U.S. Ambassador to United Nations during Tonkin Gulf crisis, 1964.

Taylor, General Maxwell. Chairman, Joint Chiefs of Staff, 1962–64; U.S. Ambassador to South Vietnam, 1964–65; consultant to President, 1965–69.

Thieu, Nguyen Van. President, South Vietnam, 1967–75.

Truman, Harry S. President, United States, 1945–53.

U Thant. Secretary General of United Nations; backer of peace initiatives, 1965–73.

Van Minh, General Duong. Premier, South Vietnam, 1963–64.

Westmoreland, General William. Commander, U.S. Forces, Vietnam, 1964–68.

Wheeler, General Earle. Chairman, Joint Chiefs of Staff, 1964–70.

Richard Nixon and After

Brezhnev, Leonid. General Secretary, Communist Party, Soviet Union, during the 1972 Moscow Summit.

Colby, William. Director of the CIA, 1973–76.

Dobrinin, Anatoly. Russian Ambassador to U.S. during the 1972 Moscow Summit.

Ellsberg, Daniel. Consultant to Johnson and Nixon Administrations; leaked Pentagon Papers, 1971.

Ford, Gerald. President, United States, 1974–77.

Gromyko, Andrei. Foreign Minister, Soviet Union, during the 1972 Moscow Summit.

Haig, General Alexander. Deputy to Henry Kissinger, 1969–73.

Helms, Richard. Director of the CIA, 1966–73.

Kennedy, Edward. U.S. Senator; critic of Vietnam War, 1960s–1970s.

Kerry, John. Founder in 1967 of Vietnam Veterans Against the War.

Kissinger, Henry. Assistant to the President for National Security Affairs, 1969–75; Secretary of State, 1973–77.

Laird, Melvin. Secretary of Defense, 1969–73.

Lon Nol. Head of State, Commander in Chief, Cambodia, 1970–75.

Martin, Graham. U.S. Ambassador to South Vietnam, 1973–75.

McGovern, George. U.S. Senator; presidential candidate, 1972.

Nixon, Richard Milhous. President, United States, 1969–74.

Nosavan, Phoumi. Rival for leadership of Laos, 1950s–1960s.

Rogers, William. Secretary of State, 1969–73.

Sihanouk, Prince Norodum. Head of State, Cambodia, 1941–70.

Souphanouvong, Prince. Rival for leadership of Laos, 1950s–1970s; close ties to Pathet Lao.

Souvannaphouma, Prince. Rival for leadership of Laos, 1950s–1970s.

Tho, LeDuc. North Vietnam's chief negotiator at Paris Peace talks, 1969–73.

Van Minh, General Duong. Temporary successor to Thieu, 1975.

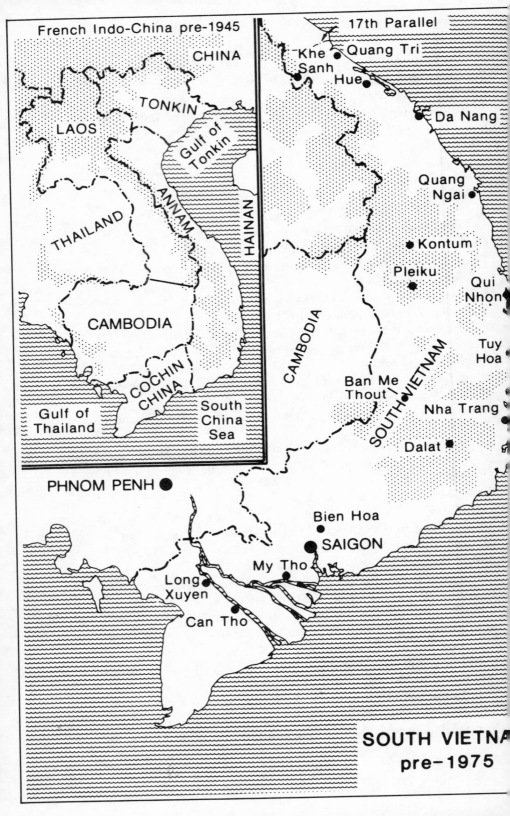

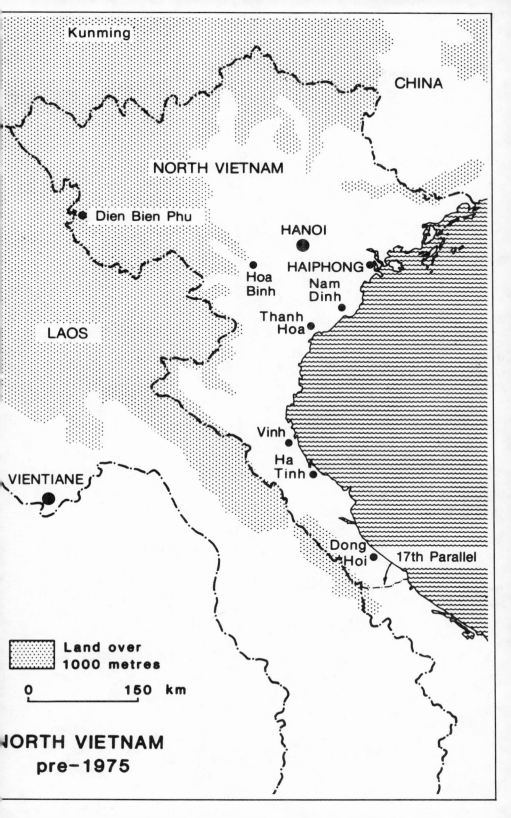

Kunming

CHINA

NORTH VIETNAM

Dien Bien Phu

HANOI

HAIPHONG

Hoa
Binh

Nam
Dinh

Thanh
Hoa

LAOS

Vinh

Ha
Tinh

VIENTIANE

Dong
Hoi

17th Parallel

Land over
1000 metres

0   150 km

NORTH VIETNAM
pre-1975

PART ONE

THE U.S./ VIETNAM INVOLVEMENT

:1

PRELUDE TO VIETNAM: ORIGINS OF THE COLD WAR

> The two systems [United States vs. USSR] are on a
> collision course. I can't tell you at what point they will
> collide, but given no change in direction in the Soviet
> way of doing things, and no change in direction of our
> way of doing things, there's bound to be an explosion
> down the line somewhere.
> —*Ambassador Thomas J. Watson*

The United States was deeply involved in Vietnam and Southeast
Asia for twenty-eight years, ten of them in active warfare—the longest war in U.S. history. We fought a war in Southeast Asia to prevent
a Communist "takeover" of South Vietnam and to prevent North and
South Vietnam from becoming a unified Communist state. All this
was a continuation of an American foreign policy known as the Cold
War. To understand what happened in Vietnam, we must also understand the Cold War.

America's antagonism toward Russia and Communism began in
1917 after the Bolshevik Revolution replaced the Emperor Nicholas
II's czarist government with a Communist regime. In 1918, the
United States dispatched troops, along with its Allies, to fight the
Bolsheviks and to support the forces opposing the revolution. The
United States also supported a movement to erect a virtual *cordon
sanitaire* around a territorially reduced Russia, and to establish well-
armed, pro-Western border states united in their fear of the Soviet
Union. The United States likewise advocated the maintenance of an
economic boycott and the isolation of the Soviet Union, diplomatically, economically, and socially, in the hope that the Russian people
would eventually overthrow the Communist regime. The seeds for
the subsequent Cold War had now been planted.

After winning the civil war, Lenin focused his attention on the economic misery of the Russian people. The Communist chairman attempted to establish economic and diplomatic contact with the West in order to encourage growth and development. The United States balked at the chance to improve relations with the new Russian government.

After the Russian Revolution, a power struggle broke out in Moscow between Lenin's potential heirs and continued for five years after Lenin's death in 1924. The main contenders were Leon Trotsky and Joseph Stalin, both of whom had helped organize the original Bolshevik Revolution. After gaining control of the Communist Party apparatus, however, Stalin was able to force Trotsky out of power and into exile. The "Trotskyite" faction immediately disintegrated, leaving Russia's sagging fortunes in the hands of Stalin and his lieutenants.

During the next twenty-five years, Stalin transformed Russia into a modern, industrialized state, but the price tag for such progress was totalitarianism and the ruthless implementation of Communist doctrines. After his accession in 1929, Stalin initiated three Five-Year Plans which increased industrial production sevenfold by the outbreak of World War II. Similarly, Stalin collectivized and mechanized Russian agriculture despite bitter opposition from the rural peasants, many of whom were killed or deported. During the 1930s, Stalin cemented his personal power even further by conducting an awesome purge of the Communist Party, the Soviet hierarchy, and the Red Army. Opponents were arrested, executed, or exiled in an attempt to "purify the revolution" and achieve the goals Stalin had set.

Meanwhile, a "Red hysteria" swept across America. Rumors of Communist infiltration in political organizations and labor unions sparked a series of early witch-hunts, foreshadowing the crazed antics of Joseph McCarthy thirty years later. In 1919, there was a wave of workers' strikes in the United States which management denounced as evidence of radicalism among organized labor. Attorney General A. Mitchell Palmer initiated a crusade against "reds"—particularly Socialists and labor radicals—which touched off violence, bombings, and public hysteria. Palmer next focused on alleged Communists, rounding up 6,000 suspects on January 1, 1920, some of whom (556) were deported. Two "anarchists," Sacco and Vanzetti, were arrested for robbery and murder in April 1920, but, according to concerned liberals, were tried for their political views and ultimately executed in August 1927. This case was a *cause célèbre* of the 1920s. Also, the wave of intolerance consumed many Catholics, Jews, and Negroes—some of whom fell victim to a revived and militant Ku Klux Klan.

Franklin Delano Roosevelt became President in 1933. FDR now for the first time attempted a cautious rapprochement with the Soviet Union, which he officially recognized in November 1933.

In August 1939, Communist Russia shocked the West by signing a Non-Agression Pact with Nazi Germany. The pact gave Moscow temporary security against a German invasion; furthermore, it allowed Stalin to start building the protective buffer zone in Eastern Europe that he desperately wanted. Germany was willing to grant Russia immediate predominance over eastern Poland, which Stalin seized at the beginning of World War II. On September 1, 1939, Hitler invaded Poland. Two days later Britain and France declared war, and World War II began in Europe. By the spring of 1940 Germany had overrun Denmark, Norway, Holland, Belgium, and most of France.

Hitler invaded Russia in June 1941. Out to conquer the immense "living space" that Russia would provide, German forces swept into Russia on a broad front, dispersing the Red Army and massacring millions of Russian civilians. The United States was drawn into the war after Japan attacked Pearl Harbor on December 7, 1941. The Western Allies came to Stalin's aid, offering supplies and Lend-Lease dollars, but the Germans continued their advance until early 1943, when the Russians counterattacked at Stalingrad and won a resounding victory. As with Napoleon a century and a half earlier, Hitler did not reckon with the vastness of Russia, the harshness of its winters, or the determination of its people. Having turned the tide, Stalin's army began a tortuous western push that lasted two years. Finally, in May 1945, Russian forces linked up with Eisenhower's army pushing east from France, and the long and bitter war against Germany ended. Germany surrendered on May 8, 1945. By then FDR had died, and Harry Truman was President of the United States. In August, Truman ordered atomic bombs dropped on Hiroshima and Nagasaki, and Japan also surrendered.

With the end of World War II in Europe, Russian troops occupied East Germany and part of Berlin and established as satellites Czechoslovakia, Poland, Romania, Bulgaria, Hungary, and other Eastern

European countries. The Russians had lost tens of millions of men women, and children in World Wars I and II. Each time their lands were invaded and devastated. The Soviets were determined to protect their lands from further invasion as far as possible and established these Eastern European nations as "buffer states." Stalin, in order to consolidate his rule and to prevent the disintegration of this Soviet sphere of influence, permitted his people only limited contact with the outside world. In March 1946, speaking in Fulton, Missouri, Winston Churchill warned that an "iron curtain" was descending across Europe.

With World War II at an end, the United States was the only nation in possession of atomic weapons. After the Soviet seizure of Eastern Europe, many voices argued for a "preventive war" to save the world from the "Communist menace." The United States rattled its nuclear sabres on many occasions, and by the end of the 1940s had surrounded the Soviet Union with a ring of forward strategic air bases with planes loaded with nuclear weapons capable of attacking the Soviet Union at a moment's notice. All of these bases with the exception of Alaska were outside U.S. territory. (Russia's subsequent attempt to establish a comparable base in Cuba was repelled by a nuclear ultimatum from the United States.)

After World War II, Harry Truman appropriated millions of dollars to bolster the Greek and Turkish economies and inaugurated what became known as the Marshall Plan whereby economic aid was sent to rebuild Western Europe. This aid, assisting friend and foe alike in Europe, sparked a remarkable recovery for these devastated nations.

Thereafter, Harry Truman became the apostle of a renewed and intense Cold War against the Soviet Union and Communism in general. Two events added to the Truman administration's fear of Communism. In January 1949, Mao Tse-tung defeated Chiang Kai-shek and established a Communist rule over all of China. America's fears climaxed in August 1949 when the Russians' first nuclear explosion occurred. The United States now knew that it no longer was the only nation capable of delivering a nuclear bomb. President Truman, in light of these developments, ordered a full-scale reassessment of American foreign policy.

The result was National Security Council Memorandum #68. NSC-68, dated April 14, 1950, encompassed a document entitled "A Report to the National Security Council by the Secretaries of State and Defense on United States Objectives and Programs for National Security," declassified on February 27, 1975. It was prepared by a "study team"[1] which had the enthusiastic backing of Secretary of State Dean Acheson, and the reluctant support of Secretary of Defense Louis Johnson.

NSC-68 shaped and reflected the major policy decisions of the Cold War. President Truman declared a state of national emergency. In a period of one year, a million soldiers were added to the U.S. military forces; the air force was provided with five times as many planes; and the defense budget climbed from $13.5 billion to $48.2 billion.

NSC-68 contended that the Soviet Union had become a permanent menace to the existence of the United States, and that ultimately it must be contained or destroyed or the United States could not continue to exist as a free society. It also contended that the existence of the idea of freedom is a continuous threat to the foundations of the USSR, which therefore regards as intolerable the existence of freedom in the world.

NSC-68 recommended that America develop a military capability and an environment within the United States and in all other areas of the world under which America and its system may survive. Toward that end, the United States must wage an unmitigated Cold War against the Soviet Union and be prepared to fight a real war with the Soviets or with their surrogates in any area of the world.

Many enlightened individuals close to the Truman administration such as James B. Conant, then president of Harvard University, and George Kennan, retiring as State Department policy planner and soon to become ambassador to the Soviet Union, warned against the emotionalism and near hysteria that surrounded the NSC analysis. Charles Bohlen, State Department counselor, said, "We must not be stampeded into unwise or hysterical action because of a 'war scare' or other type of crisis deliberately stimulated."

Robert Lovett, on the other hand, a banker and soon to be appointed President Truman's secretary of defense, supported the NSC resolution. "We should fight with no holds barred . . . exactly as though we were under fire from an invading enemy." We should cause the Russians "trouble wherever we can," including support of dissidents within the Soviet Union. In addition, Lovett urged a strong propaganda effort at home and abroad: "If we can sell every useless article known to man in large quantities, we should be able to sell our very fine story in larger quantities." The Lovett train of thought triumphed almost totally within the Truman administration.[2]

The victory of this Cold War view within the government was the catalytic force that impelled a new vitriolic anti-Communism in America, and the Truman administration now launched an "anti-Communist crusade" at home and abroad. In 1949, the administration procured the conviction of eleven "Communist Party leaders on the charge that they had violated the Smith Act by conspiring to teach or advocate the overthrow of the U.S. government."[3] The Supreme Court upheld this conviction, Chief Justice Vinson arguing that free speech was subject to containment under the "clear and present danger" doctrine. This decision gave a green light for a national campaign against any known Communist Party member.

Many espionage agents swarmed throughout America. Alger Hiss was accused and convicted of giving State Department documents to the Russians. Julius and Ethel Rosenberg were tried and executed on the still disputed charge that they had delivered atomic weapons secrets to Russian agents. Republicans now joined the wolf pack and attacked not only suspected Communists but the Democratic Party as well. Richard Nixon won his way to power by defeating Helen Gahagan Douglas in their race for election to the U.S. Senate, partly by branding her as a Communist sympathizer. Addressing the National Young Republican Convention in Boston, on June 28, 1951, Nixon alleged that Communists had "infiltrated the very highest councils of [the Truman] administration," and he promised to drive the Democratic Party from power in a "fighting, rocking, socking campaign."[4]

Soon thereafter, a little-known Senator, Joseph McCarthy, rose from obscurity to fame by falsely alleging that he had a list of 205 employees of the State Department who were members of the Communist Party. Thus began the McCarthy era, one of the darkest chapters in American history.

McCarthy captured the imagination and gained the support of the American archconservative right wing, who supported this anti-Communist crusade. Republicans followed the trail opened up for them by the House Committee on Un-American Activities. Congressman Martin Dies sponsored a committee to investigate "the extent, character and objects of un-American propaganda activities in the United States." He accused CIO president John Lewis of trying to establish a Soviet America and predicted that the "Congress of Industrial Organizations will become the Communist Party of America." He "described Eleanor Roosevelt as 'one of the most valuable assets that the Trojan Horse Organization of the Communists have [sic] possessed.'"[5]

The Silver Shirts, the Ku Klux Klan, and the government of Nazi Germany all lauded the activities of the House Un-American Activities Committee. When Dies retired, Congressman John Rankin of Mississippi took over. Rankin defended the KKK as a 100 percent American institution. The House of Representatives gave the Committee subpoena powers for the first time.

In October 1947, an investigation of the motion picture industry began. Ten screenwriters and directors who refused to discuss their political beliefs and refused to point their finger and name other individuals who may have been suspected members of the Communist Party were cited by HUAC for contempt and sentenced to a year in prison. All of the "Hollywood Ten" were denied parole and blacklisted by the motion picture industry.

To the surprise of prominent lawyers familiar with the U.S. Constitution, these convictions were upheld by the Supreme Court. The "black list" now became an American institution. As a result, hundreds of individuals in the entertainment field were unable to find employment, and some of the most brilliant, talented, and dedicated actors, entertainers, and writers had their careers destroyed. A German playwright, Bertolt Brecht, who had been summoned to testify before the HUAC, said that the dissident writer was "not deprived of his life, only of the means of life. He does not appear in the obituary columns, only on the blacklists."[6] Some Hollywood personalities, however, such as Walt Disney, Gary Cooper, Ronald Reagan, and Robert Montgomery testified before and cooperated with the HUAC.

In 1949, HUAC admitted that it maintained files on more than a million Americans. Between 1949 and 1959, it provided information on 60,000 individuals and 12,000 organizations to interested employers and listed thousands of individuals and organizations mentioned in its hearings in a *Cumulative Index*—a handy reference guide for blacklisters and superpatriots. In 1950 alone, the committee distributed 2 million free copies of its publications.[7]

Senator McCarthy became one of the most powerful men in America despite the fact that a great many of his utterances were blatantly false.

Eventually, he named a lecturer at Johns Hopkins University, Owen Lattimore—a State Department consultant who was neither a spy nor a Communist. By the spring of 1950 McCarthy had hit his stride, attacking Administration supporters for everything from Communism to homosexuality. The "pitiful squealing" of "egg-sucking phony liberals," he charged, "would hold sacrosanct those Communists and queers" who had sold China into "atheistic slavery." Promising to purge the "prancing mimics of the Moscow party line" from the State Department, he assailed Acheson and U.N. Ambassador-at-Large Philip Jessup as "dilettante diplomats," who "whined," "whimpered," and "cringed" before Communism. George Marshall, he said, was "a pathetic thing." Through it all, McCarthy remained brash and self-confident. "When did you discover Communism?" a young lady asked him at a cocktail party given by the Scripps-Howard press. "Two and a half months ago," he blithely replied.[8]

Soon what became known as the McCarran Act was railroaded through a frightened Congress. This bill destroyed the rights and privileges of anyone who was even suspected of being a member of the Communist Party, and all members were compelled to register. Many constitutional authorities and liberals believed that this bill completely abridged the constitutional rights of Americans. President Truman vetoed the measure, but his veto was overridden.

It became necessary for Dean Acheson, Truman's secretary of state, to be on the constant defensive against charges of being a Communist sympathizer despite the fact that with Harry Truman he was one of the architects of the anti-Communist crusade. Truman was forced to be more diligent in defending the Administration's anti-Communist credentials than in safeguarding civil liberties. Dean Acheson dismissed a number of Foreign Service officers associated with U.S. China policy, and by 1952 there were only two members of the China service still employed by the State Department out of twenty-two officers who had joined it a little more than a decade earlier.[9] Obviously, no one dared even suggest a rapprochement with the People's Republic of China.

Later even Eisenhower, during his race for the presidency in 1952 against Adlai Stevenson, was forced to accept Joe McCarthy. Even Stevenson failed to openly criticize McCarthy's actions, but frowned upon his methods.

Joe McCarthy ultimately made the mistake of attacking the Pentagon. An open, televised hearing was held to determine whether or not he should be censured by Congress for some of his actions. McCarthy was unable to prevail, and finally his power was broken. "McCarthyism," however, left an indelible stamp on America. One of the most deadly effects of McCarthyism concerned the U.S. Far East and China policy. When Mao defeated Chiang Kai-shek in 1949 and established the People's Republic of China, most China authorities and experts, particularly those in the Foreign Service, were of the opinion that China was well rid of the insolent tyrant Chiang Kai-shek and that the United States now had an opportunity to establish a friendly relationship with China.

Knowledgeable Foreign Service China experts at that time recommended that the United States recognize the People's Republic of China. McCarthy attacked these Foreign Service officers viciously, and most of them were swept out of office. Prodded by McCarthy, the United States established Chiang Kai-shek in Formosa as a hero and thereafter gave him large amounts of economic and military aid.

It is now generally recognized that this anti-Communist China policy was maintained largely because of the McCarthy influence. Informed individuals at the time believed that the People's Republic of China was so militarily weak that it could not even attempt to reconquer its own territories—Outer Mongolia, Formosa, Kowloon, Macao, or Hong Kong—and that China was preoccupied with its economic problems.

Nevertheless, the McCarthyites and the U.S. government acted in concert in a crusade against the "yellow peril," and an anti-China policy became firmly entrenched in the American political system, and the United States subsequently became involved in sizable wars—in Korea, Vietnam, and Southeast Asia—in order to contain Communist China.

When World War II ended, U.S. forces occupied Korea south of the Thirty-eighth Parallel and Russian forces did the same north of the parallel. The United Nations supervised elections in the South that led to a nationalistic government under Dr. Rhee, while in the North the Communists formed a people's government with a strong, aggressive army. When the United States withdrew its occupation troops in June 1949, the Thirty-eighth Parallel had become more than an unofficial barrier between North and South; it was the symbol of a divided Korea.

When on June 25, 1950, North Korea attacked South Korea in an effort to unify the divided country, President Harry Truman reacted spontaneously. Under NSC-68 he had become firmly committed to an anti-Communist stance. The anti-Communist Cold Warriors were overrunning America, and it was politically necessary to demonstrate that he was in the forefront of anti-Communist activities. Without hesitation, Truman acted. It appears that all prior study with reference to Korea indicated that Korea was not important to the defense of the United States. The Joint Chiefs of Staff, according to Secretary Acheson, had never believed that Korea had any strategic value:

> I do not think that the JCS have ever determined, or rather I think they have not determined, that Korea is of strategic importance to the United States.[10]

The Joint Chiefs' own chairman, General Bradley, confirmed this: "Korea is a poor place to fight a war, and a lot of military implications are involved in extending the war."[11]

President Truman himself had had grave doubts about Syngman Rhee when he said:

> I did not care for the methods used by Rhee's police to break up political meetings and control political enemies, and I was deeply concerned over the Rhee government's lack of concern about the serious inflation that swept the country.[12]

Truman nevertheless, on June 26, ordered sea, air, and logistical support for South Korea. The Security Council Resolution under which the United States ostensibly acted was not passed until the afternoon of June 27, 1950.

Former Secretary of State Acheson, in his memoirs, noted that:

> "Thus, some American action, said to be in support of the resolution of June 27, was in fact ordered, and possibly taken, prior to the resolution." The President confirmed the essentially unilateral American character of the intervention when he sent a note to his secretary of state on July 19 thanking him for his swift action in calling the Security Council into session: "Had you not acted promptly in that direction we would have had to go into Korea alone."[13]

General Douglas MacArthur, who was in command of U.S. forces in Korea, wanted to extend the war into mainland China. MacArthur was recalled to the United States and fired by Harry Truman. The war ended after Dwight D. Eisenhower became President, with both sides returning to the status quo. The Korean War cost the United States 33,000 dead, 115,000 wounded, and approximately $22 billion.

After the Korean War, the Central Intelligence Agency, provided with a substantially increased budget and personnel, became the primary instrument for implementing the U.S. containment policy as envisioned by NSC-68. The Truman administration authorized the CIA to undertake political, economic, and paramilitary operations to forestall any Communist moves.

The National Security Act of 1947 had placed the final responsibility for instituting covert action upon the President himself. Decisions whether to pursue covert operations and how to implement them were placed in the hands of a task force which reported to the President on matters requiring his review. The personnel of this task force changed from time to time, but at all times it was staffed by members of the highest branches of the United States government, including the Cabinet, the Departments of State and Defense, and the Pentagon.

The U.S. anti-Communist China policy was not just containment; it officially supported Chiang Kai-shek in his avowed threat, or promise, to reconquer the mainland of China. United States aid to Taiwan, totaling $2 billion during the 1950s, helped Chiang cement his rule on the island and suppress all political opposition. With the outbreak of open conflict in Korea, the United States went one step further to protect Chiang's island fortress. The Seventh Fleet moved into the Formosa Strait to shield Chiang from the People's Republic of China.

The National Security Council memorandum, NSC-64, dated February 27, 1950, now suggested that the United States take "all practicable measures . . . to prevent further communist expansion in Southeast Asia." Likewise NSC-124/2, of June 25, 1952, called Indochina "of great strategic importance in the general international interest . . . and as essential as the French interest to the security of the free world." The objective followed: "To prevent the countries of Southeast Asia from passing into the communist orbit. . . ." The basic U.S. commitment to Vietnam was now cast in stone, and few thereafter stopped to consider whether or not it was rational.

A major escalation of the Communist containment policy occurred when Dwight Eisenhower became President in 1953. The new President appointed John Foster Dulles as his secretary of state. His brother, Allen Dulles, was appointed as the director of the Central Intelligence Agency. These actions had a major effect on the future course of American history. It was John Foster Dulles who became the primary implementer of Cold Warism, while Allen directed the activities of the Central Intelligence Agency when it took over in South Vietnam in 1954.

In 1954, Dulles intensified the hard line policy toward Mao's regime, claiming that Chiang was the true master of China and should be restored to power. When Chou En-lai offered to ease tensions by negotiating a wide-ranging accord with the United States, the U.S. State Department denounced Communist China as "an outlaw-gangster regime, unpurged of its crimes and aggressions, and unfit to sit in any respectable family of nations." In 1958 Dulles, supported by Vice President Nixon, declared that U.S. policy toward Peking envisioned "a noble strategy of victory."

In September 1954, the United States concluded an alliance treaty with Taiwan which, until the late 1970s, remained the backbone of U.S. China policy. As Chiang issued threats against Mao and armed for a new war with the Communists, the United States stepped up its naval patrols, garrisoned 9,000 U.S. troops on Taiwan, and helped Chiang establish a 500,000-man Nationalist army. At the same time, it warned Communist China of the consequences of any aggressive moves against America's new ally. Five successive Presidents reaffirmed this stance. Chiang Kai-shek's dictatorship in Taiwan is only one illustration of how dictatorships were established and maintained by the United States in various areas of the world in the fulfillment of NSC-68 objectives.

After 1949, the CIA was transformed from an intelligence body, which collected and analyzed data, into an active paramilitary organization. The CIA's primary function was the destabilization of foreign governments that could be inclined toward Communism. These anti-Communist activities were a direct extension of Cold Warism and McCarthyism in the United States. In the same manner that the

United States outlawed and effectively suppressed the growth of any Communist activity in the United States, it likewise attempted to suppress and outlaw the establishment or growth of Communism in any other nation. To accomplish this objective, it first sent its shock troops, primarily CIA operators, into nations leaning toward Communism in an effort to undermine the establishment of any new Communist regime. CIA operations succeeded in ousting Premier Mossadegh in Iran and replacing him with the Shah, who was ultimately driven out by Ayatollah Khomeini. The CIA was also successful in forcing the resignation of left-leaning President Arbenz Gusman in Guatemala. Its primary failure was its unsuccessful attempt to unseat Fidel Castro. Prior to Kennedy's inauguration, the CIA had recruited, armed, and organized several thousand Cuban expatriots into a guerrilla force to invade Cuba and topple Castro. This effort led to a disastrous failure known as the Bay of Pigs episode. Finally, the CIA's efforts to assassinate Castro by hiring Mafia killers also failed. In recent years there have been well-publicized accounts of CIA intervention in Chile and Angola, all part of the U.S. anti-Communist covert containment policy. The consensus was that these CIA projects for the most part failed.

The Vietnam Syndrome thus became a direct outgrowth of Cold Warism. All the methods attempted in other areas, and many additional ones, were utilized in Vietnam, where for about eighteen years the United States made its strongest effort to accomplish the objectives of NSC-68. The United States for ten years then waged a disastrous open conflict in Vietnam in a continued futile effort to prevent the establishment of a unified Communist state. Vietnam thus became a showcase, a crucible, a symbol, and a testing ground for U.S. Cold War policies.

THE FIRST EIGHTEEN YEARS
1945–63

> All men are born equal; the Creator has given us
> inviolable rights, life, liberty, and happiness. . . .
> —*Ho Chi Minh*

On September 2, 1945, Ho Chi Minh marched into Hanoi at the head of his Vietminh forces and declared Vietnam an independent nation. He then issued his Declaration of Independence, in words notably reminiscent of the language of the U.S. Declaration of Independence. A new nation was then established in North Vietnam called the Democratic Republic of Vietnam. Its establishment was the culmination of the struggles of generations of Vietnamese against the French colonialists. Toward this goal, their leader, Ho Chi Minh, had dedicated his life. During his travels in France, Russia, and China he had worked with numerous Socialists and later Communists to create a group of Vietnamese revolutionaries, finally founding the Vietnamese Communist Party in 1930. Ho Chi Minh now, with Communist support, achieved his goal of securing independence for Vietnam. For a brief moment, the prospects of peace and permanent independence seemed bright indeed.

But Vietnam's independence was short-lived. Within a month, the French sent troops to reassert the control over Indochina that France had lost during World War II. Ho tried to negotiate with the French, hoping to find a compromise solution that would spare his people further bloodshed. He went to Paris for talks with French government officials. In the summer of 1946, an agreement was worked out in which the French officially recognized Ho as the ruler of a free state in North Vietnam. At the same time they promised free elections in South Vietnam within five years to reunify the country. Ho in return permitted 15,000 French troops to enter the Hanoi-Haiphong area to replace the Chinese troops which had left.

In retrospect, the French offer of free elections and a reunified Vietnam may have been deliberate deception. Instead of honoring their commitments, they established a separate French-controlled state in the South called "Cochinchina" and began military action against Ho in the North. In November 1946 a French cruiser opened fire on the city of Haiphong, killing more than 6,000 Vietnamese. To retaliate, Ho moved guerrilla forces into the jungles and initiated guerrilla strikes against the French. The first Vietnam War had begun.

Ho looked to the United States, the country he had supported against the Japanese in World War II, for support in his struggle with France. President Franklin D. Roosevelt had said: "The case of Indo-China is perfectly clear. France has milked it for one hundred years. The people of Indo-China are entitled to something better than that."[1] Hoping that Truman would continue the Roosevelt policies, Ho Chi Minh, in 1946, wrote a series of eight letters to President Truman, asking for aid. One read:

HANOI FEBRUARY 16 1946
President HO CHI MINH,
Provisional Government of
VIETNAM DEMOCRATIC REPUBLIC
HANOI

To the President
of the United States of America,
Washington, D.C.

Dear Mr. President,

I shall avail myself of this opportunity to thank you and the people of the United States for the interest shown by your representatives at the United Nations Organization in favour of the dependent peoples. Our Vietnam people, as early as 1941, stood by the Allies' side and fought against the Japanese and their associates, the French colonialists. From 1941 to 1943 we fought bitterly, sustained by the patriotism of our fellow-countrymen and by the promises made by the Allies at YALTA, SAN FRANCISCO, and POTSDAM.

When the Japanese were defeated in August 1945, the whole Vietnam territory was united under a Provisional Republican Government which immediately set to work. In five months, peace and order were restored, a democratic republic was established on legal bases, and adequate help was given to the Allies in the carrying out of their disarmament mission. But the French colonialists, who had betrayed in wartime both the Allies and the Vietnamese, have come back and are waging on us a murderous and pitiless war in order to reestablish their domination. Their invasion has extended to South Vietnam and is menacing us in North Vietnam. It would take volumes to give even an abbreviated report of the crimes and assassinations they are committing every day in the fighting area.

This aggression is contrary to all principles of international law and to the pledges made by the Allies during the world war. It is a challenge to the noble attitude shown before, during and after the war by the United States Government and People. It violently contrasts with the firm stand you have taken in your twelve point declaration, and with the idealistic loftiness and generosity expressed by your delegates to the United Nations Assembly, Ms. Byrnes, Stettinius and J. F. Dulles.

The French aggression on a peace-loving people is a direct menace to world security. It implies the complicity, or at least, the connivance of the Great Democracies. The United Nations ought to keep their words. They ought to interfere to stop this unjust war and to show that they mean to carry out in peace-time the principles for which they fought in war-time.

Our Vietnam people, after so many years of spoilation and devastation, is just beginning the building-up work. It needs security and freedom, first to achieve internal prosperity and welfare, and to bring its small contribution to world-reconstruction.

This security and freedom can only be guaranteed by our independence from any colonial power, and our free cooperation with all other powers. It is with this firm conviction that we request of the United States as guardians and champions of World Justice to take a decisive step in support of our independence.

What we ask has been graciously granted to the Philippines. Like the Philippines our goal is full independence and *full cooperation with the United States*. [Italics added.] We will do our best to make this independence and cooperation profitable to the whole world.

I am, Dear Mr. President,

Respectfully yours,
Ho Chi Minh.[2]

Ho Chi Minh's pleas were ignored. Instead, as the Cold War intensified, Roosevelt's views on ending French colonial rule were forgotten. Truman resolved to help the French. Almost immediately his administration began distributing millions of dollars of foreign aid to France under the Marshall Plan. It opposed French military withdrawal and complete independence on the grounds that there would be "chaos and terroristic activities." The long-term objective was bluntly stated: ". . . to eliminate so far as possible Communist influence in Indochina and to see installed a self-governing nationalist state which will be friendly to the US. . . ."³ As the State Department informed the French government, "the paramount question in Indochina now is whether the country is to be saved from communist control. . . . All other issues must be considered as irrelevant."⁴ Ideally, with American support, Ho would have established a government in Vietnam that, although Communist, was friendly towards the United States. The fiercely nationalistic Ho did not want Vietnam to be dominated by the Chinese, the Russians, or any other colonial power. Had the United States supported him at that moment, it might have avoided a costly, tragic war in Vietnam years later.

People who understood Chinese-Vietnamese relations argued then that this was so, and occasionally, a voice was raised within the State Department itself against U.S. policy. "The fundamental antipathy of the Indochinese to China is one of the factors," one official argued, to be considered in learning to live with Ho. And in any case, the French and their puppet ruler, Bao Dai, were "doomed," and cooperation with such a reactionary regime was "shameful," a "shabby business." "Whether the French like it or not, independence is coming to Indochina. Why, therefore, do we tie ourselves to the tail of their battered kite?"⁵

By early 1950, such voices were rarely raised within the government. The Truman administration refused to recognize Ho's socialist Democratic Republic. Instead, the United States committed itself to a policy of politically and militarily aiding the French and the anti-Communist groups in Indochina "to withstand Communist aggression, backed up by Chinese Communist or by Soviet assistance."⁶ The Vietnamese revolutionaries were now the enemy and would be fought by the American government for the next twenty-five years. Truman recognized the "State of Vietnam" as the true government of South Vietnam and France's puppet ruler, Bao Dai, as the region's only legitimate leader.

Ho therefore looked elsewhere for the support he needed. He envisioned a double alliance with Russia and China. But Russia at that time showed little interest in Vietnam or in the Communist movement of Ho Chi Minh. Moscow did recognize Ho's Democratic Republic of Vietnam in February 1950, but Joseph Stalin considered

Asia an area of secondary importance. In Stalin's view, the countries of Europe were more vital to the future of Russian Communism— especially France, where the French Communist Party had become that country's single largest political faction. As a result, Stalin refused to support the Vietnamese war against France, and he was not at all receptive to the idea of a second Communist front in the Far East.

China, however, was interested in assisting Ho to end the French colonization of Indochina. China, therefore, held the key to the immediate support that Ho needed.[7] Peking recognized Ho's republic in January 1950, and the Chinese took an active interest in the progress of the Vietminh. First, Mao Tse-tung opened the border between China and Vietnam. Next, after Ho visited Peking, the Chinese assigned General Lo Kwei-po to the Vietnamese Liberation Army as a military adviser. Then, in the years before the Geneva Conference, Peking supplied Ho's army with light weapons and ammunition. But China stopped short of full-scale intervention. Indeed, there is no indication that Ho, Vietnamese nationalist that he was, ever sought large-scale Chinese military forces in his country.

In June 1950, the Korean War began. Korea and Indochina were quickly seen as twin battles in the same international Communist drive to take over Asia. Thus American support for French military efforts rapidly increased as the Korean War intensified—from $150 million in 1950 to $1 billion four years later. By then, the United States was underwriting 80 percent of the entire cost of France's war in Indochina.

Peking countered by increasing its aid shipments to the Vietminh guerrillas.[8] As the war in Vietnam dragged on, writes P. J. Honey,

> Chinese aid to Ho Chi Minh increased greatly. Military advisors, munitions, artillery, medicines, and much else reached Vietnam from China, while Vietnamese troops received training on Chinese soil beyond the reach of their enemies.[9]

Thanks in part to this Chinese aid, the French army and Bao Dai were decisively defeated despite the fact that between 1946 and 1954 the French put an army estimated at 517,000 men into the field. The French army was decimated by Ho's guerrilla forces commanded by General Giap.

In desperation, the French General Staff sought to force the Vietminh into fighting conventional warfare, believing that they could then win with their greater firepower and air power. To this end, they built a great fortress in the countryside, deep in the hills of North Vietnam near Laos, in a region known as Dien Bien Phu. Giap's hit-and-run guerrilla tactics, they believed, would be useless against such a fortress, thus forcing the Vietnamese into a different kind of war.

Giap, they argued, could not possibly transport artillery up the massive hills which surrounded Dien Bien Phu. As it turned out, the French generals were wrong. The Vietnamese carried their howitzers through the hills on their backs piece by piece, anchored them in the hills, and continuously shelled the fortress and its runways. Unable to resupply their base, the French faced humiliating defeat. In desperation they called upon the United States for military assistance, requesting that the U.S. Air Force begin to bomb North Vietnam.

Secretary of State John Foster Dulles advised President Eisenhower to support the French and to bomb North Vietnam. Admiral Radford urged that American planes bomb the Vietnamese forces around Dien Bien Phu and land U.S. Marines in North Vietnam to seize the port of Haiphong. The Joint Chiefs argued that the commitment of U.S. troops made sense only if atomic warfare was not ruled out. Secretary of State Dulles, in a public speech, called for "united action" by the Allies; privately, he counseled Eisenhower to intervene. And in a background speech on April 7, Vice President Nixon stated that "if this government cannot avoid it, the Administration must face up to the situation and dispatch forces."[10]

On April 3, 1954, Dulles called a meeting of military, congressional, and administrative leaders. This group formally requested Eisenhower to authorize the U.S. Air Force to bomb North Vietnam, taking the pressure off of Dien Bien Phu, and thereafter to take whatever measures were necessary to support the French. President Eisenhower, however, refused to take such unilateral action in the absence of congressional approval and without the support of Great Britain and other European Allies.

Dulles was unable to obtain such support. Winston Churchill strongly opposed U.S. intervention and his foreign secretary, Anthony Eden, criticized Dulles for the extent to which he was "disposed to accept present risks of a Chinese war. . . ."[11] The other

Allies were against it as well. As a result, the United States acceded to the convocation of the Geneva Conference on the future of Vietnam between May 8 and July 21, 1954. Even as the conference began its meetings, Dien Bien Phu fell. The French mastery of Vietnam was at an end.

Representing the Vietminh at Geneva was Pham Van Dong, Ho's most trusted associate; also present were representatives of France and the puppet Bao Dai government in South Vietnam. Laos and Cambodia, formerly part of French Indochina, were also represented, as were the Soviet Union, China, Great Britain, and the United States.

The agreements that resulted from this conference, the Geneva Accords, were a compromise solution to the problems of Vietnam. Among the provisions of the Final Declaration of the Geneva Conference were the following:

• The Conference takes note of the clauses in the agreement on the cessation of hostilities in Viet Nam prohibiting the introduction into Viet Nam of foreign troops and military personnel as well as of all kinds of arms and munitions. The Conference also takes note of the declarations made by the Governments of Cambodia and Laos of their resolution not to request foreign aid, whether in war material, in personnel or in instructors except for the purpose of the effective defence of their territory and, in the case of Laos, to the extent defined by the agreements on the cessation of hostilities in Laos.

• The Conference takes note of the clauses in the agreement on the cessation of hostilities in Viet Nam to the effect that no military base under the control of a foreign State may be established in the regrouping zones of the two parties, the latter having the obligation to see that the zones allotted to them shall not constitute part of any military alliance and shall not be utilised for the resumption of hostilities or in the service of an aggressive policy. . . .

• The Conference recognises that the essential purpose of the agreement relating to Viet Nam is to settle military questions with a view to ending hostilities and that the military demarcation line is provisional and should not in any way be interpreted as constituting a political or territorial boundary. . . .

• The Conference declares that, so far as Viet Nam is concerned, the settlement of political problems, effected on the basis of respect for the principles of independence, unity and territorial integrity, shall permit the Vietnamese people to enjoy the fundamental freedoms, guaranteed by democratic institutions established as a result of free general elections by secret ballot. . . .

• The Conference takes note of the declaration of the Government of the French Republic to the effect that it is ready to withdraw its troops from the territory of Cambodia, Laos and Viet Nam . . . [and that] the French Government will proceed from the principle of respect for the independence and sovereignty, unity and territorial integrity of Cambodia, Laos and Viet Nam.[12]

It was understood in the agreement that Ho's armies were to be withdrawn from the South and would remain in North Vietnam and that the Vietminh would *temporarily* be in charge of the civil administration of North Vietnam, with its headquarters in Hanoi. The French and its armies were to remain *temporarily* in South Vietnam and would be temporarily in charge of the civil administration of South Vietnam, with its headquarters in Saigon, and under the control of Bao Dai. General elections were to be held in July 1956, under the supervision of an international commission, to establish a permanent government for *one* Vietnam. All parties agreed that they would be bound by the results of this election, whether it resulted in the formation of a socialist government or a government supporting a capitalistic-based society.

M. Mendés-France, representing France; Chou En-lai, representing the People's Republic of China; Anthony Eden, the conference chairman, representing Great Britain; M. Molotov, representing the USSR; and Pham Van Dong, representing the Democratic Republic of Vietnam (North Vietnam), all agreed to the terms of the declaration. Tep Phan, representing Cambodia, agreed to the resolution in principle but had reservations with reference to certain territorial provisions. Tranh Van Do, representing the French-controlled area of Vietnam, which became known as South Vietnam, agreed to the declaration in principle, taking note of the declarations of the French government. The U.S. representative, Bedell Smith, however, stated: "My Government is not prepared to join in a Declaration by the Conference such as is submitted."

John Foster Dulles did not attend the final session of the Geneva Conference because, under his direction, the U.S. government was adamantly opposed to the holding of supervised free elections to choose a single government for all of Vietnam. If this election should take place, there was little doubt of what the outcome would be. The Vietminh would almost certainly win. If that should happen, Ho Chi

Minh would certainly establish a new unified Communist government for all of Vietnam.

It was clear that President Eisenhower would not permit the utilization of U.S. military forces to prevent the establishment of a Communist government in South Vietnam unless this action was supported and participated in by America's World War II Allies. It was also clear that these Allies, who had unanimously voted at Geneva in favor of an election, obviously would never support any U.S. military action there.

Instead of using military forces, therefore, the administration elected to utilize the Office of the Secretary of State under John Foster Dulles, the Central Intelligence Agency under John's brother Allen Dulles, in conjunction with the Office of Policy Coordination to inaugurate and support the NSC-68 policies in Vietnam.

The concept for the conduct of covert activities as envisioned by a committee headed by the eminent soldier General Doolittle is illustrated by the committee's report issued in 1954:

> It is now clear that we are facing an implacable enemy [the Soviet Union] whose avowed objective is world domination by whatever means and at whatever cost. There are no rules in such a game. Hitherto acceptable norms of human conduct do not apply. If the United States is to survive, long-standing American concepts of "fair play" [sic] must be reconsidered. We must develop effective espionage and counter espionage services and must learn to subvert, sabotage and destroy our enemies by more clever, more sophisticated and more effective methods than those used against us. It may be necessary that the American people be made acquainted with, understand and support this fundamentally repugnant philosophy.[13]

The power vacuum left by the French withdrawal, the threat posed by the Communist government in the North, and the fact that the CIA was no longer needed in Korea at the close of that war insured that Vietnam should become a prime candidate for CIA covert activities, as outlined by Doolittle's committee. Colonel Edward Lansdale, a CIA operator who had successfully worked with the Magsaysay government in suppressing popular uprisings in the Philippines after the war, was now sent to Vietnam. The colorful Lansdale epitomized the newly created warrior-diplomat breed. Together with former OSS operative Lucien Conein, he attempted to set up a network of agents and guerrillas in North Vietnam prior to partition, but this ill-prepared endeavor proved unsuccessful. Henceforth the CIA concentrated on protecting its client in South Vietnam and in combatting the 5,000 to 10,000 Vietminh insurgents that remained behind in the South.

At the direction of John Foster and Allen Dulles, Lansdale assessed the domestic political scene within South Vietnam and suggested that Ngo Dinh Diem become the president of the recently established State of Vietnam, as sponsored by the United States. To begin this process, the CIA and Lansdale succeeded in obtaining Diem's appointment as premier under Bao Dai. The CIA and Diem each used the other for their own purposes. Bao Dai was still chief of state, and the French were still in control of all economic, military, and administrative operations, but under the Geneva Accords their days were numbered.

The CIA's next important objective was to get rid of Bao Dai and put Diem in his place, so as to effectively undermine the Geneva Armistice. Eisenhower wrote to Diem as "Dear Mr. President" and "Chief of State," even while Bao Dai was still in office. In his letter, Eisenhower promised American support to Diem's government in resisting the imposition of a "foreign ideology" on the "free people" of South Vietnam. Clearly it was planned that Diem, once in power, would refuse to participate in the nationwide Vietnamese elections.

Yet even in these early years there were prophetic warnings about the caliber of the man the United States picked to run South Vietnam. Eisenhower had dispatched General J. Lawton Collins to Saigon to investigate and report. He was not encouraging. In words that were to be echoed by other American officials, Collins warned that Diem "does not have the capacity to achieve the necessary unity of purpose and action" that is essential to "prevent this country from falling under Communist control." He is "practically incapable of holding this government together," he gloomily concluded.[14]

In the end, though, Eisenhower backed Diem. There seemed to be no one else, and he had obtained valuable support in the United States, where he lived much of the time from 1950 to 1953. Through his close friendship with the virulently anti-Communist Francis Cardinal Spellman, he met many prominent American political figures including Richard Nixon and Senators William Knowland, Mike Mansfield, and John F. Kennedy. He also became a friend of U.S. Supreme Court Justice William O. Douglas. Spellman introduced

Diem to the Dulles brothers, and they considered him to be the logical man to take over in South Vietnam.

A "Vietnam lobby" headed by Cardinal Spellman was established. The lobby put pressure on leading publications to support Diem. Another lobby—The American Friends of Vietnam—was set up, with similar aims. Diem himself even hired an American public relations firm to boost his image with the U.S. public.

With this heavy American backing, Diem gained the support of President Eisenhower and was able to defy both Bao Dai and the Geneva Accords. Diem refused to comply with the provision for a "supervised free election in all of Vietnam to choose a government for the entire country in 1956." Instead, he staged an obviously rigged election only in South Vietnam against Bao Dai and won with 98.6 percent of the votes. The deposed emperor withdrew to the French Riviera to drown his sorrows in champagne. With Bao Dai out, and the American puppet Diem now in full control, the French withdrew, leaving South Vietnam in the hands of the U.S. government and its surrogate.

The CIA was now firmly entrenched in South Vietnam as was Ngo Dinh Diem, who, of course, was in accord with the U.S. objective of preventing Vietnam from holding free elections that might result in the establishment of a Communist government. In the following months, Diem, with the assistance of the U.S. representatives, was beginning to achieve the capability of taking steps that he deemed necessary to prevent free elections from being held under the provisions of the Geneva Accords. Ho Chi Minh nevertheless still hoped that elections could be held that would enable him to create a unified socialist Vietnam free of foreign domination.

Meanwhile, Dulles also began to take steps that might enable him at some future date to use U.S. military support to assist him and Diem in South Vietnam, if necessary. Toward this end, he conceived the idea of a Southeast Asia Treaty Organization (SEATO) patterned after the North Atlantic Treaty Organization (NATO) in Europe. SEATO could demonstrate that the action in Vietnam was not only a U.S. undertaking, but that it had the support of other interested nations.

In order to establish SEATO, Dulles called a conference in Manila in September 1954. It was attended by Great Britain, France, Australia, and New Zealand of the West; but only three Asian nations

attended. The nations in the immediate vicinity seemed uncon-
cerned about "Communist aggression." The Asian nations who did
come already had military alliances with the United States: Pakistan,
Thailand, and the Philippines. Thus the SEATO pact was signed
only by these three Asian and the five Western governments. The
U.S. Senate formally ratified it in February 1955.[15]

Clearly, the SEATO pact was a sham and delusion to give lip
service to the theory that the United States had international support
for its actions in Vietnam. Not one of the signatories took the pact
seriously. Before long, Pakistan withdrew not only from SEATO but
from its other American alliance, CENTO. Thailand did provide
some military support, but it had been bought and paid for by the
CIA.

In later years, when Johnson called on the SEATO allies for support, the response was negligible. After intense pressure from Washington, the Philippines sent one division to Vietnam, but it was entirely noncombatant: nurses, doctors, road-building crews. Even this
nonmilitary contribution was so unpopular that President Ferdinand
Marcos promised in his reelection campaign that one of his first acts
would be to call the Philippine division home, and he lived up to his
promise. Australia sent only a token force. Even this minor aid
caused mass demonstrations in Australia, but the government explained that its dependence on the United States for defense neces-
sitated its giving America token participation in Vietnam. Indonesia,
however, refused to aid Johnson when he requested assistance. President Suharto told William Winter, when he was visiting Indonesia
during that period, that

> Vice President Humphrey is coming here to Jakarta in a few days. I
> know what he will want. He will want me to send a division of Indone-
> sian troops to Vietnam, and in return he'd give me American aid. We
> need that aid very much. But I will tell you, and I will tell him, that
> even if he offers me millions of dollars in American aid I will not send a
> single Indonesian soldier to Vietnam! It is not our war. It is not a war of
> Communist aggression. It is an American war, and if you want peace,
> all that America has to do is go home and leave Southeast Asia to the
> Asians![16]

Despite the fact that SEATO obviously was impotent and had
been created largely for show, both Presidents Johnson and Nixon in
later years continued to contend that the legal and moral basis for

U.S. military action in Vietnam was partially the solemn agreement
the United States made with SEATO nations.

By 1956, Diem, with U.S. government support, was in complete
control of the army, the bureaucracy, and the national police. The
U.S. government bought and paid for his entire regime—lock, stock,
and barrel.[17] By 1958, the United States was not only paying all costs
for his armed forces, but for 80 percent of all other government expenditures as well.

Diem's family prospered greatly during his reign. Five of his
brothers held critical positions during the 1950s. Thuc, the arch-
bishop of Hue, was the head of the Catholic Church in South Vietnam. Can, also in Hue, was the political "viceroy" of central Vietnam. Luyen, stationed abroad, was Diem's special ambassador to
England. Thuan, living in Saigon, was Diem's secretary of state.
Most important of all, however, was a fifth brother, Ngo Dinh Nhu,
who served as Diem's right-hand man. Nhu controlled the secret
police, regulated the concentration camps, and established a narcotics empire which made both him and Madame Nhu, as well as Diem
himself, extremely wealthy.[18]

Throughout the Diem years, each of these family members remained fiercely loyal to the government in Saigon. At the same time,
each found ways—like Nhu through the sale of narcotics—to filch the
scanty wealth of the Vietnamese people. The Catholic Ngo brothers
cared little for the peasants, most of whom were Buddhists living off
tiny plots of land in the countryside. Clearly, as one observer has
written, "abuse of power, nepotism, corruption, and cruel disregard
for the needs of the people were the example set by the 'Family,'"
and the head of the family was Ngo Dinh Diem.[19]

In addition to his own family, Diem at the beginning had the
support of the Catholic minority. Under the French, these Catholics
had enjoyed a privileged position not unlike the wealthy Vietnamese
landowners. They had fought against Ho Chi Minh in the First Indochina War, and nearly 750,000 migrated to the South after the Geneva Conference. Quickly, Diem resettled these Northerners around
Saigon and Hue, appointed their leaders to top bureaucratic posts,
and developed among them a "reliable and effective . . . power
base."[20]

Diem and the Saigon government also had the support of the aristocratic upper class who owned most of the land in South Vietnam.

Diem and the United States sided with these Vietnamese aristocrats, who, it is estimated, numbered about 480,000 people. Most members of this oligarchy were descendants of the feudal landowning class that had remained influential during the French colonial period. Most of them felt that the Americans were intellectually and culturally inferior to the French, but they were happy to have the Americans fill the gap left by the French. The United States and Diem permitted the old system of "rackrenting" to continue, whereby these rich landlords could remain in Saigon or elsewhere and invest their rent money in Swiss banks or in Vietnamese nightclubs and bars. Their only interest in the peasants was the money they could make from them.

British author Richard West relates a typical conversation with a Vietnamese tenant farmer:

> I asked Phan Van Que how often he saw his landlady. He replied, "My family has lived here for four generations. I am sixty-five. I have never seen the lady who owns my land. But each year at the time of the rice harvest, I see her cousins who come to collect the rent."[21]

It is easy to understand why the peasants eventually sided with the National Liberation Front and why the landowners sided with the United States and Saigon. The Saigon oligarchy did not want a repetition of what had happened during the First Indochina War, when Ho Chi Minh seized the large estates and redistributed the land among the peasants. Diem had reversed this trend and returned the land to the aristocratic barons.

The peasants, who comprised about 90 percent of the population of South Vietnam, soon realized that in lieu of living under the yoke of the French, they were now living under the rule of a tyrant who remained in office because he had the support of another foreign power. This new government likewise did very little for them, but always appeared to take something away—men for the army, money for the tax collector. There were no government programs of land reform, health and education services, public housing, or employment. As the Pentagon Papers described the situation in 1960: "45% of the land remained concentrated in the hands of 2% of landowners, and 15% of the landowners owned 75% of all the land."[22]

Based in Saigon, where the army and the landowning classes ruled society, Diem had little understanding and even less feeling for the villagers of South Vietnam. In his eyes, the peasants were almost a breed apart from the educated, city-living Vietnamese. Consequently, Diem saw to it that formal schooling remained a highly restricted venture. As one observer wrote: "It is still virtually impossible for a child born in a poor rural family to obtain a baccalaureate degree, without which he is permanently relegated to an inferior social position."[23] In this way, Diem was able to guarantee that the loyal, privileged classes would control Vietnamese society, at least in the cities. When assurances of support for his program began to pour in from Washington, Diem quickly expanded his system of control into the villages.

At the beginning, and for months and even years after the United States became involved in Vietnam, there was hope on the part of U.S. leaders that the peasant and village population could be won over to the support of the Saigon government. There was talk of "pacification" and "winning the hearts and minds of the people," but as we will see, this became a forlorn hope. Ultimately most of the peasants turned almost completely away from Saigon and the Americans, and many became active Vietcong supporters. In fact, most of the peasants hated all of the contestants: the Americans, the National Liberation Front, and the Saigon government. Their only wish was to be free of war and to live in peace. Whether their government was Communist or not was of little interest to them.[24]

Instead of trying to instigate reforms and thus gain the support of the peasants, Diem proclaimed that he would not tolerate any opposition to his regime. As early as 1955, the South Vietnamese leader moved against the old Vietminh organization, which still had support in the rural areas of the South. With the CIA's blessing, Diem organized an anti-Communist denunciation campaign to ferret out "Communist sympathizers." Relying on informers, Diem rounded up 100,000 prisoners, including large numbers of village chiefs, within the first year. While Diem supporters hailed the operation as a huge success, the real story was quite different. Thousands of innocent peasants were executed, while thousands more either went to jail or ended up in concentration camps. The United States backed Diem's denunciation campaign even though most of the victims were not hard-line Communists or even pro-Communists.[25]

In January 1956, Diem further extended his repression of the villages. He issued a harsh law which legalized concentration camps for anyone thought to be a danger to the state. This ordinance gave Diem's secret police a free hand against all potential opposition in South Vietnam. Squads of police literally invaded the hamlets outside Saigon, where they detained suspected Communists and then hauled them off to Diem's camps. Once again, as with the denunciation campaign, the press reported that many non-Communists simply disappeared overnight and were never heard of again.[26]

In May 1959, Diem established special military courts that sentenced to death anyone who threatened the security of the state or who belonged to a Communist organization. The law was so vague, yet so all-encompassing, that Diem was able to use South Vietnam's court system for political purposes. Defendants charged with treason had absolutely no rights and no recourse when brought before this judicial witch-hunt. The casualty lists continued to grow as popular resentment continued to build.[27]

In the countryside, Diem completely uprooted the popular land policy of the old Vietminh. In 1954, after defeating the French, the Communists had taken all liberated land and simply given it to the peasants. The effect of this gesture had been electric, as one guerrilla fighter recognized: "You don't understand how wretched the peasants were. When the Resistance solved the problem of the land, there was happiness and great uprising in the countryside. The concrete meaning of independence was to safeguard your land."[28] Then, suddenly, just when the villagers thought the land was theirs, Diem arrived on the scene and forcibly took it all away from them. Worse still, he transferred ownership of the land to his friends, who became absentee landlords living in Saigon. Instead of being master of a small plot of land, each peasant became a tenant once again, subject to new taxes by the government and by the privileged classes.[29]

Along with Diem's intolerable land policy were decisions in June and August 1956 to abolish all of the elected village councils throughout South Vietnam. Simultaneously, Diem dismissed over 2,500 village mayors. In place of the trusted village chiefs, most of whom had strong local ties to the Vietnamese peasants, the Saigon government created a haphazard but centralized administration responsible to Diem. Here we find one of the ultimate ironies of the Vietnam War, for most of the new village officials appointed by Diem were in fact North Vietnamese. Almost 750,000 North Vietnamese Catholics, fearful of Ho Chi Minh's new government, had migrated

South after 1954. These Northerners left *not* because of Ho's godless Communism, as U.S. officials liked to believe, but because the Catholics had had such close ties with Ho's enemy, the French. Now in South Vietnam, the Northerners formed a tight-knit element of support for President Diem, who rewarded this support with political appointments in Saigon and in the countryside. At the village level, the Vietnamese people suddenly found their own village chiefs out of office, replaced by outside "strangers who spoke a different dialect and practiced a different religion."[30] Diem's agents had little if any understanding of rural, Buddhist, Southern problems. Unable to relate to the peasants in the villages, these new officials became oppressive and corrupt. Before long, Diem's appointees actually expanded the manhunts in the villages, so much so that Phillipe DeVillers remarked in 1962:

> A certain sequence of events [has] become almost classical, denunciation, encirclement of villages, searches and raids, arrests of suspects, plundering, [and] interrogation enlivened sometimes by torture.[31]

The CIA supported wholeheartedly Saigon's program of intimidation and repression in the countryside. CIA operatives in Vietnam openly used Diem to nullify the Geneva Accords, and when the primary goal had been reached, the Agency helped Diem solidify his dictatorship over South Vietnam. Despite these draconic measures, the Diem/CIA partnership was flawed, for in the rural areas of South Vietnam, a new guerrilla movement was forming. Local assassinations, mostly of Diem's agents in the villages, were already taking place. Diem had made village life miserable, and various Southerners felt the time had come to retaliate. As one former Vietminh bemoaned:

> It was unbearable. There was only one alternative for South Vietnam. There was no hope [under] Diem. . . . Life became harder. If you asked to live in your former house, you were considered Communist and you were killed. Well, there was no other way.[32]

Diem's political enemies were incarcerated in "tiger cages"; ordinary villagers were subjected to harsh police state practices. Terrorism became widespread in the countryside. Diem was determined to stay in office with or without the support of the Vietnamese people.

In the United States, however, a propaganda campaign was undertaken to reassure the American people that Diem was very popular because he was giving his people a democratic government as an alternative to being enslaved by the Communists from the North. Specially selected news correspondents, commentators, and congressional committees were invited to view the scene at first hand. When they arrived in Saigon, they were carefully briefed by CIA public relations officers, and then taken on guided tours to specially prepared locations where everyone seemed happy and tremendously pleased with life under Ngo Dinh Diem. The visitors went home with praise for South Vietnam's democracy.

The fact was that as the Eisenhower administration drew to a close, the CIA's position in Vietnam continued to worsen. When John Foster Dulles died in 1959, two years before the expiration of Eisenhower's second term, it became increasingly difficult for his brother Allen, the CIA chief, to keep the lid on in Vietnam, and the CIA began to lose influence with the President. It was also hard to conceal the fact that Vietnamese villagers were becoming more and more resentful of Diem's rule. Many of them were still armed with weapons they had used against the French; some had obtained weapons from the departing Japanese after World War II. When government agents came to demand money and manpower, villagers began using their weapons.

It was only natural that the remnants of the old Vietminh would eventually band together in a new clandestine organization—but the Vietminh fighters were not alone. Increasingly, during the 1950s, armed religious sects, outlawed political parties, and other political and military groups had organized to oppose Diem. The most determined of these resistance fighters were the Hoa Hao and Cao Dai religious sects, and the Buddhist and student leaders who fought Saigon throughout the war.[33]

When the Southern Vietminh supporters first went underground to avoid Diem's concentration camps, there were just a few thousand cadres scattered about South Vietnam. These older guerrilla fighters had again become peasants.[34] At that time, Hanoi hesitated to support a new movement, even after the village war began, for fear that armed resistance to Diem would prevent free elections. As one authority has concluded:

Long after the date stipulated for the reunification elections, the Hanoi government . . . consistently cautioned Southern supporters of the VietMinh against the use of violence and urged them to employ peaceful methods in working towards unification.[35]

Ho Chi Minh hoped that South Vietnam would crumble or collapse as Diem alienated the people. The North Vietnamese leader decided, therefore, not to interfere. When a secret radio station in South Vietnam, calling itself the Voice of the South Vietnam Liberation Front, broadcast the theme song of the old Vietminh, Hanoi went so far as to denounce the rebel broadcasts. In June 1958, North Vietnam openly accused the front of "distort[ing] Marxist-Leninist theories" and "falsify[ing] the policies of the . . . Communist party" in Hanoi. Official statements also attacked the Voice of the South for ignoring "the urgent problems presented to our people," problems which included a reduction of armed forces and the need for a new Geneva Conference.[36] The Southern insurgency, therefore, grew in spite of Hanoi and not because of it.

This important lesson fell on deaf ears in Washington and Saigon, where the Communist threat was seen as monolithic and terribly real. Washington repeated again and again from 1960 to 1975 that the National Liberation Front, political counterpart to the Vietcong, was created and directed by North Vietnam, a claim used by the Johnson team to justify the massive air war in Southeast Asia. The truth was just the opposite.

The National Liberation Front started with the Committee of Defense of Peace, set up in Saigon in 1954. The goal of this committee was to pressure Diem into accepting the Geneva Accords. Committee leader Nguyen Huu Tho spent more than six years in Diem's prison camps, where he nurtured the idea of a National Liberation Front. Tho called his early peace committee "the embryo" of the NLF.[37]

Guerrilla activity grew during 1959 and led to a formal statement, entitled Declaration of the Resistance Veterans, issued in March 1960. The veterans claimed that Diem had "forced the people into legitimate self-defense" and that an all-out civil war would continue until South Vietnam was liberated from the U.S.-sponsored dictator. Asking Hanoi for recognition, the Southern rebels cried out: "If you don't do anything, you [Northern] communists, we will rise up against you, too."[38]

Faced with the possibility of losing all influence among the old Vietminh fighters in the South, North Vietnam finally recognized the existence of a war of liberation. In September 1960 the Lao Dong Communist Party in Hanoi sanctioned the idea of a national movement that would work to undermine the Diem government. It was just the commitment needed by the rebels. As opposition in the countryside of South Vietnam reached crisis proportions, and Diem responded with even harsher retaliation, Southerners meeting in the jungles formally created the National Liberation Front of South Vietnam on December 20, 1960. Calling for "a broad national democratic coalition administration" dedicated to reforms and to peace, the NLF offered an alternative to the peasants of South Vietnam which many villagers openly welcomed.[39] If not for the decision by the United States to back Diem to the hilt, the new movement could have forced Diem to step down or at least to moderate his repression.

The National Liberation Front grew rapidly during the early 1960s. Guerrilla activity was stepped up. Key positions in the NLF were held by non-Communists (Vice-President Humphrey was later to admit that no more than 15 percent of NLF leaders were Communist Party members), and very few of the fighting forces were Communists.[40] The uprising was directed largely by former members of the Vietminh who had waged war against French colonial rule. They had fought for freedom against one foreign power, and now they were grouped once more to fight against another.

Under the terms of the Geneva Armistice, populations could shift from one part of the newly divided country to the other as they wished. Some 100,000 party and resistance cadres and army troops had remained with Ho in North Vietnam. These Southerners had been promised that they could return home quickly and that national elections would soon reunify the country. But when elections were not held, and Diem launched his terror against the countryside, a growing number of these people began to migrate south. Some of these became advisers and leaders of the NLF military forces. Others had to win the confidence of local villagers before joining the National Liberation Front.[41] The majority of them brought no weapons with them from the North. They brought only a will to survive and a dedication to independence and nationalism for which they fought with great courage and bravery. They saw the rebellion as the only hope of ridding their country of foreign domination. Into every

South Vietnamese village went guerrilla groups, disposing of Diem's agents, driving out government troops, and then close on their heels came representatives of the National Liberation Front.[42]

When Saigon decided to relocate thousands of peasants into refugee camps—"strategic hamlets" they were called—the NLF set up a shadow government, the People's Revolutionary Party. It was avowedly a Communist Party organization and naturally adhered closely to the leadership in Hanoi. Yet regional ties and the urge for independence continued to shape the NLF, which revealed its top leadership at its first official Congress in February 1962. Tho became president; the Buddhist monk Son Vong joined four others as vice-presidents. The entire high command was Southern in origin, and the NLF program adopted that year offered as its aims freedom and democracy, gradual reunification, and a neutral and peaceful foreign policy. The Front demanded American withdrawal from Vietnam, and pledged a heroic struggle if American intervention continued.[43]

Diem was losing control. His hamlet program was turning into a disaster. President Eisenhower was becoming restless and impatient. He had been prevailed upon to increase American military personnel in Vietnam from 350 to 800, but that was as far as he would go. The U.S. public was told that those troops were simply an advisory group, showing the Vietnamese how to use modern American weapons.

The CIA at this time did not seem to have the unquestioned support of the President. Eisenhower now agreed to go to Paris for a summit meeting with the USSR's Khrushchev to try to establish coexistence between the two superpowers. By an interesting coincidence, on the eve of that meeting, the CIA sent its U-2 spy plane over the Soviet Union. The summit conference was scheduled for mid-May 1960; the U-2, piloted by Francis Gary Powers, was shot down May 2. Eisenhower did go to Paris, but the two men did not meet. Khrushchev demanded a public apology, which Eisenhower refused to give. Eisenhower's postsummit visit to the Soviet Union was canceled. Abundant circumstantial evidence, which later surfaced, showed that the CIA may have played a role in this incident.

John F. Kennedy was elected to the presidency and took office in January 1961. However, the CIA's efforts to convince him to throw full support behind its Vietnam activities were thwarted by the Bay of Pigs fiasco. Prior to Kennedy's inauguration, the CIA had recruited, armed, and organized several thousand Cuban expatriates into a guerrilla force to invade Cuba and topple Castro. Kennedy was told the Cuban people were ready to revolt and were waiting eagerly for the American invading force to spark their uprising against Fidel Castro. It was a CIA operation from beginning to end, and the Agency was firm in its belief that the landing would be safe and come as a surprise to the Castro regime. However, Castro had been forewarned, and the invading force was met with devastating gunfire.

Cuban insurgents and the CIA both frantically implored President Kennedy to assist them with American airpower, but he refused. The invaders were defeated, and the Kennedy administration was humiliated. Castro, pushed further into the arms of the USSR, invited the Russians to place missiles in Cuba to protect him from future American aggression. The result was the Cuban Missile Crisis. Kennedy had learned a bitter lesson that he did not wish to repeat in Vietnam.

The proponents of a continued involvement in Vietnam then turned to pressuring Kennedy's advisers, many of whom cooperated closely with the CIA. One of these was Robert McNamara, the newly appointed secretary of defense. McNamara was provided with mountains of statistics, reams of data, charts, graphs, and effectiveness studies concerning Vietnam—the kind of material that impressed this human computer. Next, the CIA approached Dean Rusk, the new secretary of state, a longtime hawk who had always sympathized with CIA goals. He too came to side with the Agency's war plans in Vietnam. Finally, there was General Maxwell Taylor, the former army chief of staff under Eisenhower, who had retired because of policy disagreements. Taylor became Kennedy's national security adviser and later chairman of the Joint Chiefs of Staff, reporting directly to the President. Certainly this was a man for the CIA to befriend. In his book, *The Uncertain Trumpet,* Taylor advocated the very kind of counterinsurgency the CIA had been carrying out all over the world for years, with the approval and cooperation of the White House Task Force.

Having recruited support within the administration, the Agency attempted to persuade Kennedy to help maintain Diem as the legitimate leader in South Vietnam. With Cardinal Spellman's powerful support, Kennedy naturally leaned toward supporting the Catholic Diem, whom he had known since the early 1950s. Nevertheless, he was cautious. In May 1961 he sent Vice-President Lyndon Johnson to Saigon to evaluate the situation and report back to him.[44]

When Johnson arrived in Saigon, the CIA had everything carefully planned. The Agency was expert at handling important American visitors. They had given senators, congressmen, government officials, and newsmen the official guided tour for years. Now they outdid themselves for the vice president. When he returned to Washington, Johnson reported to the President that combat troops should be sent to South Vietnam to save the Vietnamese people from the Communists. Diem himself had ambivalent feelings about that recommendation. Although he wanted American financial and military support, he feared that American military involvement might mean his own loss of control. Diem's attitude is reflected in a secret message sent by the American Embassy in Saigon to Secretary of State Dean Rusk, dated May 12, 1961, not declassified until 1974:

> General McGarr and I were present at discussions between Diem and Vice President Johnson on the introduction of U.S. forces into Vietnam. Diem told VP Johnson he does *not* want U.S. combat troops to fight in South Vietnam . . . except in case of overt aggression.[45]

Johnson did not agree, and in his report to Kennedy he said that

> the basic decision in Southeast Asia is here; we must decide whether to help those countries to the best of our ability or throw in the towel in the area and pull back our defenses to San Francisco and a "fortress America" concept. More important, we would say to the world in this case that we don't live up to our treaties and don't stand by our friends.[46]

Johnson's report carried great weight with Kennedy, who put much trust in people who had been there and seen for themselves. Similar messages came from McGeorge and William Bundy, from McNamara, and from Rusk. All seconded the CIA contentions, but Johnson's report was decisive. Ultimately the only remaining question in Kennedy's mind was how much military assistance the United States should give. The American Military Advisory Group had already been increased from 685 to 888, and Kennedy now agreed that number was insufficient. The only problem left to circumvent was Diem's refusal to ask for these "advisers." U.S. Ambassador Nolting in Saigon wired Rusk:

We badly need official guidance on Washington thinking re sending U.S. forces to SVN . . . particularly puzzled by Department press spokesman's reported statement that he did not know whether or not GVN [the South Vietnamese government] has not so requested.[47]

Finally, Diem gave in to U.S. pressure. On October 13, 1961, he reluctantly made a formal request for additional U.S. forces to be introduced into South Vietnam as combat training units. Compelled to furnish President Kennedy with a good reason for secretly introducing additional troops, Ambassador Nolting suggested to Dean Rusk that he might utilize recent flooding in South Vietnam as a pretext. Kennedy was still hesitant and finally decided to send Robert McNamara and General Taylor with other military and State Department advisers to Saigon for another look at the situation.[48] The upshot of the visit was that Taylor recommended that 8,000 to 10,000 troops be immediately dispatched under the guise of flood relief forces. He also recommended that military personnel be put under the control of CIA operatives intent on keeping the war a counterinsurgency operation.

Through 1962 and into 1963 a gradual buildup began that increased until there were approximately 18,000 U.S. "advisers" in South Vietnam. All this went on behind the closed doors of the Oval Office. There was little consultation with Congress, and of course this increased involvement was not known by most American citizens.

The introduction of these forces created new problems not only for Diem, but for the CIA. The new military leaders were difficult for the CIA to control because they took orders only from within the military chain of command. In addition, press correspondents covering the conflict began sending more truthful reports back to the United States about the status of insurgency in South Vietnam. The news that began to filter home was not encouraging. The war was going badly. Buddhist riots and sacrificial self-immolation protesting the war and the Diem regime appeared nightly on American television screens. Now there was a new public awareness, and Kennedy, ever sensitive to the popular mood, became more and more hesitant to support American involvement. Publicly he stated that while the United States could send military and economic aid, ultimately it would be up to the South Vietnamese themselves to win the war.

Before Kennedy accepted the McNamara-Taylor report, he received strong contrary opinions from other sources in the government. Roger Hilsman disagreed and strongly recommended against Taylor's proposal for sending in military advisers under the pretext of helping flood victims. Ambassador Nolting flatly informed the State Department no personnel were needed for flood relief.[49]

The strongest objections to further intervention were voiced by Kennedy's fellow New Frontiersman John Kenneth Galbraith, who was serving as U.S. ambassador to India. In a top-secret message "for the President's eyes only," Galbraith explained in great detail why the United States should not support Diem. He stated that Diem was a petty dictator who wanted only to consolidate power within his own family; he had lost touch with the Vietnamese people; his brother Nhu was running a police state; and Diem would never make the changes in his government that were necessary. "It follows from my reasoning that the only solution must be to drop Diem."[50]

In response, Kennedy considered sending Galbraith on a mission to confer with representatives of the North Vietnamese government. The trip, however, was scuttled at the suggestion of Dean Rusk, who believed that it would undermine Diem's already shaky government. Another opportunity to find a peaceful solution was lost.

Despite the introduction of 18,000 additional American military advisers, conditions in Vietnam continued to deteriorate. It became apparent that Diem's rule was disintegrating. Finally the CIA began a campaign against him. Information criticizing Diem, for example, was fed to important U.S. publications, which began to withdraw their support from him. In desperation Diem sent his sister-in-law Madame Nhu to the United States to rekindle the support that had been so forthcoming in the 1950s. But it was too late. Diem had few friends left either in the United States or in South Vietnam.

Again Kennedy dispatched McNamara and Taylor to Saigon to help him determine what to do next. Strangely enough, they brought back an optimistic report to the effect that the war was being won, and that if they could just get rid of Diem, a truly popular government could be organized around which all the South Vietnamese would rally. They predicted that if Diem were scuttled, the United States could begin withdrawing its troops almost immediately and that by 1965 a popular government would defeat the Communists and end the war.

Soon an extended debate ensued over the proposed launching of a coup against America's erstwhile ally, Diem. Ambassador Lodge insisted that the United States should not merely support a coup, but should make "all-out efforts to get [the] Generals to move promptly."[51] He quickly plunged into negotiations with various Vietnamese generals for just that purpose. The CIA station chief urged that the United States "not set [itself] irrevocably against the assassination plot" against Diem's brothers,[52] though the documents surrounding the question of Diem's own assassination are still classified.

On November 2, 1963, Diem was overthrown and assassinated.

:3

PRESIDENT JOHNSON PLANS
VIETNAM WAR
November 1963–August 1964

Everything I knew about history told me that if I got out
of Vietnam and let Ho Chi Minh run through the streets
of Saigon, then I'd be doing exactly what Chamberlain
did in World War II. I'd be giving a big fat reward to
aggression. And I knew that if we let Communist
aggression succeed in taking over South Vietnam, there
would follow in this country an endless national
debate—a mean and destructive debate—that would
shatter my Presidency, kill my administration, and
damage our democracy. I knew that Harry Truman and
Dean Acheson had lost their effectiveness from the day
that the Communists took over in China. I believed that
the loss of China had played a large role in the rise of
Joe McCarthy. And I knew that all these problems, taken
together, were chickenshit compared with what might
happen if we lost Vietnam.

Oh, I could see it coming all right. Every night when I
fell asleep I would see myself tied to the ground in the
middle of a long, open space. In the distance, I could
hear the voices of thousands of people. They were all
shouting at me and running toward me: "Coward!
Traitor! Weakling!" They kept coming closer. They
began throwing stones. At exactly that moment I would
generally wake up . . . terribly shaken. But there was
more. You see, I was as sure as any man could be that
once we showed how weak we were, Moscow and
Peking would move in a flash to exploit our weakness.
They might move independently or they might move
together. But move they would—whether through
nuclear blackmail, through subversion, with regular

armed forces or in some other manner. As nearly as
anyone can be certain of anything, I knew they couldn't
resist the opportunity to expand their control over the
vacuum of power we would leave behind us. And so
would begin World War III. So you see, I was bound to
be crucified either way I moved.

—*Lyndon B. Johnson*[1]

In May 1961, as American commitments to South Vietnam deep-
ened, President Kennedy sent Lyndon Johnson to Saigon. It proved
to be a decisive first trip. Then and there, LBJ later said, he made up
his mind never to let the "Communist bastards" take over the country. "The battle against Communism must be joined in Southeast
Asia with strength and determination to achieve success there," he
told Kennedy. Vietnam could still be saved, provided the United
States creatively managed its military aid program. The die was cast.
Either we help Vietnam or "we throw in the towel in the area and
pull back our defenses to San Francisco and a 'Fortress America'
concept."[2]

Johnson was just one of a growing number who recommended a
deepening commitment to Saigon and Diem. The lasting effect was
not on the client state, as Halberstam notes, but on Lyndon Johnson:

> *He* had given *our* word. . . . It committed the person of Lyndon John-
> son. To him, a man's word was important. He himself was now commit-
> ted both to the war and to Diem personally.[3]

Though privately he expressed reservations to Kennedy about
Diem's leadership ability, publicly he lauded him as the "Churchill
of Southeast Asia." From this time forward, LBJ's commitment to
South Vietnam never wavered.

When an assassin's bullet made him President in November 1963,
Johnson set a firm and forceful line on Vietnam. There were to be no
negotiations with the Communists, for in the end there was remarkably little to negotiate. They had only to end their aggression and
subversion and the war would cease. Johnson ordered the State Department to begin a major campaign blaming the Hanoi government
for controlling and directing the Vietcong in the South. And he publicly insisted that America's objective was only to improve the conduct of the war under the new South Vietnamese leadership with

minimum American involvement. But privately his attitude, succinctly captured in his blunt comment to Ambassador Henry Cabot Lodge two days after he became President, was: He was not about to be "the President who saw Southeast Asia go the way that China went."[4]

To accomplish his objectives, Johnson first surrounded himself with a team that he knew would carry out his orders. He was not the kind of man who tolerated disagreement from his subordinates; they agreed with him, did what he said to do, or were replaced. As Johnson himself put it, "I don't want loyalty, I want *loyalty!* I want [my staff] to kiss my ass in Macy's window at high noon and tell me it smells like roses."[5] Later he remarked that "there are many, many, who can recommend, advise, and sometimes a few of them consent, but there is only one that has been chosen by the American people to decide."[6]

Among the men willing to meet Johnson's test of loyalty was Hubert Humphrey, one of the leading figures in Congress during the late 1940s and 1950s and Johnson's choice for the vice presidency in 1964. Though a champion of liberal causes throughout his career, Humphrey reluctantly fell into line with the President's decision to support the Vietnam War:

> Many people feel today, they say, we should not be in Vietnam. Well, whether we should or not, we are. And we have been there a long time. So I am not going to argue about whether we should have been there. That is history and it cannot be repealed; it is a fact.[7]

The new secretary of state, Dean Rusk, was the President's veteran in foreign policy matters. Rusk saw America's mission in the same way his President did, and was vitally concerned with America keeping its word around the world.[7a] More and more after 1963, Rusk acted as Johnson's spokesman, endorsing policies already determined by the President. Acting on instructions from the White House, Rusk's public statements became loftier and loftier as America's war effort increased.

> Let us be clear about what is involved today in Southeast Asia. We are not involved with empty phrases or conceptions that ride upon the clouds. We are talking about the vital national interests of the United States in the peace of the Pacific. . . . We are talking about the safety of nations with whom we are allied—and in the integrity of the American commitment to join in meeting attack.[8]

The secretary of state emphasized the same themes that Johnson did, whether this involved accusing North Vietnam of "Communist aggression" or publicizing America's "vital national interests" in Southeast Asia. In every forum possible, Rusk assured the American public that the United States was in complete control of the situation in Vietnam.

Robert McNamara, the "computerized" secretary of defense, also advised Johnson. He symbolized the idea, noted one critic, that the Kennedy administration "could manage and control events in an intelligent, rational way. Taking on a guerrilla war was like buying a sick foreign company; you brought your systems to it."[9] Kennedy had lured McNamara away from the Ford Motor Company to reshape the nation's defense structure; under Johnson he continued his program, concentrating on management and analyzing quantified data. Vietnam was a problem of charts, models, and indicators of progress. McNamara believed in freedom for South Vietnam, resisting Communist aggression and preserving American security; he thought Communist control of Southeast Asia was a direct threat to national security.

Other presidential assistants also played significant roles in the Johnson administration. One was McGeorge Bundy, the national security adviser, who controlled much of the foreign policy information that reached Johnson. He argued in favor of the morality of America's commitment to help the people of South Vietnam decide their own destiny, free of external interference. Another was Walt Rostow, a former professor at M.I.T. and a foreign policy expert who chaired the State Department's policy planning council. Rostow saw Vietnam as a pivotal test case of national wars of liberation and proposed that the United States "build a fence around Vietnam."[10] Finally, there was William Bundy, older brother of McGeorge. His position was assistant secretary of state, and his Thirty-Day Plan was the most important element in the secret war plans of 1964.

These advisers represented the civilian side of the administration; the Joint Chiefs of Staff in the Pentagon represented the military side. Among the most influential military experts was General Maxwell Taylor. Taylor was appointed chairman of the Joint Chiefs of Staff in 1962, and two years later he became U.S. ambassador to Vietnam. Taylor reinforced Johnson's belief in the domino theory: "Unless we can achieve this objective [i.e., an independent, non-

Communist South Vietnam], almost all of Southeast Asia will probably fall under Communist domination," and "There's always a danger of a sort of bandwagon movement, I am afraid, among these very weak countries."[11] His successor as chairman of the Joint Chiefs, General Earle Wheeler, constantly pressured Johnson and McNamara for more troops and more planes.

When Lyndon Johnson became President, the Vietnamese were engaged in wide-scale demonstrations—in Saigon and throughout South Vietnam. Buddhists and students began protesting against the war and calling for a neutralist solution that would include Communists in the government. At the same time, the National Liberation Front sent an appeal to Diem's temporary successor, General Duong Van Minh, declaring its wish to negotiate and plan for free elections. Van Minh lent a favorable ear, but this effort by the NLF was met with silence from Washington. It represented the first of many such appeals that South Vietnam's rebel forces were to make toward the military cliques in Saigon.

The NLF was not alone in its appeal. Among others, President Charles de Gaulle of France offered his services as mediator if he could help Vietnam find peace and unity. In December of 1963 the Cambodian chief of state, Prince Norodom Sihanouk, also called upon South Vietnam's government to stop the fighting. By late 1963 the list of peace proposals had grown to impressive proportions. Perhaps the most important attempts to end the war came from Secretary General U Thant of the United Nations. He suggested that Washington support a coalition government in South Vietnam. He noted that the NLF appeared willing to work out a political solution, and that Saigon and the United States should cooperate. Later in December, U Thant brought President Johnson a personal message from Ho Chi Minh, a peace initiative from Hanoi calling for the opening of talks. U Thant hoped that Johnson would seize the opportunity to end the Vietnam conflict without further delay.[12] He waited in vain.

As the world waited, Johnson immediately rejected any conferences that might bring peace at the cost of compromise with the Communists. On November 26, 1963, Johnson approved secret hit-and-run air raids into North Vietnam and Laos. Shortly thereafter, he requested that a range of plans be drawn up for extending the war. But his advisers were pressing him with news of the deteriorating situation in Saigon. McNamara, upon his return from Saigon in December, told Johnson:

> Vietcong progress has been great during the period since the coup [against Diem], with my best guess being that the situation has in fact been deteriorating in the countryside since July to a far greater extent than we realized. . . . The Vietcong now control very high proportions of the people in certain key provinces. . . .
>
> The new government [of General Van Minh] is the greatest source of concern. It is indecisive and drifting.
>
> The situation is very disturbing. . . . Current trends unless reversed in the next two to three months will lead to neutralization at best and more likely to a communist-controlled state. . . . We should watch the situation very carefully, running scared, hoping for the best, but preparing for more forceful moves if the situation does not show early signs of improvement.[13]

McNamara further reported that "plans for covert action into North Vietnam were prepared as we had requested . . . and were an excellent job." Concluded McNamara, "they present a wide variety of sabotage and psychological operations against North Vietnam from which I believe we should aim to select those that provide maximum pressure with minimum risk."[14]

Johnson now turned to the Joint Chiefs of Staff. In January 1964 they suggested that the President "make plain to the enemy the U.S. determination to see the Vietnam campaign through to a favorable conclusion" and that the administration do away with "self-imposed restrictions" and "prepare for whatever level of activity may be required." The Joint Chiefs demanded more freedom of action, including the direct use of U.S. combat forces, American control of the total war effort, and the right to extend the war into North Vietnam and Laos.[15]

One of the new President's first actions was to instruct McNamara to proceed with Operation Switchback, a secret program in which the military was gradually to take charge of CIA activities in Vietnam. The CIA, with its own secret army, had been responsible for dealing with the South Vietnamese regime; Operation Switchback would turn Saigon over to the Pentagon, which would then continue the war in Vietnam.

In order to establish complete control in South Vietnam, Johnson needed to control General Van Minh, Diem's successor. Minh publicly leaned toward neutralism in the belief that de-escalation and the creation of a coalition government might be South Vietnam's only hope. At the beginning of 1964, Johnson sent Minh a New Year's message, hoping to change the general's mind:

> Neutralization of South Vietnam would only be another name for a Communist takeover. . . . The United States will continue to furnish you and your people with the fullest measure of support in this bitter fight. . . . We shall maintain in Vietnam American personnel and materiel to assist you in achieving victory.[16]

When Minh ignored Johnson's advice and continued to advocate neutralism, Johnson determined that Minh must go.

The President found a replacement more in agreement with his war goals in a CIA protégé, General Nguyen Khanh. With CIA help, Minh was deposed in January 1964 and Khanh was given control of the Saigon government. On March 20, 1964, LBJ cabled Henry Cabot Lodge:

> Your mission is precisely for the purpose of knocking down the idea of neutralization wherever it rears its ugly head. . . . Nothing is more important than to stop neutralist talk wherever we can by whatever means we can.[17]

Immediately, Khanh began taking orders from Washington; he rejected another offer of the Vietcong to negotiate a peaceful settlement, and he publicly attacked the "Communist conspiracy" in Southeast Asia.

But the situation in Saigon did not improve with the ousting of General Van Minh; if anything, the South Vietnamese regime had more problems than ever. Whereas Minh had shown a degree of independence from his "mentors"—the CIA and the American Embassy—his successor, the boisterous, hard-nosed Khanh, remained faithful to the CIA and the United States. Khanh pressured the United States for more military aid and at the same time cracked down on those who spoke out for peace. All the while, the National Liberation Front's campaign to win support among South Vietnam's peasants intensified, resulting in the loss of more territory for Khanh's military forces.

In February 1964 Johnson approved a secret plan, composed of three parts:[18]

• The first part—"Operation Plan 34A"—was directed by McNamara and the Joint Chiefs from the Pentagon. It consisted of flights over Vietnam by U-2 spy planes, kidnappings of North Vietnamese citizens to obtain intelligence information, the use of parachute sabotage teams against the North, and commando raids from the sea. These destructive undertakings were designed "to result in substantial destruction, economic loss and harassment to Hanoi," and were to increase throughout 1964.

• The second part was a series of U.S.-supervised air raids into Laos, conducted in large part by pilots of Air America, the pseudo-private airline run by the CIA. The new air war in Laos was a preview of the massive air war against North Vietnam, at the expense of the people of Laos. It was in response to the military advances of the North Vietnamese and reflected the administration's desire to assert pressure on North Vietnam. The target area was to expand beyond the Laotian border by the summer of 1964; by that time American planes would be hitting targets inside North Vietnam itself.

• Part three was the dispatching of destroyer patrols, code-named DeSoto patrols, into the Gulf of Tonkin, where North Vietnamese ports were located. Beginning in mid-February 1964, destroyers regularly sailed into the gulf to gather intelligence for 34A raids, to support South Vietnam's naval raids against the coast of North Vietnam, and, most importantly, to flaunt America's military might. Washington intended to react swiftly and decisively, in the event that Hanoi interpreted these patrols as a provocation.

All parts of the three-part plan were, in fact, designed to provoke Hanoi by creating an atmosphere of increasing tension. Because America's hold on South Vietnam continued to weaken, the President ordered that the "contingency planning for pressures against North Vietnam should be speeded up."[19]

Indeed, Washington became increasingly frustrated with Saigon's inability to defeat the Vietcong forces in jungle warfare. Despite ever-growing aid from the United States, Khanh simply could not contain the enemy. McNamara again visited Saigon in March 1964 and again reported that the Vietcong were continually gaining rural support. Political turmoil since September 1963 in South Vietnam had become "unquestionably . . . worse" despite the installation of the Khanh government. The secretary proposed air raids by South Vietnam into Laos as well as retaliatory bombing into North Vietnam in hopes that it would weaken Vietcong strength in the South. If such action were not enough, McNamara concluded, then the President should consider using an American air commando squadron in South Vietnam plus Saigon's air force in a general air offensive against the North. Johnson quickly approved McNamara's suggestion that these plans should start right away. McNamara also noted that the guerrilla organization had bonds of loyalty among its members that the South Vietnamese army, ARVN, did not have—a common cause, the liberation of Vietnam from foreign control.[20] Furthermore, the Vietcong had the stronger incentives: nationalism, freedom from foreign rule, and hope for a peaceful, independent national future.

In March 1964 Walt Rostow provided a theoretical framework for escalation. He suggested that this new speeded-up pressure should take the form of the bombing of industries and other selected targets in North Vietnam. The idea of bombing North Vietnam appeared again in April 1964, when Johnson's advisers met in Saigon for an important strategy session. Dean Rusk headed the delegation, which included General Earle Wheeler from the Joint Chiefs, Ambassador Henry Cabot Lodge from the U.S. Embassy in Saigon, and William Bundy from the State Department. The group discussed escalation of the war. The raids of Operation Plan 34A were a good start, according to Rusk, but he suggested moving beyond them to secret U.S. support of South Vietnamese air raids, and from there ultimately to open "aerial reconnaissance, naval displays, naval bombardments and air attacks."[21]

Before Johnson could approve these actions, however, his advisers cautioned that he would need some kind of sanction from Congress. For the first time, high-level officials broached the possibility of securing a congressional resolution to untie the President's hands in the event of the crisis worsening.[22]

On May 17, rebel Laotian forces, backed by North Vietnam, launched a sudden offensive against the forces of the Laotian government, backed by the CIA. Johnson therefore ordered the State Department to concoct yet another comprehensive military plan to rescue Saigon's battered regime. The task was assigned to William Bundy. In late May, he presented for the President's approval a step-by-step Thirty-Day Plan for open American military involvement in Vietnam. The Bundy plan proposed two different thrusts—one military, one political. First, Bundy outlined the Pentagon's military assignments: to locate the major bombing targets in North Vietnam and to gather sufficient planes to hit them. The Pentagon then would await the President's order to begin the bombing war. Next, he outlined sixteen political steps to be carried out in the ensuing thirty-day period. This plan included tactics to stall any attempt to convene a conference on Laos or Vietnam until after inauguration day, speeches by Johnson to win congressional support, and, finally, a presidential order to release the major air strike forces for service in Southeast Asia. These steps were to be accompanied by accusations pinpointing North Vietnam's aggression against the South.

The President decided not to act immediately. The crisis in Laos had died down almost as quickly as it began, so intervention would not be politically acceptable to Congress. But he now had a workable plan of action to be used later when the time was right.

In early June 1964, the President ordered still another strategy session. All of Johnson's key advisers met in Honolulu to "review for . . . final approval a series of plans for Executive action." Rusk, Lodge, McNamara, Bundy, Taylor, John McCone, head of the CIA, and General William Westmoreland, chief U.S. military leader in Saigon, debated the President's new Thirty-Day Plan. Ambassador Lodge argued that the selective bombing against military targets in North Vietnam would bolster the morale of the South Vietnamese and help support the United States' position in the South. The Joint Chiefs, to underscore their seriousness, produced a list of ninety-four targets, later to become Washington's key targets. The group quickly reached a consensus that an effective American air war against North Vietnam held the greatest chance of fulfilling the goals of the Johnson administration.

The group then shifted its attention to the need for a congressional resolution to give Johnson broad powers to prosecute the war. McNamara felt such a resolution was needed to guarantee the security of South Vietnam against retaliatory air attacks and to sanction the sending of as many as seven divisions to South Vietnam. Rusk, in contrast to Lodge, quickly agreed, adding that such a popular sanction was particularly necessary if the President decided to call up the reserves. The congressional resolution that was introduced in Congress in August 1964, therefore, was actually contemplated at this Honolulu meeting.

So President Johnson had both a comprehensive thirty-day war plan for Vietnam and a consensus that bombing was the key to defeating the "Communist conspiracy." To win the support of both the American public and Congress, the Honolulu Conference concluded that the administration increase its public relations campaign at home. Meanwhile, the Pentagon should augment its military supplies and stocks in Thailand.[23]

In July, through a Canadian official, Washington warned Hanoi that war was imminent if the North did not abandon the Vietcong in the South. On July 14, 1964, General Khanh voiced his dramatic battle cry, "To the North!" He made it based on assurances that American military involvement would soon be expanded. Two days later, Marshal Nguyen Cao Ky declared that the South Vietnamese air force was ready; it might not destroy all of North Vietnam, but Hanoi was certainly doomed.[24]

General Khanh's invasion message stunned the world. Despite a muted reprimand from Washington, observers now expected a major escalation of the war. The threat of a wider war brought forth a second flurry of peace proposals, this time more urgent than ever. Johnson and his advisers in Washington knew they had to defuse them quickly.

The peace overtures were led by U Thant. He pleaded with Washington to convene a new Geneva Conference to end the fighting in Indochina. The U.N. leader asked the warring parties—Hanoi, Saigon, *and* Washington—to consider the advantages of negotiating a settlement. ". . . The only sensible alternative," he said, "is the political and diplomatic method of negotiations which, even at this late hour, may offer some chance of a solution."[25] U Thant's initiative found fervent support in France, where President Charles de Gaulle warned of the grave dangers of escalation. He proposed that the great powers either convene a new Geneva Conference or else return to the original Geneva Accords of 1954. Only by adhering to these original accords, cautioned de Gaulle, could the opposing armies prevent Vietnam's civil war from expanding into a nightmarish general war in all of Asia. De Gaulle's message certainly added strength and credibility to U Thant's proposal, but the greatest impact of all came from two other sources.

In a move that took Washington by surprise, both North Vietnam and the Soviet Union reacted to the July 1964 crisis by calling for peace. Soviet leaders sent messages by radio from Moscow to the fourteen nations that had met at Geneva to discuss the crisis over Laos in 1961–62, proposing another peace conference to settle the Vietnam conflict. Hanoi sent out a similar message, pleading for a new conference to work out a peaceful settlement.[26] The People's Republic of China also backed the Soviet proposal.

In the face of such widespread efforts, including the message brought by the author from the Kremlin, via *Pravda*, to President Johnson, which we have previously described, it quickly became apparent that Johnson had not been moved. He rejected any and all proposals, counting on the argument that North Vietnam was responsible for the war in the South. The President explained to the public that American honor and prestige were on the line in Vietnam and that the peace offers favored only the Communists in Hanoi. "We do not believe in conferences called to ratify terror," Johnson said.[27] By the end of July 1964 his administration ordered 5,000 more troops to Vietnam. But before Johnson could accomplish his objectives, he needed not only to be chosen President in his own right in the 1964 election, but also to insure that his policies were authorized by the U.S. Congress.

TONKIN GULF:
INCIDENT AND RESOLUTION
August 1964

Many people don't even know the story of the Tonkin
Gulf Resolution. And I think it's important that
everybody know it. . . . We have made mistakes before,
but I think this is the first time in our history that we
have been deliberately deceived and lied to by our chief
executives. And that is what everybody in this country
has got to know. . . . I don't see how Lyndon Johnson
can sleep well at night, when he must know that the
blood of 50,000 Americans is on his head. And not only
50,000 Americans, but hundreds of thousands of innocent
Southeast Asians—Vietnamese, Cambodians, Laotians.
And in addition to that, of course, billions of dollars went
down the drain, funds that should have been used for
other, long-neglected uses.
—*Senator Ernest Gruening*[1]

Whlle America was engrossed in the 1964 presidential election
campaign, Johnson's staff was busy preparing the scenario for what
was to happen after Johnson was elected. The contingency plans
called for American bombing raids on North Vietnam, for the
buildup of U.S. forces in Southeast Asia, and for a propaganda campaign to stifle any opposition from the American public. The vital
question was not how to secure peace but how to start an air war—
when, where, and under what circumstances. Johnson and his staff
concluded that an open bombing war would be feasible only if it
were made to appear that the United States was defending itself.
Only then could Johnson count on all the support he needed.

The immediate problem was how to create an incident that would provoke the North Vietnamese into attack and make the United States appear to be the injured party. There were at the time no regular American combat troops in South Vietnam. North Vietnam had no air force capable of attacking American targets. However, it did have about fifty patrol boats, a small force that included a few Soviet torpedo boats. Thus the North was capable of launching a small-scale attack on ships of the U.S. Navy, provided an inviting target could be arranged.[2]

The Gulf of Tonkin seemed the ideal place for this incident to take place. The South Vietnamese had sent their boats into these Northern waters, and the U.S. Navy had been sending destroyers, the DeSoto patrols, into the gulf on intelligence-gathering missions. These destroyers had always stayed far enough at sea so as not to provoke the North Vietnamese. But now Johnson's advisers determined that the DeSoto patrols would become the bait to lure North Vietnam into an attack.

A South Vietnamese raid was scheduled for the night and early morning of July 30–31, 1964. It was not to be the usual secret attempt to land infiltrators and saboteurs. For the first time this was to be a direct shelling of the coast of North Vietnam, in order to insure a response. Immediately following the shelling, a DeSoto patrol destroyer would be ordered to enter the Gulf of Tonkin.[3]

In compliance with this directive, the destroyer *Maddox* was detached from its squadron in Japan and sent south. After a brief stop at Taiwan, where a communication van—or electronic listening post— was installed, the *Maddox* sailed to the Gulf of Tonkin, entering that area on the evening of July 30. The *Maddox* sailed past the coastal area that had been shelled and close to the area of Hon Vat and Hon Me islands, where North Vietnamese torpedo boats were known to be based. In approaching these islands, the *Maddox* probed well within the legal twelve-mile limit.

The U.S. Navy was dangling tempting bait. As far as the North Vietnamese could tell, the *Maddox* apparently had directed the South Vietnamese attack on their shore and now was brazenly intruding into North Vietnamese territorial waters on a spying mission. The *Maddox* sailed past the area and then, following orders, returned to the Gulf on August 2; North Vietnam decided to respond. Three North Vietnamese torpedo boats attacked the *Maddox* in broad daylight on August 2, launching several torpedoes which the *Maddox* evaded. The *Maddox* fired upon the torpedo boats, possibly hitting one, before the patrol boats fled. Aircraft called in for support damaged two vessels and left one dead in the water.[4]

The President thought he had the incident he wanted. The CIA/navy plot had worked well; the issue became what to tell the American people. Although the first report on the incident had been prepared in Washington, it was released to the press in Hawaii on Sunday, August 2, to give the appearance of spontaneity and to obscure the real source. The Pentagon quoted the Hawaiian release as if it was receiving the news from the Pacific. It placed the blame on North Vietnam and thereby induced a profound psychological effect on the American public.

However, possibly because of the relatively trivial nature of the incident, the country's passions were not aroused as quickly as Johnson wanted. During a Monday meeting he raged at his admirals: "You've got a whole fleet and all the airplanes, and you can't even sink three little old P.T. boats!" Later that morning the President told newsmen that he was doubling the Tonkin Gulf patrol by sending another destroyer, the *C. Turner Joy*, to join the *Maddox*, and by providing the patrol with air cover. If attacked again, said Johnson, the navy would pursue the attackers and destroy them. Secretary Rusk echoed this feeling to newsmen when he stated, "If they do it again, they'll get another sting."[5]

The question was whether or not the small North Vietnamese fleet of patrol boats would be so foolish as to attack the U.S. patrol that was now reinforced, on alert, and waiting. Johnson's military advisers warned him that the North Vietnamese probably would avoid another incident—and if they did *not* attack again, the original attack might be looked upon as an isolated incident.

The mysterious events that followed were both decisive and devastating, perhaps more so than any single episode in the entire Vietnam War.

With President Johnson and his advisers on edge, anxious to present their resolution to Congress, the destroyers *Maddox* and *C. Turner Joy* returned to the Gulf of Tonkin on August 4, 1964. There, a bad storm hampered their visibility and disoriented the technical equipment they had on board. Nevertheless, in the midst of a pitch black night, the *Maddox* broadcast that American ships were again under attack. She reported that her sonar equipment indicated something like torpedoes in the water. The sonarman aboard the *Maddox* had had little experience and his conclusions were uncertain.[5a] No one on either the *Maddox* or the *C. Turner Joy* actually saw an enemy ship, let alone torpedoes, and the veteran sonarman aboard the *C. Turner Joy* doubted that the blips on his sonar screen were torpedoes.

Nevertheless, both destroyers fired at the blips reported by the inexperienced sonarman on the *Maddox*. No one on either ship actually saw any explosions, but since the blips disappeared, navy gunners assumed that the North Vietnamese boats had been knocked out of the water. When American fighter planes arrived on the scene, they searched the battle area for hours without sighting or making radar contact with any enemy vessels. Left in an embarrassing position, Captain Ogier of the *Maddox* said three years later: "Evaluating everything that was going on, I was becoming less and less convinced that somebody was out there." Both the *Maddox* and the *C. Turner Joy* joined the search expedition the next day; still, no proof was found that enemy ships had actually attacked the American vessels or had been destroyed by them. The Gulf of Tonkin offered no evidence of a second incident—no life jackets, no debris, no oil slicks. Nothing.[6]

In view of the strange events of August 4, during which neither American destroyer had been hit by a single bullet or piece of shrapnel, Commodore Herrick, the patrol commander, sent what should have been regarded as a vitally important wire to the Pentagon. It read:

REVIEW OF ACTION MAKES MANY RECORDED CONTACTS AND TORPEDOES FIRED APPEAR DOUBTFUL. FREAK WEATHER EFFECTS AND OVEREAGER SONAR MAN MAY HAVE ACCOUNTED FOR REPORTS. NO ACTUAL VISUAL SIGHTINGS. SUGGEST COMPLETE EVALUATION BEFORE ANY FURTHER ACTION.[7]

Since President Johnson needed this second incident to obtain congressional approval for military operations in Vietnam, the message from Commodore Herrick was concealed that night from Senate and House leaders, from members of important congressional committees, and later from both the full Senate and the full House of Representatives.[8] The steamroller began to move.

When word from Tonkin Gulf that the *Maddox* and *C. Turner Joy* were "under continuous torpedo attack" reached Washington on the morning of August 4, McNamara immediately gathered his aides to discuss possible retaliation, while President Johnson broke the news to Democratic leaders at their regular Tuesday breakfast meeting. The President, despite the fact that he had Commodore Herrick's telegram in his pocket, expressed no doubts whatsoever that the North Vietnamese had actually attacked the U.S. vessels, and that it was necessary for his administration to respond. So that he would have the power to do so, he would need a congressional resolution. Throughout the meeting the Democratic leaders listened to the President and gave him unequivocal support. Their belief was that Johnson's leadership was being tested and that he must respond decisively so he would not be accused, by Goldwater and the Republicans, of being indecisive and weak. President Johnson now was confident that Congress would support American "retaliation."

At the Department of Defense, McNamara held an important meeting with the Joint Chiefs at 11:10 A.M. on August 4. The military leaders pulled their list of ninety-four bombing targets off the shelf and planned air strikes as reprisals. Secretary Rusk and McGeorge Bundy soon joined the prestigious group and, after an engaging discussion, agreed that Vietnam was a great international crisis that could be resolved only by military means.

After a quick visit with the National Security Council, the "inner Cabinet" of Johnson, McNamara, Rusk, and Bundy, as well as CIA Director John McCone, settled down for detailed decisions on Vietnam. McNamara unveiled Pentagon maps and pointed out five targets that the Joint Chiefs had chosen to hit.

By 1:30 P.M. Johnson had given approval for reprisal raids into North Vietnam, and by 3:00 P.M. he had ordered a wide-ranging deployment of U.S. air forces throughout Southeast Asia. Clearly, he was moving far beyond a tiny confrontation off the coast of Vietnam; the deployment indicated that Washington was close to a full-scale bombing attack.

Between 3:00 P.M. and 6:00 P.M. on August 4, a flaw almost crept into the plans of the Johnson administration. McNamara had returned to the Pentagon to work on the reprisal air strikes when Admiral Sharp phoned from Hawaii about the confusion surrounding the second Tonkin Gulf attack. The wire from Commodore Herrick had become a problem which needed attention, but McNamara refused to hold up the march of events. Told to check on the confusion,

Admiral Sharp called back at 6:00 P.M. to say he was satisfied that North Vietnam actually had attacked U.S. destroyers. With that, the matter was closed, and the evidence of the only man who knew firsthand what had happened in the Gulf of Tonkin was disregarded. From President Johnson, to Secretary McNamara, to Admiral Sharp, and on to Southeast Asia, the chain of command had decided that the time had come for the United States to undertake open military operations against North Vietnam.

The Johnson administration then proceeded to alert the country to the "major crisis" that had occurred and to make the country angry enough to risk a war in Vietnam. At 6:00 P.M. the Defense Department announced to the nation:

> A second deliberate attack was made during darkness by an undetermined number of North Vietnamese patrol boats on the U.S.S. *Maddox* and *C. Turner Joy* while the two destroyers were cruising in company on routine patrol in the Tonkin Gulf in International Waters about 65 miles from the nearest land.[9]

At 6:45 P.M. Johnson and his brain trust met with sixteen members of Congress, all summoned at short notice in an atmosphere of crisis. The President told the group that an unprovoked attack by the Communists had taken place and that, as a result, he had given orders for retaliatory air strikes into North Vietnam. He told the group that what he wanted was a congressional resolution of support. Standing behind Johnson, Rusk warned of the Communist threat, and McNamara pulled out his ever-present supply of maps. One by one congressional leaders—McCormack, Russell, Hickenlooper, Dirksen, Smathers—offered their support. Even J. William Fulbright, soon to be Johnson's bitter enemy over Vietnam, believed in the truth of the President's words and the need for immediate action. Johnson now had the support he needed.[10]

The evening of August 4 was full of tension. The President retired after his meeting with congressional leaders and waited for word that American planes had attacked North Vietnam. McNamara returned to the Pentagon at 8:30 P.M. and waited by the phone for the same message. At 11:30 word came that American carriers had launched their planes. With a *fait accompli* in hand, LBJ went on national television six minutes later and delivered the following address:

My fellow Americans, as President and Commander-in-Chief, it is my duty to the American people to report that renewed hostile actions against U.S. ships on the high seas in the Gulf of Tonkin have today required me to order military forces of the United States to take action in reply.

The initial attack on the destroyer *Maddox* on August 2 was repeated today by a number of hostile vessels attacking two U.S. destroyers with torpedoes. The destroyers and supporting aircraft acted at once on the orders I gave after the initial act of aggression.

We believe at least two of the attacking boats were sunk. There were no U.S. losses. The performance of commanders and crews in this engagement is in the highest tradition of the U.S. Navy.

Repeated acts of violence against the Armed Forces of the United States must be met not only with alert defense but with positive reply. That reply is being given as I speak to you tonight. Air action is now in execution against gunboats and certain supporting facilities in North Vietnam which have been used in these hostile operations.

In the larger sense, this new act of aggression aimed directly at our own forces again brings home to all of us in the United States the importance of the struggle for peace and security in Southeast Asia. Aggression by terror against the peaceful villages of South Vietnam has now been joined by open aggression on the high seas against the United States of America. The determination of all Americans to carry out our full commitment to the people and to the Government of South Vietnam will be redoubled by this outrage. Yet our response for the present will be limited and fitting.

We Americans know—although others appear to forget—the risk of spreading conflict. We still seek no wider war.

I have instructed the Secretary of State to make this position totally clear to friends and to adversaries and, indeed, to all.

I have instructed Ambassador Stevenson to raise this matter immediately and urgently before the Security Council of the United Nations.

I have today met with the leaders of both parties of the Congress of the United States and I have informed them that I shall immediately request the Congress to pass a Resolution making it clear that our Government is united in its determination to take all necessary measures in support of freedom and in defense of peace in Southeast Asia.

I have been given encouraging assurance by these leaders of both parties that such a Resolution will be promptly introduced, freely and expeditiously debated, and passed with overwhelming support. And just a few minutes ago I was able to reach Senator Goldwater and I am glad to say that he has expressed his support of the statement that I am making to you tonight.

It is a solemn responsibility to have to order even limited military action for forces whose overall strength is as vast and as awesome as those of the United States of America.

But it is my considered conviction, shared throughout your Government, that firmness in the right is indispensable today for peace. That firmness will always be measured. Its mission is peace.[11]

The morning after his August 4 television appearance, the President sent an official message to Congress calling for swift passage of the resolution. His staff worked to secure broad support. Adlai Stevenson brought to the attention of the Security Council the "acts of deliberate aggression by the Hanoi regime against naval units of the U.S." McNamara presented the technical side; he described the attack as a "great crisis in American history."[12]

The draft resolution was presented first to the Senate Foreign Relations Committee, chaired by Senator J. William Fulbright of Arkansas. It read as follows:

Whereas naval units of the Communist regime in Vietnam in violation of the principles of the Charter of the United Nations and of international law, have deliberately and repeatedly attacked United States naval vessels lawfully present in international waters, and have thereby created a serious threat to international peace; and

Whereas these attacks are part of a deliberate and systematic campaign of aggression that the Communist regime in North Vietnam has been waging against its neighbors and the nations joined with them in the collective defense of their freedom; and

Whereas the United States is assisting the peoples of Southeast Asia to protect their freedom and has no territorial, military, or political ambitions in that area, but desires only that these peoples should be left in peace to work out their own destinies in their own way: Now therefore, be it

RESOLVED BY THE SENATE AND HOUSE OF REPRESENTATIVES OF THE UNITED STATES OF AMERICA IN CONGRESS ASSEMBLED

That the Congress approves and supports the determination of the President, as Commander-in-Chief, to take all necessary measures to repel any armed attack against the forces of the United States and to prevent further aggression.

SEC. 2. The United States regards as vital to its national interest and to world peace the maintenance of international peace and security in Southeast Asia. Consonant with the Constitution of the United States and the Charter of the United Nations and in accordance with its obligations under the Southeast Asia Collective Defense Treaty, the United States is, therefore, prepared, as the President determines, to take all necessary steps, including the use of armed force, to assist any member or protocol state of the Southeast Asia Collective Defense Treaty requesting assistance in defense of its freedom.

SEC. 3. This Resolution shall expire when the President shall determine that the peace and security of the area is reasonably assured by international conditions created by action of the United Nations or otherwise, except that it may be terminated earlier by concurrent resolution of the Congress.[13]

The Fulbright committee heard Secretary Rusk's statement on behalf of the resolution. McNamara then outlined the military incident briefly without mentioning the 34A raids, the espionage mission of the *Maddox*, or the confusion about the second attack. Senator Fulbright set the pattern for the rest of the meeting by asking no questions and making a brief statement in support of the resolution.

After a discussion that lasted less than two hours, the Senate Foreign Relations Committee passed the resolution by a vote of thirty-one to one. Senator Wayne Morse of Oregon cast the only dissenting vote. Describing the resolution as a "predated declaration of war," he accused the administration of provoking the Tonkin Gulf incidents in order to carry out already prepared secret war plans against North Vietnam. The House Foreign Affairs Committee took even less time to analyze the consequences of its action and approved the resolution by a vote of twenty-nine to zero. By lunchtime on August 6, the U.S. Congress had taken its first step toward giving the President power to send U.S. soldiers to war in Vietnam.[14]

Simultaneous meetings of the U.S. Senate and the House of Representatives were convened on the afternoon of August 6 to consider the final passage of the resolution, but the ensuing debate continued into the next day. Senator Fulbright opened the proceedings and presented the administration's case for the passage of the resolution. He described the alleged attacks on the *Maddox* and the *C. Turner Joy*, calling them "without any doubt, a calculated act of military aggression." He therefore recommended "the prompt and overwhelming endorsement of the Resolution," stating that

> In Southeast Asia itself, we must leave no doubt in the minds of both adversaries and friends as to what our objectives are and what they are not. It should be clear to all concerned that our purpose is to uphold and strengthen the Geneva Agreements of 1954 and 1962—that is to say, to establish viable, independent states in Indochina and elsewhere in Southeast Asia, states which will be free of and secure from the domination of Communist China and Communist North Vietnam. . . .
>
> It should be made clear to the Communist powers of Asia, if it is not yet sufficiently clear, that they can enjoy peace and security as long—

but only as long as they confine their ambitions within their own frontiers. It should also be made clear that whenever the Communist powers show a willingness to settle the problems of Southeast Asia by peaceful and lawful means, these problems can then be placed largely or entirely under the jurisdiction of the United Nations.

It should be made equally clear to these regimes, if it is not yet sufficiently clear, that their aggressive and expansionist ambitions, wherever advanced, will meet precisely that degree of American opposition which is necessary to frustrate them.

The Resolution now before the Senate is designed to shatter whatever illusions our adversaries may harbor about the determination of the United States to act promptly and vigorously against aggression.[15]

President Johnson's request for passage of the resolution was supported by three of America's largest newspapers, whose editorials Fulbright inserted into the *Congressional Record*. One came from the *Washington Post*, which read partially as follows:

> President Johnson has earned the gratitude of the Free World as well as of the Nation for his careful and effective handling of the Vietnam crisis. The paramount need was to show the North Vietnamese aggressors their self-defeating folly in ignoring an unequivocal American warning and again attacking the American Navy on the high seas. . . .

The powerful *New York Times*, as deceived as Fulbright was about President Johnson's intentions, said:

> On July 24, President Johnson said that "the United States seeks no wider war in Vietnam," but he warned that "provocation could force a response." That provocation—twice repeated—now has brought a response that has been, in the President's words, "limited and fitting." Whether this ends the incident now is up to North Vietnam and to Communist China. The United States plans no further military strikes if there are no further communist attacks. President Johnson has made it clear that "we still want no wider war. . . ."

The sentiment of the *Philadelphia Inquirer* reflected the positions of the senators who believed in and supported the President:

> In this grim, dark hour—when the issue of peace or war hangs precariously in the balance—President Johnson has called upon the American people to meet the test of courage and determination that has been thrust suddenly and irrevocably upon us by a treacherous foe.
>
> The Nation must stand firm and united in unwavering support of the President at this crucial juncture in the history of mankind.[16]

Fulbright then responded to questions from several senators. Allen Ellender of Louisiana and George McGovern of South Dakota asked whether or not American naval forces had done anything to invite or provoke the attack. The latter asked whether in fact there had even been an attack. McGovern could not understand why a small state such as North Vietnam should seek a deliberate naval conflict with the United States given the overwhelming naval and air power that it had in that area. McGovern also pointed out that General Khanh, the South Vietnamese leader, had been quoted as saying that he wished to carry the war to North Vietnam. The senator noted that at the same time the Johnson administration had been quoted as saying that its policy was *not* to extend the war to the North, that the victory had to be won in the South, and that the United States should "take all reasonable steps to confine the war to South Vietnam." McGovern asked if there was "any danger in this Resolution that we may be surrendering to General Khanh's position our attitude as to where the war should be fought."

Senator Fulbright's reply was significant. He clearly discounted the possibility that adoption of the resolution would involve the United States in a wider war:

> I do not think there is any danger of that. There is, of course, a danger in this whole area and there has been for 10 years. It is dangerous. The policy of our Government not to expand the war still holds. That is not inconsistent with any response to attacks on our vessels on the high seas where they have the right to be.

To Senator Jacob Javits's question as to whether or not America's action was an implementation of the SEATO Treaty and whether or not the United States had consulted with our SEATO allies before taking further action, Fulbright conceded that the United States was not consulting its allies, that its action was not taken under the SEATO Treaty, and that its SEATO allies were doing too little to support its actions in Vietnam. This was a telling remark, for the administration claimed throughout the war that one of its main reasons for being in Vietnam was its obligations under the SEATO Treaty.

Senator Gaylord Nelson of Minnesota asked Fulbright how far offshore U.S. naval vessels were when the "attack" took place. Fulbright admitted that the *Maddox* was first attacked within the twelve-mile limit in North Vietnamese waters, but that the United States did not recognize anything other than a three-mile limit "for political purposes." Nelson, however, pointed out that the United States had recognized a twelve-mile limit in other instances.[17]

During the course of the debate, John Stennis of Mississippi, chairman of the Armed Services Committee, expressed fervent support for the resolution:

> . . . today we have no choice. Our flag has been attacked, and our country has been challenged in international waters—on the high seas—where we had a right to be. Our flag and our men have been fired upon. Many hundreds, if not thousands, of our naval personnel could have lost their lives had the torpedoes been more accurately aimed and hit one or more of the destroyers.
>
> We properly gave the aggressors fair warning after the first shot. Then they hit us again. Very properly, we then struck back.[18]

Others, such as Frank Church of Idaho, expressed serious misgivings about the resolution but voted in favor of it. More than perhaps any other senator, Church reflected the unease of a man torn between conscience and duty. He criticized American policy in Southeast Asia as an "addiction to an ideological view of world affairs—an affliction which affects us as well as the Communists—rather than a policy based upon a detached and pragmatic view of our real national interests." Nonetheless, also believing that "a country must live with the policy it adopts, whether it be wise or foolish," he concluded that the United States must accept the consequences of its own actions. For that reason he cast his lot with Johnson. Church's final thought, an ironic one, was that Johnson as a "man of peace" would do "everything possible to keep the war from spreading in this seething and dangerous area of the world."

For obvious reasons, Hubert Humphrey of Minnesota, the Democratic candidate for vice president, also supported the resolution. Humphrey mainly focused on America's historic right to freedom of the seas:

> Surely we cannot permit an unprovoked attack upon the forces of the United States without response. Surely, the Congress would not condone a pattern of international conduct that would deny the fleet of the United States the use of international waters. . . . The attack which was made upon our vessels had to be repulsed; and in repulsing that attack

it was essential that the particular facilities in the haven from whence the attack took place should be destroyed.*[19]

Richard Russell, of Georgia, indicated how Johnson had cleverly preempted the duty of Congress to discuss the real issues by confronting it with the pressures from the public and the press for a patriotic response, for a show of loyalty to the country in time of crisis, and the need to defend the honor of America from attack. Russell stated that

> In the present circumstances, it will serve no useful purpose to debate the wisdom of our original decision to go into Vietnam. It is unnecessary for me to state that I had grave doubts about the wisdom of that decision. It would certainly do no good to dwell on those doubts here today. Indeed, second guesses about our foreign policy, and what it should be in that area, or whether our support to South Vietnam has been too much or has been too little are not involved directly in the question before us. What is involved is our right as an independent state to operate our vessels upon international waters that have been recognized as free to all states for many centuries. Involved also is our national honor. Our national honor is at stake. We cannot and we will not shrink from defending it. No sovereign nation would be entitled to the respect of other nations, or indeed, could maintain its self-respect, if it accepted the acts that have been committed against us without undertaking to make some response. . . .
>
> Mr. President, from the beginning of our Nation, Massachusetts men have always gone down to the sea in ships. We are proud of our Navy. We know its strength and effectiveness in preserving our country and our defenses.
>
> Its prestige and the prestige of our country in the eyes of the world is [sic] at stake.
>
> It is the responsibility of the President to take immediate action to defend our country when he believes that it is under attack in one way or another.
>
> As the representative of all our people, he now asks Congress to support him in the position he has taken in this instance where our Navy has been fired upon. He made the decision to retaliate for the attack.[20]

Senators Ernest Gruening of Alaska and Wayne Morse of Oregon were the only senators to vote against the resolution. Both senators

---

* He later told the author that his remarks had literally been handed to him and that he made them against his own better judgment.

eloquently expressed reasons why it should not be adopted. Tragically, they failed to convince their colleagues, many of whom later would come to regret their affirmative votes.

Gruening noted that he had repeatedly urged that the United States get out of South Vietnam instead of escalating its involvement:

> I have stated and restated my view that this was not our war; that we were wholly misguided in picking up the burden after the French had suffered staggering losses running into tens of thousands of French young lives and vast sums of money to which the United States contributed heavily, and thereupon entering upon a policy which would be bound to result, as it has resulted, in the sacrificing of the lives of our young Americans in an area, and in a cause that in my reasoned judgment poses no threat to our national security.

Gruening dramatically pointed out that America's so-called SEATO allies were not, except for token gestures, participating in the Vietnam conflict:

> I have called attention to the fact, and do again, that whereas American boys are dying in combat, although presumably they are there as advisors, no British boys are on the firing line; no French boys are any longer at the front, they appear to have learned their lesson; no Australian youths are being killed; no New Zealand youngsters are being sacrificed; no Philippine casualties are being incurred; and the same may be said for the Pakistanis, despite the fact that we have given them close to a billion dollars in military aid.

He then challenged the contention that American security was involved in Vietnam or that the United States was supporting freedom for South Vietnam:

> While I am deeply convinced that American security is not involved, the allegation that we are supporting freedom in South Vietnam has a hollow sound. We have been supporting corrupt and unpopular puppet dictatorships which owe their temporary sojourn in power to our massive support. They have scant support from their own people, who have shown little disposition to fight. Hence our steadily increasing involvement. Yet we have persistently alleged that the war cannot be won except by the South Vietnamese. It is not happening, nor will it.

Gruening also pointed out that the United States was ignoring its obligation to support the charter of the United Nations, which provided that the parties to any dispute that might endanger international peace should first seek "a solution by negotiation, inquiry, mediation, conciliation, arbitration, judicial settlement, resort to regional agencies or arrangements, or other peaceful means of their own choice."[21]

Senator Morse, as well, forcefully stated his reasons for rejecting the resolution. His remarks indicated that he had taken the time to try to investigate what really happened at Tonkin Gulf, and that he knew enough of the facts, which he disclosed, to have caused a responsible deliberative body to investigate further before plunging the country into a war. Unfortunately, the Senate paid little attention to his words.

Morse pointed out that the alleged attack on American naval vessels took place during an engagement in which South Vietnamese naval vessels supplied by the United States were bombing two North Vietnamese islands, one approximately three miles and the other approximately five miles from the main coast of North Vietnam. He said:

> The United States knew that the bombing was going to take place. The United States has been in close advisory relationship with the military dictatorship we have been supporting as a military protectorate in South Vietnam for quite some time. We knew for quite some time that the dictator of South Vietnam has wanted to go north. We know that recently there was a big demonstration in Saigon, staged pretty much by students, but there were others, and in response to a speech made by Dictator Khanh, the cry was, "Go north, go north, go north," which meant that the cry was for escalating the war into North Vietnam. . . .

> On Friday, July 31, the war was escalated to the north. . . . This was a well thought out military operation. These islands were bombed.

> When these islands were bombed, American destroyers were on patrol in Tonkin Bay, and they were not 60 or 65 miles away. What I am about to say I can say without revealing the source and without violating my secrecy.

> It is undeniable that in the patrolling operations of our destroyers in Tonkin Bay the destroyers have patrolled within 11 miles and not more than 3 miles off the coast of North Vietnam.

> . . . If we wish to argue in one breath that we are against escalating the war, we have a little difficulty in the next breath justifying, in my judgment, the course of action that we followed in respect to South Vietnamese bombing of the two islands 3 to 5 miles off the coast of North Vietnam, and then having American navel vessels, a part of our Navy, so close to the North Vietnamese coast, although in international waters, as they were on Friday, July 31, when the bombing took place. . . .

It is bound to be looked upon by our enemies as an act of provocation; and it makes us a provocateur under the circumstances.

. . . I am taking the criticism that, in my judgment, the American armed vessels should not have been as close to the islands as they were on Friday, July 31. In my judgment, that gave cause for the North Vietnamese to assume that there was a cause-and-effect relationship between the bombardment by the South Vietnamese vessels and the presence of the American naval patrol boats in Tonkin Bay at the location where they then were. . . .

. . . I agree with those who have expressed perplexity as to why the North Vietnamese on Tuesday night in a storm, after 9 o'clock, apparently at night, attempted another armed attack on our vessels.

. . . In my judgment, we were dead wrong in proceeding to bomb the establishments on the mainland of North Vietnam and then out of the corners of our mouths saying, "Well, we are not seeking to expand the war. We do not want to widen the war. We are just going to defend ourselves."[22]

One final challenge was presented by Gaylord Nelson, the Democratic senator from Wisconsin, who proposed one simple amendment to clarify exactly what powers the resolution would give to Johnson. The amendment read:

Our continuing policy is to limit our role to the provision of aid, training assistance and military advice, and it is the sense of Congress that, except when provoked to a greater response, we should continue to attempt to avoid a direct military involvement in the Southeast Asia conflict.[23]

Given the fact that direct involvement had *already* been America's secret policy, Johnson could hardly accept such an amendment. Fearing that some senator might try to limit the meaning of the resolution, the administration requested that Fulbright accept no changes in the wording. Fulbright quickly dismissed Nelson's proposal. The House had already approved the resolution by a vote of 416 to 0, and any further discussion in the Senate would only confuse and delay matters. Fulbright thereby canceled the last hope Congress had to stop Johnson's war. The final Senate vote was 88 to 2. Lyndon Johnson had his war.

Within a year, Fulbright realized that he had been set up and used by Johnson. In 1966 and again in 1968, the Arkansas senator led investigations into American policy in Southeast Asia. Three years later Fulbright said:

Imagine, we spent all of an hour and forty minutes on that resolution. A disaster; a tragic mistake. We should have held hearings. The resolution would have passed anyway, but not in its present form. At the time, I was not in a suspicious frame of mind. I was afraid of Goldwater.[24]

In the three days following the passage of the Tonkin Gulf Resolution, Johnson praised the Congress for its "patriotic, resolute and rapid action." The first week of August 1964 had been "highly gratifying" and "deeply reassuring," he said, although his double meaning was unknown to the American people. On August 10 Johnson went on national television once more, to sign the "Joint Resolution to promote the maintenance of international peace and security in Southeast Asia." With important cabinet members, military men, and congressional leaders gathered behind him, the President explained the significance of the historic moment:

One week ago, half a world away, our nation was faced by the challenge of deliberate and unprovoked acts of aggression. . . . [As of] today, our course is clearly known in every land. There can be no mistake—no miscalculation—of where America stands. . . . Americans of all parties . . . can be justly proud—and justly grateful. Proud that democracy has once again demonstrated its capacity to act swiftly and decisively against aggressors. . . . It is everlastingly right that we should be resolute in reply to aggression. . . . But it is everlastingly necessary that our actions should be careful and should be measured. . . . So, in this spirit and with this pledge, I now sign this Resolution.[25]

PART TWO

LYNDON BAINES JOHNSON'S VIETNAM WAR

LBJ, PEACE CANDIDATE/ WAR PLANNER
August 1964–January 1965

President Lyndon Johnson, by means of the Tonkin Gulf Resolution, obtained what Wayne Morse correctly called his "predated declaration of war." Now, with the power to begin the war he envisioned at the appropriate time, LBJ concentrated on his political campaign, pretending to be the peace candidate, and portraying Barry Goldwater as the warmonger. Secretly, however, LBJ planned to unleash a full-scale war as soon as he was safely ensconced as President of the United States in his own right.

Johnson's strategy, as in the past, was to direct his appeal to the center of the American political spectrum. The President would be all things to all people—firm but peaceful, decisive but restrained, determined but patient. He continued to downplay the Vietnam crisis, outlining his political position as infrequently as possible, and then only in vague, artful terms. One speech, given to the American Bar Association convention in New York City on August 12, 1964, only ten days after the Gulf of Tonkin incident, formed the essence of Johnson's campaign position on Vietnam:

> Some are eager to enlarge the conflict. They call upon us to supply American boys to do the job that Asian boys should do. They ask us to take reckless action [bombing?] which might risk the lives of millions and engulf much of Asia, and certainly threaten the peace of the entire world. . . . Such actions would be no solution at all to the real problem of Vietnam. . . . Our firmness at moments of crisis has always been matched by restraint. Our determination by care. And I pledge you that it will be so long as I am your President.[1]

Like Theodore Roosevelt, LBJ was talking softly and carrying a big stick. Johnson seemed to treat the Vietnam issue carefully, focusing

on America's commitment to the Vietnamese people, never emphasizing the possibility of war. As he said to the American Bar Association:

> In Vietnam we work for world order. . . . First, the South Vietnamese
> have the basic responsibility for the defense of their own freedom.
> Second we [will] engage our strength and our resources to whatever
> extent needed to help others repel aggression. . . . Some say that we
> should withdraw from South Vietnam. . . . But the U.S. cannot, and
> must not, and will not turn aside and allow the freedom of a brave
> people to be handed over to Communist tyranny.[2]

Tactfully, Johnson stressed the danger of Communism, the weakness
of a free South Vietnam, and American determination to help an ally.
With American help the people of South Vietnam could defeat the
Communist aggressors.

When Johnson boldly retaliated against the alleged North Vietnamese aggression in the Gulf of Tonkin, Senator Goldwater lost a
campaign issue; much of his campaign had hinged on accusing Johnson of being soft on the Communists in Vietnam. Stripped of his
primary campaign issue and neutralized by Johnson's tactics, Goldwater reversed his criticism of LBJ. He charged that the President
was courting war and possibly nuclear war through his actions at
Tonkin Gulf.[3]

To this and other Goldwater attacks, Johnson coolly replied that
his only goal was peace in Vietnam and freedom for its people. Such
tactics worked superbly. Before long, Goldwater found himself
hopelessly on the defensive.[4]

Another successful Johnson tactic was his public focus on domestic issues rather than war. Johnson increasingly de-emphasized Vietnam as he concentrated on popular Great Society issues—medical
care for older Americans, farm supports, housing availability, higher
employment and victory in the war against poverty. Americans tradi-
tionally had voted their pocketbooks, and that is what Johnson cun-
ningly exploited. He offered both peace and prosperity.

Meanwhile, in Vietnam the military and political situation continued to deteriorate. In the last week of August, General Khanh lost
control of his own government. When it fell, there was no one to take
over. Said one observer: "There was only anarchy at the top to deal
with anarchy in the streets."[5] Johnson knew that he had to defuse the
situation in Saigon quickly before it could become a campaign issue.

Accordingly, he launched a massive publicity campaign to disguise the situation and to assure the American public that all was well in South Vietnam. When the issue absolutely could not be avoided, he stressed that stability was already returning to the South and that continued progress was being made in the field against the Communist Vietcong.[6]

To support the President, Rusk, Taylor, and Lodge all issued similar public statements and held corresponding press conferences to convince the public that all was well in Saigon, and to mollify any congressional unrest. Secretary Rusk categorically reassured the American people about the turmoil in Saigon:

> In the first place, this is not a coup situation. This has not been a sweeping change in the administration of the leadership of the Government. . . . Secondly, these events have not interfered with the persecution of the effort against the Vietcong in the countryside.

And Ambassador Taylor was equally reassuring:

> The military situation, in spite of the disturbances of the last 10 days in August, remained essentially normal. If General Westmoreland were here, I think he would say he feels there is a general upward trend. . . . I am happy to say . . . the activities in the provinces where the war is being conducted show no visible signs of retardation. This is a small unit war—the war of the squadron, the platoon, and the company. So by the very nature it does not require the centralized government direction which would be the case in a so-called conventional war.[7]

However, no sooner did one crisis fade than another one appeared. On September 18 the United States found itself involved in another Tonkin Gulf incident. According to the *New York Times,* "Two United States destroyers fired upon, and presumably hit, what they took to be four or five hostile targets in the Gulf of Tonkin." Only a month earlier Johnson had seized upon precisely such an incident to justify retaliatory air strikes against North Vietnam and to push his Gulf of Tonkin Resolution through a docile Congress. But this time, only six weeks later, both he and the Department of Defense blithely ignored it.[8]

Johnson's sudden restraint was smart politics. Firmly entrenched as the peace candidate, the President wanted no new incidents to jeopardize his position. He could ill afford widespread publicity on the latest attacks. Indeed, because American "sightings" of enemy ships had been only by radar, some questioned whether or not they had occurred at all. Johnson knew that if public questioning of this new attack reached back to the first, all his carefully laid plans might be destroyed. So, as quickly as it surfaced, the incident disappeared. No protest was made to North Vietnam, even though evidence was stronger than the evidence for the August 4 Tonkin Gulf attack.

Three characteristic speeches pinpoint LBJ's deception of the public during his campaign. Responding to one of Goldwater's attacks, Johnson retorted that

> I have had advice to load our planes with bombs and drop them on certain areas that I think would enlarge the war . . . and result in our committing a good many American boys to fighting a war that I think ought to be fought by the boys of Asia.[9]

Yet in Washington he was planning this very action. In another speech he stated that

> I have not thought that we were ready for American boys to do the fighting for Asian boys. What I have been trying to do was to get the boys in Vietnam to do their own fighting. We are not going north and bomb at this stage of the game.[10]

Again he had already decided that bombing North Vietnam was the only solution. In the closing weeks of the campaign, Johnson categorically intoned: "We are not about to send American boys nine or ten thousand miles away from home to do what Asian boys ought to be doing for themselves."[11]

Even as he spoke, however, a small Asian war was growing larger by the day, and soon American troops would be involved. While LBJ was preoccupied with his reelection, his advisers became more eager than ever for a free hand in Vietnam. On August 11, 1964, William Bundy suggested to Johnson that the United States begin a full-scale air war against North Vietnam at the appropriate time. Bundy suggested limited bombing until after Johnson won the election, when the administration could embark on an escalation of military pressure.[12]

Both General Taylor and General Westmoreland supported Bundy, agreeing that unless something was added in the coming months, the National Liberation Front would topple the Saigon government. In an August cable from Saigon, Taylor proposed "a carefully orchestrated bombing attack on [North Vietnam], directed primarily at infiltration and other military targets" to slow down enemy advances. This attack would only work if Hanoi failed to respond favorably to previous actions. If General Khanh then could not pacify the South, suggested Taylor, Washington should consider bombing North Vietnam anyway, even though an air war would increase the likelihood of U.S. involvement in ground action.[13]

The Joint Chiefs also exerted pressure on Johnson to widen the war. Their collective position was that an accelerated program of action against Vietnam was "essential to prevent a complete collapse of the U.S. position in Southeast Asia," that it would be foolish to think "that we should be slow to get deeply involved until we have a better feel for . . . our ally," and that because the United States was "already involved . . . only significantly stronger military pressures" on North Vietnam could bring relief and provide the psychological boost necessary to maintain government stability. The Joint Chiefs suggested a strategy of continued provocation by established methods even though they might cause more incidents like the two in the Tonkin Gulf.[14]

To explain and clarify the military's position, Assistant Secretary of Defense John McNaughton sent his opinion to McNamara on September 3. Because of the upcoming election, he said, we must act with special care. Nevertheless, he urged that the United States consider serious escalation in the form of secret air strikes into Laos, more 34A raids by South Vietnamese boats, and a resumption of the DeSoto patrols in the Gulf of Tonkin. The idea was to provoke a military response from North Vietnam which would "provide good grounds for us to escalate if we wished." McNaughton timed his report so that President Johnson and his top advisers would feel pressure from the military at an important White House meeting on September 7.[15]

Johnson, Rusk, McNamara, Wheeler, Taylor, and McCone gathered at the White House for the September 7 strategy session. It had been the consensus that LBJ should unleash the military against North Vietnam within a matter of months. The only questions left to be answered were how much to unleash and when. As an interim measure, the President approved more DeSoto patrols in the Gulf of Tonkin, but he refused to risk the deliberate provocation of North Vietnam during the election. A more significant reason was the weakness of the Saigon regime. Since Khanh's government was still struggling to stabilize its position, Johnson felt it wise to avoid escalation until Saigon became stronger.

On September 10 the President issued a National Security Action Memorandum to continue current operations until the New Year and then begin military operations against the North. In the meantime, he planned to send naval destroyers back into the Gulf of Tonkin, to send planes on missions into Laos, to instruct Saigon to step up its 34A commando raids, and to be prepared to launch more reprisal air raids into North Vietnam.[16]

Even though Johnson decided not to follow the advice of the Joint Chiefs—to provoke Hanoi into immediate escalation of the war—the results of the White House meeting in early September had exactly that effect. The next DeSoto patrol goaded North Vietnam into another Gulf of Tonkin incident on September 18, but the President waited to retaliate until after the election.

The military leaders in Saigon also continued to lobby for expansion of the war. Naval bombardments, 34A raids, acts of sabotage, and continued U-2 spy plane missions, all of which occurred throughout October 1964, formed the main part of their strategy.

An important part of the administration's plan was its desire to hinder the peace talks being held in Paris among various political factions from Laos. The Pentagon argued that a Laotian cease-fire was incompatible with current U.S. interest; rather, the President needed even more secret bombing of infiltration routes along the Laotian border. Presumably, if the Paris peace talks led to a new Geneva Conference on Southeast Asia, the United States would almost be forced to negotiate with North Vietnam.

During October a special fighter squadron flew combat strikes over Laos to continue the destruction that had been begun by the CIA and Air America. While Johnson asked the Laotian leader, Prince Souvannaphouma, if the United States could increase the number of air strikes in Laos, he did not think it necessary to tell the prince that South Vietnamese troops had unofficial orders to raid North Vietnamese strongholds along the Laotian border.[17]

Johnson's preparations for war, although restrained, provoked a response in the form of a mortar attack on Bienhoa airfield near Saigon on November 1. Four Americans were killed and six U.S. B-57 bombers were destroyed. Still mindful of the election, Johnson publicly ignored Bienhoa, but privately he was outraged. The airfield was a base for B-57 strikes against the Vietcong and a possible base for raids into North Vietnam. The military hawks privately demanded that Johnson retaliate.

Again Johnson held back. On November 2, the day before the election, in a meeting with Secretaries Rusk and McNamara, "the decision was made to do nothing." In effect, LBJ was telling the nation that in August an unconfirmed and suspicious group of radar blips and sonar images were cause for retaliation against North Vietnam, but that the killing of four U.S. servicemen and destruction of six jet bombers in an attack on a U.S. base was not. In addition, he feared that retaliatory strikes might bring further counterstrikes from North Vietnam against American bases and civilians in the South, thus marring the peace image he had so carefully carved for himself during the campaign.

The Joint Chiefs, enraged by Bienhoa and dissatisfied with Johnson's reluctance to act, continued to apply pressure for retaliation. Calling the attack "a deliberate act of escalation and a change of the ground rules," the military demanded a "prompt and strong response."[18] Specifically they wanted to:

1. Conduct air strikes in Laos and reconnaissance on targets in North Vietnam;

2. Land the marine special forces at DaNang and airlift army or marine units from Okinawa to Saigon;

3. Use aircraft in evacuation of United States dependents from Saigon;

4. Assemble and prepare necessary forces for progressive air strikes into North Vietnam, against the targets listed in the Pentagon's ninety-four target study;

5. Conduct air raids on a sustained basis from Thailand, after securing authority for unlimited use of Thai bases.[19]

Certainly the risks of such actions were grave, but again Johnson reacted with restraint. He appointed an interagency working group under William Bundy to draw up various political and military options for direct action against North Vietnam. Increasingly, William Bundy began to play a key role in formulating America's Southeast Asia policy.[20]

Johnson was reelected in a landslide on November 3. The Johnson-Humphrey ticket won 61 percent of the popular-vote and 486 electoral votes; it was the largest popular vote plurality in U.S. election history. With such a resounding victory behind him and the congressional resolution in his pocket, Johnson felt little reason to hold back any longer. The first order of business was avenging the attack on Bienhoa. The interagency working group, which had advocated immediate retaliation, still clamored for action. William Bundy suggested that

> Bienhoa may be repeated at any time. This would tend to force our hand, but would also give us a good springboard for any decision for stronger action. The President is clearly thinking in terms of maximum use of a Gulf of Tonkin rationale, either for an action that would show toughness and hold the line till we can decide the big issue, or as a basis for starting a clear course of action under the broad options.

Bundy set forth his objectives in a report dated November 21: breaking the will of North Vietnam; forcing Hanoi to end the Vietcong rebellion in the South; and setting up a pro-American, non-Communist government in South Vietnam. He also cautioned that the Johnson administration should not negotiate with North Vietnam until the impending air war put the United States in a stronger bargaining position.

Washington's next step, according to Bundy, should be one of the following choices:

• First, reprisal air raids, more 34A coastal raids, more DeSoto patrols, and more CIA air strikes into Laos, in other words, to continue present policy.

• Second, the "fast full squeeze." The United States would bomb the North "at a fairly rapid pace and without interruption until we achieve our central present objectives." Everything would be subordinated to constant and intense military pressure against North Vietnam in order to bring her to the conference table.

• Finally, the "slow squeeze" method, which included air strikes "against infiltration targets, first in Laos and then in . . . North Vietnam." This option would "give the impression of a steady deliberate approach . . . designed to give the United States the option at any time to proceed or not, to escalate or not, and to quicken the pace or not." Another blue chip for bargaining might be included under the slow squeeze approach: significant ground deployment to the northern part of South Vietnam. The wording of this option made it the likely choice when the National Security Council met again on November 24 to review the Vietnam situation.[21]

The broad options mentioned by Bundy did not include American withdrawal from South Vietnam, or a holding action by American forces, or a supporting action while Saigon attempted one last push. The Bundy group thought only in terms of escalation. They preferred an all-out military solution in Vietnam.

Vice Admiral Mustin, a member of the Bundy group, summarized the thinking of the Joint Chiefs:

> In short, we believe that certain strong U.S. actions are required in Southeast Asia, that we must make them regardless of opinion in various other quarters, and that results of our failing to take them would be substantially more serious to the United States than would be any results of world opinions if we did take them.[22]

On November 24, Rusk, McNamara, McCone, General Wheeler, McGeorge Bundy, and George Ball gathered to thrash out their views on the three options. Only George Ball, the under secretary of state, questioned why the United States had to fight a war in Vietnam in the first place. Ball did not believe in the domino theory and he argued against bombing North Vietnam. He suggested working with Great Britain and the Soviet Union in arranging an international conference which would work out a compromise political settlement. Forced to make a choice among the three Bundy options, Ball preferred the first, but the other committee members rejected his advice.

While Rusk and McNamara leaned toward the slow squeeze, Wheeler pushed hard for the second option. The military wanted to use military force to its full limits to acheive U.S. objectives. Wheeler believed that smashing air strikes carried less risk of a major conflict. This position was rejected when costs were balanced against risks.

The November 24 meeting ended with the group agreeing that no decision would be reached until Ambassador Taylor expressed his views.[23] Taylor arrived in Washington on November 27, 1964, and met with the National Security Council. He quickly made his views known. "If, as the evidence shows, we are playing a losing game in South Vietnam, it is high time we change and find a better way. First, establish an adequate government in South Vietnam; second, improve the conduct of the counterinsurgency campaign; and finally, persuade or force North Vietnam to stop its aid to the Vietcong." Taylor emphasized that the United States should get tough with Saigon by demanding political reforms.

What Taylor proposed, and what the select group of listeners on November 27 agreed to, was a combination of two of the Bundy group's proposed three steps. For thirty days, the United States would intensify its secret acts of war—coastal raids, air strikes in Laos, and several reprisal attacks into North Vietnam. After phase one was completed and Taylor had Khanh under control, the air war would begin, the slow squeeze would force Hanoi to its knees, and negotiations would finally take place—on terms favorable to U.S. interests.

This secret November plan, approved by the National Security Council, was the final step in triggering an aggressive United States air war in Vietnam. As Bundy wrote to Johnson, the bombing "would consist principally of progressively more serious air strikes over a period of two to six months, of a weight and tempo adjusted to the situation as it develops." If North Vietnam protested the raids, the United States would convey its "determination and grave concern to the Soviets, not in the expectation of change in their position but in effect to warn them to stay out," and with some hope they would pass on the message to Hanoi and Peking.[24]

Meanwhile, South Vietnam remained in political turmoil. The government was not, contrary to Johnson's assurances to the U.S. public, stabilizing, nor was all going well. Ten days after Johnson's election, Khanh was ousted in a military coup by General Phat. This coup, accomplished while Ambassador Taylor was in the United States, caught the administration by surprise. In a few days, however, Khanh regained power and the United States renewed its pledge of support. But the Phat interlude illustrated the fact that no legal government existed in Saigon to claim the allegiance of even a small portion of the populace. The United States could have used that fact as reason to depart from Vietnam. Instead, the Johnson administration relentlessly proceeded to plan for more American involvement.

While war plans were being finalized in Washington, Johnson relaxed at his ranch in Texas. At a November 28 news conference, when asked about the possible expansion of the war into Laos and North Vietnam, the President replied:

I have just been sitting here in this serene atmosphere [Texas ranch]
. . . for the last few days reading about the wars that you [newsmen]
have involved us in and the additional undertakings that I have made
decisions on or that General Taylor has recommended or that Mr.
McNamara plans or Secretary Rusk envisages. I would say, generally
speaking, that some people are speculating and taking positions that I
think are somewhat premature.[25]

At a White House meeting on December 1, 1964, however, Johnson heard the report by Ambassador Taylor, listened to McNamara
and Rusk, discussed the paper written by William Bundy, and issued
several directives:

• That Taylor pull the South Vietnamese together before the
United States made public its commitment to bomb; clearly he har-
bored doubts about the efficiency of the bombing unless the South
Vietnamese government was reformed.

• That the State Department win "new, dramatic [and] effective"
forms of assistance from those U.S. allies concerned about Vietnam;

• That further direct consultations with leaders of Congress were
not necessary because the joint resolution "remained in full force";
and

• That "only a brief, formal statement" be issued to the news media after the meeting, with no mention of the proposals and decisions
made.

Several results emerged from the meeting:

• First, the President approved Phase One of the National Security
Council plan, the thirty-day secret war with special bombing in Laos
under the code name "Operation Barrel Roll";

• Second, he approved in principle the second phase of Bundy's
war options, the slow squeeze bombing campaign in the Laotian
panhandle, which would move in gradual stages into North Vietnam;

• Third, the President ordered Taylor to meet with South Vietnamese leaders and present American requests for specific reforms; and

• Finally, Johnson sent William Bundy to Australia and New
Zealand on December 4 to brief those countries' leaders on both
phases of the bombing. He also made sure that British Prime Minister Harold Wilson was thoroughly briefed on the forthcoming U.S.
actions during his visit to Washington on December 7, and that Canada too was kept informed.[26]

Events moved quickly after the President approved the November
bombing plan. William Sullivan, U.S. ambassador to Laos, pressured
Prince Souvannaphouma into agreeing that American planes could

bomb the Ho Chi Minh Trail, just as McNamara ordered still more raids by CIA planes from Thailand. Bombing was to focus on the corridor areas close to the North Vietnamese border. Operation Barrel Roll began on December 14 as American jets struck targets of opportunity in the panhandle of Laos. It was "agreed that there would be no public . . . statements . . . unless a plane were lost," a decision that "fulfilled precisely the President's wishes."[27]

In Saigon, Ambassador Taylor badgered General Khanh and Premier Huong into promising reforms. Despite such efforts, political turmoil continued in Saigon. General Khanh joined with Marshal Ky to dissolve the High National Council on December 20, 1964, in a coup that angered U.S. officials. Taylor immediately reprimanded Khanh and his young associates:

> I told you . . . that we Americans were tired of coups. Apparently I wasted my words . . . because . . . you evidently didn't understand. I made it clear that all the military plans which I know you would like to carry out are dependent on government stability. Now you have made a real mess. We cannot carry you forever if you do things like this.[26]

News of increased American aid and military action in Vietnam began to surface in the United States. Although few details were released, officials in Saigon did report that the United States decided to increase its military assistance to South Vietnam for new action against the infiltration routes from Communist North Vietnam. Washington officials continued to assure the American public that the increased military and economic aid to South Vietnam did *not* foreshadow a move to expand the war to Communist North Vietnam.[29]

By the end of 1964, the situation in Saigon had deteriorated further. On Christmas Eve, a bomb was planted in the Brinks Hotel U.S. Officers' Billet in downtown Saigon, killing or injuring fifty-two Americans and knocking the American Forces Radio Station off the air. Bob Hope, appearing at an air base in Saigon at the time, cracked, "When I arrived, I got a twenty-one-gun salute—and three of them were ours."

The Joint Chiefs and General Westmoreland pressed for an immediate air war against the North. As soon as Johnson gave the signal, U.S. bombers were ready. But Johnson's inauguration was several weeks away, and he still did not want to adopt a warlike posture.

On January 13, 1965, the *New York Times* announced that two U.S. jet fighters were shot down on combat missions over Laos. The news was out, so Johnson had nothing to lose by at last putting his plan into action. The next day he asked for $500 million in military aid for South Vietnam, along with an additional standby authorization. The Pentagon, for its part, admitted that U.S. Air Force planes were flying regular bombing and strafing missions over Laos.

Meanwhile the political instability in South Vietnam continued; the American public became more aware of events in Vietnam, more restless and more critical; and the deception of the Johnson team began to unravel in the face of increasing public skepticism.[30] Wayne Morse was openly critical and well informed. Dean Rusk's attempts to defend the actions of the administration were undermined by Morse, who charged that the administration was following "the jungle law of military might" and warned that he saw "no hope of avoiding a massive war in Asia" unless the United States policy was reversed immediately.[31] Nevertheless, the hour for Johnson's war was near.

Ironically, in his January 20, 1965, inaugural address, President Johnson completely ignored the question of Vietnam. Instead, he insisted with due solemnity:

> How incredible it is that in this fragile existence we should hate and destroy one another. There are possibilities enough for all who will abandon mastery over others to pursue mastery over nature. There is world enough for all to seek their happiness in their own way.
>
> And our nation's course is abundantly clear. We aspire to nothing that belongs to others. We seek no dominion over our fellow man, but man's dominion over tyranny and misery.[32]

THE AIR AND GROUND WARS
1965–68

In January 1965, with the election and inauguration behind him, Lyndon Johnson was now in a position to wage war in Vietnam with or without the consent of the American people. He needed only to plan the military strategy, eliminate voices of dissent in the White House and in Saigon, disregard peace offers and world opinion, assume his rightful role as commander in chief of the armed forces, and thus be ready for war and victory on his own terms.

There were three problems that LBJ needed to solve in order to wage his war in Vietnam: the need to solidify the support of his advisers; the need to overcome the pressures from the United Nations and many foreign countries for a peaceful solution of the conflict; and the need to procure a stable government in Saigon.

The first requirement for solidifying support for his Vietnam War was to eliminate the degree of uncertainty that now existed among the members of his team. Several of his advisers were not sure that there should be an open bombing war against North Vietnam. Now that the moment of truth had arrived, some of the planners drew back from their earlier recommendations.

Just about everyone who had expressed any reservations about Johnson's war policies was quietly and effectively purged. Robert Johnson, Rostow's deputy and part of the Policy Planning Council, discovered that no one would even listen to him after his special 1964 report which concluded that bombing North Vietnam would not bring victory. Other key figures such as Roger Hilsman, Paul Kattenburg, Bill Truehart, Michael Forrestal, and even elder statesman Averell Harriman were likewise forced out of positions of authority.

The secretary of state, Dean Rusk, made certain that LBJ had a faithful bureaucracy. As David Halberstam has written:

Without attracting much attention, without anyone commenting on it, the men who had been the greatest doubters on Vietnam . . . were moved out, and the bureaucracy was moved back to a position where it had been in 1954, more the old Dulles policies on Asia than anyone realized.[1]

George Ball became perhaps the only official at the State Department who was able to oppose escalation of the war and yet remain at the center of things. He was the token "No"-man, the administration's official worrier and inner-circle critic, but neither the President nor the secretary of state paid much attention to Ball's warnings.

Within a month of his inauguration, Johnson had virtually overcome the first of the three obstacles to his policies. The principals on his team were falling in line with the ideas of Walt Rostow, whose star was rising fast in the President's eyes. Rostow had previously mentioned the advantages of bombing North Vietnam; his recommendations were made the basis for all the secret war planning that went on during the Johnson election campaign. Now Johnson and Rostow drew closer together, agreeing in their new camaraderie on the merits of all-out bombing. In the words of David Halberstam, "Walt was no longer the semicomic, peripheral figure. He was a zealot with an answer." Johnson liked him and wholeheartedly adopted the Rostow plan for bombing North Vietnam.[2]

Only two others were yet to be convinced that Johnson and Rostow were right: Vice President Hubert Humphrey and National Security Adviser McGeorge Bundy. Whatever inner turmoil Humphrey experienced he kept to himself, emerging in public in 1965 as someone who loyally accepted the President's decisions. Bundy's position was different. He supported the basic policy but felt the CIA, not the military, ought to run the show, clandestinely, as it was doing in Laos. Further, Bundy was not completely sure that bombing was necessary now that the situation in South Vietnam, as he put it, was holding steady. Instead of replacing Bundy, Johnson sent him to South Vietnam on a special review mission. While he was there, the NLF fired mortar shells into the U.S. barracks at Pleiku. Eight American advisers were killed and sixty were wounded. This experience turned Bundy completely around. He became an all-out bombing advocate and even telephoned the White House with a recommendation that the United States retaliate for Pleiku.[3] When he returned to Washington, Bundy sent a special memo dated February 16 to the

President with a strong recommendation that he mount continuing pressure on Hanoi rather than episodic retaliation. Johnson quipped: "Well, they made a believer out of you, didn't they? A little fire will do that."[4] By early 1965, there was no meaningful dissent among the men around Johnson.

LBJ's second problem was his need to counteract world opinion. In early 1965 Johnson faced a flurry of peace pressures. As military activity intensified in Vietnam, particularly after the Pleiku incident, many nations feared the consequences of what appeared to be the beginning of a new massive American intervention. These nations then began to exert strong efforts to convince Washington that it would be in its best interest to work toward a peaceful settlement. Johnson, however, viewed these peace efforts as unwarranted and in error, and tackled the problem with the ingeniousness he had demonstrated in his years as Democratic majority leader in the Senate.

The Soviet Union stood at the forefront of the initiatives for a negotiated end to the war. Moscow announced in January that Premier Kosygin would visit Hanoi the following month, and that he would like to meet with President Johnson first. But the Johnson-Kosygin meeting never took place. Washington saw Kosygin's planned visit to Hanoi as an opening move in an attempt by the Soviet Union to mediate between North Vietnam and the United States. In the absence of a Johnson-Kosygin meeting, the Soviet Union hoped for high-level conversations as a preface to a reconvening of the Geneva Conference. Now Moscow warned that American retaliation bombing after Pleiku would make agreement more difficult to achieve. The Soviet Union would take further measures to safeguard the security and strengthen the defense capability of North Vietnam.

While the Soviet offer was being considered in the White House, Secretary General U Thant of the UN urged all parties involved to move "from the field of battle to the conference table." He too seemed to fear that a bombing war was imminent. The planning, it seemed to fear that a bombing war was imminent. U Thant proposed "negotiation and discussion" that might lead to political stability; thus the United States would be able to "withdraw . . . with dignity"—and, of course, to avoid great losses and great risks. U Thant's appeal was made directly to the American public:

> I am sure the great American people, if they only knew the facts and the background of the developments in South Vietnam, will agree with me that further bloodshed is unnecessary. . . . As you know, in times of war and of hostilities the first casualty is truth.[5]

U Thant's warning made little impression. Johnson denied publicly that he had received any real proposal for peace, and further charged U Thant with being naive.[6] Americans believed their government and the President. LBJ insisted that the 1954 Geneva Accords guaranteed the independence of South Vietnam, which, of course, was clearly not the case. And Rusk argued that LBJ needed to escalate the war because South Vietnam was under attack by the forces of North Vietnam, when he must have known that at that time there were no regular North Vietnamese units in South Vietnam.[7]

Of all the obstacles Johnson faced early in 1965, the politics of South Vietnam proved to be the trickiest. LBJ's team had supported the General Khanh dictatorship during most of the previous year, but Khanh apparently was planning to negotiate with the Communists. Moreover, Khanh became intransigent, at one point accusing General Maxwell Taylor of interfering in South Vietnamese affairs, and hurling open insults at the United States. The White House was unanimous; once Johnson was safely installed in the presidency, Khanh must go. Yet some way had to be found to keep a measure of stability in South Vietnam and to find and maintain a regime which would continue the war and not undermine American military plans.[8]

A search was made for a new man. Premier Huong seemed a possible choice. He was definitely under the thumb of the Armed Forces Council, and he was reputed to be pro-American. The chicanery began January 27. As premier of the government, Huong was pressed to defy Khanh by appointing four new generals to his cabinet without Khanh's concurrence. Among the appointees were Nguyen Cao Ky and Nguyen Van Thieu, two men making their first appearance in the upper levels of government. For a time it looked as if the Khanh clique might be toppled. In the end the feisty general prevailed, and Huong was forced to resign. The scheme had failed. Khanh, now more firmly entrenched, not only continued to ignore the Americans, but entered into an alliance with the Buddhists, who bitterly opposed all American involvement in their country. The Buddhists wanted peace first and foremost, and they were willing to join forces with questionable leaders like Khanh to achieve this goal.[9]

Khanh would not listen to Maxwell Taylor, who urged a more cooperative replacement for Huong. Instead he heeded the urgings of his Buddhist supporters and chose Dr. Quat as the new premier. Quat, after wavering between the army and the Buddhists, formed a cabinet seemingly determined to negotiate an end to the war. Anger mounted in the White House, as it did in South Vietnamese military circles. Something had to be done, and at once. It seemed as if the ostensibly pro-American puppet might assume independent power and defy American wishes.

On February 19, 1965, the military establishment, prompted by the CIA, revolted against Khanh and drove him into permanent exile. The two young Turks, Ky and Thieu, worked quickly to consolidate their power. They took over the Armed Forces Council, molded it to their own design, and laid the groundwork for eliminating Premier Quat. At that point, however, Johnson intervened. He would rather have a weak and subservient premier like Quat, provided he made a public pledge to fight an all-out war against the Communist insurgency. There had been so much instability in Saigon that Johnson wanted to reassure the American people that a strong and stable government existed in Saigon, deserving of U.S. support. A guarantee by the Quat government that the war would continue was essential if the United States was to make further air strikes against the North.

However, Quat was not cooperative. Despite relentless pressures from the generals and the American Embassy, he favored the Buddhist peace plan. During the infighting that February, Quat said: "Vietnam is suffering too much. We want to end the war with honor." It now became obvious that the United States needed a strong military government in Saigon to cooperate with its own growing military forces. They found two new leaders and collaborators: Air Marshal Nguyen Cao Ky and Nguyen Van Thieu. These two "leaders" ruled independently or together for various periods until the final evacuation in 1975. Ky helped to push aside Premier Khanh and then his successor Premier Quat during the latter months of 1964. From that time on, Ky and then Thieu were in practical effect *the* government in Saigon.

Ky and Thieu reached an uneasy truce in June 1965. Thieu settled for a behind-the-scenes post as chairman of the National Leadership Committee. He bided his time for almost two years. Finally, in late 1967, Thieu rigged a countrywide presidential election and, as part of his power play, forced Ky to accept the vice-presidency. With that, Thieu inaugurated an eight-year rule.[10]

In the early 1960s, when Diem and his brother Nhu ran a widespread narcotics ring which smuggled opium from Laos into South Vietnam, Nguyen Cao Ky was in charge of the actual smuggling operation. Then, when Diem and Nhu were assassinated, Ky reacted quickly, seizing the entire narcotics organization for himself and expanding the opium and heroin trade. In effect, Marshal Ky, from 1965 to 1967, controlled every aspect of the importation and sale of narcotics in South Vietnam.[11]

During this period, Nguyen Van Thieu was also part of the Diem regime, as commander of an infantry division, and he was apparently jealous of the enormous profits he knew Ky was depositing in Swiss banks. For that reason, Thieu quickly sought to break Ky's grip on the narcotics traffic in Southeast Asia. During the Tet offensive in early 1968, Thieu ordered the assassination of a number of Ky's henchmen, and he wasted little time in replacing these people with loyal followers of his own. Soon he controlled Ky's operation. The profits were passed up the military chain of command, with each level skimming off a percentage, until the final payoffs were made to the South Vietnamese legislators, government leaders, customs and police officials, and ultimately to President Thieu and Vice-President Ky.[12]

For his part, Thieu controlled the South Vietnamese army and navy, and as president he controlled the South Vietnamese National Assembly, many of whom assisted his drug trade. The legislators went to Laos, Thailand, or Hong Kong and returned with large supplies of heroin; the South Vietnamese navy aided in the importation of narcotics by sea; and the army helped distribute them throughout the country.

President Johnson and the United States now had in place the government that was to rule Vietnam until the defeat of Thieu in 1975. The United States poured out American blood, treasure, and honor to sustain this corrupt government for a period of over ten years, and its primary leader, Nguyen Van Thieu, supported the U.S. war in Vietnam not for the benefit of his people, but for his own personal power and enrichment.

LBJ now had everything under control. He had in place a government in Saigon that would force the people of Vietnam to support the war or be eliminated; he had a docile and loyal team in Washington; and he had squelched any talk of peace not only in Vietnam but in nations throughout the world. The time had come when Lyndon could begin to implement the agreed-upon strategy to win the war by bombing Hanoi and North Vietnam into submission.

As Johnson ignored peace efforts, he also ignored intelligence reports that predicted that the North Vietnamese would unite to withstand bombing attacks, just as the British people did in response to the relentless attacks of the Luftwaffe in 1940. Washington's policy of declaring its war in Vietnam a war against Communism, and of attacking North Vietnam, had an effect that was exactly the opposite of the intended result. Johnson increasingly forced North Vietnam to support the Vietcong and in turn forced Peking and Moscow to support both North Vietnam and the Vietcong.

At the beginning, Ho insisted that the Vietcong in South Vietnam fight their own battles as he in turn gave them foreign aid by transferring food and supplies for their support. The intensive U.S. bombing of North Vietnam ultimately forced the North Vietnamese to defend themselves and the National Liberation Front, particularly after 1966, and to send their own ground forces into the fray whenever they believed that conventional warfare would be effective.

Washington literally forced Hanoi's fellow Communists—The People's Republic of China and the Union of Soviet Socialist Republics—to give support to the Vietnamese. The Chinese government believed that if the Democratic Republic of Vietnam was crushed and eliminated, China would find an entrenched enemy—the United States—encamped on its border with thousands of planes loaded with nuclear and other weapons poised to bomb China. Chinese officials were also concerned about the fact that since the United States was constructing military camps capable of housing tens of thousands of ground forces, and were building naval bases capable of accommodating the U.S. naval forces, that these military and naval bases could threaten the security of China.[13]

It appears that the Soviet Union had its own "domino theory." If

Vietnam came under U.S. domination, and even if China was not attacked by the United States, the Chinese Communists, who had cooperated with Russia during the Vietnam War, would now be free to resume their hostile attitude toward the Soviet Union, and Russia could face the possibility of the United States cooperating with the Chinese in an attack upon the Soviet Union. During the Vietnam War, however, even though the latent hostility between China and Russia remained, the U.S. involvement in Vietnam literally compelled both countries to make common cause in assisting North Vietnam and the NLF.

The first bombing attack on North Vietnam was called Flaming Dart I, but this was just the harbinger of bigger things to come; Flaming Dart II was launched February 11, 1965.[14] This was the beginning of an air war that was to continue for almost a decade in an effort to bomb the enemy into submission. On February 13 the President formally ordered "measured and limited" air action jointly with the South Vietnamese, against military targets in North Vietnam below the Nineteenth Parallel. Operation Rolling Thunder began on March 2, nineteen days after the last of the Flaming Dart raids. Twenty-five F-105s and 20 B-57s of the U.S. Air Force struck the North Vietnamese ammunition dump at Xom Bong, thirty-five miles north of the north-south demarcation line. Ten days later came the second Thunder attack. After that, there were two American raids every week. The raids were at first limited to bridges and radar posts between the Seventeenth and Nineteenth Parallels—about two-hundred miles into North Vietnamese territory.

General Westmoreland pressed for other measures. He wanted to use air power against the Vietcong in the South. This authority was granted, and the deadly bombing of South Vietnam began—on March 6—without the fanfare that accompanied the strikes in the North, but with far greater intensity. With these developments, a new dimension was added to the American war in Vietnam. There was no longer the pretense that South Vietnamese pilots were flying their own bombing missions to save their compatriots from Communism. The U.S. Air Force took over the show, both in North and South Vietnam, and made no effort to hide either its direct involvement or its total control.

Civilian targets can never be distinguished completely from military ones. There was inevitable destruction of homes, wholesale killing of people in the vicinity, even though the intended target was purely military. Before many months had elapsed, the Pentagon all but lifted even the restriction against attacking civilians. There was direct instruction to destroy villages and hamlets suspected of harboring the Vietcong. One young pilot admitted: "I killed 40 Vietcong today. That's the number they told me were in the village. Anyway, I leveled it."[15]

The Strategic Air Command began to employ B-52 bombers— huge, heavy, powerful craft capable of long-range flying and heavy bomb loads—as early as June 1965 over South Vietnam. Within a year, by April 1966, B-52s were flying Rolling Thunder raids into North Vietnam as well. The devastation was vast, and as spring moved into summer the furor of the air war grew even more intense. However, the prediction of the intelligence services that persistent bombing strengthens rather than weakens the determination of the victims to resist, proved valid in Vietnam.

Ho now requested increased military aid from both Communist China and the USSR. Peking agreed to continue to send weapons to Hanoi and to help build railroads over which Russian aid could be transported. China, however, stipulated that unless the United States actually invaded North Vietnam, it would not intervene in the Vietnam War.[16] China evacuated large areas of South China, established civil defense posts, and promised military intervention if the United States invaded North Vietnam.[17] Ho's agreement with China not only provided for shipments of small arms, but also for an alleged 50,000 "Chinese engineering troops" to serve as "work brigades" in North Vietnam.[18] Food trains chugged across the border every few days, and Vietnamese workers unloaded rice, milk, canned goods, and vegetables before sending the trains back into China. Southern Chinese communes, acting as factories, manufactured radios, ammunition, clothing items, and medical supplies for use in North Vietnam. Along several large pipelines, free oil flowed from pumping stations in Canton to storage facilities in Hanoi and Haiphong.

Increased Russian aid also became available. Soviet Premier Kosygin was in Hanoi for a state visit when United States planes bombed North Vietnam on February 7 and 8, 1965. Ho quickly requested Russian antiaircraft guns and a token number of MIG jets, which Kosygin agreed to send. The Russians also helped establish a system of antiaircraft defense for beleaguered North Vietnam.[19] Agreements were entered into between Hanoi and Moscow, providing for some Russian weapons, which Hanoi sent to the Vietcong, and for antiaircraft equipment. As the war intensified, North Vietnam received an increased commitment for both military and economic assistance. Russia sent MIG jets in April 1966, radar systems for the surface-to-air missiles, and military advisers to direct the antiaircraft sites.

Until very late in the war, Hanoi received 90 percent of these supplies by rail from Communist China, so that Ho could never ignore the wishes of Peking as he sought sophisticated weapons from Russia.[20] The Sino-Soviet rivalry thus remained a most important factor in Ho's diplomacy, forcing the Vietminh leader to walk the tightrope repeatedly.

Early in April, 1965, only five weeks after Operation Rolling Thunder began, American bombers met precisely targeted attacks by Soviet surface-to-air (SAM) missiles. SAMs were first detected by a U-2 aircraft on April 5, 1965. By the end of that year, fifty-six SAM sites had been detected. United States strikes against SAM sites began in late July 1965. Just as the bombing brought greater determination to the victims who introduced new defensive weapons, so the attacks by the SAMs brought more American bombers to Vietnam. The V-4 fighter-bomber arrived, the most advanced American bomber at the time. The number of sorties increased, as did the total weight and destructive power of the bombs.

After two months of this, Johnson called a temporary halt to the bombing raids on the North. The pause was to last only six days, long enough for him to make it appear that he genuinely sought peace, but not long enough to afford sufficient time for diplomats to achieve any results. After the pause, he ordered the air force to ignore previous restrictions on bombing north of the Nineteenth Parallel. Now the air war was to be brought close to Hanoi itself. Planes began bombing north of Hanoi. In July 1965 the first bomber was downed by a SAM; the bombers, in Operation Iron Hand, attacked SAM launching sites. But it took Hanoi no time at all to replace destroyed SAMs. In fact, old SAMs were replaced by newer Soviet models, and more launching sites than ever before were created.[21] As the war progressed, the Russians continued to supply increasingly efficient antiaircraft artillery, which was manned by thousands of expert Chinese gunners.[22]

Despite the increase in the number of American planes shot down, and the constant replacement of SAMs destroyed by air attacks, officials at the Pentagon and in the White House continued to assume that Hanoi would sooner or later sue for peace. It did not happen, however, and Johnson began to worry. He sent Army Chief of Staff Harold K. Johnson to Vietnam with the following exhortation:

> You generals have all been educated at the taxpayers' expense, and you're not giving me any ideas and any solutions for this damn little piss-ant country. . . . I want some solutions. I want some answers.[23]

General Johnson found in Saigon that there was a basic disagreement between the embassy and the American military command. Westmoreland had up until then been willing to act as Ambassador Taylor's military chief of staff. As he confirmed in his memoirs: "After I assumed command of the MACV, there was never a question as to my relationship with Ambassador Taylor. He was the boss; I was in effect, his deputy for military affairs."[24] However, after the air war got under way, Westmoreland felt it was time to bring more ground troops into Vietnam. He argued that since the United States was bringing in hundreds of jet aircraft and their crews and maintenance personnel, ground troops were needed to protect U.S. air bases from attack by the Vietcong. He pressed the argument on the ambassador until Taylor grudgingly agreed.

General Johnson sent his report to President Johnson, and the first U.S. ground combat units were ordered to South Vietnam. The Ninth Marine Expeditionary Brigade landed at Da Nang on March 8, 1965. The men were told they were to protect the U.S. Marine Air Base at Da Nang; nothing more. They were not to engage in day-to-day actions against the Vietcong.

The marines had hardly gotten their feet dry, however, when several proposals emanated from Generals Johnson and Westmoreland for an active American ground war. General Johnson wanted a full U.S. infantry division sent to Vietnam to operate in the central highlands to secure various bases. Ambassador Taylor was not yet sold on the idea of combat troops, but he felt that if they were sent they should be used along the coast in a series of defensive enclaves. This would free the South Vietnamese ARVN for fighting the NLF. Westmoreland leaned toward General Johnson's view that more American combat units should be sent. He requested two more marine battalions—for Da Nang and nearby Phu Bai. He also wanted more freedom to maneuver the new troops, and that was precisely what the Joint Chiefs had in mind back in Washington.[25]

After listening to General Johnson on his return from Saigon, the President recalled Ambassador Taylor for consultation. Soon the ambassador recognized that the President and most of his advisers were close to a decision to commit more American troops, even though Rolling Thunder was less than two months old. As Halberstam wrote:

> What was significant about these meetings was the timing. After six weeks of Operation Rolling Thunder, the massive bombing of the North, it had become obvious that the bombing was not going to bring Hanoi either to its senses or its knees, and that as a political weapon against the North it had probably failed.[26]

Ambassador Taylor, in his effort to limit the number of U.S. ground combat troops in Vietnam, saw that he had been outmaneuvered by the Joint Chiefs of Staff, who teamed up with McNamara and Westmoreland. He compromised and modified his position. Instead of continued opposition to the buildup of American armed forces, he would simply try to hold down their number and restrict their activities.

With Taylor's objections out of the way, the President was ready for an entirely new phase of the Vietnam War—all-out ground action in the South. With sights set on building up U.S. ground forces in Vietnam, LBJ approved a change in the mission for the marines around Da Nang. The President decided they could operate offensively on pacification missions within fifty miles of the base. Even though this was a major change in the use of American armed forces, introducing an entirely new phase to American involvement in Vietnam, there was no announcement from the White House. Indeed, as Halberstam noted, "quite the reverse; everyone was [told] to minimize any change, to say that the policy had not changed. The President had enough problems with his domestic programs without being hit from the other side about going to war. . . . [As a result] the word did not slip out for another two months."[27] All during that time, Johnson and his advisers avoided any consultation with Congress. The new phase of the war was carried out in secret.

The White House issued National Security Action Memorandum

(NSAM) 328, which called for a general increase of 18,000 to 20,000 United States logistical and support forces to be sent to Vietnam immediately. In that memorandum the President also approved Westmoreland's request for two additional marine battalions for Da Nang and Phu Bai and "a change of mission for all Marine battalions deployed in Vietnam to permit their more active use. . . ." These reinforcements would be sent under conditions to be established and approved by the secretary of defense in consultation with the secretary of state.

The military leaders quickly asked for larger increases in the number of troops. Westmoreland no longer felt restrained by Ambassador Taylor; he simply sent his requests through the military chain of command. Johnson's staff then put pressure on Taylor to support the new presidential policy, and to obtain approval from the government in Saigon. The pressure was relentless, as Schandler has indicated:

> . . . Ambassador Taylor was bombarded with messages and instructions from Washington testifying to an eagerness to speed up the introduction to Vietnam of U.S. ground combat forces far beyond anything that had been authorized in NSAM 328.[28]

Taylor hesitated, afraid that Ky and Thieu would oppose the buildup of U.S. troops. In addition he wrote to Washington that he was not sure where the buildup would lead:

> Before I can present our case to the GVN I have to know what the case is and why. It is not going to be easy to get ready concurrence for the large-scale introduction of foreign troops unless the need is clear and explicit.[29]

Taylor argued with Westmoreland about troop requests, but the more he argued, the more he isolated himself from the Johnson team. The war was being run from Washington, not from Saigon, and the South Vietnamese were compelled to comply. Westmoreland went behind Taylor's back to ask for the 173d Airborne Brigade to be sent to Bienhoa Air Base. The Joint Chiefs and McNamara promptly approved, without bothering to hear Taylor's argument. When he heard what had been done, Taylor was shocked, but there was nothing he could do about it. In theory, Taylor remained the chief U.S. spokesman in Vietnam, but Westmoreland bypassed him and went straight to the Pentagon.

The Taylor-Westmoreland split required Johnson to clarify his policy. He called all hands to Honolulu to get everything straightened out. The Honolulu Conference set the pattern for America's ground war in Vietnam. Ambassador Taylor was there to present his case, but ran counter to McNamara, JCS Chairman General Wheeler, Westmoreland, and Admiral Sharp. The military leaders paid polite lip service to Taylor's argument that U.S. forces merely guard the enclaves along the Vietnamese coast. They even promised to consider the enclave strategy further. However, the Pentagon carried the day. U.S. troop strength in South Vietnam would increase to thirteen battalions, a total strength of 82,000 by the summer of 1965.[30] Clearly, the President intended to send as many soldiers to South Vietnam as were necessary to do the job.

Returning to Saigon, Ambassador Taylor stressed the limited nature of America's role in the war. Westmoreland did not interpret his mandate in that way:

> When President Johnson changed the mission of the American units from a defensive posture and authorized them to engage in counterinsurgence combat operations, that was to me a broad authority.[31]

Consequently, troop requests continued. In June, Westmoreland pushed for a total of thirty-five battalions, plus nine more for later deployment. Because the ARVN suffered so many defeats in May and June, Westmoreland claimed there was simply "no course of action open to us except to reinforce our efforts in SVN with additional U.S. or Third Country forces as rapidly as is practicable during the critical weeks ahead. I am convinced," the general concluded, "that U.S. troops with their energy, mobility and firepower can successfully take the fight to the VC."[32]

This message was well received in the White House. Westmoreland received even wider authority than before. The President informed his general he could hereafter commit U.S. forces anywhere in the country when in his judgment they were needed to strengthen the South Vietnamese forces. Westmoreland responded by sending U.S. forces into War Zone D, northwest of Saigon, for the first time—less than one day after Johnson gave him the go-ahead.

Nevertheless, Johnson wished to reexamine all options before further deployment. Therefore, he sent McNamara back to Saigon. Westmoreland told McNamara he now needed forty-four battalions in 1965 and that additional forces would be required in 1966 to fight the VC. McNamara returned to Washington and recommended this forty-four-battalion request to the President, who promptly agreed to consider the idea. The President held a series of meetings with congressional leaders and his advisers on the proposal. Maxwell Taylor and his deputy, U. Alexis Johnson, were against any new increases. Senator Mansfield and George Ball felt the same way. But Rusk joined McNamara and Johnson and approved a force buildup to 175,000 troops, to be completed by the end of the year. Moreover, the President approved Westmoreland's newly adopted strategy that American forces would now act freely and offensively in South Vietnam. Instead of holding back defensively in coastal enclaves, Westmoreland's troops would now search for the Vietcong and destroy them militarily. The restrictive enclave strategy was finally rejected, and there was a new catchphrase for the war: Search and Destroy.[33]

Lyndon Baines Johnson had crossed his Rubicon. He had committed the wealth and manpower of the United States to a land war in Asia. He had deliberately plunged the United States into a full-fledged war without the consent of Congress and without fully informing the American people. Johnson had ordered the U.S. military establishment to take over the conflict, making it not a Vietnamese but an American war.[34] No end was in sight. It was now a war that would be waged on the ground as well as in the air.

The air war was fought primarily by U.S. Air Force units based in Thailand—and by U.S. Navy aircraft flying from aircraft carriers in the Gulf of Tonkin. The air war, which began in 1965, was called Rolling Thunder. It was fought under the personal direction of President Johnson.

> In undertaking air strikes, political considerations were usually paramount. . . . The President retained such firm control of the air campaign against the North that no important target or new target areas could be hit without his approval.[35]

At first LBJ approved only a limited group of targets between the Seventeenth and Nineteenth Parallels in North Vietnam. Somewhat later he extended this attack area to the Twentieth Parallel, but from the start, LBJ and his advisers selected the specific targets in *Washington* and then sent an up-to-date list to the commander in chief of

Pacific operations in Hawaii. He, in turn, divided the targets between the U.S. Air Force and the U.S. Navy aircraft waiting in Southeast Asia.

The first few Rolling Thunder missions were flown primarily by
U.S. Air Force planes in South Vietnam, aided by some South Vietnamese and U.S. Navy aircraft. Soon, however, American planes
began flying missions from six newly constructed U.S. Air Force
bases in Thailand. These bases grew from about 1,000 personnel and
83 aircraft in early 1965 to a peak of 35,000 personnel and 600 aircraft
in 1968. The intensity of these early Rolling Thunder raids increased
throughout 1965; strikes against North Vietnam multiplied from
1,500 sorties in April to 4,000 sorties in October. Industrial sites,
major factories, and other targets near populated areas were officially
off limits. In addition, North Vietnamese airfields and missile sites,
as well as the area around Hanoi and Haiphong, were officially outside the scope of the bombing raids. LBJ wanted to drive the North
to its knees, but he decided the process should be gradual and painful.[36]

In February 1966, after a short pause in the bombing, Johnson met
in Honolulu with the new leaders of South Vietnam, Ky and Thieu.
There LBJ made his famous statement that now was the time to "nail
the coonskins to the wall" in Vietnam.[37]

> [Soon thereafter Johnson] approved a series of heavier air strikes
> against North Vietnam. Added to the target list were storage facilities.
> . . . Others included a power plant and a cement factory in Hanoi, an
> important road and rail bridge . . . and an early warning and ground
> control intercept reader facility at Kep. . . .[38]

On April 10, 1966, the powerful B-52s made their first raid over
North Vietnam. In June, air force F-105s, flying from Thailand, attacked a storehouse for petroleum-oil-lubricants less than four miles
from Hanoi, destroying 95 percent of its capacity. Beginning July 9,
1966, U.S. aircraft bombed additional storage facilities and began
heavier bombing of rail lines north of Hanoi. The tempo of the raids
increased throughout September, when 12,000 sorties were flown by
U.S. planes. In November, Johnson approved still more targets, including for the first time railroad yards on the outskirts of Hanoi. By
the end of 1966, the United States had flown 106,500 sorties over the
North and dropped 165,000 tons of bombs. But the toll was high: 455

aircraft were shot down over the North in 1966. Nine were lost in aerial combat against North Vietnamese MIG jets, which entered the air war in September. The rest fell victim to SAM gunners on the ground.

To counter the growing success of Hanoi's MIG jets, the U.S. Air Force conducted Operation Bolo in January 1967. A number of F-4s, the fastest fighter-bomber at the Pentagon's disposal, were disguised as heavily laden F-105s. When the MIGs rose to attack what they thought were the slower F-105s, the F-4s attacked the MIGs and shot down seven aircraft in twelve minutes. This incident ended the MIG attacks for some time and gave LBJ more freedom of action. He increased the bombing and authorized raids nearer to North Vietnam's metropolitan areas. In March and April 1967, U.S. planes bombed the Thai Nguyen iron and steel plant, thirty miles from Hanoi, and destroyed a railway bridge only four miles from Hanoi. Each step closer to Hanoi increased the chance of civilian casualties, but LBJ and the military continued to blast a growing number of targets.

In late July 1967, Johnson tightened the screws still further by approving yet another target list. On August 2, U.S. bombs hit the Paul Doumer railway bridge in Hanoi, an important transportation link, and leveled an entire span. After it was repaired, the bridge was hit again on October 25. U.S. aircraft returned again on December 19 to finish the job. Other targets to receive a massive pounding in the summer of 1967 were the MIG airfields. Up until this time the MIG bases had not been attacked, but authorization came from the White House in mid-1967. During raids against the Kep, Hoa Lac, Kien An, and Phuc Yen MIG bases, the North's meager supply of MIGs was destroyed or damaged, except for the eighteen MIGs based at Hanoi's civilian airport, Gia Long. This action initially ended the threat of MIG attacks upon U.S. aircraft. During 1967 the United States had downed a total of seventy-five MIGs in combat and had lost twenty-five U.S. aircraft to them.

From the date LBJ transferred responsibility for Operation Rolling Thunder to the U.S. Air Force units in Thailand, the aircraft based in South Vietnam were used to support Westmoreland's ground operations. From an original limit of three air bases in 1965, the air force and marines in the South had built six new bases, to which LBJ added more fighter-bomber squadrons.

One of the first jobs assigned to the bolstered air forces was a bombing campaign against the DMZ, which began in June 1966. Meanwhile, the giant B-52 flying fortresses based on Guam continued to raid suspected enemy enclaves in the jungles of South Vietnam, as they had done since the middle of 1965. By the middle of 1966, the B-52s had flown nearly 4000 sorties against territory controlled by Saigon. When the statistics from ground action and from these Southern air raids are added to the destructive capabilities of defoliant sprays and toxic gases, the evidence clearly indicates that the tempo of Johnson and Westmoreland's war in the South increased remarkably within the first year.[39]

Between 1965 and 1968 a major land war developed in the South. When the Marines landed at Da Nang in March 1965, the President became committed to a ground war in which U.S. servicemen would search out and defeat the Vietcong and, if need be, the North Vietnamese. At the end of July 1965, the U.S. First Infantry and 101st Airborne Divisions arrived in Vietnam, supplemented by two more brigades of U.S. Marines.

General Westmoreland fully understood and supported the change of strategy, and he quickly began using his new authority on the battlefield. In early August 1965 he sent the marines into battle near Chu Lai in Operation Starlight. This was the first of the search-and-destroy missions in which large U.S. military units took the war to the enemy. Operation Starlight resulted in 700 Vietnamese deaths, which the Pentagon labeled as Vietcong but which definitely included civilian casualties.

Throughout the remaining months of 1965, the U.S. buildup continued at full force, as did Westmoreland's search-and-destroy missions. By September the First Cavalry Division arrived at Qui Nhon in the central highlands, the first division completely equipped with helicopters. Able to transport infantry to the battle scene and wounded away from the fighting, helicopters were soon used to hunt down suspected Vietcong and to devastate villages suspected of harboring them. The First Cavalry Division wasted little time getting into action in Vietnam. In October a major battle developed in the Ia Drang Valley, and Westmoreland threw his fresh units into combat. By the end of the Ia Drang operation, U.S. troop strength in Vietnam had reached 148,300, a figure that included two brigades from Korea. Around Qui Nhon, the Koreans formed their own closed society but nevertheless joined the First Cavalry Division in its maneuvers against the Vietcong. The use of Korean troops further served to alienate the peasant population around Qui Nhon.

Westmoreland now reported to Washington that his authorized limit of 165,000 was not high enough, and on November 22, 1965, requested additional troops. Johnson sent McNamara to Saigon for a meeting with Westmoreland. On November 28 the secretary of defense arrived in South Vietnam. Westmoreland convinced his visitor that he needed a total of seventy-four battalions, a figure which would increase U.S. troop strength to about 400,000 by the end of 1966.

McNamara presented this request to Johnson, but LBJ decided not to act upon the proposal for the time being. Johnson was not opposed to an increase in troop strength, but he wanted to avoid the kind of commitment that would make it necessary to call up reserve forces. LBJ feared that this would shock the nation and hurt his reelection chances in 1968. He determined, therefore, that the buildup would continue but that troop levels would be met from active-duty forces.

During January 1966, while LBJ made demands on Hanoi and threatened to increase the air war, the jungle war continued in the South except for a short cease-fire from January 20 to January 23 for the Tet holiday. Westmoreland, quick to utilize his ever-expanding combat forces, won approval from LBJ and the Pentagon for two more search-and-destroy missions in January.

In February 1966, Westmoreland made yet another request for more troops. Attending a special conference held in Honolulu, he personally asked LBJ for seventy-nine battalions, which he felt, along with the twenty-three allied battalions he already had, would enable him to turn the tide of war. The President promised to discuss the request with his advisers in Washington, and Westmoreland returned to Saigon to prepare for the next round of offensive action.

In the meantime, U.S. forces in Vietnam continued to grow as the Twenty-fifth Infantry Division arrived from Hawaii. By March 1966, U.S. troops strength totalled 215,000, with 20,000 more en route; Westmoreland was ready for further escalation. In March and April, with Johnson's approval, he sent his forces on three major search-and-destroy missions that swept through heavily populated areas of South Vietnam and left several hundred burned-out villages in their wake.

By the time these operations had ended, Westmoreland finally received an answer to his troop request. On April 10, 1966, Johnson approved a plan for giving Westmoreland seventy of his requested seventy-nine battalions and increasing U.S. forces to 383,500 by the end of the year. It was a dramatic decision on the part of LBJ, who continued to give the military more of a free hand in South Vietnam than ever before.[40]

In the summer of 1966, the Fourth Infantry Division arrived in Vietnam and Westmoreland continued his major search-and-destroy missions in June and July. By August the 196th Light Infantry Brigade arrived and U.S. troop strength rose to 300,000. But still Westmoreland was not satisfied. On August 5, McNamara came to Saigon and Westmoreland submitted a request for a total of 542,585 troops by the end of 1967. This request, on the heels of Westmoreland's assurances that the war was going well for the United States, stunned McNamara and disturbed even Ambassador Lodge, who wanted to slow the influx of new troops. Lodge told McNamara that the presence of so many Americans in South Vietnam was causing inflation and other serious internal problems, an issue which the military would not address.

Therefore, when McNamara returned to Washington he recommended a partial change of strategy to Johnson. The United States should limit its forces to 470,000 men, cease search-and-destroy missions, fall back into an enclave strategy, hold the Rolling Thunder missions to the present level, and pursue vigorously the pacification program. McNamara was gradually coming to see that LBJ's Vietnam policy merely invited further escalation. The secretary was still on the Johnson team, but his trip to South Vietnam in August 1966 paved the way for yet more drastic suggestions.

While Westmoreland's request and McNamara's ideas were being debated in Washington, both U.S. and auxiliary forces continued to arrive in Vietnam. In September the Australian Eleventh Armored Cavalry arrived, but, more importantly, the infamous Korean Ninth Infantry Division made its appearance in South Vietnam. With the Ninth, or White Horse, Division, the Koreans had two full divisions plus another brigade in Vietnam. They soon gained a reputation for their brutal treatment of suspected Vietcong, treatment which the U.S. military command overlooked. Westmoreland repeatedly praised their military operations and congratulated the Koreans for "some of the most imaginative and effective pacification operations in the entire war."[41]

Finally, in mid-1966, Westmoreland brought the U.S. Coast Guard into a major role in South Vietnam. He set up a coast patrol, which relied on Aluminum Swift boats and eighty-two coast guard boats to patrol South Vietnam's shoreline and to fire upon enemy positions. There seemed to be no limit to U.S. ingenuity.[42]

A major change in strategy came about in October 1966, but it was not the change that McNamara had recommended several months earlier. At a highly publicized conference in Manila from October 24 to October 30, President Johnson met with Ky and Thieu. Theodore Draper writes that LBJ had finally decided to drop the pretense that U.S. forces were merely aiding the ARVN in the war. The President wanted victory in 1967.

> The hard, stark decision reversing the [official] roles of the American and South Vietnamese forces in the war was made at about the time of the Manila Conference. . . . It entailed an increase in the number of American troops in Vietnam by approximately 100,000 for a total of nearly 500,000 by the end of 1967. The justification for this enlarged force was a new strategy. . . . As the South Vietnamese Defense Minister tersely described this strategy, "the entire Vietnamese Army will switch to a pacification role in 1967 and leave the major fighting to American troops."[43]

THE FULBRIGHT CHALLENGE
1966–68

Senator William Fulbright, who had guided the Tonkin Gulf Resolution through the Senate in 1964, emerged as Johnson's principal
critic on Vietnam. The Arkansas senator had witnessed firsthand the
effects of the Tonkin Gulf operation. In stunned silence, he had
watched President Johnson escalate a foreign involvement into a
full-fledged war. The first sign of things to come had taken place in
May 1965, when LBJ requested an additional $700 million to meet
mounting military costs in Vietnam. The President told Congress:

> This is not a routine appropriation. For each member of Congress who
> supports this request is also voting to persist in our effort to halt Com-
> munist aggression in South Vietnam. . . . The Communist aim in Viet-
> nam is not simply the conquest of the South. . . . It is to show that
> American commitment is worthless. Once that is done, the gates are
> down and the road is open to expansion and endless conquest. . . . Our
> conclusions are plain. We will not surrender. . . . I see no choice but to
> continue the course we are on. . . . Nothing will do more to strengthen
> your country in the world than the proof of national unity which an
> overwhelming vote for this appropriation will clearly show.[1]

With little discussion, Congress overwhelmingly approved the
President's request. The vote in the House was 408 to 7; the vote in
the Senate was 88 to 3. Fulbright, however, began to doubt Johnson's sincerity. He sympathized with Wayne Morse when Morse
announced, "I say bitterly, sadly and solemnly, out of deep conviction that today my government stands before the world drunk with
military power."[2] Like Morse, Fulbright was moving toward a position opposed to the war—and LBJ's leadership.

By June 1965, Fulbright went on record as an opponent of escalation. When the President met with congressional leaders and announced an immediate increase of 50,000 troops for the war in Vietnam, Fulbright refused to give his approval. After another cold exchange in August, the break between these old allies was complete and irreversible.

By the end of 1965 Fulbright realized that Johnson was seeking military victory at any cost, despite the fact that antiwar activity in the United States was increasing. Fulbright was particularly concerned about the growing deception practiced by the White House, for example, over the question of peace initiatives.[3] He was convinced that Johnson's war in Vietnam was wrong. As Anthony Austin has written:

> All the fears that had been voiced during the Senate debate on the Gulf of Tonkin Resolution had come true—and all of Fulbright's reassurances that the fears were groundless had come back for him to eat, bitter as wormwood.[4]

The United States was now fighting a land war in Southeast Asia; the military was bombing North Vietnam around the clock. Since the passage of the Tonkin Gulf Resolution, Johnson made no effort to consult Congress except to ask for continuing appropriations. The infamous "502 to 2 Resolution" had come back to haunt the American people. Fulbright, realizing his colossal mistake in supporting the Tonkin Gulf Resolution, was ready to try to undo his error. When Johnson asked for $415 million to continue the war in Vietnam, the request fell under Fulbright's jurisdiction, and the Arkansas senator was ready to challenge the administration.[5]

On January 28, 1966, Fulbright's Senate Foreign Relations Committee held a public meeting to discuss the new appropriation request. This developed into one of the only official hearings on the Vietnam War. For four days, presidential advisers, generals, supporters and opponents of the Vietnam War were examined and cross-examined before the Fulbright Committee.

Dean Rusk testified that the extra millions were utterly indispensable for the American war effort. As Rusk explained to the committee:

> The United States has a clear and direct commitment to the security of South Vietnam against external attack. The integrity of our commit-

ments is absolutely essential to the preservation of peace right around
the globe. At stake also is the still broader question: whether aggression
is to be permitted, once again, to succeed. We know from painful experience that aggression feeds on aggression. [If] the other side [refuses]
to sit down and make a peace . . . there is no alternative . . . [except] to
meet this force with force. . . . While we look—and work and fight—for
the day when South Vietnam will enjoy peace, we must apply our
resources [several billion dollars in 1965!] and ingenuity to building
the foundation for that future.[6]

Instead of complying with the request, Fulbright turned the public hearing into a larger investigation. When did the United States
first get involved in Vietnam; why did the United States help the
French in their war against the Vietnamese; why was the United
States now involved in a disastrous war of its own; what exactly was
the U.S. commitment to Saigon; and when would U.S. involvement
end? Fulbright explained his reasoning:

Something, it seems to me, is wrong or there would not be such a great
dissent among the American people. . . . I do not regard all of the
people who have . . . protested the war as irresponsible. I think it is
our duty, the duty of the Committee and the Administration and others
to try to clarify the nature of our involvement in Vietnam and what it is
likely to lead to and whether or not the ultimate objective justifies the
enormous sacrifice in lives and treasure. I think, in all honesty, that is
why there is such interest in this matter.[7]

Several committee members joined Fulbright. Wayne Morse expressed his complete and total opposition to everything the administration was doing in Vietnam and called upon Congress to initiate in-
depth hearings on the Vietnam crisis. Albert Gore asked Rusk if the
recent bombing pause was anything more than a publicity gimmick,
claiming that "Many people . . . [and] many members of Congress
do not believe that the costs, the risk of a nuclear war, [and] the
dangers of war . . . with both China and Russia" are worth our involvement in Vietnam. Joseph Clark challenged Rusk on the idea
that Vietnam was vital to U.S. security. "Why," asked Clark, "have
we turned this into . . . an American war? In your opinion is this
essential to the security of the United States?" Eugene McCarthy
directly attacked the President. How could Johnson accuse Hanoi of
outright aggression while the United States continued to bomb and
strafe North Vietnam? "What is the difference?" he asked.[8]

Secretary Rusk was unable to reply at length and asked for a recess. Before adjourning the session, Fulbright raised one final ques-

tion. "Don't you think," the chairman concluded, "that we ought to understand what we are in for, and that the Congress should give its further approval of this changed situation in Vietnam?"[9] An alarmed Rusk left to prepare the administration's defense, as Fulbright scheduled four more days of public hearings and invited key witnesses to testify.

President Johnson, uneasy about Fulbright's intentions, tried to steal his audience by holding a well-publicized high-level meeting in Hawaii with the leaders of South Vietnam in early February 1966. The major TV networks nevertheless covered the Senate hearings extensively, and millions of Americans tuned in for the extraordinary sessions that probed the President's conduct of the war.[10]

At the February 8 hearing of the Senate Foreign Relations Committee, General James Gavin, a former army chief of plans and operations, testified that he had opposed the idea of sending troops to Indochina as early as 1954, not to mention the U.S. buildup in Vietnam in the 1960s. He feared a confrontation with Red China, the general weakening of America's international strategic position, and the undermining of its economic strength. Gavin questioned whether the vast expenditures in Vietnam were justified and argued that U.S. bombing raids into North Vietnam constituted cruel and unusual punishment which, in any case, would not break the Vietnamese will. Similarly, Gavin announced his opposition to the U.S. buildup on the ground as lacking clarity and purpose. He suggested that the United States establish enclaves or defensive strong points in Vietnam, avoid excessive combat, and let world opinion push Hanoi to the conference table. If the Johnson administration would reevaluate its commitments and the costs of the war, Gavin concluded, possibly a way out could be found.[11]

On February 10, George F. Kennan, former ambassador to Russia and one of the country's most distinguished scholar-diplomats, made his views on the Vietnam situation known:

> The first point I would like to make is that if we were not already involved as we are today in Vietnam, I would know of no reason why we should wish to become involved, and I could think of several reasons why we should wish not to. Vietnam is not a region of major military, industrial importance. It is difficult to believe that any decisive developments of the world situation would be determined . . . on that territory. If it were not for the considerations of prestige that arise precisely out of our present involvement, even a situation in which

South Vietnam was controlled exclusively by the Viet Cong, while regrettable, . . . would not, in my opinion, present dangers great enough to justify our direct military intervention.

Kennan dismissed the domino theory, claiming that a Communist regime in South Vietnam would follow a fairly independent course between Russia and China. Furthermore, he opposed U.S. efforts to control the government in Saigon; such intervention and control was both unwise and unnecessary. The main problem, Kennan argued, was Washington's commitment to South Vietnam at the expense of other legitimate political interests elsewhere in the world. "Our action [in Vietnam]," Kennan pointed out, "has failed to win either enthusiasm or confidence even among peoples normally friendly to us." America's relations with the Soviet Union "have suffered grievously." The ambassador did not favor a "disorderly withdrawal" from Vietnam, but he agreed with General Gavin that U.S. actions should be strictly defensive until its troops could be evacuated. Under no circumstances, Kennan warned, should the United States escalate its involvement:

I have great misgivings about any deliberate expansion of hostilities on our part directed to the achievement of something called "victory," if by the use of that term we envisage . . . the formal submission by the adversary to our will, and the complete realization of our present stated political aims. I doubt that these things can be achieved even by the most formidable military successes. There seems to be an impression that if we bring sufficient military pressure to bear, there will occur at some point something in the nature of a political capitulation on the other side. I think this is a most dangerous assumption. . . . Any total routing out of the Viet Cong . . . could be achieved . . . only at the cost of a degree of damage to civilian life and of civilian suffering . . . for which I would not like to see this country responsible.

In response to Chairman Fulbright's question as to whether the Communist threat in Vietnam required an all-out military effort by the United States, Kennan stated:

I think that we should do all that we can with due regard to our own security and to our own interests in world peace to prevent [a Communist takeover in South Vietnam], but I think that we should also be careful not to overrate or to misinterpret the implications of it. . . . I have a fear that our thinking about this whole problem is still affected by some sort of illusions about invincibility on our part, that there is no problem . . . in the world which we . . . could not solve. I disbelieve in this most profoundly.

On the broader question of U.S.-Soviet relations, Kennan warned against distorting and applying the containment doctrine to Southeast Asia, and then losing sight of the central and pivotal issues. "I think," Kennan said, "if there was any point where we went wrong, it was putting fighting men ashore for purposes of combat, without knowing how and at what point to get them out again." Kennan concluded by warning against further escalation:

> I would submit that there is more respect to be won in the opinion of the world by a resolute and courageous liquidation of unsound positions than by the most stubborn pursuit of extravagant and unpromising objectives.[12]

In reply and in defense of the President, General Maxwell Taylor appeared before Fulbright's Senate committee on February 17, 1966. The Communist-inspired war in Vietnam, according to Taylor, represented a great test for the United States, since the Communist chain of command went straight from the Vietcong to Hanoi and on to Peking and Moscow. Obviously, Taylor commented, the immediate Communist goal was the takeover by aggression of the freedom-loving country of South Vietnam, a country to which the United States had a clear commitment. Without U.S. aid and manpower, the general reasoned, Saigon would fall and the remaining nations in Southeast Asia would have to face the Communist onslaught alone. As a next step, the Communists would skillfully export the "war of liberation" to other areas of the world. It was clear, therefore, that the United States had a vital stake in Vietnam.

U.S. strategy, in Taylor's words, consisted of four parts. The first was the buildup of South Vietnam's army, since "this is a Vietnamese war." The second part was America's air war against "the source of the aggression," North Vietnam, designed "to change the will of the enemy leadership." The third ingredient was U.S. efforts to "stabilize the government, the society and the economy" of South Vietnam. Finally, the United States sought a peaceful settlement of this conflict, but as yet Hanoi was unresponsive. Taylor ended his formal statement with these words: "The key, I believe, is inexorable pressure at all points, directed at the will, the ability and the means of the Communist aggressors."

Under questioning, Taylor defended LBJ's assumptions and policies. South Vietnam was not racked by civil war but faced foreign aggression supported from Hanoi. The Vietcong were the military arm of North Vietnam. The leadership, the direction, and all the vital supplies came from North Vietnam. He denied knowledge of U.S. air raids on Laos and seemed assured that escalation of operations in Vietnam would not lead to war with China.[13]

Wayne Morse, predictably, was not satisfied. He remained resolutely opposed to the war, and warned Taylor against ignoring or attempting to smear those who dissented by suggesting that dissent aided the Communists and the enemies of the United States. The final exchanges were revealing:

> *Morse:* I know that that is the smear that you militarists give to those of us who have honest differences of opinion with you, but I don't intend to get down in the gutter with you and engage in that kind of debate, General. I am simply saying that in my judgment the President of the United States is already losing the people of this country by the millions in connection with this war in Southeast Asia. All I am asking is, if the people decide that this war should be stopped in Southeast Asia, are you going to take the position that is weakness on the home front in a democracy?
>
> *Taylor:* I would feel that our people were badly misguided and did not understand the consequences of such a disaster.
>
> *Morse:* Well, we agree on one thing, that they can be badly misguided, and you and the President in my judgment have been misguiding them for a long time in this war. . . .[14]

Fulbright then asked Taylor why the United States was demanding that Hanoi surrender unconditionally as a prerequisite to any peace conference.

> *Taylor:* No, sir, I am not asking for anyone to surrender.
>
> *Fulbright:* I don't see how else you can explain it. I don't understand this play on words. . . .
>
> *Taylor:* This is simply to make them see pursuing their present course of action is so disadvantageous, it is to their interests to come to the table.
>
> *Fulbright:* Yes, I think that to me means surrender.
>
> *Taylor:* No, sir, it is not surrender.
>
> *Fulbright:* Let me make the contrary point: I would think a limited war would be where our real efforts are to seek a conference and propose a compromise in which we don't necessarily get our way and they don't surrender. We don't surrender, but we seek a settlement of it.

Taylor: How do you compromise the freedom of fifteen million South Vietnamese, Senator? I don't understand that. . . . They are either free or not free.

Fulbright: You can [extend] that reasoning—how do we compromise the freedom of two hundred fifty million Russians? We don't go over there and free them?

Taylor: That is not the issue for the moment.

Fulbright: I know it is not the issue, and I don't think your answer is responsive. I think that this is a war, a most unfortunate war; I am very unhappy about it. But we are trying to develop just what is our objective.[15]

On February 18, 1966, Secretary of State Dean Rusk appeared once again before Fulbright's committee. In his opening statement, Rusk promised to answer any questions about U.S. policy in Vietnam. Lest the committee forget, Rusk reminded the senators that their main job was to discuss and approve the President's request for more money for the war in Vietnam. The United States was involved

. . . because the issues posed there are deeply intertwined with our own security and because the outcome of the struggle can profoundly affect the nature of the world in which we and our children will live. What are our world security interests involved in the struggle in Vietnam? . . . We must recognize that what we are seeking to achieve in South Vietnam is part of a process that has continued for a long time—a process of preventing the expansion and extension of Communist domination . . . through force and threat.

In Rusk's view, it was America's duty to oppose Communism anywhere in the world, and especially in Asia, where the SEATO treaty required the United States to intervene in Vietnam's war. "It is this fundamental SEATO obligation which has from the outset guided our actions in South Vietnam." He seemed to have forgotten that in August 1964 he had said that the United States was *not* acting in Vietnam under the SEATO treaty. As proof of America's commitment to Saigon, Rusk cited President Eisenhower's 1954 letter to Diem, calling it a "bilateral commitment and assurance [made] directly to the government of South Vietnam." The United States, he said, was protecting

. . . South Vietnam as a part of protecting our own peace and security. We have sent American forces to fight in the jungles of that beleaguered country because South Vietnam has . . . been the victim of aggression

by means of armed attack. There can be no serious question as to the
existence and nature of this aggression. The war is clearly an armed
attack, cynically and systematically mounted by the Hanoi regime
against the people of South Vietnam. The North Vietnamese regime has
sought deliberately to confuse the issue by seeking to make its aggression appear as an indigenous revolt [civil war]. But we should not be
deceived by this subterfuge. It is a familiar Communist practice. [They
have] developed . . . over many years . . . an elaborate doctrine for so-
called "wars of national liberation" to cloak their aggressions in ambi-
guity.

The road to peace would be difficult, Rusk acknowledged, mainly
because the Communists could not understand ". . . the limited
nature of our purpose. . . . We wish only that the people of South
Vietnam should have the right and opportunity to determine their
future in freedom without coercion or threat from the outside." In
contrast, Rusk insisted, Hanoi has refused to negotiate:

> For months now we have done everything possible to make clear to the
> regime in Hanoi that a political solution is the proper course. If that
> regime were prepared to call off the aggression in the South, peace
> would come in almost a matter of hours. . . . This is the simple message
> that we have tried to convey to Hanoi through many channels. We have
> sought in every way to impress upon the Communist world the ease
> with which peace could be attained if only Hanoi were willing. We
> have used every resource of diplomacy. I know of no occasion in history
> where so much effort has been devoted . . . to bring about a political
> solution to a costly and dangerous war.

Rusk said that neither Marshal Ky nor President Johnson was at
fault; the blame and the responsibility for continued war and aggression rested with Hanoi.

After brushing aside a reference to General de Gaulle's criticism of
the war and seeking to remind the committee of America's global
responsibilities and of the Gulf of Tonkin Resolution, Rusk stood
firm on the question of North Vietnamese aggression. Senator Aiken
pointed out that almost 275,000 Vietcong were fighting in the South,
compared to only 60,000 infiltrators from the North. Wasn't this really a civil war? Rusk answered:

> There are elements of civil war in this situation, but the heart of the
> problem of peace is the external aggression. The great problem of inter-
> nal peace is . . . the violence that is going on there for which the North
> must take the heaviest responsibility.[16]

Wayne Morse asked why, if the North had indeed invaded South Vietnam, had LBJ not placed the problem before the United Nations? Rusk replied that the Soviet Union would veto any U.N. move to censure North Vietnam or to organize a conference. Senator Church asked whether the administration felt that the United States faced in Vietnam a case of Chinese or North Vietnamese aggression. Rusk replied that

> the instrument of aggression, that is the active agency of the aggression, is Hanoi. The doctrine which is used to support this aggression is from Peking, and there is indication that Peking even more than Hanoi has blocked the path toward a conference table.

Fulbright remained skeptical. He disputed the premise that the United States had a clear commitment to go to war in Vietnam, and rejected as oversimplified the view that the issue was one of clear-cut aggression by North Vietnamese Communists against a free independent nation. The United States, he felt, had not been completely honest about its desire to negotiate, especially since LBJ seemed intent on excluding the real enemy in the field, the Vietcong. As Fulbright saw it, part of the problem was that both our allies and the neutral nations feared that the United States desired a permanent presence in Vietnam. He blamed himself for the congressional failure to fully discuss the Tonkin Gulf Resolution and for the consequences of it.

> [Now it appears that our Vietnam involvement is] not a limited war, that we intend to pursue it to victory even though that may result in bringing in the Chinese, and possibly the Russians, which would force World War Three. . . .

Finally, after a heated exchange between Fulbright and Rusk, Senator Symington asked Rusk for a pledge of good faith.

> *Symington:* Do you believe the President is doing everything that he can to obtain a just peace, but with honor?
>
> *Rusk:* I would think this is the overriding problem. . . . I do not believe that there are procedures or forums or diplomatic channels that are available or that could be created that have not been pursued. . . . [The President] has approached this matter with the greatest solemnity. . . . [I]t is the President who must guide us in choosing among the real alternatives.[17]

The Fulbright hearings, although heard with interest by millions of Americans, actually had no appreciable effect on the continuation of the war. A growing number of Americans were joining the antiwar movement, but Congress refused to follow Senator Fulbright's lead and review the Gulf of Tonkin Resolution and its consequences. Only five Senators—Morse, Fulbright, Gruening, McCarthy, and Stephen Young of Ohio—supported the attempts to repeal the resolution. Congress, in 1966, continued to appropriate the funds that Johnson requested to continue the war. When LBJ asked Morse how he stayed healthy, he replied: "Well, Mr. President, I'll tell you. Every time I read in the papers what you're doing in Vietnam, it makes my blood boil. That purges me; it keeps me fit."[18]

Within three months of the televised hearings, Fulbright began to probe into the details of the Tonkin Gulf affair. He suspected that Johnson and his advisers had been covering up what appeared to be important information, and he set out to bring the matter into the open. On May 3, 1966, the Arkansas senator expressed in public his doubts about the 1964 incident. "I still don't know whether we provoked that attack in connection with supervising or helping a raid by the South Vietnamese or not." No one, he found, seemed to have proof that the North Vietnamese boats actually fired upon the *Maddox* and *C. Turner Joy,* and, according to reports, "there was no physical damage. They weren't hit by anything. I heard one man say there was one bullet hole in one of those ships. One bullet hole!"[19]

Later that month, Fulbright questioned John McNaughton, assistant secretary of defense, and discovered that, indeed, the U.S. destroyers had violated North Vietnamese waters in August 1964. When Fulbright asked who fired the first shot, however, McNaughton refused further comment and left the interview. Fulbright next approached William Bundy, who admitted that the State Department had prepared a draft congressional resolution *long before* Tonkin Gulf occurred. He said that as a part of routine planning, officials had anticipated the possibility that things might take a more drastic turn. That may be, Fulbright replied, but why did Tom Wicker of the *New York Times* write in November 1965 that Johnson carried the resolution "around in his pocket for weeks waiting for the right moment"? On this subject, the senator ran into a brick wall of vague and evasive answers.[20] He felt it necessary to warn that power has a way of undermining judgment, of planting delusions of grandeur in the minds of otherwise sensible people and otherwise sensible nations. The idea of being responsible for the whole world seems to have dazzled us, giving rise to what I call the arrogance of power. . . . If the war goes on and expands, if that fatal process continues to accelerate until America becomes what she is not now and has never been, a seeker after unlimited power and empire, . . . then Vietnam will have had a mighty and tragic fallout indeed.[21]

Fulbright renewed his investigation in the summer of 1967, when a constituent from Little Rock sent him an article from the *Arkansas Gazette,* which was a reconstruction of the Gulf of Tonkin incident by a ten-person team from the Associated Press. In this article, various crew members from the *Maddox* and *C. Turner Joy* described the events of August 2 and 4, 1964. Their inside story seemed to confirm what Fulbright had learned from retired Admiral Arnold True, an expert on destroyer tactics. True had questioned the official version of the Tonkin Gulf attacks and pointed out that "there is no provision in international law for 'firing a warning shot' at another man-of-war on the high seas. [McNamara, Wheeler, and Rusk claimed the United States fired three warning shots on August 2, 1964.] . . . It seems to me," he concluded, "that . . . the U.S. fired the first shot in the war with North Vietnam, . . . and that the resolution was passed on false premises."[22]

The evidence began to show that Admiral True's surmise was correct. Weapons Officer Connell admitted that on August 2, 1964, the destroyer *Maddox* had orders to shoot to kill. There were no warning shots; "we were definitely aiming right at [the North Vietnamese boats]." The article also revealed that, prior to its mission, the *Maddox* had taken aboard a mysterious black box containing electronic espionage equipment, hardly standard for a ship on routine patrol. As for the alleged second attack against the *Maddox* and the *C. Turner Joy,* crewmen from both ships remembered a night that was "darker than the hubs of hell." Radarman Stankevitz and Weapons Officer Connell explained that the engagement was conducted by radar, and that no targets were ever clearly identified.

No one from either U.S. ship could positively remember torpedoes, explosions, clouds of smoke, or debris scattered across the Gulf of Tonkin. In fact, the report suggested that Johnson and his advisers may have concocted the second incident as an excuse to bomb North

Vietnam and win passage of the Tonkin Gulf Resolution. Fulbright, in response, decided to initiate another Senate probe.[23]

On August 28, 1967, Fulbright sent a special request to Secretary McNamara at the Pentagon. The senator wanted to see the ships' logs from the *Maddox* and *C. Turner Joy*—specifically the logs for August 1964. He hoped to reconstruct the events that had led to the Tonkin Gulf Resolution. McNamara ignored this initial request. In October Fulbright tried again, but the result was the same. Finally, to force McNamara's hand, the senator publicly outlined his suspicions of an administration cover-up. "In spite of my many inquiries to the Pentagon," Fulbright explained, "I cannot be sure it [the August 2 attack] was [not] a provoked incident."

Soon after Fulbright's public statement, the Pentagon sent over copies of several radio messages intercepted from the North Vietnamese in August 1964. According to McNamara, this proved that the U.S. ships had been attacked. Fulbright was not convinced, however, and asked to see all of the radio messages in the Pentagon's files. Deputy Secretary of Defense Paul Nitze met with Fulbright on December 14, 1967, and tried to persuade Fulbright to call off his investigation. Nitze warned the senator of the ill effects that would accompany any exposé. Unwanted publicity would damage the national interest, stir up Communist propaganda, and undercut the President's Vietnam policy. Fulbright asked once again for a copy of all the messages in the ships' logs.[24]

In the midst of these exchanges between Fulbright and the Pentagon, Fulbright received an anonymous letter which revealed the existence of a top-secret Pentagon report titled "Command and Control of the Tonkin Gulf Incident, 4–5 August 1964." According to the informant, this secret report verified that the North Vietnamese attack on August 2, 1964, took place because Hanoi thought the *Maddox* was part of the CIA's 34A raids. It also concluded that the alleged second attack on August 4 was probably imaginary. The letter judged the Tonkin Gulf affair to be "a confused bungle" and recommended that Fulbright continue with his investigation, doubting, however, that he would penetrate to the truth.[25]

As a result, Fulbright asked Secretary McNamara, on January 8, 1968, for a copy of the secret "Command and Control" report. In the meantime, he instructed his staff to review the evidence that had become available since the summer of 1967. This staff report asserted that the *Maddox* had indeed been involved in a special electronic espionage mission in 1964, that it had sailed into North Vietnamese waters to bait a Communist attack, and that the lack of evidence suggested an imaginary second attack. Furthermore, the study concluded, McNamara had consistently misled the Senate Foreign Relations Committee in 1964. Fulbright, therefore, persuaded the Committee to demand a new hearing on the Tonkin Gulf episode, and asked that McNamara himself appear as the primary witness.[26]

After evading the committee's invitation for several weeks, McNamara finally appeared before the senators on February 20, 1968, nine days before his intended resignation as secretary of defense. As a precaution, McNamara had asked for a copy of the report compiled by Fulbright's staff, but Fulbright refused the request. Instead, the senator proposed an exchange, the staff report for a copy of the Pentagon's "Command and Control" report. Only then, Fulbright claimed, could the hearing evaluate the decision-making process of our government in time of crisis. The exchange was never made.

With the issue of the two reports unresolved, McNamara testified in closed session on February 20. In his formal statement, the secretary revealed, contrary to his official testimony in 1964, that the officer commanding the *Maddox* had indeed known about the South Vietnamese naval bombardment of North Vietnam. McNamara argued that "Congress, at the time of the debates on the Tonkin Gulf Resolution, was aware that . . . electronic surveillance . . . was one of the purposes served by the DeSoto patrol," an allegation hotly denied by Fulbright. McNamara went on to cite radar reports from both destroyers, eyewitness accounts, and "intelligence reports from a highly classified and unimpeachable source" as proof that the second attack on August 4 actually occurred. He insisted that "No one within the Department of Defense has reviewed all of this information without arriving at the unqualified conclusion that a determined attack was made on the *Maddox* and *C. Turner Joy* in the Tonkin Gulf."[27]

Near the end of his formal statement, McNamara digressed long enough to label as "monstrous" the "insinuations" that the United States "induced the incident on August 4 with the intent of providing an excuse to take the retaliatory action which in fact we took." No conspiracy, McNamara said, involving the entire chain of military command reaching to the President himself, had existed. Fulbright remarked that nobody had said anything about a conspiracy, and warned McNamara not to attempt to intimidate the committee. Fulbright then questioned McNamara directly and pointedly:

> Were there, in fact, recommendations by the U.S. military at any time from late 1963 until July of 1964 to extend the war into the North by bombing or any other means?

McNamara could not recall; he would be ". . . happy to check the record and put the proper answer in the record." Had McNamara seen the Bundy resolution of May 1964? "I don't believe I ever saw it," replied the secretary of defense, "but I can't testify absolutely that I didn't. My memory is not clear on that." Did the movement of aircraft into Southeast Asia in 1964 take place *before* or *after* Tonkin Gulf? "I don't recall that information," McNamara answered.[28] Why were U.S. ships gathering intelligence in the Gulf of Tonkin in 1964? Why did McNamara claim at the time that the U.S. destroyers had no knowledge of the 34A raids? Why did the administration retaliate without double-checking every piece of evidence? At this point, McNamara, in danger of exposing the administration, refused to answer any further questions on the grounds that his answers would contain "classified information" which the members of Fulbright's committee were not cleared to hear or discuss. Fulbright took this and other responses to be sheer evasion.

Eugene McCarthy asked McNamara if, as part of the DeSoto mission, the *Maddox* had supplied intelligence information to the South Vietnamese before their 34A raids took place. The secretary of defense could not remember, calling that type of assistance extremely unlikely. Wayne Morse accused the U.S. destroyers, acting on official orders, of luring the North Vietnamese boats away from the coast before the secret raids by the South Vietnamese. How then, Morse asked, could the military claim that U.S. ships were not involved in the 34A raids? McNamara responded, "The North Vietnamese boats knew that our boats had no hostile intent and played no hostile role."

Albert Gore challenged McNamara on the entire thrust of his opening statement, claiming "once again the facts have been twisted." McNamara protested and continued to evade, but without the Pentagon's secret "Command and Control" report, Fulbright could not directly refute McNamara's testimony. The February 20 hearing, therefore, was not nearly as revealing as Fulbright had hoped. Congress had failed to challenge the administration effectively, although the validity of the Gulf of Tonkin Resolution had been destroyed.[29] Meanwhile, the war in Southeast Asia continued.

General Vo Nguyen Giap (*left*), Vietnam commander who defeated the French at Dien Bien Phu, and Ho Chi Minh (*right*), September 1945. *Wide World Photos*.

President Johnson and his top advisers at Camp David, Maryland, after conferring on Vietnam, April 10, 1968. *Left to right:* Defense Secretary Clark Clifford, U.S. Ambassador to Vietnam Ellsworth Bunker, the President, Ambassador-at-large Averell Harriman, Secretary of State Dean Rusk, General Earle Wheeler, chairman of the Joint Chiefs of Staff, Assistant Secretary of State William Bundy, Presidential Adviser Walt Rostow. *Wide World Photos.*

Top-level U.S. team meets top-level South Vietnamese team in Honolulu, February 8, 1966. *Left to right:* Dean Rusk, Premier Nguyen Cao Ky, Ambassador Henry Cabot Lodge (behind Ky), President Johnson, Robert S. McNamara, and Head of State Nguyen Van Thieu. *Wide World Photos.*

Official U.S. Navy photographs of Phu Lang military area before (*top*) and after (*bottom*) U.S. bombing, July 1966. *United Press International Photo.*

U.S. Marines in helicopters capture suspected Vietcong guerrillas, November 1965. *United Press International Photo.*

A 101st Airborne Division demolition team stands clear as they blow a house apart west of Saigon; the house was suspected of belonging to a Vietcong, September 1968. *United Press International Photo.*

Prince Norodom Sihanouk in happier days shakes hands with his people at Sihanoukville, Cambodia, November 1968. *Wide World Photos.*

Secretary of Defense Robert McNamara (*right*) talks to Chairman William Fulbright of the Senate Foreign Relations Committee before appearing at a closed session, March 3, 1966. *Wide World Photos.*

President Johnson in a television address, March 31, 1968, says: "I shall not seek, and I will not accept, the nomination of my Party for another term as your President." *Wide World Photos.*

CITIZEN PROTEST
1965–68

"Somehow this madness must cease."
—*Dr. Martin Luther King*

When President Johnson ordered air strikes against North Vietnam in February 1965, there was little or no criticism from the American people. Even after the bombing war and the buildup of ground forces got under way, the majority of the American people supported the President. There were several minor demonstrations in March and April 1965 but no mass outcry against the U.S. escalation in Vietnam.

The first major challenge to Johnson's war policy came from the United Nations. Secretary General U Thant, reacting quickly to the news that America had intervened militarily in Southeast Asia, called upon Washington to cease hostilities and to negotiate a fair settlement, and pleaded with President Johnson to reveal the true facts about Vietnam to the American people.

Johnson immediately sought to undercut U Thant as well as critics in Congress. Spokesmen for the President lashed out at U Thant, Wayne Morse, and Ernest Gruening, accusing them of falsely alarming the American people. McGeorge Bundy met privately with Senators McCarthy, Nelson, Young, McGovern, and Church to explain White House actions and warn against any Senate effort to restrict the President. Johnson himself tried to reassure longtime friends, especially Fulbright and Mike Mansfield, of the absolute necessity of going to war in Vietnam. If a presidential pep talk failed, LBJ responded with threats against the political careers of those deemed vulnerable. He was determined to suppress opposition to his Vietnam policy.[1]

Behind the scenes, a different kind of opposition was forming, composed not of political leaders but of ordinary people. As the war intensified, this opposition grew in strength and in conviction. At the forefront of the new movement were those whose lives were completely disrupted by the war, in particular students and black Americans. The war galvanized both university and ghetto like no issue before it.

The student movement had its roots in the fight for civil rights among American blacks. Student activists had traveled to Alabama and Mississippi each summer since 1961. There, side by side with black leaders, the students had worked to correct a host of racial injustices. When fall arrived, these activists had returned to their campuses and demonstrated against the "establishment." In 1962 student leaders in Michigan had organized Students for a Democratic Society to protest a variety of government policies. Likewise, at the University of California at Berkeley, students gathered in September 1964 to air grievances before several university officials. When the university refused to listen, students formed the Free Speech Movement and eventually won the right to conduct political activity on the Berkeley campus.[2]

When President Johnson decided to bomb North Vietnam, hundreds of students and faculty members signed an open letter to LBJ, urging negotiation of the Vietnam crisis. As the students learned, however, the administration ignored all efforts to bring about a peaceful solution. Undaunted, a group of intellectuals approached Adlai Stevenson, U.S. ambassador to the United Nations, in June 1965. The group asked Stevenson, known for his liberal beliefs, to resign as a protest against U.S. escalation in Vietnam. He refused. Still, these early and perhaps naive efforts by student leaders and intellectuals to change the course of the war carried with them a very important lesson.[3] If dissent was to flourish, if students wanted a forum for discussing the war, they would have to go into the streets.

The academic community responded with great vigor when the administration began drafting students for combat in Vietnam. One form of protest which galvanized the universities was the "teach-in." Faculty members at the University of Michigan organized the first teach-in on March 24, 1965. Over 3,000 students gathered to study the war and make recommendations. The idea spread to other campuses—Columbia, Wisconsin, Oregon—as the fledgling student movement attempted to educate the public and to convince President Johnson that his Vietnam adventure was irrational and immoral. As interest grew, plans for a national teach-in materialized. The Inter-University Commission for a Public Hearing on Vietnam chose Columbia University as the site for a debate between McGeorge Bundy, speaking for the administration, and several prominent antiwar scholars. The scheduled date was May 15, 1965.

The White House tried to silence its critics from the academic world. The State Department issued an important white paper to prove three points: that the war in Vietnam was, without doubt, a case of Northern aggression; that South Vietnam could not be abandoned in good conscience; and that U.S. national security was at stake. The administration also established a "truth team" headed by William Jorden to visit college campuses and inform students of the history of U.S. involvement in Vietnam. And McGeorge Bundy announced that, due to a busy schedule, he would not be able to participate in the scheduled teach-in after all.[4] The students went ahead with the debate, but the absence of an administration spokesman doomed the event; there was little drama to a teach-in where only one side was represented. Student activists needed a more effective means of change. The teach-in, popular and instructive as it was, simply did not hold the answer.[5]

By mid-1965 it was obvious that Johnson intended to expand and intensify the war, despite the efforts of the peace movement. As a result, when 18,000 people congregated on June 8 in New York City, the consensus was that those opposed to the war must go into the streets. On this point, however, the SDS was already one step ahead of the peace movement. Several weeks earlier student radicals had organized a huge demonstration in front of the Washington Monument. Twenty thousand protesters gathered, listened to speeches, and then marched from the Washington Monument to the White House. This event marked the emergence of a second avenue of dissent—the mass demonstration. When the administration ignored the SDS-led procession, the opposition announced that civil disobedience would be employed in future marches. During the next six months, numerous demonstrations took place and hundreds of students accepted arrest, yet LBJ still held to the view that "There is no substantial division in this country, in my judgment, and no substantial division in the Congress."[6]

By the fall of 1965, the idealism of the early 1960s was brushed with anger. The peace movement decided that Johnson was unmoved on the subject of Vietnam, and that the only way to influence the President was to organize a gigantic rally. To this end, thirty-three separate antiwar groups pooled their resources and formed the National Coordinating Committee to End the War in Vietnam. The committee announced nationwide demonstrations for the weekend of October 15–16, 1965, and decreed that most protesters were ready to challenge the authorities. When the protest weekend began, thousands marched to the Army induction terminal in Oakland, California, but were turned back by a wall of police. In New York City, a mass of protesters marched down Fifth Avenue while an equally determined group of hecklers threw eggs and insults. At the Whitehall Street army induction center, a crowd watched as David Miller stepped forward and burned his draft card, thus demonstrating his moral outrage against the war.

In Washington, Congress quickly passed a harsh law against those who defied the Selective Service by burning their draft cards—five years in jail and a $10,000 fine. Several weeks after the October demonstrations, two young men went even further. Norman Morrison, a young Quaker, and Roger LaPorte, a young Catholic, burned themselves to death in public, one in front of the Pentagon and the other before the United Nations. Their peace suicides revealed that, for many individuals, the war had become a life-and-death issue.[7]

In the wake of the October marches, the State Department argued that the noisy demonstrations did not represent the vast majority of Americans, who supported the President's war policy. General Maxwell Taylor told reporters that the protesters were not promoting peace but postponing it. Columnist James Reston of the *New York Times* warned that such lawless demonstrations would only spark political represssion in the United States. J. Edgar Hoover of the FBI concluded that:

> Anti-Vietnam demonstrators in the U.S. represent a minority for the most part composed of halfway citizens who are neither morally, mentally nor emotionally mature. This is true whether the demonstrator be the college professor or the beatnik.[8]

As the government heaped ridicule on the peace movement, the protest gained new life. In November 1965, U.S. forces fought the bloody battle of the Ia Drang Valley in Vietnam. The battle cost the United States 240 lives in only seven days and demonstrated the toughness of their opponents. Outraged by Ia Drang, the National Coordinating Committee staged a massive demonstration on November 27, 1965, before the Washington Monument. A crowd of 25,000 heard angry speeches denouncing Johnson's war. Dr. Benjamin Spock demanded that elected officials break their silence and oppose the warmongering Johnson administration. Norman Thomas proclaimed, "I'd rather see America save her soul than her face." Carl Oglesby of the SDS challenged all concerned Americans to turn against the administration before it was too late. What brought the protesters together was a moral indignation about a war "conducted with such cold impunity by a handful of men in Washington."[9] In the minds of the protesters, there simply had to be a way to stop the bloodshed.

The antiwar movement was strangely quiet for most of 1966. There were cases of draft-card burnings, but for the most part, the protesters watched anxiously as the confrontation between Johnson and Fulbright developed. These initiatives by Fulbright, however, did not produce the desired results, and, as Fulbright himself forecast,

> . . . when the Congress fails to challenge the Executive, when the opposition fails to oppose, when politicians join in a spurious consensus behind controversial policies, . . . the campuses and streets and public squares of America are likely to become the forums for a direct and disorderly democracy.[10]

The students, however, tried once again, in the fall of 1966, to make the system work. They focused their full attention on the midterm congressional elections and, in fact, transformed the elections into a referendum on Johnson's war in Vietnam. The students rallied behind antiwar candidates like Robert Scheer in California, who was attempting to oust Jeffrey Cohelan, a longtime hawk and friend of President Johnson. During the campaign, LBJ joined the fray pulling strings, making threats, and traveling extensively to keep the Democratic majority in Congress. The result was both a victory and a defeat for the antiwar forces. Peace candidates showed surprising strength but could not win the allegiance of a majority of the voters. Scheer received 45 percent of the vote but suffered a narrow defeat. On the national level, LBJ supporters did lose forty-seven seats in the House of Representatives, three Senate seats, and eight governorships, but, of course, the Republicans—and not the antiwar candidates—benefited most from the swing of the pendulum.

Growing more restless with each passing day, the students resolved that, if elections could not further the cause, only direct action was left.[11] The stage was set for 1967, an explosive year.

The war in Vietnam had also destroyed the hopes and dreams of many black Americans. In the early 1960s, the civil rights movement had made progress. In 1965 President Johnson signed both the Civil Rights Act and the Economic Opportunity Act. Few observers realized at that time, however, that the Johnson administration had committed the United States to two wars simultaneously: the war against poverty and the war in Vietnam. The results would prove to be catastrophic to the American economy and to the civil rights movement.

Part of Johnson's policy was keeping the Vietnam War "undeclared"; no tax increases were passed to pay for the massive military spending. But the economy could not provide both guns and butter, and within a matter of months, the bad effects were felt at home, as social programs slowed. When the first marine detachment landed at Da Nang in 1965, the U.S. economy had just experienced five years of prosperity. Unemployment was at 4.5 percent, inflation was modestly increasing by 2 percent annually, prices were stable, and corporate profits were rising.

> War costs piled on top of domestic spending, without a tax increase, spelled large budget deficits. With monetary and credit expansion proceeding on a large scale, the result [was] a huge increase in total spending, both governmental and private. As prices rose and wages followed, the classic inflationary spiral uncoiled.[12]

Clearly, the cost of the war in Vietnam overheated a strong American economy and wrecked much of the domestic reform inherent in the Economic Opportunity Act (EOA). The appropriation for the Office of Economic Opportunity was only $800 million for 1964–65, and $1.5 billion for 1965–66. At the same time, the war in Vietnam cost *$4.7 billion* during 1965–66 and rose to more than *$30 billion a year* by 1967! Dr. Martin Luther King, founder of the Southern Christian Leadership Conference, described perfectly the unfolding situation: "I fear, with the escalation of the war, a cutdown and damage to the social programs here. Do we love the war on poverty, or do we love the war in Vietnam?"[13]

As early as January 1966 the disparity began to hit home. The President's budget message for 1966 cut the Great Society program back to a pace which reflected the claims of the commitment in Southeast Asia. Funds for education and for school milk programs were the first to go, disappearing just as the administration asked for and received from Congress $12 billion in supplemental funds for Vietnam. During the year, wages, prices, and interest rates skyrocketed, the VA began paying out millions of dollars in benefits, and the total amount of short-term international debt built up by the United States was twice the amount of gold on reserve in Treasury vaults. By the summer of 1967, the President was forced to ask for a 10 percent tax surcharge to finance the war, but the damage was already done.[14]

The group most affected by the massive military spending was, of course, black America. Almost immediately, the civil rights movement fell victim to the widening war in Southeast Asia. Dr. King spoke out against the consequences of the war in July 1965:

> It is worthless to talk about integration if there is no world to integrate in. I am certainly as concerned about seeing the defeat of Communism as anyone else, but we won't defeat Communism by guns or bombs or gases. We will do it by making democracy work. . . . The war in Vietnam must be stopped. There must be a negotiated settlement.[15]

After making this statement King and his organization received several warnings from the administration, and the FBI stepped up its surveillance of King's activities.

White House pressure and policies aggravated an internal split within the black movement. The Student Nonviolent Coordinating Committee had been part of King's Southern Christian Leadership Conference through 1964, but the SNCC played a more independent role during 1965. Gradually, the SNCC, angry about the draft and about Johnson's threats, moved closer to radical action.[16] By early 1966, black leaders were encouraging resistance to the draft, which continued to induct a higher percentage of poor, uneducated blacks. Likewise, the SNCC made it very clear that the fight for civil rights should be linked to the progress of the antiwar movement. The SNCC declared:

The murder of Samuel Younge [SNCC activist, killed on January 3, 1966] in Tuskegee, Alabama, is not different than the murder of people in Vietnam, for both Younge and the Vietnamese sought, and are seeking, to secure the rights guaranteed them by law. In each case, the United States government bears a great part of the responsibility for these deaths. Samuel Younge was murdered because United States law is not being enforced. Vietnamese are murdered because the United States is pursuing an aggressive policy in violation of international law. . . . We believe that work in the civil rights movement is a valid alternative to the draft. We urge all Americans to seek this alternative, knowing full well that it may cost them their lives—as painfully as in Vietnam.[17]

During several black rallies in 1966, Stokely Carmichael, militant leader of the SNCC, abandoned caution and demanded an end to the draft. After the shooting of James Meredith in Mississippi, Carmichael stepped closer to radicalism with the call for "Black Power," and for "Negroes not to go to Vietnam and fight but to stay . . . and fight here."[18] The system both denied freedom to blacks and sent them to die in Vietnam.

Feeling cheated and abused, blacks rioted in many American cities during 1966 and 1967. There were several ugly precedents, most notably in Harlem in 1964 and in the Watts ghetto of Los Angeles in 1965. The latter, more than any black rally or demonstration, sent a chill through the country. The viewing public watched on television as arsonists set hundreds of fires and looters helped destroy $45 million worth of property. In the wake of this devastating riot, the U.S. Army Intelligence Command organized a special program to preserve internal security, a program which included surveillance and infiltration. The Pentagon, meanwhile, outfitted a domestic war room to deal with antiwar protesters, students, and blacks suspected of aiding the Communists.

Subsequently, in July 1967 black bitterness over the failure of the war on poverty sparked another round of massive riots in Newark, New Jersey, and in Detroit, Michigan. In each city, black, urban America terrorized itself and terrified the nation as a whole. President Johnson insisted that America's riots were in no way political, but black militants like H. Rap Brown insisted they were highly political—and aimed at two things: the plight of the poor and the war in Vietnam. By the end of Johnson's term in office, the Black Panthers had emerged and rumors were widespread, if groundless, that revolution was near.

The Student Nonviolent Coordinating Committee split the civil rights movement over the issue of how blacks should respond to administration injustices. After 1965 the SNCC moved more and more in the direction of violence and radical action. Martin Luther King, meanwhile, continued to preach the gospel of nonviolence and Christian love as the best method for ending both the war in Vietnam and discrimination at home. After moving to Chicago in 1966, King encountered the problems of a Northern ghetto, problems similar to but more intense than those of rural, Southern blacks. Only a compromise agreement with Mayor Richard Daley halted the demonstrations and riots predicted for the summer of 1966, after which King retired to analyze the dilemma facing blacks. King was opposed to the militance of Carmichael's SNCC, but at the same time he was deeply concerned about the draft, the killing, and the ongoing war in Vietnam. Finally, in early 1967, King emerged from his temporary exile more determined than ever before to take the offensive and to speak out against Johnson's war. He had decided that the war was destroying both the civil rights movement and the country, squandering resources in a cause that was wrong.[19] In a speech in Los Angeles on February 25, 1967, he stated that

> . . . the promises of the Great Society have been shot down on the battlefield of Vietnam. . . . It is estimated that we spend $322,000 for each enemy we kill, while we spend in the so-called war on poverty in America only about $53 for each person classified as "poor." . . . We must combine the fervor of the civil rights movement with the peace movement. We must demonstrate, teach and preach until the very foundations of our nation are shaken.

On April 4, 1967, in New York, a similar outburst:

> Somehow this madness must cease. We must stop now. . . . I speak for the poor of America who are paying the double price of smashed hopes at home and death and corruption in Vietnam. The great initiative in this war is ours. The initiative to stop it must be ours. . . . Every man of human convictions must decide on the protest that best suits his convictions, but we must all protest.

Quickly the administration's contacts in the media moved to discredit Dr. King. A *Washington Post* editorial proclaimed that King "has [gravely] diminished his usefulness to his cause, to his country, and to his people." The fact remained, however, that King had once and for all broken with LBJ. The black leader was convinced that "the great tide of reform in American life, so long needed and so late in coming, was being destroyed by an evil war."[20]

The antiwar movement, made up of students, blacks, and a growing number of concerned citizens, considered 1967 a pivotal year. Johnson's war was over two years old, and experts were predicting the need for a million U.S. troops to stop the Communist "invasion" of Vietnam. For the first time, a majority of Americans began to feel uneasy about the growing body counts, the lost expenditures, and LBJ's apparent obsession with the war. As the casualties mounted, so did the exposure of death and destruction through television and newspaper accounts. The Johnson team had created the Joint U.S. Public Affairs Office in Saigon in 1965 to control and, in effect, to censor the news sent back to America, allowing only reports that "made the United States look good."[21] In 1967, however, dedicated newsmen began to break through the wall of censorship.

Harrison Salisbury of the *New York Times* was one of the first. He reported from Hanoi that American bombs had fallen on Hanoi itself, despite vehement denials by the U.S. State Department. Salisbury was an eyewitness to widespread destruction in North Vietnam's capital city and in areas where no military targets existed. His reports stunned the reading public even though Johnson organized a campaign to prove Salisbury's "disloyalty." Others followed Salisbury's lead: depicting children ravaged and maimed by the war; what pacification actually meant for so many villages; and the impact of special weapons like defoliant sprays and napalm. It seemed, based on the news accounts, that "the vast resources of American technology were turning whole sections of the country into moonscape, black, lifeless, crater-pocketed deserts where no one could move or live."[22] The antiwar movement, utilizing the information provided by journalists, demanded an end to the U.S. bombing and, choosing a specific target, launched a major offensive against Dow Chemical Company, the maker of napalm.

Alongside the protesters, however, were increasing numbers of ordinary citizens, former members of the silent majority. More individuals than ever before, ashamed, worried about the costs, the domestic dissension, and the moral consequences for the United States of the war, were beginning to turn away from it and from LBJ himself.[23]

The news revelations of early 1967 brought the antiwar movement out of its passive phase. A new group calling itself the Spring Mobilization to End the War in Vietnam began preparations for still another demonstration in Washington, this one scheduled for April 15, 1967. The dean of the peace movement, A. J. Muste, chastised the fainthearted who hesitated to join the Spring Mobilization.[24] The organizers concentrated on persuading more marchers than ever before to protest Johnson's war, and on April 15 a great flood of people, numbering 300,000 to 400,000, descended upon Washington. Included among the protesters were students who burned draft cards, black leaders, concerned citizens willing to show their support, and a group of Vietnam veterans who soon formed their own organization to oppose the war. Faced with this unprecedented protest march, the administration used Dean Rusk to warn the public of the President's concern that the authorities in Hanoi might misunderstand and that the effect of the demonstrations would be to prolong rather than shorten the war.

Antiwar forces throughout the country applauded the Spring Mobilization of 1967. Leaders of the protest realized that the movement's base of support was dramatically larger than before, and that with increased action the base might grow. Before long, students began to organize a nationwide draft card turn-in. Scheduled for October 20, 1967, the turn-in was to be the culmination of an antiwar convention outside the Department of Justice. The peace movement was ready for an open confrontation with LBJ.

By October 1967, when Senator Eugene McCarthy announced his candidacy for President, the more militant antiwar forces had gained a greater prominence, since protests and civil disobedience seemed to be the only weapons left to influence government policy. The Mobilization Committee in the East and a group called the Resistance in the West both envisioned an all-out effort against the draft and against the military in general. When the moment for action arrived, the Resistance led a peaceful sit-in at the Army induction center in Oakland, but during the next day, October 17, 1967, police clubbed demonstrators in an act of brutality that shocked even the militants. By the end of the week, police had once again assaulted the marchers, who took the blows, retreated, and then reappeared elsewhere.

The mobile tactics employed in Oakland inspired the Washington protesters, many of whom invaded the plaza of the Pentagon on October 21. Federal officers and soldiers waited until midnight, when the reporters had left, before moving in, clubbing the demonstrators, and dragging many away. The futile invasion ended on October 22, when police arrested the remaining protesters and removed them from the steps of the Pentagon.

Opponents of the war now marched when any administration official dared to risk a public appearance, as Dean Rusk discovered in New York City in November 1967. In addition, angry demonstrations against the draft were more widespread then ever before, as were antiwar efforts to organize an underground railroad to aid resisters in getting to Canada. There were numerous confrontations between police and protesters, little evidence that the administration understood the seriousness of the problem, and a growing danger of violence for violence's sake.[25]

The events of early 1968 only made matters worse for the Johnson administration. First there was the humiliating surprise of the Tet offensive in South Vietnam. In twenty-eight cities the forces of General Giap and the Vietcong attacked U.S. and ARVN outposts, displaying more firepower than Washington ever expected. There were other equally humiliating incidents: the North Korean capture of the U.S. *Pueblo,* the bloodbath at Khe Sanh, and the dramatic plunge of the U.S. dollar on the world market. World leaders openly criticized American "aggression" in Vietnam. The media concentrated on the war, as American cities continued their decline, becoming less livable and less governable each day. American youth seemed more deeply alienated than ever from the cherished values inherited from previous generations, and parents wondered what to do about their sons and daughters. Finally, common anxiety about the prudence and morality of our presence in Vietnam led more than ever to a questioning of America's nature and national purpose; somehow an unbearable gap loomed between promise and achievement. For the first time, public opinion polls showed more than 50 percent of the American public opposed to the war.[26]

Farsighted politicians realized that a major shift in policy was badly needed, not only to reflect the latest polls but also to buy peace at home and abroad. Eugene McCarthy offered some hope, especially in academic circles, but it was the announcement by Robert Kennedy that he was a candidate for the presidency that galvanized antiwar forces all over the country.[27] It is well to recall his promise and his challenge:

> Here, while the sun shines, our brave young men are dying in the swamps of Southeast Asia. Which of them might have written a poem? Which of them might have cured cancer? Which of them might have played in a World Series or given us the gift of laughter from a stage or helped build a bridge or a university? Which of them would have taught a child to read? It is our responsibility to let these men live.[28]

His campaign could neither be ignored nor contained. "His speeches expressed the deepest misgivings in people's hearts and blamed them squarely on the President and the President's war." President Johnson realized that his hold on the Democratic Party was slipping, and he decided to capitulate. He announced a partial bombing halt on March 31, 1968, and, in the same speech, declared that he would not run for reelection. Minutes later, thousands of antiwar protesters appeared in the streets to celebrate a great victory. Johnson had been defeated—or so it seemed—but the leaders of the movement recognized that much work remained to be done. The war itself was not over, and, unfortunately, the trend to violence in the United States did not dissipate either.[29]

In the spring of 1968, the nation focused most of its attention on the presidential candidacy of Robert Kennedy. Charismatic energy flowed from the late President's brother as he swept through the Democratic primary battles with one lone defeat in Oregon. Kennedy promised new policies "to end the bloodshed in Vietnam and in our cities, policies to close the gap that now exists between black and white, between rich and poor, between young and old, in this country and around the rest of the world."[30]

But Kennedy was not to live beyond his triumph in California on June 4, 1968. He was assassinated by Sirhan Sirhan. Already, on April 1, 1968, the day after Johnson decided not to run for reelection, James Earl Ray had shot and killed Dr. King in Memphis, Tennessee. These senseless murders touched off weeks of unrest and racial violence in American cities. Within minutes of King's death, the news reached Washington D.C., and stunned crowds gathered in the black ghetto. Angry vigilante bands invaded the downtown shopping district, setting fires, breaking windows, and looting stores. In three days of rioting, 700 fires destroyed much of downtown Washington, resulting in $13 million worth of damage. National Guardsmen guarded the White House and the Capitol, while 15,000 troops patrolled the streets.[31] The turmoil spread quickly to Detroit, Boston, and 165 other U.S. cities.

> In Chicago flames destroyed a large black residential area and Mayor Richard Daley ordered his police: "Shoot to kill arsonists, and shoot to maim looters." Eleven persons were killed and 2,900 blacks arrested.[32]

The riots following Martin Luther King's death, and the countermeasures by Johnson's administration, demonstrated the violent division in American life and the tortured gap between the races that Robert Kennedy had hoped to close. The events of 1968 were tied indirectly but so very closely to the war in Vietnam, and that war continued. Dr. King's dream, and other examples of progress, would simply have to wait. Despite the convening of peace talks in Paris, Johnson decided to send 50,000 more men to Vietnam in early April 1968, not merely the 13,500 announced by the President on March 31. The troop increase of 50,000 included, for the first time, U.S. reservists, who were thrown immediately into Operation Total Victory, a last-ditch effort to crush the Vietcong.

Likewise, the partial bombing halt ordered by Johnson on March 31 was no more than a play on words. The Joint Chiefs simply rearranged the list of targets and then increased the total tonnage of bombs dropped. To make matters worse, the arbitrary line across North Vietnam, north of which U.S. planes were not supposed to fly, was nothing more than a propaganda ploy. According to correspondent Alexander Kendrick, "within thirty-six hours following the stipulation of the new bombing line twelve heavy raids were made far above it, dangerously close to the Chinese border."[33] The war's end, it seemed, was no closer than before LBJ's "abdication."

Little wonder, therefore, that the antiwar protest continued in the spring and summer of 1968. Responding to news of Operation Total Victory and Martin Luther King's assassination, the SDS (Students for a Democratic Society) demonstrated against Columbia University for accepting grants from the Defense Department for military research. The universities, with their CIA-sponsored research, their ROTC training, and the recruitment campaigns by Dow Chemical and other companies, symbolized what the students felt to be the ills of society. Universities, they claimed, were participating in the destruction of Vietnam and the uprooting of America's youth. Out of fear, frustration, and anger, the students lashed out in protest. After a student march in April 1968, Columbia President Grayson Kirk slapped the antiwar leaders with an indefinite suspension from school. This action sparked a sit-in demonstration inside several university buildings. Kirk immediately called the police and demanded the forceful removal of all students taking part in the sit-in. The police attempted to do so, but the students regrouped and quickly seized five university buildings, demanding reform of the university and an end to the war. Again the police responded, and the violence escalated. The takeover at Columbia lasted five days, after which all remaining classes were canceled for the semester. In addition, Grayson Kirk resigned the presidency of the university.

Following Columbia's example, other confrontations took place at Northwestern, Stanford, Michigan State, and other universities. In the main, the students wanted nothing more than responsible government and an end to the Vietnam War. Unfortunately, this message was not clearly understood during the summer of 1968.[34]

In May 1968, amidst the city riots and campus upheavals, the U.S. Army Intelligence network revived and expanded the internal security measures it had established in 1965. The Pentagon proceeded to infiltrate almost every U.S. peace organization and antiwar rally. Using 1,000 agents, the army spied on an estimated 18,000 American citizens, including many elected officials. In addition, the army compiled more than 100,000 dossiers on alleged dissidents. By treating these Americans as enemies, the administration fostered the myth that all protesters were Communists and traitors, bent on stabbing America in the back during a time of war. Flooded by prowar propaganda, many Americans believed what the government told them. The result was the creation of a wider generation gap than ever before and the disruption of thousands of families.[35]

The assassination of Robert Kennedy on June 4, 1968, shook the nation generally, and seemed to threaten particularly the future of the peace movement. The symbolic and critical confrontation took place in August, 1968, in Chicago at the Democratic National Convention. The peace movement met Mayor Richard Daley in open combat. Jules Archer, an authority on the rioting in the 1960s, described the battle in all its viciousness and brutality:

> All week long appalling scenes have swirled across the nation's TV newscasts, showing helmeted cops clubbing teen-agers on bloodied pavements, and national guardsmen in gas masks spraying tear gas at choking antiwar demonstrators at the Democratic National Convention. . . . For the most part the demonstrators have been non-violent but strident, shouting insults at the Chicago police. When rushed, beaten, and scattered, some demonstrators have hurled bottles . . . and eggs at their uniformed assailants.

What newsmen labeled the Battle of Chicago left over 800 people injured, 90 percent of whom had intended to be peaceful demonstrators. Nearly 700 persons went to jail, including a number of reporters who just happened to be in the way. Subsequent inquiries concluded that, although there was provocation, the police of Chicago had actually perpetrated the riots that occurred by overreacting to the demonstrations. Even President Johnson's National Commission on the Causes and Prevention of Violence blamed Daley's police for instigating a "Chicago police riot." Attorney General Ramsey Clark denied both that police violence was necessary and that it was efficacious. "It did not maintain order, enforce law, prevent crime, or protect lives and property. It did the opposite."[36]

The violence in Chicago partially crippled the antiwar movement, draining from it the emotional fervor that had built up prior to August 1968. New conspiracy laws passed by Congress resulted in conspiracy trials and jail terms for many of the antiwar leaders arrested in Chicago.[37] The bulk of the protesters, however, their commitment to politics deflated by the defeat of Eugene McCarthy, returned to their homes and campuses weary and disillusioned. Hubert Humphrey, still following the party line on Vietnam, had won the Democratic nomination and would face Richard Nixon. Within a year, however, the antiwar movement would regroup once again to protest the ongoing war in Vietnam and its hold over the new President.

THE EMBATTLED PRESIDENT
1967–March 1968

During the early months of 1967, Secretary of Defense Robert McNamara developed serious misgivings on the advisability of continuing the Vietnam War under circumstances that began to develop. He became unwilling to give unquestioned support to presidential policies and began to recommend steps that would enable the President to reevaluate his position. Among them were the following:

On May 19, 1967, he delivered a message to President Johnson which said in part:

> The time has come for us to eliminate the ambiguities from our minimum objectives—our commitments—in Vietnam. Specifically, two principles must be articulated, and policies and actions brought in line with them: (1) Our commitment is only to see that the people of South Vietnam are permitted to determine their own future. (2) This commitment ceases if the country ceases to help itself.
>
> It follows that no matter how much we might *hope* for some things, our *commitment* is *not:*
>
> . . . To ensure that a particular person or group remains in power, nor that the power runs to every corner of the land (though we prefer certain types and we hope their writ will run throughout South Vietnam),
>
> To guarantee that the self-chosen government is non-Communist (though we believe and strongly hope it will be), and
>
> To insist that the independent South Vietnam remain separate from North Vietnam (though in the short-run, we would prefer it that way).

McNamara also recommended that after the South Vietnamese presidential election in September 1967 the United States should insist that Saigon begin to seek a political statement with the non-Communist members of the NLF—to explore a cease-fire and to reach an accommodation with the non-Communist South Vietnamese who are under the VC banner; to accept them as members of an opposition political party, and if necessary, to accept their individual participation in the national government—in sum, a settlement to transform the members of the VC from military opponents to political opponents.[1]

On June 17, 1967, McNamara now ordered the preparation of what has since become known as "The Pentagon Papers," a top-secret history of the U.S. role in Indochina. A year and a half later, this work, consisting of a fully documented analysis and history of the Vietnam War, was delivered to the President. It was highly classified, and only fifteen copies were made.[2] The Pentagon Papers appear to have had little impact on Lyndon Johnson. Other advisers continued to urge the President to step up the war sharply, to consider invasions of Laos, Cambodia, and even North Vietnam. The President was called upon to mobilize the reserves and increase the army's strength and capability of waging an all-out military engagement.

In November 1966, McNamara pressured the Joint Chiefs of Staff to limit their troop requests to 470,000, the figure McNamara had recommended in the spring of 1966. He wanted to avoid passing the half-million mark, much less reach the 542,000 figure Westmoreland favored. Despite McNamara's growing disillusionment, the scheduled buildup in South Vietnam continued.

In early 1967, Westmoreland began his most ambitious plan of action, in part to prove to Johnson that the military was on top of the war in Vietnam. Five search-and-destroy missions were launched in the heaviest one-month barrage of the entire ground war. Then, in February, after a four-day Tet cease-fire, Westmoreland began three more operations.

In March 1967, when it was announced that Ellsworth Bunker would soon succeed Lodge as U.S. ambassador to Saigon, Westmoreland saw a chance to secure acceptance of his latest troop request. Ambassador Lodge had opposed any large troop increases, but with his departure, Westmoreland, on March 18, 1967, requested 200,000 more troops.[3]

By April 20, 1967, Westmoreland's request had found its way through military channels and the JCS formally asked McNamara for more troops for Vietnam. McNamara opposed the idea of having 670,000 U.S. soldiers in Vietnam, and a struggle developed between the DOD civilian leadership and the Pentagon. As a result, Westmoreland was recalled to the U.S. to meet with the President on April 27. The issue was clear, as Westmoreland recounted in his memoirs:

> [On] April 27, I met twice with President Johnson in the Cabinet Room of the White House, along with Secretaries McNamara and Rusk, Deputy Secretary of Defense Vance, . . . the chairman of the Joint Chiefs, General Wheeler, and the President's adviser on national security affairs, Walt Rostow. At issue in both meetings was the possibility of additional American troops for Vietnam. . . . Before coming to Washington I had submitted two plans for additional American troops beyond the 470,000 already approved for 1967. [One plan] involved an additional two and one-third divisions and five tactical fighter squadrons, which meant 80,500 additional troops, for a total of 550,000. [The other] involved four and one-third divisions and ten tactical fighter squadrons which would entail an additional 200,000 men, for a total strength of about 670,000.[4]

To the Pentagon's dismay, nothing was decided during Westmoreland's visit to Washington, primarily because McNamara argued effectively against any further buildup, warning LBJ that U.S. reserve forces would have to be called into active duty if the new increase was granted. But the postponement of Westmoreland's request did not end the battle between McNamara and the Joint Chiefs. The argument about strategy continued throughout the summer.

In July 1967 the President, in search of a solution, sent Maxwell Taylor and Clark Clifford to America's allies to get them to commit more troops to South Vietnam. Finally, on August 3, 1967, Johnson told Congress that he had decided to send 45,000 more troops to South Vietnam for a total authorization of 525,000. This figure was less than Westmoreland wanted, but it was an increase that could be accomplished without calling up the reserves.

This decision finally turned McNamara against the policy of President Johnson. Their differences were aired in detail during hearings before the Senate Armed Services Committee in August 1967. The committee listened politely as McNamara discussed the air and ground wars in Vietnam, but a hawkish group of senators supported the military's desire to hit North Vietnam even harder. On August 31, 1967, the committee backed the military against McNamara. Although it was not apparent at the hearings in August, McNamara's testimony marked the beginning of the end for him. He had dared to oppose the President and would pay for his independence.

On September 1, Johnson praised the military leadership during a White House press conference. On September 10, he authorized the air force to raid a previously restricted target in North Vietnam, Cam Pha, against the advice of McNamara. It was only a matter of time before the split led to major changes within the administration.[5]

On September 7, 1967, McNamara announced his decision to construct an anti-infiltration barrier just south of the DMZ, consisting of strong points, obstacles, and electronic devices. This barrier, to be known as the McNamara line, was intended to slow the infiltration of enemy troops into South Vietnam, and if carried through to completion would have been a strong argument against accepting the requests of General Westmoreland for additional troops. LBJ and the Joint Chiefs drowned McNamara's idea in ridicule.

Then, in November, when U.S. troop strength reached its previously authorized limit of 470,000, McNamara tried again to influence Johnson's position on Vietnam. The secretary sent a memorandum to the President in which he recommended against expansion of the air war in the North; against expansion of troop levels in the South; and for a bombing halt and a review of U.S. military strategy in South Vietnam. Each of these suggestions ran directly counter to the proposals of the Joint Chiefs of Staff; since LBJ supported the Joint Chiefs, McNamara's ideas also ran strongly counter to the thinking of the President.[6]

The President then proceeded to study McNamara's proposals for the next several weeks. Finally, on December 18, 1967, Johnson dictated a personal memo for the permanent files, giving his views on McNamara's recommendations. He would not order a bombing halt; he agreed not to increase U.S. ground troops in Vietnam above those already authorized; and he agreed to review the strategy of the war.[7] Shortly after the December 1967 exchange, Johnson announced that McNamara would take a job at the World Bank, confirming the rumors that McNamara was about to be dismissed for arguing in public against Johnson's Vietnam strategy. Still, the Joint Chiefs had not won a clear-cut victory, since LBJ held firm to his decision not to increase the U.S. troop limit and not to call up the reserves.

In this manner, the decision was finally made to limit the buildup in South Vietnam, but the actual cessation of troop movements to

Southeast Asia was still months away. In December 1967 the remainder of the 101st Airborne Division and the Eleventh Infantry Brigade arrived, bringing total U.S. troop strength in South Vietnam to 486,000. The total would eventually reach 542,000 troops before the gradual withdrawal began. Alongside the U.S. forces at the end of 1967 were 47,800 Koreans and 10,000 troops from Australia, New Zealand, and Thailand.

By the end of 1967, Washington watched Johnson reveal publicly the irascibility he always had shown in private, as he defended his Vietnam policies and chastised the people at home who disagreed with him. LBJ's close advisers began to notice more subtle changes. His face was growing lined and worried, his hair was graying, and his posture was beginning to sag. He seemed to be withdrawing, and the number of people to whom he would listen was shrinking. The tired President spent more and more time in the rolling hills of his Texas ranch. Not in decades had a United States President been so burdened with troubles: The 1967 deficit was unexpectedly high—$4 billion; in December alone the speculative panic on the U.S. dollar in the world market cost $1 billion in gold. Johnson's dream of a Great Society was fading; it was impossible for him to make it work and at the same time to pay for the war. His conduct of the war was being questioned more severely every day. The deception and cover-up that had previously helped him avoid this criticism was no longer successful. In the latest polls his popularity had plummeted from 83 percent in 1964 to 39 percent. He must either reassert himself and regain his hold on the Democratic Party, or abdicate.

In 1968, a mood of cautious optimism concerning the course of the war began to permeate the Johnson administration. Previously authorized troops were still arriving in Vietnam, all the new air bases throughout South Vietnam and Thailand were in operation, and America's fighting forces were exacting a heavy toll of Vietcong casualties. Westmoreland assured Johnson that the war in the South was steadily being won. Although Congress was growing restless and there were violent public protests, Johnson still had the support of his "Wise Men."* Johnson, therefore, took on very briefly renewed

---

* The *Wise Men* was a term applied to a group of elder statesmen whose counsel and advice the President sought on foreign policy issues from time to time. The group included Dean Acheson, George Ball, McGeorge Bundy, Matthew Ridgeway, Douglas Dillon, Arthur Dean, Henry Cabot Lodge, Cyrus Vance, Robert Murphy, Abe Fortas, Omar Bradley, and Maxwell Taylor.

144 : Lyndon Baines Johnson's Vietnam War

confidence early in 1968, hoping that his Vietnam policy was the correct one and that Westmoreland's campaign would soon begin to show dramatic results.[8]

The mild and fleeting euphoria of early January was suddenly shattered when the North Vietnamese began a protracted siege of a small ARVN base at Khe Sanh near the North Vietnamese border. It was a change of strategy for the North Vietnamese; for the first time the enemy was making direct, offensive assaults on a military base over an extended period of time. Unfortunately for Johnson, this sudden change of tactics coincided with his own efforts to convince the American public that—contrary to press reports and the pessimistic predictions of antiwar critics—genuine progress was being made in Vietnam.

North Vietnam's Defense Minister Vo Nguyen Giap personally directed the siege, massing 40,000 North Vietnamese opposite Khe Sanh, where 6,000 marines were dug in bunkers ready for battle. Near two main North Vietnamese supply and infiltration routes into South Vietnam, fifteen miles below the DMZ and less than ten miles from the Laotian border, Khe Sanh was surrounded by hills on every side.

Westmoreland assured Johnson he could hold Khe Sanh. The United States, with its superior firepower, could inflict a great defeat on the enemy. For Johnson the battle for Khe Sanh became a symbol of ultimate victory or defeat. During the next three months, more than 45,000 American men were deployed to Khe Sanh from bases further south. As the weeks wore on, U.S. planes trying to land with men and supplies were hit by enemy fire; runways were blocked, cleared, and then blocked again.[9]

The similarities between the Khe Sanh battle and Dien Bien Phu were widely noted in the press. As General Westmoreland admits in *A Soldier Reports*:

> Khe Sanh was isolated enough and bore enough similarities to Dien Bien Phu to excite armchair strategists. President Johnson . . . had begun to develop a fixation about it. General Taylor had to set up a special White House Situation Room to depict and analyze American and enemy disposition, complete with large aerial photographs and a terrain model. The President asked General Wheeler to submit a memorandum on how Khe Sanh was to be defended, which led to the apocryphal story that the President had required the Joint Chiefs to "sign in blood" that Khe Sanh could be held. "I don't want any damned Dien Bien Phu!" raged Johnson.[10]

Then, in the early hours of January 31, 1968, the Communist forces launched their nationwide Tet offensive, ripping into twenty-eight South Vietnamese cities. Vietcong squads simultaneously attacked ARVN bases throughout the country. As the Vietcong brought the war into downtown Saigon right to the doors of the American Embassy, it was captured in vivid detail by U.S. television cameramen. The daily showing of this film on American television for days and weeks and the detailed description of the brutality of the South Vietnamese against captured Vietcong shocked the American consciousness as nothing in the war had done before. The view of the Tet offensive portrayed by American television and the press was not a totally accurate one. The American public was given the story of a great Communist victory, when in fact the Communists paid dearly for their boldness. They lost an estimated ten men for every American or South Vietnamese killed.

The Tet offensive, however, had a stunning effect on America. As Herbert Schandler has recounted:

> A feeling of frustration and gloom had settled over official Washington. The government had been shaken. . . . Even the usually imperturbable Rusk began to show the pressure and strain. At a backgrounder press conference at the State Department on February 9, Rusk blew up at persistent questions concerning the failure of the U.S. intelligence in Vietnam. "There gets to be a point when the question is whose side are you on?" the Secretary upbraided the startled newsmen. "I don't know why . . . people have to be probing for the things that one can bitch about."[11]

The military reacted by considering how to lash out at the North Vietnamese. The Joint Chiefs of Staff "renewed an earlier proposal for reducing the restricted [bombing] zones around Hanoi and Haiphong."[12] Dean Rusk and Clark Clifford supported this idea, although Johnson rejected it because it would not have any immediate and direct effect on the fighting in South Vietnam. Everyone in Washington was out of bright ideas: There were 600,000 new refugees in Saigon, the city was in rubble, the economy stunned, and fear rampant. In desperation, Westmoreland raised the possibility of using tactical nuclear weapons!

> There was another possibility at Khe Sanh: tactical nuclear weapons. . . . If Washington officials were so intent on sending a message to Hanoi, surely small tactical nuclear weapons would be a way to tell Hanoi something, just as two atomic bombs had spoken convincingly to

> Japanese officials during World War II. . . . I felt at the time . . . that to
> fail to consider this alternative was a mistake.[13]

The administration rejected his proposal, but Johnson was willing to provide Westmoreland with military reinforcements. General Westmoreland initially asked only for some C-130s and helicopters, and told Wheeler that he was making a further study of his long-range requirements. Apparently Westmoreland did not fully realize that Johnson, as a reaction to the Khe Sanh situation, was willing to ignore the 525,000-man ceiling secured by McNamara in December 1967.[14]

General Wheeler, however, grasped immediately the significance of the opportunity and told Westmoreland, "The U.S. Government is not prepared to accept a defeat in South Vietnam. In summary, if you need more troops, ask for them." Westmoreland initially sent only a vague request for reinforcements. Finally, on February 12, 1968, Westmoreland made a specific request for additional troops.[15]

> It seemed to me that for political reasons or otherwise the President and
> the Joint Chiefs of Staff were anxious to send me reinforcements. We
> did a little sparring back and forth. My first thought was not to ask for
> any, but the signals from Washington got stronger.[16]

The response to Westmoreland's formal request revealed the reasoning of General Wheeler and the Joint Chiefs. The JCS saw the Tet offensive as an ideal occasion for a decisive military effort to win the war and to strengthen the armed forces in general. For many months they had been pressuring Johnson to call up the reserves, but for political reasons Johnson had refused. Now, with Westmoreland's latest troop request in hand, and the crises of Tet and Khe Sanh gravely endangering the entire American war effort, the JCS told Johnson that they could not fill Westmoreland's request without a call-up of reserves.

Johnson faced the obvious dilemma brought on by political considerations and military reasoning. He agreed to send Westmoreland the first part of his request (the first brigade of the 82nd Airborne and the marine regimental landing team), but he delayed authorizing the remainder of the two divisions, and refused to authorize a reserve call-up.

The Joint Chiefs of Staff, therefore, sent General Wheeler to Saigon, on February 23, 1968, to confer directly with Westmoreland. The latter believed Wheeler came at the request of the President, and together they worked out a deployment plan for 206,000 men. Their request staggered many of the President's advisers, including McNamara, Clifford, Rusk, Humphrey, Rostow, General Taylor, and CIA Director Helms. They saw little alternative, however, and decided to study the new plan carefully and to examine how these needs could be met in an election year. They were fully aware of the political repercussions of escalated involvement in Vietnam.[17]

President Johnson appointed Clark Clifford, who was soon to replace McNamara as secretary of defense, to supervise this study.[18] Clifford began to ask some important questions that others in the bureaucracy were afraid to consider. Others took heart: Paul Nitze, who wanted a complete halt of the bombing of North Vietnam; Townsend Hoopes, the undersecretary of the air force, who had sent Clifford a letter telling him that "U.S. victory in Vietnam is a dangerous illusion"; Paul Warnke, assistant secretary for international security affairs in the Department of Defense; and Phil Goulding, assistant secretary for public affairs in the Defense Department, who with Nitze participated in many meetings with Clifford, where the "battle to end the bombing and turn the war around was fought out, in the first stages."

Clifford, as one of his first actions, asked Westmoreland to provide more information to back up his troop request. Westmoreland understood what was afoot; he later said:

> The request may have been doomed from the first in any event, for it ran into another proposed new strategy. That was de-escalation, to include a bombing halt, that Secretary McNamara had begun to promote in November. The cut-and-run people had apparently gotten to McNamara. Although the proposal had put the departing secretary in President Johnson's disfavor, he had nevertheless implanted an idea in the minds of a number of civilian colleagues that was to prove persistent.[19]

Clifford's sharply divided task force debated the various recommendations to be made to President Johnson;[20] approximately fifteen separate proposals were made. Pleas for reinforcements for Vietnam met demands for a full review of the entire involvement.

> For the first time it was recognized and made explicit that new strategic guidance was required, that a reassessment of our strategy in Vietnam was needed, that a limit to United States involvement in South Vietnam had to be determined.[21]

Secretary McNamara's position was now untenable. He continued long enough to permit Clifford, LBJ's choice for a successor, to become indoctrinated and to complete the task force recommendation. On March 1, 1968, he became head of World Bank as Clifford became the new secretary of defense.

On March 4 Clifford's task force presented a final compromise report to the President. The report recommended that about 22,000 additional troops and three squadrons of aircraft be sent to Vietnam, that the rest of Westmoreland's request be held in abeyance, and that there be a partial mobilization of some reserve units, with a week-by-week reexamination of the need for future troop deployments. Johnson responded by instructing General Wheeler to inform Westmoreland that only 22,000 additional troops would be sent to Vietnam. Wheeler, however, refused to accept this as the final word on the subject.[22]

At this point, the loyal Dean Rusk also wavered. He began to question the wisdom of meeting Westmoreland's requests for reinforcements. On March 4, he met secretly, as he sometimes did, with Rumania's First Deputy Foreign Minister Gheorghe Macovescu, who had direct access to Hanoi. His staff then leaked the word that the time might be right to arrange peace talks if the bombing stopped. Rusk began to push for a bombing halt. He supported the Clifford report, except that he opposed even the minimal 22,000-man troop increase. Rusk's new strategy was to suggest a policy of fighting and negotiating at the same time, getting the negotiations started with a bombing halt.

Johnson was now faced with attacks on his policy from two of his closest advisers. Clifford felt he was

> going through an intensive period of education and of soul searching. He was beginning to be convinced that the military course being pursued by the United States in Vietnam was endless as well as hopeless, and would lead neither to victory or [sic] peace.[23]

Lyndon Johnson faced further problems in March 1968. On March 12, Senator Eugene McCarthy almost defeated him in the New

Hampshire primary. The near upset revealed to the President that his growing unpopularity had undermined his control of his own political party. On March 15, Dean Acheson, the former secretary of state under President Truman, told the President that the Joint Chiefs "didn't know what they were talking about," "were leading the President down the garden path," and that his recent Vietnam speeches were so out of touch with reality that no one believed him at home or abroad.[24] On March 16, sensing Johnson's vulnerability, longtime rival Robert Kennedy announced his entry into the Democratic presidential race, bitterly attacking Johnson's policies and record. Finally, Arthur J. Goldberg, the U.S. ambassador to the United Nations, recommended to the President a complete and immediate bombing halt.[25] Goldberg's recommendation caused the matter of a bombing halt to be broached in a meeting between Johnson and his principal advisers. The President exploded with rage:

> "Let's get one thing clear," he said. "I'm *not* going to stop the bombing! Now, I don't want to hear any more about it. Goldberg has written to me about the whole thing and I've heard every argument. I'm *not* going to stop it! Now is there anybody here who doesn't understand that?"[26]

It was typical of the shaken Johnson to conceal his real feelings from the public. A few days later, he stood before a crowd in Minneapolis and said, "Make no mistake about it—we are going to win. . . . America will prevail."[27] Despite such public statements, he took Acheson's warning seriously. On March 22, Johnson announced that Westmoreland would be leaving Vietnam to become the army chief of staff. On the same day, however, he told his advisers that he was going to make a speech which contained no new peace proposals, rejected a bombing halt, and proposed a call-up of 50,000 reserves. Both Clifford and Rusk opposed the suggestion and argued for at least a partial bombing halt.

In desperation the President requested Arthur Goldberg to meet with the Wise Men on March 25. After receiving several briefings, the Wise Men were divided and reported their differences to the President. Bundy, Acheson, Dillon, Vance, Goldberg, and Ridgeway wanted a scaling down of the war. Taylor and Justice Fortas wanted to escalate. Lodge and Bradley were wavering. Clark Clifford proposed that the United States send only a small increase of 12,500 men to Vietnam. Dean Rusk repeated his proposal that they try negotiations coupled with a partial bombing halt. A majority, however, seemed to prefer to change existing policies and to reduce American involvement in Vietnam. The group met with Johnson on March 26. Although they remained divided, they did bring home to the President that further escalation would not be acceptable to a large segment of the American public, and that it would be necessary for him to change policy. There was no doubt that Johnson had not expected such a report. "Somebody poisoned the well," he mused.[28]

Only among his friends did Johnson show the strain. He began reading and answering voluminous quantities of letters that had poured into the White House mail. Many came from personal friends in Texas whose sons had been fighting 10,000 miles away as he sat in the serenity of the White House—where these young men showed up at his dinner table as statistics. Suddenly, in human terms, all the statistics became meaningful. The President seldom smiled. Every so often he would talk wistfully about Khe Sanh to his friends:

> They're tired out on the DMZ tonight. . . . They don't complain about their taxes or a damned thing, just to get out alive. . . . I read their letters. They know what is at stake.

On March 27, Johnson talked with Senator Mike Mansfield about the speech he was to give on March 31. He did not hold out much hope for peace, and Mansfield told the President that making the speech would be a mistake. Clark Clifford confirmed Mansfield's assessment of the proposed speech. The next day Clifford, Rostow, William Bundy, and the President's speech writer, Harry C. McPhearson, Jr., met with Rusk to change the thrust of the speech and to work in the partial bombing halt.[29] The final draft of the speech announced a small troop increase of 13,000 men, instead of the 206,000 that had been requested, and proclaimed a partial bombing halt in an effort to get the North Vietnamese to the conference table.

When Johnson addressed the nation on March 31, 1968, not even Lady Bird knew how her husband would end his speech. His conclusion was in his pocket, self-prepared, and not in the text that had been distributed to newsmen:

> . . . The ultimate strength of our country and our cause will lie not in powerful weapons or infinite resources or boundless wealth, but will

lie in the unity of our people. . . . What we won when all of our people are united must not now be lost in suspicion, distrust, selfishness and politics among any of our people.

Believing this as I do, I have concluded that I should not permit the Presidency to become involved in the partisan divisions that are developing in this political year. With America's sons in the fields far away, with America's future under challenge right here at home, with our hopes and the world's hopes for peace in the balance every day, I do not believe that I should devote an hour or a day of my time to any causes other than the awesome duties of this office—the Presidency of your country.

Accordingly, I shall not seek, and I will not accept, the nomination of my Party for another term as your President. . . .[30] (emphasis added)

As part of his March 31 speech, the President ordered a partial bombing halt over North Vietnam:

I have ordered our aircraft and our naval vessels to make no attacks on North Vietnam, except in the area north of the demilitarized zone, where the continuing enemy buildup directly threatens allied forward positions.[31]

North Vietnam reacted promptly. On April 4, 1968, Hanoi agreed to begin peace negotiations. The news that both sides finally wanted to sit down and talk about Vietnam fired the national consciousness and raised hopes everywhere. Unfortunately, Johnson did not press for a quick settlement.

On April 1, Westmoreland had launched a major search-and-destroy mission known as Operation Pegasus to win the slow war of attrition. In Westmoreland's view, as long as enemy losses remained greater than allied losses, the war would be won—eventually. On April 7 and 10, 1968, Westmoreland assured President Johnson that "militarily, we have never been in a better relative position in South Vietnam." To prove his point, the U.S. commander immediately stepped up offensive operations with the young draftees that continued to pour into Vietnam.[32] Convinced that the announced change in policy had been forced on a reluctant President, Westmoreland resolved to serve his commander in chief by fighting just as hard as he could until his replacement arrived.

In Washington, the President continued his litanous refrain: "Now, as in the past, the United States is ready to send its representatives to any forum, at any time, to discuss the means of bringing this war to an end."[33] Yet, for several weeks after Hanoi agreed to negotiate, Johnson stalled over the site for the talks. After rejecting Phnom Penh and Warsaw, the President finally gave approval to meet with North Vietnamese representatives in Paris some time in May 1968.

Westmoreland's actions were clearly a source of delay. The North Vietnamese were suspicious of the new offensive sweeps conducted by U.S. and ARVN forces. It seemed to Hanoi that since Washington intended to negotiate only from strength, a response of some kind was necessary. Hoping, therefore, to seize the initiative, North Vietnam launched a major offensive on May 4, 1968, the day scheduled for the beginning of the peace talks. On May 7, Communist units struck at Saigon. Westmoreland countered as quickly as possible, hurling allied forces into battle under Operation Total Victory. By the end of May, the general felt confident enough to return to the United States for a conference with the President. He assured Johnson that "the enemy seems to be approaching a point of desperation; his forces are deteriorating in strength and quality. I forecast that these trends will continue. . . . Time is on our side." One month later, on June 24, 1968, Westmoreland reaffirmed to LBJ that "our side is getting stronger whereas the enemy is getting weaker," but it turned out to be his last statement as commander of U.S. forces in Vietnam. Within a week General Creighton Abrams had replaced him.[34]

Under Abrams, the ground war remained intense even though the new commander did not share his predecessor's love of search-and-destroy missions. In the air, U.S. bombers continued to pound at targets below the Twentieth Parallel. With LBJ's consent, the air force practically doubled the number of air strikes in the area where bombing runs were not prohibited.

These new operations were bound to hamper the peace talks, which finally opened in Paris on May 13, 1968. Johnson clearly wanted to negotiate from strength and only after he had several fresh victories in Vietnam. After instructing his negotiators, Averell Harriman and Cyrus Vance, not to accept a "fake" solution to the conflict, Johnson announced that his administration would not recognize the National Liberation Front or the Vietcong. Furthermore, the President demanded two concessions: that South Vietnam be permitted to determine its own political future, and that America be permitted to maintain a "presence," presumably military, in Southeast Asia. The

North Vietnamese, on the other hand, demanded a complete and immediate bombing halt, and thus wanted more than Johnson had promised on March 31. Deadlock ensued in Paris, and the war in Vietnam that had occupied the attention of Lyndon Johnson and drained American resources during his entire term of office dragged on.

On the ground, the U.S. Army was fully in charge of the war in South Vietnam, and more than a half million U.S. soldiers were waging a relentless struggle against the enemy, with more on the way. According to official air force sources, over 304,000 combat sorties were flown against North Vietnam during the three years and nine months that Rolling Thunder had been in operation. In addition, 2,380 B-52 raids, which were not actually part of Rolling Thunder, were included among the statistics.[35] The Committee of Concerned Asian Scholars, using official Pentagon sources, estimated that nearly 100,000 B-52 strikes alone were flown against the North, each flight dropping seven tons of bombs. Instead of 600,000 tons of bombs released over North Vietnam, which the Pentagon calculated, the committee felt the figure was at least twice that number.[36] In any event, Rolling Thunder was a massive air campaign that escalated over the years and changed its scope—from a six-month "example" of United States power when it started to a four-year, round-the-clock bombardment. As LBJ's presidency was drawing to a close, there was still no indication that he was now willing to attempt to find a nonmilitary solution to this deadly war.

PART THREE

RICHARD MILHOUS NIXON'S VIETNAM WAR

PRESIDENT NIXON
ASSUMES COMMAND
January–November 1969

> A problem that strikes one in the study of history,
> regardless of period, is why man makes a poorer
> performance of government than of almost any other
> human activity. . . . Why do men in high office so often
> act contrary to the way that reason points and
> enlightened self-interest suggests? Why does intelligent
> mental process so often seem to be paralyzed? . . .
>
> In the case we know best—the American engagement
> in Vietnam—fixed notions, preconceptions,
> wooden-headed thinking, and emotions accumulated into
> a monumental mistake and classic humiliation.
>
> . . . It was our misfortune during the Vietnam period
> to have had two Presidents who lacked the
> self-confidence for a change of course. . . . They did not
> want to hear the truth or to face it.
> —*Barbara W. Tuchman[1]*

From the beginning of his career, Nixon has been one of the United
States' leading proponents of the Cold War. Elected to Congress in
1946, Nixon first gained a national reputation by his work on the
House Un-American Activities Committee. He helped draft some of
the legislation dealing with the threat of Communist subversion to
internal security; he also played a key role in the celebrated Alger
Hiss case, which helped to inspire Joseph McCarthy's anti-Communist outburst in 1950. In that same year, Nixon defeated Helen Gahagan Douglas, a liberal, in the race for a Senate seat from California.
During the campaign, he called Mrs. Douglas "The Pink Lady" and

accused her of voting the same way as an unnamed notorious Communist-line congressman from New York—tactics that won the election with a margin of 700,000 votes.

In 1952, at the age of thirty-nine, Nixon was propelled to the vice presidency under Eisenhower on a wave of anti-Communist hysteria. The extent of his hatred for Chinese and Russian Communism, and what he thought it represented, is well illustrated in his *Memoirs:*

> For twenty-five years, I had watched the changing face of communism. I had seen prewar communism, luring workers and intellectuals with its siren call of equality and justice, reveal itself as an aggressive imperialistic ideology during the postwar period of the Marshall Plan. Despite the most nobly ringing rhetoric, the pattern was tragically the same: as soon as the Communists came to power, they destroyed all opposition. . . . At home I had seen the face of underground subversive communism when it surfaced in the Hiss case, reminding people not only that it existed, but that its purpose was deadly serious.
>
> . . . I had seen communism spread to China and other parts of Asia, and to Africa and South America, under the camouflage of parties of socialist revolution, or under the guise of wars of national liberation. And, finally, during the 1960s I had watched as Peking and Moscow became rivals for the role of leadership in the Communist world.
>
> Never once in my career have I doubted that the Communists mean it when they say that their goal is to bring the world under Communist control.[2]

Nixon had equally strident views on the war in Vietnam and the need for total military victory against the forces of Communism. As vice president, Nixon visited Vietnam and exclaimed:

> The threat to this nation, although it has taken the form of a civil war, still derives its strength from an alien source. This source, to call it by its name, is totalitarian communism.[3]

In 1954, faced with the possibility of France's defeat in Vietnam, Nixon advocated that the United States and its allies provide air support. Should France be forced to withdraw he would support intervention on a larger scale, not necessarily excluding ground forces. In 1962 he encouraged Kennedy to increase the American presence in Vietnam, and in 1964 he demanded harsh retaliation for the Tonkin Gulf incidents. In 1966 he recommended sending U.S. forces into Laos and North Vietnam:

. . . President Johnson has got to make it clear to the world and to the people of South Vietnam that our objective is a free and independent South Vietnam with no reward and no appeasement of aggressors.[4]

During the Johnson administration, Nixon remained convinced of the need for total victory. He stressed the grave consequences of losing the war and being thrown out of Vietnam. He reminded his listeners that American involvement was "the cork in the bottle of Chinese expansion in Asia." Nixon argued that America should increase air and naval action "despite any risk of conflict with China." The stakes were high. The loss of South Vietnam

would mean ultimately the destruction of freedom of speech for all men for all time, not only in Asia but in the United States [and] throughout the world.[5]

With the Republican Party in disarray after Goldwater's crushing 1964 defeat, Nixon let it be known that his temporary "retirement" from politics had ended. He appeared in numerous cities, spoke to audiences of all sizes, and built up a sizable following. By 1967, Nixon began to focus exclusively on his own candidacy for office. He attacked the Johnson administration for costly new social programs. He argued in favor of reducing taxes and restricting the Great Society. When the subject of Vietnam arose, Nixon lashed out at Johnson's policy of slow escalation. He urged a faster buildup of U.S. forces and a more determined effort to win the war. "It can be said," Nixon declared, "that the defeat of Communist forces in South Vietnam is inevitable. The only question is how soon."[6] A rejuvenated Nixon continued to broadcast his hawkish views on the war in Vietnam. During the campaign Nixon did not reiterate these views, and few people remembered his apparent obsession with military victory.

In 1968, however, after the Tet offensive, public opinion was strongly in favor of finding a way to end the war. Nixon responded with vague promises that would appeal to both hawks and doves. During the New Hampshire primary, the Republican front-runner announced: "I pledge to you new leadership to win the war and win the peace in the Pacific." In another speech, Nixon zeroed in on LBJ: "When the strongest nation in the world can be tied down for four years in the war in Vietnam, with no end in sight . . . I don't think

America can afford four more years of Lyndon Johnson in the White House."[7]

With such statements, Nixon was able to please everyone without really saying anything. The hawks assumed that Nixon wanted to win the war. The doves assumed that he wanted to end it. Middle America simply assumed he would do "what was best for the country."

After Johnson announced he would not seek reelection, Nixon realized he had nothing to gain and everything to lose by taking a position on Vietnam. He told reporters he would "observe a personal moratorium," a statesmanlike silence, on comments relating to the war in Vietnam, so as not to upset the opening of peace talks in Paris. When asked about his plan to end the war, Nixon repeated his intention not to undermine the Paris peace talks. As his speechwriter so aptly phrased it, "All in all, Nixon's withdrawal into silence was a brilliantly executed political stroke."[8]

By August 1968 it was obvious that Nixon's do-nothing strategy was a complete success. Having swept the primary races, Nixon arrived in Miami for the Republican National Convention assured of receiving the party's presidential nomination. The only obstacle left was the writing of a Vietnam plank in the party platform, but by deft maneuvering the Nixon camp was able to cloud over the Vietnam issue—"we must build bridges of understanding"—and to focus almost entirely on law and order. "The first civil right of every American," Nixon reaffirmed, "is to be free from domestic violence. The forgotten Americans, the nonshouters, the nondemonstrators, they're decent people." While "we will not tolerate violence," he continued, the party will accept change, "even fundamental social change," if the people want it. As the convention ended, Nixon was in rare form, taking every opportunity to stroke the constituency that he hoped would make him President.[9]

While Nixon basked in the Republican Party's newfound sunshine, the Democrats were engaged in an old-fashioned dogfight. By default, the President's mantle passed to Vice President Hubert Humphrey. Despite inner misgivings about the course of the war, Humphrey had never been disloyal to his leader. The big question now was how long would he continue to support Johnson's war.

Because of his late start, Humphrey was unable to compete against Kennedy and McCarthy in the state primaries. Instead, while Democrats went to the polls in Indiana, Oregon, and California, Humphrey concentrated on building up a professional staff and preparing for the Chicago Convention. Like Nixon, Humphrey had a fistful of political IOUs which would prove decisive in the coming months, especially after June 6, when Robert Kennedy was assassinated in Los Angeles. Humphrey mourned the loss of a friend and colleague, but he realized he stood to gain politically from Kennedy's death.

During June and July, as the convention neared, Humphrey agonized over Vietnam. At heart he disagreed with Johnson's policy, but the vice president found it very difficult to overcome his steadfast loyalty to the man in the White House. A group of advisers on Humphrey's staff, led by George Ball, Zbigniew Brzezinski and Edwin Reischauer, tried to induce the vice president to deliver a speech they had prepared which would have broken all ties with Johnson once and for all. Humphrey refused, but his friends knew that he must do so if he wanted to win.

> What was Humphrey to decide? His dilemma was worse than ever. Could he loyally take issue with the President when the Republican nominee had [not made his position clear]? . . . Humphrey could imagine only too well the grim satisfaction with which the President would drive in the nails. He made up his mind not to make up his mind.[10]

Choosing to avoid questions about Vietnam, Humphrey went to the Chicago Convention still tied to the President's apron strings. His only opposition was the vocal McCarthy, whose supporters organized protest marches out in the streets, and an uncertain McGovern, who never mustered much of a challenge. By midweek it was apparent that Johnson's shadow was still in control of the Democratic Party, and as long as Humphrey agreed to a Vietnam plank that was "harsher than his heart desired," the Johnson machine made sure he walked away with the nomination. While the bloody riots raged outside Convention Hall, Humphrey accepted the nomination without ever coming to grips with the Vietnam War issue.[11]

Labor Day marks the traditional start of the presidential campaign. A Gallup poll on September 3 revealed that Nixon held a commanding early lead over Humphrey. As the campaign heated up, Humphrey fell further behind. Faced with financial problems that made it difficult to buy television time and advertising spots, Humphrey also had to deal with hostile crowds of antiwar demonstrators everywhere he went; often the boos were so loud that he had to leave the platform without finishing his speech. By the end of September he had slipped from 31 to 28 percent in the polls.[12] "Humphrey's main predicament," writes Lewis Chester, "was not his shortcomings as a campaigner." Instead, "it was becoming all too plain that he could achieve his political objective only by [releasing] a statement on Vietnam . . . that marked him off from the President on the war."[13]

At the end of his rope, Humphrey finally dug out the speech that Ball, Brzezinski, and Reischauer had urged him to make back in July. The speech had been filed away when Humphrey rejected their pleas to sever all ties with Johnson and his war policy. Now, two months later, Humphrey was desperate for some kind of catalyst to save his dying campaign. On September 30, Humphrey went before a national television audience to "cut the umbilical cord" which had bound him to the Johnson administration. For the first time, Humphrey was introduced not as the vice president but as the Democratic candidate for the presidency. Without wasting time or mincing words, Humphrey announced that "as President, I would stop the bombing of [North Vietnam] as an acceptable risk for the peace because I believe it could lead to success in the negotiation and thereby shorten the war."[14]

Now that Humphrey had taken the initiative, Nixon found himself on the defensive. He counterattacked with a worn-out refrain that had been at the center of his political strategy since April 1, 1968. "I hope," Nixon repeated, "that Vice President Humphrey would clarify his position and not pull the rug out from under the [Paris] negotiators."[15] What sounded noble and statesmanlike in April, however, sounded clumsy and evasive in October. The press began to pepper Nixon with questions about his secret plan. Could he be more specific? Could he elaborate on the details? Repeatedly, Nixon's staff urged its candidate to speak out on Vietnam, but, as Theodore White recounts, Nixon refused. By the middle of October, Nixon's once insurmountable lead had closed to only eight percentage points.[16]

In the midst of the final election countdown, two unexpected events gave Humphrey more support. On October 11, the North Vietnamese agreed to several of Washington's negotiating demands in exchange for a bombing halt. There is no clear evidence that Hanoi was trying to help Humphrey's campaign, but it seems likely that this was so. In response to North Vietnam's concessions, President Johnson finally announced a total U.S. bombing halt over North Vietnam, effective November 1, 1968. The President made his announcement on October 31, declaring: "I have now ordered that air, naval and artillery bombardment of North Vietnam cease." With that, the devastating air raids of Operation Rolling Thunder ended, and the President helped Humphrey inch closer than ever to his Republican opponent. On November 3 the *Los Angeles Times* reported that Nixon's lead had shrunk to less than one percentage point. By the morning of November 5, election day 1968, the race was too close to call.[17] When the final tallies were in, Nixon managed to squeak out a victory by less than one percent of the popular vote. The victory margin was less than 500,000 votes out of more than 73 million votes cast. By practically ignoring the major issue facing the country—the Vietnam War—Nixon was able to win a narrow victory. And, just as happened after Johnson was elected, Vietnam became President Nixon's main preoccupation.

Soon after the election, President-elect Nixon was given a briefing by Dean Rusk, Clark Clifford, Earle Wheeler, Richard Helms, and Walt Rostow. The main subject was Vietnam. As Nixon remembers:

> They all emphasized that the United States must see the war through to a successful conclusion—with negotiation if possible, but with continued fighting if necessary. They agreed that an American bug-out, or a negotiated settlement that could be interpreted as a defeat, would have a devastatingly detrimental effect on our allies and friends in Asia and around the world.[18]

One month later, on December 12, 1968, Nixon received a lecture from President Johnson as the two leaders conferred in the Oval Office. LBJ was bitter about the war and the criticism his administration had endured. He cautioned Nixon to maintain total secrecy and to pounce on national security leaks. According to Nixon, the outgoing President said:

> Let me tell you, Dick, I would have been a damn fool to have discussed major decisions with the full Cabinet present, because I knew that if I said something in the morning, you could sure as hell bet it would appear in the afternoon papers. It's the same thing with the National Security Council. Everybody there's got their damned deputies and note-takers with them sitting along the wall. I will warn you now, the leaks can kill you. I don't even let Hubert sit in on some of those

> meetings for fear his staff might let something out. And even with all
> the precautions I take, things still leak. . . . If it hadn't been for Edgar
> Hoover, I couldn't have carried out my responsibilities as Commander
> in Chief. Dick, you will come to depend on Edgar. He is a pillar of
> strength in a city of weak men.[19]

Nixon listened intently and then promised a bitter and beleaguered Johnson that he would do everything possible to end the
Vietnam War with honor: "I told him he could be proud of having
stood up to his critics, particularly those in his own party."

Henry Kissinger was at Nixon's side throughout the transition period from November 1968 to January 1969. He was the perfect complement to Richard Nixon. Born in Germany, Kissinger immigrated
to the United States as a youth in the 1930s. When Kissinger completed his graduate studies, he launched his career in two comple-
mentary directions—one toward the sedate, scholarly life of a historian and political scientist, the other toward the glamour of
Washington politics. His first book, A World Restored, glorified
Prince Metternich and his managing of the European balance of
power after the Napoleonic Wars. It stated Kissinger's belief that
forceful, secret negotiations between the world's great powers was
the only way to achieve stability and order. Although Kissinger denied that he patterned his career after Metternich's, the similar use
of cunning and duplicity, the unscrupulous manipulation of people
and events, the resort to force, and the reliance on secrecy were evident.[20]

During the Kennedy and Johnson administrations, Kissinger
served as a part-time consultant and committee chairman. As a firm
and unyielding enemy of Communism, Kissinger supported the
American war effort in South Vietnam. In his memoirs, Kissinger
states:

> Insofar as I held any views, I shared the conventional wisdom that the
> war was an effort by North Vietnam to take over South Vietnam by
> military force. This I continue to believe.[21]

When President Johnson ordered U.S. combat troops into the war,
Kissinger applauded the decision "to resist Hanoi's now clear direct
involvement." At the urging of Henry Cabot Lodge, Kissinger made
three trips to Vietnam in 1964 and 1966. He toured several government-held villages and concluded that Johnson "knew neither how

to win nor how to conclude" the war.[22] Yet he would soon demonstrate that his own plan for ending the war differed little from Johnson's.

Even before he took office, Nixon requested a special review of Vietnam policy to be undertaken by Kissinger and the Rand Corporation. The President-elect wanted to know what options would be available to him after entering the White House.

The Rand study confirmed that in government circles opinion about U.S. Vietnam involvement was divided. Clark Clifford and his supporters held a pessimistic view of America's ability to win a clear-cut military victory. The Joint Chiefs of Staff, on the other hand, along with certain officials in the State Department, believed that North Vietnam could not fight much longer and would surrender if the United States renewed its bombing war in the North.[23]

Almost immediately, Nixon sided with the Pentagon. He commissioned Kissinger to review all policy options from massive escalation to immediate unilateral withdrawal and to provide possible military options in the search for victory. Among the courses suggested were:

1. Remove the restrictions which saddled U.S. commanders in the field, allowing them to use America's massive power to defeat the enemy.
2. End the bombing halt and resume air strikes against the North Vietnamese.
3. Mine Haiphong Harbor while threatening to invade North Vietnam.
4. Pursue enemy units into Laos and Cambodia, seeking to destroy their sanctuaries and disrupt their supply lines.

Although the above options were not immediately implemented, all of them were ultimately utilized by Nixon and Kissinger.[24]

After reviewing these possible courses of action, Nixon concluded that he could not secure a rapid military victory. He decided, therefore, to remove the restraints that Johnson had imposed on the military forces, thus giving them every opportunity to conduct military operations of such intensity that North Vietnam would be forced to accept the United States' terms for ending the war. In this way, Nixon could secure what he felt would be a fair and negotiated settlement. The terms would include two items that, according to Nixon, were not negotiable. First, North Vietnam would return all American prisoners of war and account for all personnel missing in

action. Second, General Thieu must remain as president of a South
Vietnam that was a free and independent nation. As Nixon put it:

> I would not agree to any terms that required or amounted to our over-
> throw of President Thieu.
>
> I was aware that many Americans considered Thieu a petty and corrupt
> dictator unworthy of our support. I was not personally attached to
> Thieu, but I looked at the situation in practical terms. . . . The South
> Vietnamese needed a strong and stable government to carry on the fight
> against the efforts of Vietcong terrorists . . . [and] the North Vietnam-
> ese Army [which sought] to impose a Communist dictatorship on . . .
> South Vietnam. My determination to honor our commitment to Thieu
> was [therefore] a commitment to stability.[25]

In making his decision, there was one course that Nixon never
seemed seriously to consider: the immediate U.S. withdrawal from
Vietnam. Millions of Americans had hoped this was the option Nixon
would choose when, during his political campaign, he had said, "I
have a plan to end the war." It became apparent, however, that
withdrawing from Vietnam was never a part of his plan. As Nixon has
written:

> At the other end of the spectrum from escalation was the case for ending
> the war simply by announcing a quick and orderly withdrawal of all
> American forces. . . . As I saw it, however, this option had long since
> been foreclosed. A precipitate withdrawal would abandon 17 million
> South Vietnamese . . . to Communist atrocities and domination. When
> the Communists had taken over North Vietnam in 1954, 50,000 people
> had been murdered, and hundreds of thousands more died in labor
> camps. . . . We simply could not sacrifice an ally in such a way. If we
> suddenly reneged on our earlier pledges of support, because they had
> become difficult or costly, . . . or because they had become unpopular
> at home, we would not be worthy of the trust of other nations and we
> certainly would not receive it.[26]

Richard Nixon's concept of how to achieve peace thus envisioned
a policy of escalation and war. He would wage a merciless campaign
to destroy Hanoi's will to fight, to force it to the conference table, and
to insure that General Thieu remained the dictator of South Vietnam.
To do this, he needed to make it appear that he was winding down
the war while actually intensifying it. He was sure Congress and the
American people would not support his military policies unless they
believed he was at the same time leading the nation toward peace.

To prevent any disclosure of his actual policies, Nixon determined that he and Kissinger alone would have absolute control over the decision-making process; he remembered Johnson's warning. So he revived the National Security Council and put it under the direction of Henry Kissinger. The influence of the Departments of State and Defense was downgraded, while Kissinger would rule over all committees responsible for the defense budget, the CIA, clandestine military operations, and crisis management.

The National Security Council became the only forum for reviewing and making policy at the highest level. Kissinger gathered information and formulated options; Nixon made the ultimate decisions. Not even Congress could penetrate and monitor the processes and actions of the President and his national security adviser. As Kissinger once said, "The only way secrecy can be kept is to exclude from the making of decisions all those [i.e., Congress and the bureaucracy] who are theoretically charged with carrying [them] out."[27]

As Nixon prepared to assume the reins of power, Kissinger published some very definite ideas on the war in Vietnam. In the January 1969 issue of *Foreign Affairs,* he stated that "ending the war honorably is essential for the peace of the world. . . . The United States cannot accept a military defeat." Until Hanoi understood that fact, all the new administration could do was "to strengthen the Vietnamese army to permit a gradual withdrawal of *some* American forces."[28]

Kissinger's article foreshadowed the policies of Nixon's first year in office, hinting that victory and honor, not withdrawal, were the new administration's ultimate definitions of peace. In his memoirs, Kissinger repeated the same theme, claiming the United States simply could not "walk away from [the war]" and expect to salvage the respect and confidence of other nations.

> No serious policymaker could allow himself to succumb to the fashionable debunking of "prestige" or "honor" or "credibility." For a great power to abandon a small country to tyranny simply to obtain a respite from our own travail seemed to me—and still seems to me—profoundly immoral and destructive of our efforts to build a new and ultimately more peaceful pattern of international relations.[29]

Nixon and Kissinger were smugly confident that North Vietnam would soon buckle under. "Nothing to worry about," Kissinger told friends at Harvard. "We'll be out in a matter of months." At his inauguration ceremony, Nixon reiterated his devotion to peace. "The greatest honor history can bestow is the title of peacemaker. This honor now beckons America."[30]

In June 1969 the President broadcast that he was finally bringing American men home. This was the first step in his plan to camouflage the actual military escalation. A token 25,000 troops (out of 520,000) would be withdrawn by August. Nixon did not reveal his schedule for further troop withdrawals, claiming that such a disclosure would only benefit Hanoi.[31]

Nixon was convinced that the United States could win despite the reduction in manpower. Such a step clearly would quiet critics of the war. Furthermore, he would compensate for the reduced manpower by relying on greater technological expertise. Nixon believed he could now turn the ground fighting over to the South Vietnamese military forces. This policy he called "Vietnamization." The United States would "train, equip and inspire the South Vietnamese . . . to defend themselves."[32] In order to make this possible, the United States would supply the ARVN with whatever weapons and supplies were necessary. The American people were told that South Vietnam could, within a reasonable period, be in a position to defend itself.

Nixon, Kissinger, and the Pentagon should have known, however, that General Thieu and the ARVN would never be able to defeat the Vietcong. The evidence was clear. Practically every military operation conducted by the ARVN resulted in defeat. The chances that Vietnamization would work were slim. Nixon and Kissinger simply used it as a cover-up and public relations ploy. As Kissinger has admitted:

> Nixon's strategy in the early months . . . was to weaken the enemy to the maximum possible extent, speed up the modernization of Saigon's forces, and then begin withdrawals. He thought that would be a public relations coup.[33]

Within the administration, there was much discussion as to how troops should actually be withdrawn. Secretary of Defense Laird suggested the withdrawal of from 50,000 to 100,000 troops; "Laird, conscious of the views of the Joint Chiefs of Staff, officially supported the smallest figure (50,000) but indicated privately that he would not mind being overruled."[34] For the longer term, Laird supported withdrawals stretching over a period of forty-two months, although he favored leaving in Vietnam a "residual" force of 260,000 men. It would take three and a half years to withdraw slightly more than half of America's ground forces, with the others remaining in Vietnam indefinitely.

Debate over the rate of withdrawal continued for some time; in the end the timing and extent of troop withdrawals were linked cynically to the volume of protest against the continuation of the war. Whenever Nixon needed a political advantage, he could always announce that a few more men were coming home; he trusted that no one would ask what else was happening.

General Thieu vehemently and publicly opposed Nixon's program of U.S. troop withdrawal coupled with Vietnamization. Although he had a million men under his command, he realized that without total U.S. support he could never hope to win. To bring Thieu into line, Nixon arranged a meeting at Midway Island to reassure the Vietnamese leader. Thieu was in an unenviable position, Kissinger has argued. He was expected, by his American critics, to install a "Western-style democracy if not a coalition government," but that was impossible in the midst of a civil war. He was simultaneously being asked to win a war, "adjust his own defense structure to the withdrawal of a large American military establishment, and build democratic institutions in a country that had not known peace in a generation or democracy in its history."[35]

Thieu's cooperation was secured at the Midway conference; Nixon gave him a hint of his real policy and intentions. The President then began his "public relations" program, and as Kissinger has noted:

> Nixon was jubilant. He considered the announcement [of troop withdrawal] a political triumph. He thought it would buy him the time necessary for developing our strategy.[36]

The next step in Nixon's strategy of camouflage was promulgation of the "Nixon Doctrine" to explain U.S. policy in Southeast Asia. While making an around-the-world trip, the President and his advisers stopped on the island of Guam on July 25, 1969. During an informal news conference, Nixon outlined America's future role in Asia to the leaders of Southeast Asia and, through the press, to the American public.

The United States is going to be facing, we hope before too long—no one can say how long . . .—a major decision. What will be its role in Asia and in the Pacific after the end of the war in Vietnam? [I am] convinced that the way to avoid becoming involved in another war in Asia is for the United States to continue to play a significant role. . . . Asians say . . . they do not want to be dictated to from outside. Asia for the Asians . . . that is the role we should play . . . [but, nevertheless, we must] keep the treaty commitments that we have.[37]

The newsmen had a difficult time deciphering Nixon's message. He seemed to say that the United States would hereafter provide aid but *not* troops if another country in Asia faced the threat of a Communist takeover. At the same time, the President promised to rescue our Asian allies in time of war, or in other words, to intervene militarily, as we had done in Vietnam. Nevertheless, Nixon assured his audience that the Nixon Doctrine was the key to the future. In private, he explained that

the Nixon Doctrine was not a formula for getting America *out* of Asia, but one that provided the only sound basis for America's staying *in* and continuing to play a responsible role in helping the non-Communist nations and neutrals as well as our Asian allies to defend their independence.[38]

If Nixon had truly wanted a compromise solution to end the war immediately, he had the best possible opportunity when he first took office. The peace talks under Johnson were largely a charade. Unfortunately, Nixon's theory of negotiation was the same as LBJ's: He would go through the motions while the United States used its massive military power to force a North Vietnamese surrender.

Immediately upon taking office, Nixon relieved Averell Harriman and Cyrus Vance of their duties as U.S. negotiators in Paris. The new team would be headed by a holdover from the Johnson years, Henry Cabot Lodge. The President immediately rejected a bargaining bid from Hanoi, probably the most significant peace initiative yet made. To show its desire to begin real negotiations with the new administration, North Vietnam withdrew some of its forces from South Vietnam. Nixon ignored Hanoi's gesture and remained adamant about the preservation of the Thieu regime, which he identified with the concept of a free and independent South Vietnam.[39]

The position of North Vietnam was best expressed by Ho Chi Minh in a letter to Nixon dated August 25, 1969; it was a reply to a threatening letter Nixon wrote to Ho in July, setting a deadline for capitulation and warning that "there is nothing to be gained by waiting. Delay can only increase the dangers and multiply the suffering."[40] Ho said that U.S. intervention had transformed a local civil war into an American war of aggression against the Vietnamese people. "I am extremely indignant," Ho declared, "at the losses and destruction caused by the American troops to our people and our country. I am also deeply touched at the rising toll of death of young Americans." The solution was a just and lasting peace complete with "independence and real freedom." Ho did not believe that Nixon wanted the war to end:

> You [Nixon] have expressed the desire to act for a just peace. For this the United States must cease the war of aggression and withdraw their troops from South Vietnam, respect the right of the population of the South and of the Vietnamese nation to dispose of themselves, without foreign influence. This is the correct manner of solving the Vietnamese problem. . . . This is the path that will allow the United States to get out of the war with honor.[41]

Instead of seizing upon this opportunity to begin meaningful peace negotiations, Nixon denounced Ho's letter, claiming that it revealed "the other side's absolute refusal to show the least willingness to join in seeking peace." Nixon was also miffed because "Ho did not even write 'Dear Mr. President' in his letter, just 'Mr. President.' " A White House aide said, "Now that's damned rude!"[42]

Top White House advisers dismissed Ho's letter as a "cold rebuff." "Whether [the letter] was based on real or feigned outrage," Kissinger concluded, "it once again made clear that Hanoi would be satisfied only with victory."[43] It was also once again clear that Richard Nixon would be satisfied only with victory. Nixon told a group of Republicans that he was doing his damnedest to end the war and would not make it hard for the North Vietnamese if they genuinely wanted a settlement, but he would "not be the first President of the United States to lose a war."[44]

Thus the chance for peace slipped away. In less than two months of renewed heavy fighting in 1969, the total number of Americans killed in Vietnam reached 33,641, passing the final death count from the Korean War.

On January 13, 1969, 4,000 marines began the largest amphibious operation of the war south of Da Nang. Three weeks later, the U.S. military command reported 700 Vietcong sympathizers killed near Saigon, as American units rounded up 12,000 civilians for transportation to a resettlement camp. In March 1969 an allied force using artillery and B-52 bombers swept through the Michelin rubber plantation at Dau Tieng, searching out the VC and destroying suspected Communist villages. Attacks from both sides became more indiscriminate than before, and reported atrocities almost equaled the number of pitched battles. By the end of the year, 9,249 more Americans had died.

The most egregious example of the desperate warfare of that year was the Battle of Hamburger Hill in May 1969. American paratroopers charged the Vietcong stronghold ten times in five days, finally storming the hill with massive air support on May 20. Most of the Vietcong had already slipped away into the jungle, leaving the Americans with an empty hilltop. The U.S. commander called in helicopters to retrieve several hundred U.S. casualties and then withdrew the remaining forces. Why? Some experts contend that the position was worthless and that the only aim of the battle had been to kill Communists. That week, 430 Americans were killed in Vietnam.[45]

The attention given to such battles by the American press, coupled with the waves of protest that continued to sweep the United States, made Nixon anxious to gain immediate support for his policies. He had already issued an ultimatum to Hanoi. On August 4, 1969, Kissinger met secretly in Paris with Xuan Thuy and Mai Van Bo, the North Vietnamese representatives. Their rendezvous was the first of many secret meetings between Kissinger and North Vietnamese negotiators during the next three years. Kissinger opened with a personal warning from President Nixon, who felt the United States had already taken significant steps toward a Vietnam settlement. As Xuan Thuy listened intently, Kissinger said:

> I have been asked to tell you in all solemnity, that if by November 1 no major progress has been made toward a solution, we will be compelled—with great reluctance—to take measures of the greatest consequences. [You have called the war] Mr. Nixon's war. We do not believe that this is in your interest, because if it is Nixon's war, then he cannot afford not to win it.[46]

Xuan Thuy did not crack under this pressure. He repeated Hanoi's position, which called for the withdrawal of all American forces, free elections in South Vietnam, and the ousting of General Thieu. Yet Nixon still hoped that his threat of escalation would induce Hanoi to accept the American terms. If not, he would unleash all the military might at his disposal to force a surrender.

As he waited for Hanoi's response, Nixon considered the problem of public opinion. He intended to carry out his threat made to the North Vietnamese, but he feared a renewed wave of public protest such as had already surfaced with the antiwar movement's call for a Vietnam Moratorium on October 15.

> I had to decide what to do about the ultimatum. I knew that unless I had some indisputably good reason for not carrying out my threat of using increased force, . . . the Communists would become contemptuous of us and even more difficult to deal with. I knew, however, that after all the protests and the Moratorium, American public opinion would be seriously divided by any military escalation of the war.[47]

Nixon's solution to this dilemma was a typical one—he decided to make a propaganda speech. On October 24 he isolated himself at Camp David, and one week and twelve drafts later, after staying up most of the final night, he finished an address which he hoped would win him the support of the "great silent majority of Americans."[48]

Before a television audience on November 3, 1969, Nixon delivered what he clearly regarded as one of the most important addresses of his career.

> The message of my November 3 speech was that we were going to keep our commitment in Vietnam. We were going to continue fighting until the Communists agreed to negotiate a fair and honorable peace or until the South Vietnamese were able to defend themselves on their own—whichever came first. At the same time we would continue our disengagement based on the principles of the Nixon Doctrine: the pace of withdrawal would be linked to the progress of Vietnamization, the level of enemy activity, and developments on the negotiating front. I emphasized that our policy would not be affected by demonstrations in the streets.[49]

In other words, something for everyone. He pledged to continue fighting, to continue withdrawing, and to continue negotiating. He asked for unity at home:

The more support I can have from the American people, the sooner that pledge [to end the war] can be redeemed; for the more divided we are at home, the less likely the enemy is to negotiate at Paris.[50]

Nixon claimed that he received more than 50,000 telegrams and 30,000 letters in response to his address and that 75 percent of those letters and telegrams supported his position. Subsequent investigation has revealed, however, that many of these responses were orchestrated by Republican state committees and had actually been sent to the White House before Nixon even gave the speech.[51]

In his *Memoirs*, Nixon says:

The November 3 speech was both a milestone and a turning point for my administration. Now, for a time at least, the enemy could no longer count on dissent in America to give them the victory they could not win on the battlefield. I had the public support I needed to continue a policy of waging war in Vietnam and negotiating for peace in Paris until we could bring the war to an honorable and successful conclusion.[52]

Nixon believed he was ready to lead the nation to the victory he envisioned.

NIXON'S SECRET END-THE-WAR PLAN: AN AIR WAR *1970–73*

> Victory in this struggle will come
> through perseverance, by never giving
> up, by coming back again and again when
> things are tough. . . .
>
> If we determine to win, if we resolve to
> accept no substitute for victory, then
> victory becomes possible. Then the spirit
> gives edge to the sword, the sword preserves
> the spirit, and freedom will prevail.
> —*Richard M. Nixon*[1]

Having achieved, he believed, the support of the American people for his Vietnam policies, Nixon was now ready to unleash his secret plan to end the war: to withdraw American ground troops and curtail the search-and-destroy missions, yet at the same time to wage an all-out technological war against both North and South Vietnam. The Hanoi peace negotiators were told that if they failed to capitulate to U.S. terms, they would face the possibility of being obliterated by a greatly intensified bombing attack.

Journalists dubbed the multibillion-dollar network of communications systems, computers, and weaponry to be used by the dwindling U.S. forces the "electronic battlefield." It included acoustic sensors to pinpoint targets, digital computers to store information, closed circuit TV screens to control helicopter fire, infrared riflescopes to see the enemy at night, radioactive dust monitoring systems, and even radio-controlled robots that could arm and detonate themselves by computer signal. It was estimated in late 1970 that the cost for this automated battlefield program would exceed $20 billion within several years. Although much of this project was experimental, the price tag was deemed acceptable by both Nixon and Kissinger.[2]

By 1970–71 the air force was flying an estimated 10,000 sorties a month over Cambodia, and an estimated 25,000 sorties a month over Laos. By 1970–71 the United States had dropped almost 5 million tons of bombs on Vietnam, Cambodia and Laos, more than doubling the tonnage dropped in World War II. In the first five months of 1970 alone, 600,000 tons of bombs were dropped on Vietnam, a figure far surpassing the amount of bombing during the entire Korean War. Each year thereafter, the total tonnage of bombs dropped averaged about 1.4 million tons. B-52 raids alone cost over $1 million a day, and the level of destruction in Southeast Asia exceeded 20 million bomb craters and untold numbers of civilian deaths.[3]

By late 1971, the skies over South Vietnam were filled with spotter planes, jet bombers, gunships, flare ships, reconnaissance planes, rescue helicopters, refueling ships, command-and-control planes, and high-flying spy planes. B-52s regularly attacked free-fire zones and suspected enemy positions in every corner of South Vietnam. They dropped fragmentation bombs, anti-personnel bombs, tons of napalm, and eventually the new "smart bombs" directed onto a target by means of laser beams and TV signals. Claimed to be foolproof, the smart bombs actually fell at random; 50 percent of the new bombs landed outside their target area.[4] The result was greater destruction than ever inside South Vietnam. When one realizes that the military defoliation program had already ruined over 5 million acres of forest land in South Vietnam by the end of 1971, the overall impact of U.S. action is almost inconceivable.[5]

The most newsworthy target for America's bombs continued to be North Vietnam. In 1970, Nixon lifted most of the restrictions on bombing north of the demilitarized zone. The Pentagon chose to call the renewed air attacks over North Vietnam "protective reaction strikes," but the results were the same for the people who suffered on the ground. U.S. planes, flying in groups of 250, carried out nearly 200 protective reaction strikes in 1971. The most violent air raids of the year occurred in December, when Nixon ordered 1,000 sorties in a five-day period. According to Alexander Kendrick:

The weather was bad. Pilots could not see the ground. The Pentagon nevertheless declared that "only military targets" had been hit, while President Nixon called the raids "very successful." With the increase in "protective reaction" strikes, supposedly to protect the American withdrawal, more planes were lost and more pilots captured.[6]

By December 17, 1971, when the heaviest raids were in progress, the military announced that 8,051 U.S. aircraft had been lost since the war started in 1965. Of these, almost 4,500, or more than half, had been lost because of accidents and "non-hostile" causes. The remainder had been shot down by the Vietcong and by North Vietnamese and Chinese antiaircraft gunners. These statistics told only part of the story; the tragedy of the American POWs and those missing in action followed hand in hand with the air war.

By the end of 1970, the highly publicized withdrawal program had reduced the U.S. combat force to approximately 300,000. But even though the number of troops was reduced, the overall casualty figures and the level of combat remained tragically high. There were nearly 400,000 casualties throughout Indochina in 1970 alone, most of them innocent civilians. The President told newsmen that U.S. troops would remain in Vietnam until South Vietnam could defend itself, and Defense Secretary Melvin Laird announced that U.S. ships and planes would stay in Indochina even after the last U.S. soldier had been evacuated, as "part of the realistic deterrent which we shall maintain in Asia."[7]

Hanoi responded by constantly improving its antiaircraft defense, which ultimately shot down thousands of U.S. planes. Meanwhile, Hanoi chose not to fight a conventional war against the U.S. military juggernaut. Instead, in Nixon's first year in office, North Vietnam withdrew as many as 60,000 troops from the South. Each year thereafter, until a peace treaty was signed, it withdrew some forces. North Vietnamese commanders were ordered to conserve their main-force troops and not to risk being targeted by U.S. air power. Hanoi's military leaders thought that the Tet offensive in 1968, with its concentration on conventional warfare, had been too costly. They preferred to have the guerrilla army in South Vietnam carry on the struggle alone until "final victory" became possible.

North Vietnam never forgot that the war was a political war, and that the Vietcong could achieve final success only by rallying the people in the South to its cause. Thus, in 1970, instead of furnishing major military support, Hanoi urged the Vietcong to increase its agitation among those elements opposed to President Thieu. The Thieu regime was alienating more and more of the population in South Vietnam, and political groups previously unaffiliated with the NLF were joining the resistance at an increased rate. In contrast, Hanoi maintained a low military profile in the South.

Another reason why North Vietnam withdrew some of its forces was the hope that the new President, either from choice or the pressure of public opinion, would begin serious peace negotiations. It assumed that Nixon at some point would have to respect the will of the people and begin a serious search for peace. But such was not to be the case. Nixon and Kissinger chose to ignore the defensive posture of North Vietnam throughout 1969–71. Their reply was to invade Cambodia and intensify the massive air war over all of Indochina.[8]

Attempts to bring the United States and North Vietnam into serious peace negotiations continued to fail. On April 1, 1970, the foreign minister of France, Maurice Schumann, proposed a peace conference on Indochina. He secured Soviet approval initially, although by April 18 Moscow described Schumann's proposal as "unrealistic at present." North Vietnam rejected this French initiative in April before the United States invaded Cambodia in May. In 1970, the North Vietnamese offered to reduce their involvement in Laos if the United States would halt the bombing of the Ho Chi Minh Trail in that country. Nixon rejected this idea immediately.

At the same time, the Soviet Union continued to press for a solution of the Vietnam problem, but Nixon was in no mood to deal with the Soviets.[9] Likewise, the People's Republic of China attempted, to no avail, to begin a peace initiative. Instead, the United States "threatened" China by its invasions of Cambodia and Laos. General James Gavin pointed out that "there may be those who would be tempted to the ultimate confrontation, war with Red China."[10] There is also some evidence that commando raids were being carried out against China by the sending of Nationalist guerrillas from Taiwan into China, action which minimized any breakthrough in U.S./China relations in 1970.[11]

North Vietnam nevertheless remained open to further talks with the United States at Paris. The new United States envoy was David

Bruce. Hanoi's position was simple: North Vietnam demanded U.S. withdrawal from South Vietnam and the formation of a provisional, coalition government. This had been Hanoi's position throughout 1969, and it remained unchanged during the meetings in September 1970. North Vietnam proposed that the coalition government consist of three elements: representatives of the NLF's government-in-exile; representatives from Saigon believing in peace, independence, and neutrality; and representatives from nonaligned religious groups.[12] When North Vietnam spoke of neutrality, it meant "neutral" in terms of future Vietnamese relations to China, Russia, or America. However, when the NLF spoke of neutrality, it meant a transitional government that would eventually become socialist and would remain neutral from any power blocs. To Nixon, neither definition was "neutral." He refused to accept Hanoi's proposed coalition government without the consent of Thieu and Ky, who of course turned down the proposal.

At these September meetings, the United States unveiled its new plan to the North Vietnamese. Nixon and Kissinger still demanded a cease-fire in all of Indochina but proposed that the NLF be allowed to keep its forces in the areas of South Vietnam that it already controlled. The catch was that the NLF would have to recognize Saigon's ultimate sovereignty over all of South Vietnam. There would be neither a chance for NLF leaders to participate in the national government, nor a coalition government. Nixon spoke of a readiness to "seek a political solution that reflects the will of the South Vietnamese people," but the offer patently excluded any real compromise with the NLF.[13]

In 1971, Nixon shifted the emphasis of negotiation to secret meetings between Kissinger and representatives of North Vietnam. Kissinger flew to Paris six times that year. He made his first trip in May, apparently confident that North Vietnam would finally accept America's peace terms. In fact, the invasion of Laos seemed to strengthen North Vietnam's will.

Kissinger presented the U.S. peace proposal to Le Duc Tho on May 31, 1971, a proposal which "was carefully conceived, like its predecessors, to yield nothing of substance."[14] Kissinger offered a cease-fire, followed by the eventual but unscheduled withdrawal of U.S. troops, thereby preserving the ability of the United States to reenter the war at any time. Furthermore, the United States offer ignored Hanoi's position that as long as Thieu remained the ruler of South Vietnam, free elections could never take place. Hanoi contended that Thieu would have to step down so that fair elections could be held.[15]

The remaining five secret meetings in 1971 between Kissinger and North Vietnam's representatives revolved around this central theme of President Thieu and the elections in South Vietnam, scheduled for October 1971. Hanoi wanted some sign that Washington would not, once again, impose the Thieu regime on the people of South Vietnam. Toward that end, Le Duc Tho presented Kissinger with a nine-point package on June 26, 1971, calling on the United States to "stop supporting Thieu . . . so that there may be set up in Saigon a new administration standing for peace, independence, neutrality and democracy."[16] These four goals formed the basis of Hanoi's negotiating strategy until the end of the war.

After two exchanges in July, Kissinger flew back to Paris on August 16, 1971, to present a response to North Vietnam's nine-point package. The United States was ready, according to Kissinger, to negotiate a withdrawal date, and, to show its good faith, Washington would declare itself neutral in the upcoming election in South Vietnam.

Le Duc Tho listened intently as Kissinger spoke; a U.S. pledge of neutrality was exactly what Hanoi wanted. If nothing happened during the next several weeks to discredit Kissinger's response, then perhaps the long-awaited breakthrough in negotiations could occur. His government, Tho declared, would reply at the next meeting. In the meantime, Hanoi would watch Thieu's actions—and Washington's attitude—very closely.

Since the beginning of American involvement in Vietnam, each President had told the American public that South Vietnam's right to free elections was a major goal of the war. But free elections never occurred. In fact, as the U.S. involvement in Vietnam intensified, America's presence had the opposite effect. With U.S. support, Thieu continued to manipulate the election process and remain in power against the wishes of most of the people of South Vietnam. A final futile effort was made, in the 1971 presidential election, to hold a meaningful free election.

As the campaign began, the non-Communist opposition to Thieu finally coalesced around General Duong Van Minh. He was the same "Big Minh" who had ruled South Vietnam briefly in 1963, before the

CIA engineered his downfall. Now retired from the army, Minh was known for his neutralist stance. With him in the race, the election promised to offer a real choice to the people of South Vietnam for the first time in thirty years.

Although Minh was not a Communist, his program was almost identical to that of the National Liberation Front. Minh called upon the United States to stop supporting Thieu and to leave Vietnam altogether. In Minh's words, only a "positive and constructive neutrality" by the United States would guarantee a free election in October.[17]

In August, President Thieu moved to eliminate all possibility of a free election in October. On August 5, the Supreme Court of South Vietnam, under orders from Thieu, disallowed the candidacy of Vice President Ky, Thieu's partner and erstwhile competitor. Then, on August 12, Big Minh revealed a seedy government plot whereby Thieu planned to use South Vietnam's army and administrative apparatus to insure victory at the polls.

In the face of these provocations, Minh decided to pull out of the elections, leaving Thieu alone in the race and revealing the election for the charade it was. When election day arrived, a number of riots broke out in South Vietnam, but the farce was played out to the bitter end. Thieu emerged victorious with over 90 percent of the votes.[18] With continued U.S. backing, he would rule Saigon until the end, ruthlessly making war against his own people and their neighbors.

The Nixon team tried to tell the world that Thieu's one-man election was neither extraordinary nor unusual. Kissinger and Nixon denied that the United States helped manage the election. Ambassador Bunker, who had urged Big Minh to accept American financial support to stay in the race and lose so that he could emerge as leader of the opposition, consoled himself with the fact that "even after two hundred years we still have gross irregularities in our own elections." The most unusual comment, however, came from Ronald Reagan, who carried Nixon's personal congratulations to Thieu. Reagan noted that George Washington had also been elected without opposition.[19]

Predictably, another consequence of Thieu's one-man election was the complete breakdown of talks between Kissinger and Le Duc Tho. During the election campaign in South Vietnam, Washington assured Hanoi of its neutrality. In turn, North Vietnam could only repeat its demand that Washington stop imposing Thieu on an unwilling people. There was little common ground.

On October 11, 1971, with Thieu firmly in control again, the United States offered one last peace package for 1971, calling for some kind of independent commission to organize new elections. Kissinger hoped for a favorable reply, but North Vietnam said no. Obviously, in the wake of Thieu's reelection, Hanoi had lost all hope that the United States was seriously interested in peace.[20]

Nixon's plan to procure peace by an intensified air war was not working. Neither Nixon nor the Pentagon, however, seemed willing to change this policy. At this stage Congress still failed to take any action. Nixon, invoking the memory of President Kennedy in the Cuban missile crisis, made it clear that he would consult Congress whenever possible on foreign and defense matters, but that the President had the constitutional right and responsibility to act quickly and without consultation to protect American lives and interests.[21]

However, a few authoritative voices were raised in criticism of the conduct of the war and its basic premises. Senator Edward Kennedy compared the violence at home with the war in Vietnam and concluded that both conflicts were the product of that "strange and tragic fascination [with] military victory which [has] cast a mad spell over two successive Presidents. . . . Can any of us," Kennedy asked, "fail to realize now what Vietnam has done to our spirit, our nation, and our sons? . . . Dear God, help us. The war must end."[22] Senators George McGovern and Mark Hatfield proposed an amendment to the Defense Procurement Bill which would have cut off all Vietnam war funds by the end of 1970, later extended to the end of 1971. After three months of haggling and petty debate, however, the Senate voted fifty-five to thirty-nine to kill the measure.[23]

Then, for a brief moment, the Congress was stirred to strong protests. W. R. Anderson of Tennessee and Augustus Hawkins of California were part of an official delegation from the House of Representatives to Saigon, but instead of following the standard official tour, they slipped away to investigate an alarming rumor. They found Con Son, the famous penal island. They were sickened by

> inhuman conditions in the "tiger cages," which were concrete cells set in the ground and covered by bars. The inmates were shackled constantly, so that their legs were paralyzed, and the congested cells had no sanitary facilities, no water, and no sunlight. Any who complained

were sprinkled with lime dust from above. Most distressing to the Americans was the fact that the "tiger cage" inmates were political prisoners, of whom the island commandant said, "These are very bad people. They won't salute the flag. They won't salute the American flag." The number of political prisoners was a reminder that despite American intervention Vietnam had remained essentially a civil war.[24]

The congressional party reacted angrily to the discovery that South Vietnam's regime kept hundreds of prisoners in tiger cages. The visitors heard stories of hunger, thirst, and multiple beatings by military guards. The congressmen expressed their sense of outrage to the CIA agent who accompanied them, only to be told: "You have no right to interfere with Vietnamese affairs. You have come here trying to stir up trouble. You are guests . . . here. You aren't supposed to go poking your nose into doors that aren't your business." Congressman Hawkins reminded the CIA agent that, because the United States provided 95 percent of all funds used by Saigon, it was indeed their business. The CIA man tried to change the subject and at one point even suggested that Hawkins and Anderson spend their time buying souvenirs at the prison gift shop. Hawkins left Con Son with the promise, "I'm going to stop this. I'm going to stop this."[25]

Nothing substantial, however, came of the tiger cage controversy. The newspapers were hesitant to expose the situation; the reporter who tipped off the congressmen about Con Son was harassed and then thrown out of South Vietnam.

A more serious challenge to Nixon's Vietnam policy emerged with the trial of Lieutenant William Calley in November 1970. After being kept for more than two years as a military secret, the story of My Lai exploded into view during 1970. The Pentagon, uneasy about the publicity surrounding the My Lai affair, dropped the charges against twenty-four other soldiers. Calley, however, was brought before a military court to answer charges that he had murdered 102 civilians at My Lai village. There was never any question that Calley had gunned down the entire population of this village. The only issue under debate was whether or not the killing of these civilians was murder.

Calley's unit was engaged in a routine search-and-destroy mission, and the villagers of My Lai were suspected Vietcong sympathizers. So on the direct orders of Calley, all the villagers were shot to death. Calley's defense was that he was simply carrying out the orders given by his company commander, Captain Ernest Medina. Medina, himself awaiting court-martial, denied that he had given Calley orders to kill civilians. The trial ended when the military tribunal sentenced Calley to life imprisonment, and dropped the case against Captain Medina. Calley appealed his sentence, which was first reduced to twenty years and then quietly dropped altogether.[26]

Outside the courtroom, the trial raised many questions about the war in Vietnam. How many more such incidents were there? To what extent were the United States forces inflicting casualties on a noncombatant population? Where did the responsibility for this policy ultimately rest? Most disturbing of all, was there really a difference between the avowed enemy and the civilian population of Vietnam? Was the United States fighting a war, not against the Communist menace but against the Vietnamese people? And what of the conduct of a war where American forces meted out quick death to anything that moved in the jungles, and allowed blanket bombing and burning of Vietnamese villages?

> Some Vietnam veterans said that if Calley was guilty, so were they, as indeed they may have been. Antiwar veterans saw Calley as the victim of American policy, as they felt they themselves had been. Some critics of the verdict called the entire nation guilty, as "all Germans" had been held to be because of Hitler. . . . To those like John Kerry, one of the leaders of Vietnam Veterans Against the War, the trial, the principles of military justice, the Pentagon, and the Commander-in-Chief had failed because they had not distinguished between guilt and responsibility.[27]

The year 1971 ended with a startling revelation about the state of public opinion: A Harris poll showed that 65 percent of the American people now believed it was

> "morally wrong" for the United States to be fighting in Vietnam, instead of merely a "mistake" as before, and [that] a 3-to-1 majority favored "getting completely out" by May 1972, leaving no residual force and discontinuing the use of air power in support of South Vietnamese troops. For the first time Nixon's rate of withdrawal was found "too slow" by a majority, 53 percent. "Get out" of Vietnam was widely favored over "winding down."[28]

This attitude followed Nixon into 1972, as disillusionment with the Vietnam War continued to grow. Senator Edmund Muskie, a leading Democratic candidate for President, set the tone early in the year, when he attacked the war as immoral. The United States had "no right to kill, wound, or displace over 100,000 civilians a month" in Vietnam, just as Nixon had no right "to send young Americans to Vietnam as bargaining chips for the freedom of prisoners of war who would be free if those young Americans were not sent at all." Too many Americans had died "not for a cause but for a mistake."[29]

THE INVASION OF CAMBODIA
1969–73

One of the saddest episodes in U.S. history was the massacre of millions of innocent Cambodian peasants and the virtual destruction of their land by massive U.S. air and ground attacks. Prince Sihanouk, the enlightened and competent Cambodian ruler, had for years attempted to maintain a neutral position regarding the U.S./ Vietnamese struggle. Nixon decided, however, that neutrality was not good enough, which resulted in Sihanouk's overthrow by an incompetent dictator, Lon Nol, approved by the United States. As a result, the United States now had to cope with another major war, which was unwinnable despite the enormous military and financial burdens the United States was compelled to assume.

Even before he took office, Nixon made it clear that he considered Cambodia a vital link in achieving victory in Vietnam. On January 8, 1969, Nixon wrote to Kissinger:

> In making your [preliminary] study of Vietnam I want a precise report on what the enemy has in Cambodia and what, if anything, we are doing to destroy the buildup there. I think a very definite change of policy toward Cambodia probably should be one of the first orders of business when we get in.[1]

The new President wasted little time. On his first day in office, Nixon told the Joint Chiefs he wanted a plan to "quarantine" Cambodia by swift military action. General Creighton Abrams in Saigon responded by requesting B-52 strikes against Base Area 353, a suspected Communist sanctuary in Cambodia. Abrams insisted that Base Area 353 housed the elusive enemy known to the Pentagon as COSVN (Central Office for South Vietnam). If the military could successfully destroy the COSVN, it could severely handicap any large-scale offensive against the Saigon area and significantly disrupt enemy operations throughout South Vietnam.[2]

The idea of bombing Cambodia intrigued Nixon and Kissinger, both of whom were hesitant to defy public opinion by immediate resumption of air raids over North Vietnam. "Thought then turned to bombing of the North Vietnamese sanctuary areas in Cambodia," Kissinger has recorded, "not from a desire to expand the war, but to avoid bombing North Vietnam. . . ."[3] An air war over Cambodia could be kept secret and still fulfill the goals of disrupting enemy supply lines and destroying enemy bases. Most important of all, it might force Cambodia to abandon its long-held policy of neutrality.

Prince Norodom Sihanouk had governed Cambodia since the beginning of the Second World War, at the behest of the French and then by a significant measure of popular support.[4] During that time he had guided the nation to independence and maintained neutrality in foreign affairs. In the 1950s and 1960s, Cambodia was an oasis in war-torn Indochina—fertile, peaceful, relatively united.[5] Sihanouk's ability to disassociate Cambodia from the growing turmoil in Vietnam was particularly frustrating to American leaders, who applied great pressure on him. In 1956, John Foster Dulles tried to bring Sihanouk under the wing of SEATO and, when the attempt failed, decreed that Washington should "reverse the drift towards pro-Communist neutrality" in Cambodia.[6] In 1956 and 1958, the CIA acquiesced in plots to overthrow Sihanouk. In 1959 the Pentagon participated in an undercover campaign aimed at wooing both the middle class and the army away from the prince.

Despite a decade of intrigue, Sihanouk refused to buckle under American pressure. When he realized that Cambodia's elite had become heavily dependent on the United States, the prince canceled the American aid program and broke relations with Washington. The United States feared a "lean to the left" in Phnom Penh, but Sihanouk continued to play off Russian, Chinese, and American influences during the early 1960s.[7]

Cambodia's balancing act began to crumble in 1964, when Lyndon Johnson escalated the Vietnam War. To escape the U.S. search-and-destroy missions, the Vietnamese Communists moved westward to the Cambodian border, where they established sanctuaries and base areas for the war in Vietnam. The network of paths known as the Ho Chi Minh Trail became the supply route from North Vietnam to

them. Sihanouk opposed the presence of foreign troops on Cambodian soil but could do little to stop the intrusion. If the American
army with all its men and modern equipment could not overcome
the Vietcong's guerrilla tactics, what chance would Cambodia's
army—smaller and less well equipped—have of being more successful? And Sihanouk did not want to run the risk of war with Hanoi. So
he looked the other way and tried to ignore the intermittent violation
of Cambodian neutrality. He did act to suppress the small Communist movement *inside* Cambodia, the Khmer Rouge. He purged the
leftists from his Cabinet and allowed his prime minister, General
Lon Nol, to crush a suspected Communist revolt in the province of
Battambang.

   Nevertheless, these actions did not satisfy the Johnson administration. At the beginning of 1968, American emissary Chester Bowles
traveled to Phnom Penh for a meeting with Sihanouk. He attempted
to persuade Sihanouk to launch an attack against the Communist
sanctuaries. If he was unable to do so, Bowles explained, then it
might be necessary for U.S. forces to defend themselves by crossing
the Cambodian border. Sihanouk vehemently opposed both suggestions. Four years later, Henry Kissinger declared under oath that
Sihanouk asked for U.S. military action against the sanctuaries, but
the evidence suggests that this was not so. The prince recognized
that Cambodian neutrality had been abused by the Vietnamese
Communists, but he hoped desperately to avoid U.S. intervention on
a grand scale.[8]

   When North Vietnam launched a small-scale offensive in South
Vietnam during mid-February 1969, Nixon seized the opportunity
and gave tentative approval for a B-52 raid against Cambodian Base
Area 353. Nixon later called the enemy offensive

   > a deliberate test, clearly designed to take the measure of me and my
   > administration at the outset. . . . If we let the Communists manipulate
   > us at this early stage, we might never be able to negotiate with them
   > from a position of equality, much less one of strength.[9]

After the Joint Chiefs devised a schedule for bombing the sanctuaries, Nixon and Kissinger briefed Secretaries Laird and Rogers in
February. On March 16, 1969, Nixon met with Kissinger, Laird, Rogers, and General Wheeler. Rogers expressed reservations about the
bombing, fearing an outburst of domestic criticism. The President

assured him that every precaution would be taken to keep the strike secret. Nixon wanted to do "something," militarily, as soon as possible. On March 18, therefore, the first of a series of deadly B-52 attacks took place inside Cambodia. The Pentagon called it Operation Breakfast. Nixon called it "the first turning point in my administration's conduct of the Vietnam War."[10]

The most frequently expressed view is that Sihanouk did not denounce the bombing. It is true that his denunciations were not widely reported in the United States. However, the B-52 operations began on March 18, 1969, and on March 26 the Cambodian government issued statements condemning the bombing and strafing of "the Cambodia population living in the border regions . . . almost daily by U.S. aircraft," and demanding that "these criminal attacks must immediately and definitively stop." On March 28 Sihanouk called a press conference in which he emphatically denied reports circulating in the United States that he "would not oppose U.S. bombings of communist targets within my frontiers." He pointed out how there were growing numbers of Cambodian victims. And then he said, "I appeal to you to publicize abroad this very clear stand of Cambodia—that is, I will in any case oppose all bombings on Cambodian territory under whatever pretext."[11]

Nixon and Kissinger nevertheless authorized Operation Lunch in April and a cluster of new attacks—Dessert, Snack, Supper, etc.—in May 1969. On each occasion, B-52s pounded the Cambodian countryside with several hundred tons of bombs, inflicting only minor damage to the mobile sanctuaries. But a number of Cambodian villages were destroyed and the sparse border population was decimated. After August 1969, the Menu raids were institutionalized; the White House no longer bothered to approve each attack. Menu continued on a regular basis until the 1970 invasion of Cambodia, after which the bombing intensified, expanded, and shed its veil of secrecy.[12]

For more than a year, Menu was a well-kept secret. The Pentagon specifically ordered all military personnel involved to deny its existence. "Due to the sensitivity of this operation," General Wheeler stressed, "all persons who know of it, who participate in its planning, preparation or execution should be warned not . . . to discuss it with unauthorized individuals." With Nixon's approval, the Joint Chiefs devised a method of dual reporting to hide the Menu attacks from

Congress. After each raid, officers falsified documents to conceal the actual targets of the mission. The final report for each run specified that all bombs had been dropped over South Vietnam. In this way, the military was able to deceive both Congress and the American people.[13]

The same mentality dominated at the White House. Henry Kissinger "saw no sense" in acknowledging the Cambodian bombing campaign, which he described as a "minimum defensive reaction fully compatible with international law."[14] If revealed, Menu might spark an international crisis or complicate the Vietnamization process. Furthermore, the issue would probably unleash a new wave of protest at home. Nixon later wrote that a major "reason for secrecy was the problem of domestic antiwar protest. My administration was only two months old [when Menu began], and I wanted to provoke as little public outcry as possible at the outset."[15]

The secret was not revealed until 1973, when Major Hal Knight testified before the Senate Foreign Relations Committee that he had systematically falsified all documents relating to Operation Menu. All told, more than 3,600 secret B-52 sorties were flown against supposed enemy sanctuaries in Cambodia from 1969 to 1970. More than 100,000 tons of bombs were dropped on a neutral country whose international position was fragile at best. These raids constituted 60 percent of all B-52 operations throughout Indochina during the period in question.[16]

The 1973 hearing also raised the question of why Congress had not been informed of the Cambodian raids. In fact, on June 11, 1969, Nixon and Kissinger had briefed Senator John Stennis, the chairman of the Senate Armed Services Committee, and Senator Richard Russell about the bombing; later the White House informed Everett Dirksen, Mendell Rivers, and Gerald Ford. "Not one," recounts Kissinger, "raised the issue that the full Congress should be consulted."[17] Furthermore, he insisted, it was an accepted practice that when dealing with classified military operations, the executive consulted only with key members of Congress. As a result, the legislative branch of the United States government, empowered by the Constitution to declare war and appropriate funds, knew nothing about the bombing war over Cambodia. "By informing only a few sympathetic legislators in a general way of the bombing," William Shawcross concluded, "the White House was deliberately usurping the Congress' constitutional rights and responsibilities."[18] When Operation Menu was exposed, many Congressmen agreed with Congressman Robert Drinan's indictment in 1974 that Nixon's secret war was "more shocking and more unbelievable than the conduct of any President in any war in all of American history."[19] Drinan, as a member of the House Judiciary Committee, went on to propose an article of impeachment against Nixon for concealing the Cambodian war from Congress.

What were the results of the secret war? Night after night for more than a year, the giant stratofortresses crossed Cambodia's border and pulverized the jungle areas below. Contrary to Kissinger's assertions, the Menu raids did not localize or contain enemy resistance in the sanctuaries. As the Joint Chiefs admitted, the bombing actually forced the North Vietnamese and Vietcong to disperse over a greater area than before. In effect, the enemy simply moved its sanctuaries deeper into Cambodia, where U.S. bombs were not falling. Predictably, Sihanouk found it more difficult than ever to maintain Cambodia's neutrality. Very rapidly, the Vietnam War was spreading westward into Cambodia.[20]

In the spring of 1970, Cambodia finally succumbed to the upheavals of war. By allowing the Vietnamese Communists to use parts of eastern Cambodia as a sanctuary, Sihanouk had managed to sidestep a major confrontation with Hanoi. At the same time, by acquiescing in Operation Menu, the prince had blunted the antineutralist pressures emanating from Saigon and Washington, but only temporarily, since the White House had adopted a dual strategy to permit escalating operations in Cambodia.

On the one hand, to satisfy Congress, administration officials denied any aggressive intentions toward Cambodia. When, for example, the Senate Foreign Relations Committee called upon Secretary of State Rogers to explain Nixon's intentions toward Cambodia, Rogers assured the committee that the President had no incentive to escalate the war, since military operations into Cambodia would disrupt the process of Vietnamization. On behalf of the White House, Rogers promised that the United States would avoid any act which appeared to violate Cambodian neutrality. As far as Sihanouk was concerned, he said, "our hands are clean and our hearts are pure."[21]

On the other hand, Nixon and Kissinger encouraged Sihanouk's enemies—primarily business and military leaders—in order to exploit any political crisis that resulted. They did not have long to wait. On January 7, 1970, Sihanouk left Phnom Penh and journeyed to France for one of his periodic rest cures; before returning home, he planned to visit Moscow and Peking to discuss the North Vietnamese presence in eastern Cambodia. During Sihanouk's absence, General Lon Nol, the prime minister, and Sirik Matak, a leading businessman and cabinet member, ran the government. Both men were anti-Communist and pro-American.

On March 8, 1970, the acting government staged demonstrations in Svay Rieng province, along Cambodia's eastern border, to protest the presence of Vietnamese Communists. Three days later, the same thing happened in Phnom Penh. Thousands of students and soldiers marched down Norodom Avenue and sacked the official embassy of the Vietcong. Military police, disguised in civilian clothes, led the assault. From Paris, Sihanouk denounced the demonstrations and considered returning home immediately. But, after receiving assurances from the CIA that he had nothing to worry about, the prince decided not to change his plans. Lon Nol and Sirik Matak, therefore, had the opening they needed.

On March 12, the government canceled Cambodia's trade agreement with the Vietnamese Communists and closed the port of Sihanoukville. On March 13, Lon Nol broadcast an ultimatum demanding that all Communist forces leave Cambodia within two days. On March 15, when the ultimatum expired, the general asked for and received South Vietnamese artillery bombardment of the sanctuaries. Finally, on March 18, Lon Nol and Sirik Matak completed their coup d'etat by ousting Prince Sihanouk altogether.[22]

In the midst of the crisis, Sihanouk delivered a televised address in Paris in which he accused the CIA of interfering in Cambodian politics and plotting with Cambodian rightists. In their memoirs, both Nixon and Kissinger denied the allegations. Nixon wrote that "Lon Nol's coup came as a complete surprise."[23] Kissinger maintained that "we neither encouraged Sihanouk's overthrow nor knew about it in advance."[24]

Although it is uncertain whether or not the CIA gave direct assistance to Lon Nol and his clique, there is no doubt that the CIA, which had been operating in Cambodia since the 1954 Geneva Accords, contributed to the idea of a coup. For years, the Agency had fomented anti-Sihanouk subversion aimed at replacing Cambodia's neutralist regime with a more pro-Western government. This clandestine activity increased noticeably in the months before March 1970. One source argues that Lon Nol received funds for the coup against Sihanouk from a Cambodian banker purported to be in the service of the CIA.[25] Other evidence strengthens the theory that, despite Kissinger's claim, Washington knew of and encouraged the plans of Lon Nol and Sirik Matak. In any event, as Frank Snepp of the CIA noted, "We were in a position to rub our hands and take advantage of it [the removal of Sihanouk]."[26]

With little hesitation, the United States accepted the transition of power in Cambodia, as a small group of pro-American army officers, businessmen and aristocrats replaced Sihanouk. Eventually, Sihanouk found asylum in Peking, where he ended his neutral stance and called for the overthrow of Lon Nol. Several weeks after the coup he declared, bitterly:

> I had chosen not to be with either the Americans or the Communists, because I considered that there were two dangers, American imperialism and Asian Communism. It was Lon Nol who obliged me to choose between them.[27]

In Phnom Penh, the new government immediately issued a call to arms against all Communists. By mid-April, 70,000 volunteers had enlisted in Lon Nol's makeshift army. As one journalist vividly recalled:

> Their induction was cursory, their training on a golf course outside Phnom Penh was erratic, and their equipment was nonexistent. Every day they could be seen setting out from the city, hanging on the sides of Coca-Cola trucks or brightly painted buses, wearing shower clogs or sandals, shorts or blue jeans, . . . old French uniforms or oversized American fatigues, some empty-handed, some carrying . . . [weapons], laughing as they headed for the war in the plains.[28]

As the fighting intensified and the last remnants of Cambodian neutrality dissolved, villagers began to resist the new military government. Some joined the growing non-Communist rebel movement, still loyal to Prince Sihanouk. The Communists among them gravitated to the left-wing Khmer Rouge. This group received aid from Hanoi but remained fiercely independent. The majority of Khmer Rouge leaders were nationalist Cambodians who opposed the increasingly harsh and autocratic Lon Nol government.[29]

Soon, five separate wars were in progress in Cambodia. Along the eastern border, U.S. warplanes continued to bomb a narrow strip of territory containing enemy sanctuaries, Cambodian villages, and thick jungle. When the pace of the bombing slowed, South Vietnamese units crashed across the border, burning, looting, and raping anything Cambodian that they encountered. A short distance to the west, Lon Nol's army engaged a combined force of Khmer Rouge rebels and North Vietnamese troops that had pushed toward Phnom Penh to escape the intense U.S. air war. Within the "liberated" provinces, Khmer Rouge and North Vietnamese units battled each other, literally at times, for control of the expanding war. Finally, within government-held territory, Lon Nol's army unleashed a brutal campaign against the 400,000 ethnic Vietnamese who lived in Cambodia.

President Nixon, in the face of the Cambodia situation, remained unrepentent. He wanted, as he noted on a memorandum from Kissinger, to aid the government of Lon Nol, and he ordered the CIA to open an official station in Phnom Penh. He asked Director Richard Helms to organize a pro-U.S., pro–Lon Nol propaganda campaign as soon as possible. In addition, Nixon asked the Pentagon for alternative scenarios in case he decided to retaliate against the Communist "invaders" in Cambodia. One suggestion was to send the Special Forces teams deeper into Cambodia; another was to expand the target area for Operation Menu; General Wheeler proposed that they organize a 30,000-man amphibious invasion against Sihanoukville, Cambodia's major port. As the crisis intensified, the Pentagon decided that massive escalation was the only answer. The Joint Chiefs sided with General Abrams in Saigon, who recommended a wider Cambodian air war and an allied ground invasion of eastern Cambodia.[30]

President Nixon took the situation in Cambodia as yet another challenge to his leadership. He was especially miffed because, that spring, the Senate rejected two proposed appointees to the Supreme Court (Clement Haynsworth and G. Harold Carswell). Cambodia was one way to get even with his opponents on Capitol Hill. "Those senators think they can push me around, but I'll show them who's tough," Nixon fumed. "The liberals are waiting to see Nixon let Cambodia go down the drain just the way Eisenhower let Cuba go down the drain."[31] Curiously, the President seemed to gain sustenance from private showings of his favorite movie, *Patton*. The way to overcome Communism, Nixon felt, was to strike out no matter what the odds or the costs. By doing so, he, like Patton, would probably save the day.[32]

By April 20, 1970, an unofficial countdown began. In response to a request by Lon Nol, $10 million of war materiel had already been shipped to Cambodia. Lon Nol's arms, however, had not stopped the antigovernment forces, which continued their drive toward Phnom Penh. As the situation became more desperate, Nixon and his advisers contemplated further action. Nixon threatened to slow down U.S. troop withdrawals from Vietnam unless the Vietcong guerrillas in Cambodia surrendered. The President also threatened North Vietnam. "If increased enemy action jeopardizes our remaining forces in Vietnam," Nixon warned, "I shall not hesitate to take strong and effective measures to deal with that situation."[33]

Before meeting with the National Security Council on April 22, the President sent Kissinger an important memorandum. The message was clear. "I think we need a bold move in Cambodia . . . to show that we stand with Lon Nol. . . . [The Communists] are romping in there, and the only government in Cambodia in the last twenty-five years that had the guts to take a pro-Western and pro-American stand is ready to fall. If I decide to take aggressive action," the President continued, Kissinger should summon "the lily-livered Ambassadors from our so-called friends in the world" and stress that their position on Cambodia would reveal "who our friends are." In any event, Nixon concluded, "I will talk to you about this after the NSC meeting."[34]

That afternoon, Nixon, Kissinger, Rogers, Laird, Spiro Agnew, Helms, and the Joint Chiefs debated the crisis in Cambodia. Three options emerged during that tense meeting. The United States could do nothing, it could direct a South Vietnamese invasion of the sanctuaries, or it could, in Kissinger's words, "neutralize all of the base areas . . . using whatever forces were necessary, . . . including American combat forces."[35] Of particular concern to the group were the Parrot's Beak and Fishhook sanctuaries, both northwest of Saigon, where the Communist Pentagon was supposedly located. These sanctuaries had already been devastated by fourteen months of secret B-52 attacks, but still the military believed that COSVN was intact and operational. The next logical step in a policy of escalation was a ground assault into Cambodia.

Nixon listened to the arguments of his inner circle and then decided that a huge ARVN force would invade the Parrot's Beak sanctuary on April 28, 1970. Without committing himself further, Nixon hinted that U.S. troops might be used to attack the Fishhook sanctuary. Until a final decision was reached, Kissinger would coordinate the administration's secret planning.[36]

Kissinger agreed wholeheartedly with Nixon's decision to apply massive force in Cambodia. In Kissinger's view, the emergence of Lon Nol had served to clarify the situation. By 1970 the war in Southeast Asia was

> a single war. . . . Strategically, Cambodia could not be considered a country separate from Vietnam. . . . [T]he enemy in [both countries] was the same one. Whatever forces we fought in Cambodia we would not have to fight in Vietnam and vice versa.[37]

To extend and escalate the war would strengthen the prospects for total victory.

Between April 22 and April 30, 1970, Kissinger held dozens of meetings with aides, advisers, and members of the National Security Council. Understandably, he wanted complete cooperation, almost blind allegiance, from those around him. Several NSC members, notably William Watts, Tony Lake, Larry Lynn, and Roger Morris, could not accept the idea of escalation and resigned. Kissinger railed against the "bleeding hearts." When William Safire asked if an invasion of Cambodia would not contradict the Nixon Doctrine, Kissinger replied, "We wrote the goddam doctrine, we can change it." He reminded his staff that "we are all the President's men" and that, during a crisis, it was necessary to stand firm and not buckle under the pressure. As Alexander Haig added, "The basic substance of all this is that we have to be tough.[38]

On the evening of April 26, Kissinger drafted and Nixon signed a directive authorizing the use of American troops in an attack against the Fishhook sanctuary. The next day, in response to an observation that the campuses of the nation would be in flames if the United States invaded Cambodia, Nixon ordered his inner circle to refrain from any criticism whatsoever. "If I decide to do it [invade Cambodia], I don't want to hear of it again. If I decide to do it, it will be because I have decided to pay the price."[39]

The President was anxious for immediate action, but Kissinger advised him to wait another day or two, in order to pacify the "doubting Thomases," especially the secretaries of state and defense. Rogers was concerned about congressional reaction if the White House invaded Cambodia without proper consultation. To ease such concern, Nixon asked Kissinger to consult and inform Senator Stennis. When Kissinger explained White House planning to Stennis, the senator, ever reliable and compliant, expressed no objections to an American thrust into Cambodia. Rogers was also worried, justifiably, about testifying before the Senate Foreign Relations Committee. He feared charges of perjury if he concealed plans for war against a neutral country. To solve this dilemma, Nixon and Kissinger settled on an ingenious ploy. The President simply retracted the directive he had already signed, instructed Rogers to deny allegations that a major escalation was planned, and then reinstated the directive after Rogers's congressional appearance. Relieved, apparently, by these maneuvers, Rogers supported the escalation of the war.[40]

Secretary of Defense Laird objected not to the idea of invading the sanctuaries, but only to the use of American troops. He advised the President to minimize direct U.S. involvement and concentrate instead on the South Vietnamese phase of the operation. Nixon rejected Laird's suggestion. As he later told Nelson Rockefeller, in characteristic language:

> the recommendation of the Department of Defense was the most pusillanimous little nit-picker I ever saw. "Just bite off the Parrot's Beak." I said you are going to have a hell of an uproar at home if you bite off the Beak. If you are going to take the heat, go for all the marbles. . . . I have made some bad decisions, but a good one this was: When you bite the bullet, bite it hard—go for the big play.[41]

Kissinger had reached the same conclusion, as he observed in his memoirs:

> With respect to the use of military force, [a President's] basic choice is to act or to refrain from acting. He will not be able to take away the moral curse of using force by employing it halfheartedly or incompetently. There are no rewards for exhibiting one's doubts in vacillation; statesmen get no prizes for failing with restraint. Once committed they must prevail. . . .[42]

On April 28, 1970, ARVN units crossed the Cambodian border and launched an attack against the Parrot's Beak sanctuary. Two nights later, on April 30, a combined United States/ARVN attack force entered the Fishhook region of Cambodia with orders to locate and destroy COSVN, the fortified Communist Pentagon. U.S. fighter-bombers accompanied each expedition. Air raids against Cambodia were no longer secret; Operation Menu was superseded by an escalated U.S. air war which, during the next three years, threatened most of Cambodia.[43]

In a televised speech on April 30, 1970, President Nixon announced that U.S. troops had entered Cambodia. Combative and openly belligerent, the President declared, with little justification, that the United States had scrupulously respected Cambodian neutrality during the past five years while North Vietnam occupied the border areas and created sanctuaries. Since the threat to American servicemen in Vietnam had grown to dangerous proportions, he had decided to strike out and dislodge the Communists. A military thrust was undertaken, according to Nixon, not for the purpose of expanding the war into Cambodia, but for the purpose of ending the war in Vietnam. It was a test of "our will and character" in a time of grave crisis:

> If, when the chips are down, the world's most powerful nation . . . acts like a pitiful, helpless giant, the forces of totalitarianism and anarchy will threaten free nations and free institutions throughout the world. If we fail to meet this challenge, all other nations will be on notice that despite its overwhelming power, the United States, when a real crisis comes, will be found wanting.[44]

A month later, Nixon proclaimed that the invasion of Cambodia was "the most successful operation of the Vietnam War." In fact, however, the COSVN was never discovered. U.S. troops expected to find a fortified bunker thirty feet underground with 5,000 officials directing the Communist war effort. Instead, all they encountered was scanty evidence of a mobile enemy headquarters that had already been moved deeper into Cambodia.[45] Allied forces engaged the local guerrillas, pounded Cambodia with B-52 raids, and destroyed a certain amount of supplies, including the rice harvested by Cambodian farmers for their families. That was all the military action. Yet Nixon and Kissinger repeatedly expressed great satisfaction with the operation. On June 30, 1970, their mission "complete," U.S. forces withdrew from Cambodia amidst great fanfare and television coverage.

Kissinger's account, in his memoirs, of what happened in the United States as a result of Nixon's Cambodian invasion is both interesting and revealing:

> The tidal wave of media and student criticism powerfully affected the Congress. . . . On June 30 the Senate approved the Cooper-Church amendment [forbidding the further use of American troops in Cambodia]. . . . The pattern was clear. . . . Senate opponents of the war would introduce one amendment after another, forcing the Administration into unending rearguard actions to preserve a minimum of flexibility for negotiations. Hanoi could only be encouraged to stall, waiting to harvest the results of our domestic dissent.
>
> The practical consequence was that in the absence of any serious alternative the government was left with only its own policy of capitulation. . . .
>
> The very fabric of government was falling apart. The Executive Branch was shell shocked. After all, their children and their friends' children took part in the demonstrations. Some 250 State Department employees, including 50 Foreign Service Officers, signed a statement objecting to Administration policy. . . . The President saw himself as a firm rock in this rushing stream. . . . Pretending indifference, he was deeply wounded by the hatred of the protesters. . . .
>
> Exhaustion was the hallmark of us all. . . . Despite the need to coordinate the management of the crisis, much of my own time was spent with unhappy, nearly panicky colleagues. . . .[46]

Opposition to the attack on Cambodia strengthened the antiwar movement:

> So we ended the Cambodian operation still on the long route out of Vietnam, confronting an implacable enemy and an equally implacable domestic opposition. . . .
>
> The ultimate victims of our domestic anguish were the gentle people of Cambodia.[47]

In effect, Kissinger argues that the Cambodian people were the victims of dissent in the United States. Nixon, no doubt, prefers the same interpretation. History will record, however, that the "gentle people of Cambodia" were the victims of sustained U.S. air operations. 539,129 tons of bombs were dropped on Cambodia up to the end of the bombing war on August 15, 1973; many of these bombs fell in 1973 after the Paris Peace Agreement and three years after the invasion of Cambodia.

The U.S. invasion and the bombing of Cambodia had devastating consequences. Even after the withdrawal of U.S. ground units, entire South Vietnamese divisions remained in Cambodia, where they unleashed a particularly violent racial war against the people of Cambodia. ARVN troops went on a rampage of rape, murder, and pillage. Neither congressional action nor U.S. protest was able to save Cambodia and its people. In addition, the Cambodian civil war, pitting the Khmer Rouge rebels against the forces of Lon Nol, continued, while North Vietnamese troops, no longer encamped on the borders, engaged Lon Nol's Cambodian army on several fronts. Meanwhile, massive U.S. bombing continued throughout Cambodia to bolster Lon Nol and to punish the Communists.

Lon Nol had become an American client. As soon as U.S. troops were withdrawn from Cambodia, Alexander Haig traveled to Phnom Penh to meet with Lon Nol. He found Cambodia's strong man visibly shaken and unsure. The Communists, he complained, instead of occupying the desolate border areas, had now spread out all across Cambodia. While Haig reassured Lon Nol that Nixon would send as much aid as possible, the Cambodian leader gazed out the window and wept; perhaps he understood that he was, in part, responsible for the destruction of Cambodia.

When Haig returned to Washington, planning began in earnest on how the United States could underwrite the war in Cambodia. The Pentagon recognized that Lon Nol was in deep trouble. His army lacked training and equipment, his officers were incompetent and corrupt, and his air force was obsolete. With the help of the Joint Chiefs, Haig devised a series of "quickfix" measures to bolster the Phnom Penh government.[48]

During the summer of 1970, $50 million was funneled secretly to Lon Nol and his generals. At the same time, the administration increased the direct military involvement of the United States in Cambodia. Tactical aircraft and B-52s ranged deeper into that country. Their pilots were free to bomb any targets they wanted, since nearly all reports were falsified or destroyed. The Pentagon also encouraged South Vietnamese attacks on Cambodia; South Vietnamese pilots bombed Cambodian villages, while ARVN units "behaved as if they were conquering a hostile nation, rather than helping a new

ally." President Nixon also wrote Lon Nol several encouraging letters, exhorting him to resist Communist advances and maintain a
pro-U.S. posture.[49]

By September 1970 the secret funds channeled to Lon Nol had run
out; Nixon was forced to turn to Congress. To protect what Secretary
Laird called "our already significant investment in terms of military
equipment and prestige," the White House insisted that Congress
appropriate an additional $260 million for military-assistance pro-
grams. Of that total, $60 million went to Cambodia.[50]

Clearly, Nixon and Kissinger wanted an aggressive strategy that
would save Lon Nol and secure the new battlefield in Southeast
Asia. On September 15, 1970, Kissinger recommended a plan to the
President. They should attempt to create an effective Cambodian
army, which, with South Vietnamese and Thai ground and air support, and American air support, could try and hold half of Cambodia
against the Communists. Laird felt that the plan was both too ambitious and too expensive, but Kissinger and the Joint Chiefs prevailed, securing the President's endorsement.

The plan was operationalized in National Security Decision Memorandum 89, "Cambodian Strategy," which committed the administration to a military solution in Cambodia. Because of the Cooper-
Church amendment, U.S. combat troops could not be used in
Cambodia, but almost every other weapon from the war in Vietnam
would play a role.[51]

The buildup of Lon Nol's army proceeded at a steady pace. The
Pentagon supplied weapons, uniforms, equipment, and vehicles to
an army that had no previous experience and, for many months,
actually went off duty at 3:00 every afternoon. When Kissinger issued another Decision Memorandum nine months later, calling on
Lon Nol to take the offensive in Cambodia, he asked the military
what Lon Nol would need to do the job. The answer: a fully
equipped army of 220,000 men costing $350 to $400 million a year.
Ignoring the issue of legality, Kissinger conferred with Nixon and
then approved the military's plan for the accelerated buildup of
Cambodian troops.[52]

It was already apparent, however, that the program was not effective. Their stress on quantity created a ridiculous situation in which
Cambodian commanders invented the names of imaginary new soldiers to meet their quotas, and then personally collected the salaries

of these phantom troops. Conscription squads roared down the streets of Phnom Penh, snatching males of any age; many such draftees were missing again before the day was over.

Even authentic increases in the size of Lon Nol's army meant nothing when government forces were put to the test. At the battle of Chenla II, for example, in late 1971, Cambodian soldiers walked into an obvious trap near Kompong Thom. The monsoons had flooded the fields, but Lon Nol, who retained personal control of the expedition, saw no reason to scout the low-lying areas or to protect the column's flanks. After the Cambodians opened up a front forty miles long and two feet wide, the North Vietnamese and Khmer Rouge counterattacked and decimated the government column.

Chenla II, a stunning defeat for Lon Nol's army, pointed to a major deficiency in U.S. strategy. The Cambodian army simply could not win the war. On occasion, individual Cambodians fought bravely and tenaciously, but the army as a whole was a failure. Leadership was almost nonexistent. The officer corps lacked imagination, intelligence, and experience. Officers ignored the chain of command and acted impulsively in battle.

After Chenla II, Lon Nol's own leadership abilities were called into question, and rumors of a coup abounded in Phnom Penh. Sirik Matak and others, aware that Lon Nol had suffered a stroke in April 1971, pleaded with the general to step aside or at least to surrender part of his power. But Lon Nol refused, and Washington supported his decision. As time passed, Lon Nol, exhibiting signs of mental illness, began to meddle constantly in the conduct of battles. At the same time, his political attitude grew more autocratic. He dismissed the National Assembly and assumed emergency dictatorial powers. Then he removed the chief of state and issued a new anti-Communist constitution. In June 1972, he rigged the presidential election and won a resounding, but fraudulent, victory.

Throughout this period, the United States never wavered in its support for Lon Nol. Kissinger described the general as the key to stability in Cambodia. The official position was that his overthrow would be contrary to U.S. interests in Southeast Asia.[53]

The Nixon-Kissinger strategy for Cambodia depended substantially on air operations. Initially designed to support Lon Nol's ground war, the air strikes gradually turned into a substitute for the ineffective Cambodian army. Under the Cooper-Church amendment, Nixon could authorize air strikes only to "interdict men and supplies en route to Vietnam." From the beginning, however, the President ignored this restriction on bombings in order to support Lon Nol's ground forces. In effect, he ordered an aggressive U.S. and RVNAF (South Vietnamese) air campaign in Cambodia. By substituting helicopters and attack planes for foot soldiers, as he had already done in Vietnam itself, Nixon maintained an intense level of combat while pretending that the war was winding down.

The air force began to extend the air war westward. Pilots referred to the new target area as "Freedom Deal," presumably because every village, field, or convoy inside the eastern half of Cambodia was considered a legitimate target. If U.S. bombs fell outside Freedom Deal, especially in the more populated areas of the Mekong Delta, reports were altered to conceal air force mistakes. Interservice rivalry developed between air force, navy and army bombers, all of whom staked a claim to the new war zone and contributed to the destruction. Nixon and Kissinger also encouraged Lon Nol and his generals to utilize B-52 strikes outside the Freedom Deal target area.

It was important, from Washington's perspective, to keep as many U.S. planes in the air as possible. A high sortie level demonstrated toughness to the North Vietnamese, and increased air action would also ease the sting of Vietnamization failures. When the South Vietnamese botched the invasion of Laos in February 1971, for example, bombing runs in Cambodia immediately picked up, and plans for new air raids were set. "The roof would come flying off the Capitol," Laird mused, "if they knew we were seriously considering flying large numbers of sorties in 1973 and 1974."[54] Escalation was less visible to the American people, but Nixon believed its message would be apparent to the enemy.

In 1971, more than 61,000 sorties (14 percent of all combat sorties in Southeast Asia) were flown over Cambodia. The upward climb continued until April 1972 when Hanoi launched its 1972 spring offensive, which tied down the bulk of America's air armada for the rest of the year. As a result, Cambodia was granted a reprieve from the incessant bombing of the previous three and a half years. The reprieve was only temporary; it ended in January 1973, when Washington and Hanoi signed the Paris agreement and implemented a shaky cease-fire in Viétnam. At that point, as William Colby admits, Cambodia became "the only game in town," and the bombing was resumed.[55]

The Paris agreement did not include a Cambodian cease-fire, because the United States would not compromise its support for Lon Nol. The North Vietnamese said that they had no control over the Khmer Rouge, who in any case would not recognize Lon Nol. In a not-very-persuasive demonstration of good faith, the United States asked Lon Nol to suspend offensive operations on January 28, 1973, one day before the Paris agreement went into effect. But Lon Nol's army had been on the defensive since its defeat at Chenla II, so suspending "offensive" operations was an empty gesture. When Kissinger rejected a possible meeting with Sihanouk, the nominal leader of the Cambodian rebels, the Khmer Rouge announced that its struggle against Lon Nol's government would continue.[56]

In turn, Nixon and Kissinger were not prepared to compromise. Alexander Haig visited Lon Nol and pledged continuing support for the Cambodian war effort. The U.S. ambassador to Cambodia promised that air power based in Thailand would be deployed whenever Lon Nol needed it. Even Vice-President Spiro Agnew assured Lon Nol of continuing military aid. Sustaining a friendly government in Phnom Penh, Agnew reported, was Washington's primary goal.[57] Following these words of reassurance, the White House ordered an escalation of the Cambodian bombing war on February 9, 1973. This decision killed what hope remained for a negotiated settlement and ushered in the final phase of Cambodia's destruction.

The United States Seventh Air Force shifted its headquarters from Vietnam to Thailand. Kissinger summoned Ambassador Swank to Bangkok and informed him that his embassy would coordinate the new bombing war in Cambodia. Swank in turn chose Tom Enders, deputy chief of mission, to handle the day-to-day conduct of the bombing campaign. Working with General John Cleland, ranking military officer in Cambodia, Enders set up an embassy command post and authorized wave after wave of B-52 strikes into the very heart of Cambodia. Requests from Lon Nol's generals were approved, regardless of the danger to and destruction of civilian lives and property.

During March 1973, B-52 bombers dropped 24,000 tons of bombs on Cambodia. The figure rose to 35,000 during April and 36,000 during May. This aerial campaign stirred criticism on Capitol Hill, but Kissinger assured Congress that Lon Nol needed U.S. air support. When the Senate Foreign Relations Committee sent an investigative team to Phnom Penh, it reported that "the political, military and economic performance of the Lon Nol government had reached an all-time low."[58] The bombing had done little to improve the situation, but it had caused tremendous suffering for the Cambodian people.

Unrest about the continuing air war (and about the growing Watergate scandal) provoked a congressional debate in May 1973. The debate centered around a proposed War Powers Bill which was designed to restrict the President's ability to wage secret war without the consent of Congress. Finally aroused, the House voted on May 10 to refuse a supplemental appropriation for the bombing war in Cambodia. It was the first time Congress had denied funds for Southeast Asia.

On June 25, 1973, both houses of Congress passed an amendment to stop the bombing of Cambodia by the end of that month. Nixon immediately vetoed the amendment, claiming that air raids were the only means of enforcing the Paris peace agreement. He pleaded with Congress:

> After more than ten arduous years of suffering and sacrifice . . . it would be nothing short of tragic if this great accomplishment, bought with the blood of so many Asians and Americans, were to be undone now by Congressional action.[59]

Conservatives mustered enough support to sustain Nixon's veto, but Senator Mansfield warned that similar amendments would be passed "again and again and again, until the will of the people prevails."[60] Nixon finally agreed to compromise with the Congress. Both sides set August 15, 1973, as the deadline for a bombing halt.[61]

During the remaining forty-five days, the administration literally buried Cambodia in bombs. Tactical bombing increased 21 percent, and B-52 raids increased to the maximum level possible. By mid-August the tonnage of bombs dropped on a country without military or industrial targets had reached frightening proportions. The campaign that began with Operation Breakfast ended with the final assault in the summer of 1973. "On Air Force maps of Cambodia, thousands of square miles of densely populated, fertile areas [were] marked black from the inundation."[62] Thousands—perhaps millions—of innocent Cambodians lost their lives because Nixon and Kissinger insisted on victory for Lon Nol.

Congress put an end to Nixon's ability to wage war on Cambodia, but by then the country had been transformed. Its farms and villages had been devastated by U.S. bombs. Its economy had been undermined by U.S. aid. The country's three leading exports—rice, fish, and rubber—were no longer even being harvested. Inflation was a staggering 250 percent a year. Cambodia's capital, once a charming city of 600,000, now bulged with a population in excess of 3 million. The refugees from the bombings congregated in shanty towns and run-down slums where food was scarce, health care nonexistent, and prostitution a way of life.

The military government of Lon Nol, wallowing in graft and corruption, did little that was effective to defend the country. Huge amounts of U.S. aid went directly into the pockets of Lon Nol's officer corps. Weapons of all kinds poured into Phnom Penh, but the Cambodian army was totally unprepared to use—much less maintain—the sophisticated weapons systems Washington forced it to accept. Instead of concentrating on the war, Lon Nol worried about whether his title should be "Supreme Commander" or "Commander in Chief." Instead of taking the offensive against the enemy, Cambodian units devoted their energy to expanding the black market in U.S. supplies and equipment. The Khmer Rouge became one of the profiteers' best customers.[63]

In the jungle, the Khmer Rouge watched and waited. The rebels numbered only 60,000 when the bombing stopped, but they were well disciplined and fought according to a clear and carefully thought-out strategy. They attacked government outposts and destroyed vital roads and bridges. They conducted limited offensives, seeking ultimately to surround Phnom Penh and force Lon Nol's surrender.

During 1974 an attitude of fanaticism began to appear within Khmer Rouge ranks. Radicals like Saloth Sar (later to be called Pol Pot), Ieng Sary, and Son Sen gradually ousted the moderates and broke all ties with Hanoi; in their view, the North Vietnamese had betrayed the revolution by signing the Paris agreement. The radicals also began to disassociate themselves from Prince Sihanouk and to engage in terrorist activities. They experimented with "purification" techniques: emptying the cities, banning religion and family, and eliminating undesirables.

The United States continued to reject any compromise settlement for Cambodia. John Gunther Dean, who replaced Swank as ambassador to Phnom Penh, argued for negotiations and pointed out that Sihanouk was still willing to meet with Kissinger. But Kissinger refused. He told Dean, "Your job is to improve the military situation to enable us to negotiate from strength. I don't want to hear about Laos-type compromises."[64] When French President Giscard d'Estaing broached the possibility of bringing Sihanouk back to Phnom Penh before the radicals claimed total victory, Kissinger sabotaged the proposal by revealing it to the press. Similarly, before his resignation, President Nixon wrote to a sick Lon Nol:

> I am convinced that under your vigorous leadership and that of your government, the republic will succeed. . . . The United States remains determined to provide maximum possible assistance to your heroic self-defense and will continue to stand side by side with the republic in the future as in the past.[65]

On New Year's Day, 1975, the Khmer Rouge launched what turned out to be the final offensive of the war. All across Cambodia the rebels shelled government enclaves, severed transportation and communication links, and engaged the remnants of Lon Nol's army. As a last resort, the government appealed for U.S. intervention. Before Washington could respond, the Khmer Rouge surrounded Phnom Penh, seized the Mekong River, and fought its way to the outskirts of the capital. There the offensive stalled as disguised U.S. planes, prohibited from flying combat missions, began a massive seven-week airlift into Phnom Penh.

Shipments of fuel and ammunition kept Lon Nol's tottering regime alive, but the airlift did little to help the frantic refugees. Thousands of malnourished children died as food supplies ran out. Thousands more, unable to receive proper medical care, fell victim to disease. Still, the White House announced, "We seek only to keep them alive and fighting through the remainder of this fiscal year."[66] When the President requested emergency funds, Congress sent a fact-finding mission to Phnom Penh, headed by Congressman Pete McCloskey of California. The team came away convinced that U.S. policy toward Cambodia was the main culprit behind the unfolding tragedy. As

McCloskey stated:

> . . . I can only tell you my emotional reaction, getting into that country, if I could have found the military or State Department leader who has been the architect of this policy, my instinct would be to string him up. Why they are there and what they have done to the country is greater evil than we have done to any country in the world, and wholly without reason, except for our own benefit to fight against the Vietnamese.[67]

At the end of March 1975, sources indicate that Lon Nol accepted a bribe of $500,000 and, on April 1, boarded a plane for Hawaii, never to return. Four days later, Ambassador Dean asked permission to evacuate U.S. personnel, but Kissinger refused. In tears, Dean told a British journalist, "I've got orders to fight to the last Cambodian."[68] By April 11 the Khmer Rouge broke through the last government defenses and threatened to seize the city before the embassy could be evacuated. At last Kissinger relented. The next morning, 82 Americans, 159 Cambodians, and 35 "third-country nationals" boarded U.S. helicopters and left Phnom Penh. Ambassador Dean, carrying the American flag, supervised the orderly evacuation. For all intents and purposes, the war was over.[69]

On April 17, 1975, the Khmer Rouge marched into Phnom Penh. Unsmiling, dressed in black, the victorious rebels wasted little time implementing their radical plans. With the end of the U.S. role in Cambodia, the food sources for the most part were gone. It appears from U.S. Embassy reports that at least 1 million people might have died from starvation in the three-week period after the U.S. evacuation. The Khmer Rouge and Pol Pot therefore faced this possibility with great brutality. It was almost like an Adolph Hitler–type of "final solution." The millions of people of Phnom Penh were given only a few hours to gather their possessions and evacuate the city. Soldiers dragged the unwilling from their homes and the sick from the hospitals. Another long march began: the sick, the lame, women, children—everyone. Those who could not keep up were killed. The survivors were herded into collectivized work camps to provide food for the population. It was Pol Pot's theory that modernization was the enemy, so he forced a return to the land. Merchants, teachers, former government workers were all marked for execution because they were a drain on those who worked the land. The infirm and unfit were eliminated. The cycle of brutal and purposeless blundering was complete.

:13

THE DEVASTATION OF LAOS
1969–73

When Richard Nixon came into power, the CIA had been deeply and secretly involved in Laos for almost twenty years. The CIA had established its own air force and army, and had waged a secret war in an independent country without the knowledge or consent of the American people or Congress.

The Laotian story is best told by first describing the background of this little-known country. Laos, a landlocked country in the interior of Southeast Asia, had a population of 3 million prior to U.S. involvement there. The country had been ruled by France since the late 1800s, first as several principalities and then, after World War II, as a unified kingdom. Laos, under French control, was the least exploited and therefore the least developed region of Indochina. It was a peaceful country with little economic or strategic value, and, unlike the Vietnamese, the Laotians never rebelled against the French.

After Laos was granted its autonomy by the French, a political cleavage developed in the country. For the next twenty-five years, two half-brothers, both princes of the royal family, competed for control of Laos. Prince Souvannaphouma and Prince Souphanouvong were both ardent nationalists, but they disagreed about the political future of their country. Souvannaphouma wanted Laos to remain neutral in international affairs, whereas Souphanouvong wanted Laos to support the Communist revolutions underway in China and Vietnam. Souvannaphouma began to work closely with French officials who had remained in the Laotian administrative capital of Vientiane. Souphanouvong, on the other hand, moved into the countryside and formed a national Communist movement known as the Pathet Lao.

In the early 1950s, Souvannaphouma became the official prime minister of a French-backed government in Laos, while Souphanouvong continued to build a grass-roots guerrilla movement in the northern part of the country. All remainded quiet until 1953, when the Vietnamese war spilled over the Laotian border. Vietminh forces under Ho Chi Minh entered northern Laos, where they joined up with Souphanouvong and the Pathet Lao to fight the French. Together, they captured most of northern Laos and threatened the royal capital of Luang Prabang.

The fighting in Laos stopped temporarily when the French were defeated at Dien Bien Phu. After this defeat, the Geneva Conference was held in 1954. Although it dealt primarily with the Vietnam conflict, a compromise was also worked out for Laos. The parties agreed that Laos would be neutral and that all foreign armies would leave the country.

The Geneva Conference of 1954 had attempted to secure a peaceful, neutral, and demilitarized Laos, free of foreign troops and control. This solution was not acceptable to U.S. Secretary of State John Foster Dulles. He wanted Laos firmly bound in the pro-Western camp, rather than neutral.

> Secretary Dulles interpreted the Geneva Accords not as providing for a neutralist solution in Indochina but as a "deal" in which, by handing over half of Vietnam to the Communists, he had "eliminated the possibility of a domino effect in Southeast Asia" by "saving" Laos and Cambodia.[1]

He attempted to tie Laos to SEATO, barely two months after the Geneva Accords were signed. Then, U.S. economic aid, which had been trickling into the country since 1951, was greatly increased. Finally, under pressure from Dulles, the Pentagon agreed to set up a 25,000-man Royal Laotian Army. In violation of the Geneva Accords, Dulles sent U.S. military advisers into Laos to train the newly formed army. By claiming that these advisers, who worked in civilian clothes, were only State Department "observers," Dulles managed to camouflage the U.S. program of military assistance. In addition, Dulles worked to insure that a pro-American regime secured power, one that did not attempt to involve Communists in the government.

Even as he accepted U.S. aid, Souvannaphouma was attempting to open talks with his half-brother Souphanouvong; it was the first of many efforts to end the threat of civil war by making the government a true coalition. But before he could make any progress, Souvannaphouma was forced out of power by events touched off by the assassination of his neutralistic minister of defense, Kou Voravong. Many suspect that this assassination might have been engineered by the CIA. Whether or not that is true, the outcome was certainly just what the State Department wanted. The pro-American prime minister, Katay Don Sasorith, replaced Souvannaphouma, broke off talks with the Communist Pathet Lao, and seemed able to save Laos from Communism.

But U.S. aims in Laos soon suffered setbacks. In December 1955 the elections called for under the Geneva Accords returned Prince Souvannaphouma to power. He immediately announced that his government would reopen talks with the Pathet Lao. Secretary Dulles's attempts to interfere were ineffectual, and Souvannaphouma's flirtations with the Communist regimes in Peking and Hanoi "sent shivers of dread through the United States and Thailand."[2] Both countries feared that Souvannaphouma would sell out to the Communists.[3]

Finally, in November 1957, the two half-brothers reached an agreement to integrate the Pathet Lao into the royal government. All Pathet Lao military forces were either disbanded or merged into the Royal Laotian Army. A new government of "National Union" was formed, with two cabinet posts for the Pathet Lao. New elections were set for 1958. This coalition government was a neutralist government of the type envisioned by the Geneva Conference.

The elections of 1958 were designed by Souvannaphouma and Souphanouvong to complete the merger of the royal government and the Pathet Lao. But U.S. policymakers were afraid of free elections in Laos just as they were afraid of free elections in Vietnam. They feared that a government sympathetic to Communism might be elected. Consequently, the U.S. counterinsurgency attempted to rig the election through "Operation Booster Shot." In an attempt to buy votes, for example, U.S. officials flooded rural Laos with food and other gifts. When the vote was in, however, the Pathet Lao and their allies had won thirteen out of twenty-one contested seats, giving them a majority.[4] This result was a blow to U.S. policy. As J. Graham Parsons, U.S. ambassador to Laos, told a congressional committee, "I struggled for 16 months to prevent a coalition."[5]

Alarmed by the results of the election, the United States set out to topple the newly elected government of Laos. The United States withheld aid payments, making it very difficult for the coalition government to function. The CIA entered the Laotian political arena, seeking to form a political bloc from a group of young national-assembly members. This right-wing bloc forced Souvannaphouma out of power on July 23, 1958, and installed pro-Western Phoui Sananikone as the new prime minister. Sananikone immediately formed a new government and ousted Souphanouvong and the other Pathet Lao member from the cabinet.[6]

Prime Minister Sananikone quickly abolished democratic rule and won the right to rule by decree. He used his power to embark on an anti-Communist crusade. Government agents began to persecute the Pathet Lao soldiers who had been integrated into the Royal Laotian Army. Several battalions escaped and returned to their jungle headquarters to await the arrival of Prince Souphanouvong. But before the prince could rejoin them, Sananikone arrested him along with all other Pathet Lao leaders who had remained in Vientiane.

During the summer of 1959, the Pathet Lao forces went on the offensive in the northern provinces of Laos. The CIA encouraged the Laotian government to call the offensive a North Vietnamese invasion. The Agency then used the fighting as a rationale for reinforcing its own personnel, thus extending its operations in Laos. Journalists from all over the world began to converge on Laos to cover the "invasion." Joseph Alsop, for example, arrived in Laos and wrote immediately of the massive attack on Laos by at least three and perhaps five battalions of enemy troops from North Vietnam.

After the death of Secretary Dulles, the U.S. Department of State was unable to maintain close control over the efforts in Laos. It appears that the CIA was now in more complete control of the Laotian operation. Its private airline, known as Air America, became more active, and there were even some U.S. Air Force pilots operating in Laos.[7]

In late 1959, the puppet government of Laos went so far as to lodge a complaint with the United Nations about the so-called North Vietnamese invasion. The UN responded by sending an investigative team to Laos. While it was at work, press reports continued to flow out of Laos describing fierce battles between Royal Lao and North Vietnamese forces. The reports became more and more absurd, culminating, as Bernard Fall pointed out, in the "assertion that no one else but Red Chinese Field Marshal Peng Te-Huai was masterminding Communist operations in Laos and that Red Chinese troops had captured a Lao Army post."[8] When the UN investigation was completed, the truth finally emerged; there was no evidence of a North Vietnamese invasion.[9]

These findings left the CIA in an awkward position. With no Communist invasion, there was no reason for an American military buildup in Laos. The Agency sought a scapegoat, and on Christmas Day, 1959, a violent coup toppled Prime Minister Sananikone and brought a new face onto the scene. The new strongman was Phoumi Nosavan, a dictatorial general whom the CIA called "our boy." Nosavan took control of the government at a key moment, since new elections were scheduled for April 1960. With the help of the CIA, election returns were falsified. For example, in one province, known to be a Pathet Lao stronghold, the government candidate received 18,189 votes to only 4 for his opponent. The elections gave a legal facade to the regime of CIA-backed General Nosavan, and U.S. policy seemed to be successful. Yet 1960 proved to be a most unsettled year as Nosavan battled with his political opponents and resorted to military actions to retain control.

In April 1961 the United States, under President Kennedy, and the Soviet Union orchestrated a cease-fire and convened a new Geneva Conference to resolve the conflict in Laos. The proceedings at the conference were often interrupted by violations of the cease-fire. Nosavan's position deteriorated sharply, and Secretary of Defense Robert McNamara persuaded Kennedy to send 5,000 troops to northeast Thailand, ostensibly to defend the Thai border against the Communists.[10] Despite several such incidents, the Geneva Conference reached an agreement on July 23, 1962; a neutral coalition government would rule Laos. Within a few weeks, a new coalition government was formed in Vientiane with Prince Souvannaphouma as prime minister. Prince Souphanouvong of the Pathet Lao and General Phoumi Nosavan were to serve as deputy prime ministers.[11]

The 1962 Geneva agreement, however, was not the end of U.S. involvement in Laos but the beginning of a new phase. As Roger Hilsman, assistant secretary of state for Far Eastern affairs, admitted: "We all understood perfectly well [it] was just the starting gun."[12] This time the United States would insure that Prince Souvannaphouma would be on the American side, to help isolate the Pathet Leo and defeat them more easily. The State Department, therefore,

quickly recognized Souvannaphouma's coalition government and resumed the flow of aid. Washington also resumed its role with the
Royal Laotian Army, and placed Phoumi Nosavan in charge of defense. In effect, Prince Souvannaphouma slowly became a dependent of the United States. As a result, by April 1963, the Pathet Lao
began to fight again, and the civil war in Laos resumed.[13]

For more than five years, American involvement in the Laotian
civil war was covert, but it was nevertheless very real. The CIA
began to recruit, as a private army, hill people known as the
Hmong.[14] These hill people, whose simple culture revolved around
agriculture and hunting, began to receive food and goods supplied
by the CIA and delivered by its private air line, Air America. The
CIA then relocated the Hmong tribes into mountain redoubts and
organized their young men into a formidable fighting force. These
new soldiers were at first delighted to be given all the advantages
that the CIA made possible. The older tribe members, living off the
subsidies of the CIA, were in no position to make an effective protest.

Soon all the Hmong lived in these mountain fortresses, which
were located in territory controlled by the Pathet Lao. They became
entirely dependent on the CIA for food and supplies. They could not
disagree with CIA policies because there was nowhere else for them
to go. Their ancestral villages had been abandoned or destroyed, and
the areas where they lived became, in fact, mountain prisons.

From 1962 to 1964, the CIA built the Hmong tribes into a large
guerrilla army which stabbed repeatedly at Communist positions in
northern Laos. According to William Colby:

> The CIA was authorized to revive, supply and increase the tribal units
> it had started to build before the Geneva Accords. Moreover, it was
> authorized to send its harassing parties deep into areas "controlled" by
> North Vietnamese to locate its depots, ambush its trucks, mine its roads,
> and mortar its outposts. The tribal patrols . . . were airlifted to battle in
> Air America's helicopters.[15]

The Hmong fought bravely against impossible odds, unaware that
the CIA often sent them on suicide missions from which they were
not expected to return. They had no concept of Laos as a nation, or of
Communism as a form of government, nor did they understand politically why they were fighting.

After 1964, when the United States stepped up its direct military involvement throughout Southeast Asia, the role of the Hmong tribes began to change. They began to take on the characteristics of a more conventional fighting force. More tribesmen chose to wear uniforms. Their weapons became more sophisticated. The number of airfields serviced by Air America grew to more than 300. Yet the major difference between 1962 and 1965 was the influx of foreigners to fight the Pathet Lao. The CIA brought Thai forces into the war to fly bombing missions against them. U.S. military advisers poured into Laos to lead the Royal Laotian Army into battle. The Hmong had to learn how to coordinate their ground attacks with air raids by U.S. jets. They also had to learn how to take part in large military operations involving many different units. "Three Arrows," a sweeping maneuver in July 1965, was just such an operation.

Even though foreign troops were brought in, the CIA war in Laos always revolved around the Hmong tribesmen who fought the Pathet Lao continuously for more than eight years. By 1968, nearly an entire generation of Hmong tribesmen had been killed; almost all males between the ages of eighteen and thirty-five were gone. The tribes were forced to use small boys to continue the war, but, even then, they did not call a halt. It appears that this quiet, peaceful race of people had been used.

Years after the war in Vietnam was over and the Communists had prevailed not only in Vietnam but also in Laos, the few survivors of the Hmong tribes were refugees, persecuted by the victorious Pathet Lao. The Hmong had nowhere to go; their villages had been destroyed, they had lost the skills of hunting and farming, and the United States gave them little, if any, assistance.

The CIA remained in full charge of clandestine U.S. activities in Laos throughout the Johnson presidency. Even the bombing in Laos fell under its jurisdiction. Using Thai or Air America pilots, the CIA harassed the Pathet Lao at every opportunity. The CIA was able to run a show in Laos because President Johnson focused almost exclusively on North Vietnam. Most of the United States Air Force bombers used against North Vietnam flew from bases in Thailand, but Laos was all but ignored until 1968.[16]

The activities in Laos were also substantially ignored by Congress. For some reason, Congress viewed the CIA as off limits for any investigation. William Colby wrote that

occasional attempts to establish new committees to supervise [the] CIA
. . . were regularly voted down. . . . And when Senator Leverett
Saltonstall [for example] expressed his "reluctance, if you will, to seek
information and knowledge on subjects which I personally, as a Member of Congress and as a citizen, would rather not have, . . ." Senator
Mike Mansfield replied that "The Senator is to be commended." In
short, the Congress was satisfied to consider the CIA the particular
preserve of the Executive branch, a tool for the President alone to use
as he saw fit . . . and it voted the Agency its funds with little or no
discussion about the kinds of operations for which those funds were
used.[17]

But J. William Fulbright remarked:

We got along pretty well in this country for a long time without any
interest in Laos at all. . . . What is there about Laos that justifies the
spending of a billion dollars? . . . If we have any sense left we ought to
liquidate the mistake [of replacing the French there] in the most efficient manner we can and leave it there. . . . I do not think it is of any
consequence today whether they [the North Vietnamese] control it or
not. . . . If I could get up on the floor and say . . . how ridiculous this is,
a lot of my colleagues would say, "For goodness' sakes, this is nonsense
throwing [deleted] millions a year pretty nearly down a rat hole."[18]

During the closing months of the Johnson administration, Johnson
authorized the U.S. Air Force to begin an intensive bombing of Laos.
When, in March 1968, LBJ called a temporary bombing halt against
North Vietnam, the air force began to bomb Laos. The war there was
still relatively secret. There were no military targets of any value in
the country, but as the U.S. deputy chief of missions in Laos stated,
"Well, we had all those planes sitting around and couldn't just let
them stay there with nothing to do."[19]

The devastation in Laos certainly equaled that inflicted upon Vietnam from 1965 to 1972. Air force jets bombed villages and farms,
forcing hundreds of thousands of civilians to flee into the jungle or to
live in caves. Another 600,000 peasants became refugees in government camps.

[T]hese people speak most of 1969, after the bombing halt in North
Vietnam and the diversion of jets into Laos. During this period jets
came over daily, bombing both day and night, dropping 600-pound
bombs, delayed-action bombs, napalm, phosphorus bombs and . . . an-
tipersonnel bombs. They say that American jets . . . bombed both the
villages and their outskirts, that they themselves spend most of the time
in holes or caves, and [that] they suffered numerous civilian casualties.

Everything was attacked—buffaloes, cows, rice fields, schools, temples, and tiny shelters erected outside the villages.[20]

The bombing was mindless, devastating, and without military justification. Militarists with little understanding of Laotian politics simply lumped Laos into the same category as Vietnam and applied the same logic of saving the Laotians by destroying them. One official actually declared that

> for the country finally to make some progress, everything would have to be leveled. The inhabitants would have to be reduced to zero and rid of their traditional culture, which is blocking everything.[21]

In that spirit the air war raged over Laos.

> The inhabitants ask themselves the reasons for this deluge of fire and steel. "I don't even know where America is," says a peasant woman whose daughter has just been killed and who has lost all her belongings. [Another] peasant remarked: "Before, I understood nothing about what was said against American aid, against the United States. After the raids on my village, I know what they mean." Everything American, far and wide, is hated by the people.[22]

Rumors about a possible U.S. invasion of Laos began to circulate in late 1970. At that point, as the American people emerged from the shock of Nixon's invasion of Cambodia, the tales of bombing and secret warfare in Laos began to make sense. Nixon defended the bombing campaign, calling it a firm deterrent to the success of the Pathet Lao. Yet as Branfman and others have shown, the

> air war probably has been—on the whole—militarily counterproductive [in Laos]. . . . In early 1965, about 30 percent of the young men volunteered for the Pathet Lao army in the Plain of Jars area. Five years later [after years of heavy bombing] volunteers were in the order of 95 percent. The attitude was "better to die fighting than to die hiding from the bombs."[23]

In his *Memoirs*, Richard Nixon noted that during the Kennedy administration he had been disappointed that JFK did not desire to become militarily involved in Laos. At the beginning of the Johnson administration Nixon believed that "we should 'quarantine' the war in Vietnam by using our air and sea power to close off outside interference from Laos."[24]

Once Richard Nixon became President, the opportunity to invade Laos, despite a congressional prohibition against using any U.S. forces for such a purpose, seemed irresistible. The bombing campaign during 1969 and 1970 had failed to close the labyrinth of paths and small trails making up the Ho Chi Minh Trail. So the Pentagon asked for the chance to get the job done once and for all. Calling the trail a "lucrative" target, the generals proposed a ground assault across Vietnam's border into Laos.[25]

The American people had no idea that Nixon and the Pentagon were planning a new invasion. Throughout 1970 the State Department increased its propaganda campaign. The air force increased its bombing of the Ho Chi Minh Trail. Then, on March 6, 1970, the President made a major speech about Laos in which he finally admitted two startling facts: that the United States was already bombing *all* of Laos, not just the trail, and that, in addition, the United States was financing the unpopular government of Prince Souvannaphouma. These actions, according to Nixon, were necessary to protect American lives in Vietnam and to meet North Vietnam's military escalation in Laos.[26]

There were some North Vietnamese troops in Laos, but the vast majority never left the border areas where the Ho Chi Minh Trail was located. These forces had been sent to guard the trail when the CIA began its secret war in Laos, and their numbers had increased only after the United States began full-scale bombing of all of Indochina. There was, in fact, no invasion on a significant scale of northern Laos by North Vietnam. The war there remained essentially a civil war, fought by the rebel Pathet Lao against the U.S.-supported Souvannaphouma government in Vientiane. Yet, in his speech, Nixon was seeking the support of the American people for the bombing of Laos, and for the invasion which was to follow.

By early 1971, military planners thought the time ripe for a large-scale invasion of Laos. Under orders from Nixon and Kissinger, they ironed out the details of an operation designed to cut the Ho Chi Minh Trail and smash the Communist sanctuaries in Laos. The President wanted to use American ground troops in the invasion, but Congress had foreclosed that option by the passage of the Cooper-Church amendment. So the invasion would have to take place using only ARVN ground troops.[27]

The Pentagon ordered U.S. forces to cover ARVN's rear, but to

remain on South Vietnam's side of the border. An exception was
made for U.S. airmen, whose participation was allowed by Congress.
As Marvin and Bernard Kalb pointed out:

> Once again, as in the case of Cambodia, this air support was critical;
> without it—without U.S. planes bombing, strafing, ferrying ARVN
> troops, hauling heavy artillery, transporting supplies and food—the op-
> eration could not have moved one foot across the border.[28]

"One foot" was about as far as the ARVN got. The invasion began
on February 8, 1971. Approximately 20,000 South Vietnamese troops
pushed across the border and set their sights on Tchepone, a town
twenty miles inside Laos. Despite a massive pounding of eastern
Laos by American bombers, the ARVN made little headway in the
first phase of the operation, bogging down in rain, mud, and fog.
When the weather cleared on February 17, the Vietcong surprised
the American rear guard in South Vietnam and easily cut the main
supply line behind the ARVN invaders. Then North Vietnamese
units, using tanks for the first time, counterattacked inside Laos and
overran each newly established ARVN position. Faced with widespread defeat, the ARVN had to be evacuated by its U.S. protectors at
the end of February 1971.

The second phase of ARVN's attack only accelerated the disaster.
On March 4, U.S. helicopters, loaded to the brim with South Vietnamese ground forces, leapfrogged the enemy strongpoints and
landed the invaders near the target of Tchepone. Only four days
later, on March 8, 1971, units from Hanoi's army easily forced the
South Vietnamese troops to evacuate Tchepone.[29]

As the North Vietnamese continued their counteroffensive, the
ARVN continued to abandon its positions inside Laos. Despite intensive U.S. air support, the ARVN was soundly defeated. The invasion was a failure, and the ARVN retreat was literally a rout. The
ARVN force of almost 25,000 suffered casualties to the tune of 1,445
dead and 4,016 wounded. The humiliation was viewed on television
by millions of Americans. Even with massive air support and the
direction of the Pentagon, they had failed miserably.[30]

Kissinger's and Nixon's description of both the events and the
results of the Laotian invasion are remarkable. In his *Memoirs*, published in late 1979, Nixon gave his version of the action. He recounted that after the successful Cambodian invasion in 1970, heavy

arms and supplies came overland through Laos and down the Ho Chi Minh Trail. Strangely, he contended that the invasion of Cambodia, which took place in March 1970, was successful, when by December of that same year it was evident that "Laos was clogged with men and supplies, the bulk of which would be moved into Cambodia for a 1971 spring offensive."[31]

Nixon's explanation of the Laos invasion is most revealing:

> Because of the problem of American domestic opinion and because the South Vietnamese wanted to prove how successful Vietnamization had been, we decided that the operation would be an ARVN exercise; the United States would supply only air cover and artillery support. The principal American contribution would be ferrying troops and supplies by helicopter, gunship support, and B-52 raids. Even the operation's codename was Vietnamese: Lam Son 719.[32]

A cogent example of Nixonian logic is his subsequent explanation of the ARVN's defeat, which he nevertheless called a substantial success:

> The South Vietnamese forces quickly recovered from these initial setbacks, and most of the military purposes of Lam Son were achieved within the first few weeks as the Communists were deprived of the capacity to launch an offensive against our forces in South Vietnam in 1971.
>
> In view of the operation's substantial success and because of signs that the Communists were trying to prepare a major counteroffensive, the ARVN commanders decided to withdraw early. On March 18 they began what was to have been a strategic retreat. Our air support was inadequate, however, and under severe enemy pounding some of the ARVN soldiers panicked. It took only a few televised films of ARVN soldiers clinging to the skids of our evacuation helicopters to reinforce the widespread misconception of the ARVN forces as incompetent and cowardly.

Nixon finally admitted that

> the net result was a military success but a psychological defeat, both in South Vietnam, where morale was shaken by media reports of the retreat, and in America, where suspicions about the possibility of escalation had been aroused and where news pictures undercut confidence in the success of Vietnamization and the prospect of ending the war.

Nixon sought aid from Kissinger when he wrote:

I still agree with Kissinger's assessment of Lam Son at the end of March 1971 when he said, "If I had known before it started that it was going to come out exactly the way it did, I would still have gone ahead with it."[33]

However, Kissinger concluded:

It was a splendid project on paper. Its chief drawback, as events showed, was that it in no way accorded with Vietnamese realities. South Vietnamese divisions had never conducted major offensive operations against a determined enemy outside Vietnam and only rarely inside. They would be doing it this time without American advisers because these were barred by the Cooper-Church amendment. The same amendment proscribed even the American officers who guided our tactical airstrikes, thus sharply reducing the effectiveness of our air support. . . . The South Vietnamese divisions were simply not yet good enough for such a complex operation as the one in Laos.[34]

By the spring of 1971, the invasion of Laos was history. It was the second largest ground operation of the entire war up to 1971, surpassed only by the invasion of Cambodia in 1970. The results were the same as in Cambodia. Nixon's invasion pushed the North Vietnamese away from the Ho Chi Minh Trail and deeper into Laos. The North Vietnamese joined forces with the local guerrillas, the civil war intensified, and thousands of innocent Laotian peasants died. The intensified fighting removed what hope existed that Souvannaphouma's government and the Pathet Lao might reach a compromise in their civil war; such a compromise had seemed likely in January 1971. In addition, the joint U.S./ARVN action into Laos sparked another American project, the importation of troops from Thailand to fight the Pathet Lao.[35]

Laos was now consumed by war; its future was no brighter than that of Vietnam or Cambodia. In all three countries bombing and invasion had been a way of life. With Nixon in control, the United States was at war in all of Indochina.

The invasion of Laos should have exposed the fallacy of the contention that Vietnamization would save South Vietnam and allow the United States to withdraw. Laos revealed that Vietnamization was nothing but an exercise in semantics, an effort to create reality by publicizing a word. The United States made every effort to support its client regimes, by equipping their forces with tanks, helicopters, artillery, planes, small weapons, and ammunition, but to no avail.

The U.S.-supported troops not only lacked experience and leadership, but most of them also lacked a will to fight and die. On the other hand, the peasant soldiers fighting against them believed they were fighting for their freedom as well as to expel external aggressors. History will record how many years and thousands of additional deaths later, the Laotians finally achieved the right to rule their country without outside interference.

:14

THE NIXON WAR AT HOME
1969–73

> . . . [W]e were confronted by public protests and
> demonstrations and quickening demands in the media
> and the Congress for unilateral concessions in the
> negotiations. They had one common theme: The obstacle
> to peace was not Hanoi but their own government's
> inadequate dedication to peace.
>
> Future generations may find it difficult to visualize the
> domestic convulsion that the Vietnam war induced. . . .
>
> The very fabric of government was falling apart. The
> Executive Branch was shell-shocked. After all, their
> children and their friends' children took part in the
> demonstrations. . . .
>
> Exhaustion was the hallmark of us all. I had to move
> from my apartment ringed by protesters into the
> basement of the White House to get some sleep.
> —*Henry Kissinger[1]*

On January 18 and 20, 1969, 7,000 activists gathered in Washington to protest Nixon's inauguration. Led by the National Mobilization Committee to End the War in Vietnam, the demonstrators called for a mass protest against "another four years of war, political repression, poverty and racism."[2] For three days, the activists organized rallies, listened to speeches, and broadcast their suspicions about Richard Nixon.

The new President, they argued, had not repudiated the war policies of his predecessor. Moreover, he had refused to discuss, let alone reveal, his secret plan for peace. As Kissinger acknowledged, the protest sprang from a deep conviction that "the obstacle to peace was not Hanoi but their own government's inadequate dedication to peace."[3] On signs and banners, the demonstrators printed their warning: "Nixon's the One—#1 War Criminal."

On January 20, as Nixon delivered his inaugural address, groups of protesters lined the parade route from the Capitol to the White House. When the Presidential limousine passed, they chanted antiwar slogans and waved homemade flags. Except for one incident where smoke bombs landed in the street, the demonstrations were orderly and nonviolent. Nevertheless, Nixon reacted with characteristic paranoia. On the eve of the counterinaugural, he ordered undercover agents from the FBI and the Department of Justice to infiltrate the crowds and disrupt all antiwar activity. At the same time, he approved plans to use hundreds of policemen from the Civil Disturbance Unit along the inaugural parade route. Brandishing thirty-inch riot batons, squads of police surrounded the protesters. In case of an emergency, the new administration was prepared to activate hundreds of National Guardsmen, poised in the wings with rifles and bayonets.[4]

When the inaugural parade was over, unfounded rumors began to circulate that radicals were advancing on the White House, sparking several episodes of police brutality in which innocent bystanders were clubbed by police and dragged away to jail. Within a few hours, police attacks subsided as most of the demonstrators boarded buses and left the city, but helicopters patrolled the streets from above until dusk on Nixon's first day in office.

Dissent continued. Several weeks after the inauguration, members of Clergy and Laymen Concerned About Vietnam (CLCAV) urged Kissinger to negotiate a fair settlement of the war. They reminded Kissinger that thousands of religious Americans, including the 900 demonstrators waiting outside, opposed the war as immoral and unjust.[5]

In May 1969, seven student leaders met with Kissinger to press for immediate changes in the Vietnam strategy. The group asked whether Nixon's policy would indeed be different from Johnson's. "We don't talk about winning the war now. We are talking about achieving peace," Kissinger said. It would be "a waste of time to argue against the morality of [our] Vietnam involvement." The President had already decided that "it would be immoral to pull out precipitously. Nor could we admit to everyone that our involvement was a mistake." The students left with Kissinger's closing remark ringing in their ears: "Give us a year. . . . If you come back in a year and nothing has happened . . . then I can't argue for more patience."[6]

A week before the inauguration, on January 12, 1969, Chalmers Roberts, a diplomatic correspondent, said: "At a guess, the country and Congress will give the new President six months to find the route to disengagement with honor from the Vietnam War. But very probably six months, or any limited extension that public attitudes may grant, will not be enough."[7] And so it was that as the first six months of Nixon's term expired, there was a marked acceleration in the number of protests and demonstrations.

On various campuses, scores of students protested the draft or boycotted graduation ceremonies, while others turned their backs on government speakers or walked out of political debates. In Philadelphia, demonstrators organized a dramatic rally during which the names of 34,000 Americans killed in Vietnam were read aloud. Antiwar women raided a New York draft office in order to burn draft records and publicize their discontent. A group of protesters stormed Fort Lewis on July 15, while others staged weekly demonstrations outside the Pentagon and the White House. On August 28, representatives of Business Executives for Vietnam Peace warned Nixon and Kissinger that the country's patience was wearing thin. On September 3, 225 psychologists proclaimed that Vietnam was "the insanity of our times." A month later, their sentiments were echoed by eighty university presidents, led by Kingman Brewster of Yale, who argued for unconditional withdrawal from Vietnam. In each instance, the protesters agreed that Vietnam had become, in the words of Whitney Young, "a moral and spiritual drain" on the American people.[8]

Antiwar leaders announced plans for a nationwide Vietnam Moratorium on October 15, scheduled to be the largest demonstration against the war. The initial response from media and congressional critics of Nixon's policy was highly favorable, but Nixon immediately attacked the idea of a moratorium:

> Now, I understand that there has been and continues to be opposition to the war in Vietnam on the campuses, and also in the nation. As far as this kind of activity is concerned, we expect it. However, under no circumstances will I be affected whatever by it.[9]

This statement angered antiwar activists across the country and intensified the media blitz in the fall of 1969. Newspapers and newsmagazines concentrated on the unending array of antiwar speeches, teach-ins, and rallies which preceded the moratorium. *Time* labeled the first week in October as "Nixon's Worst Week" in office. "It did not take an alarmist of Chicken Little proportions," editorialized *Time*, "to discern that bits of sky were falling on the Nixon Administration." David Broder wrote in the *Washington Post* that

> it is becoming more obvious with every passing day that the men and the movement that broke Lyndon Johnson's authority in 1968 are out to break Richard Nixon in 1969. The likelihood is great that they will succeed again.[10]

At the same time, organizers of the moratorium were thrilled by the enthusiastic support of key congressmen. In early September, Senator Edmund Muskie lashed out at the President's war policy, complaining that Nixon remained very ambiguous about efforts to achieve peace in Vietnam. Two weeks later, Edward Kennedy accused Nixon and Thieu of sabotaging every chance for a Vietnam cease-fire. On September 25, Congressman Allard Lowenstein offered to mobilize a "dump Nixon" coalition, while Senator Charles Goodell announced plans to introduce a resolution requiring U.S. withdrawal from Vietnam by the end of 1970. Between late September and mid-October, 1969, ten additional antiwar resolutions were introduced in Congress, including one from Mark Hatfield and Frank Church which would have forced Nixon to reveal his timetable for military withdrawal from Vietnam. None of the resolutions passed— Nixon supporters closed ranks and killed each measure—but the publicity surrounding these congressional outbursts strengthened the potential impact of the moratorium.[11]

One day before the nationwide demonstrations, the House of Representatives held a spirited debate on the subject of Vietnam. Representative Andrew Jacobs of Indiana expressed his support for the goals of the moratorium—the immediate and unilateral withdrawal of American forces from Vietnam. In Jacobs's words:

> The fact is that our war in Vietnam has not enhanced our national security but [has instead] weakened our national foundations. Since the Vietnam war began in earnest four years ago, our society has been subject to strains that have virtually torn it apart. . . . Look at what has happened to us. First, the campaign to end poverty has ground to a virtual halt.

Second, our inequitable and undemocratic draft system has become an unconscionable burden to us all. . . .

Third, inflation has ravaged our economy, sparing no American. . . . Fourth, our educational system . . . has fallen progressively behind. . . .

Fifth, our air and water have become more polluted. Sixth, our cities are in crisis . . . and

Seventh, our preoccupation with Vietnam has led to serious neglect of our relations [with other countries].[12]

Jacobs concluded, "If this country ever goes to war it should be because we have to, not because we have a chance to."[13]

President Nixon urged Americans not to buckle under radical pressure. The White House announced that Nixon would deliver a major address on Vietnam on November 3 to outline plans for securing peace. In the meantime, Nixon recruited important Republicans to denounce the upcoming demonstrations. Hugh Scott and Gerald Ford sharply criticized the antiwar movement and its backers in the Congress, while Senators Tower and Goldwater recommended increased military action in Vietnam as an answer to any protests. A resolution was drafted commending Nixon on the troop withdrawals and, by inference, on his handling of the war.[14]

On October 15, 1969, the long-awaited Vietnam Moratorium finally took place. Over one million concerned Americans marched in the streets and attended noisy antiwar rallies. In Washington, 250,000 protesters gathered at the Washington Monument and listened as Benjamin Spock discussed "limitations on [Nixon's] personality" which prevented him from ending the war. In New York, 100,000 activists assembled in Bryant Park to voice their opposition to the war, while 20,000 others rallied at the noon hour in the heart of New York's financial district. In Boston, 100,000 protesters converged on Boston Common chanting, "Peace Now, Peace Now." They applauded Edward Kennedy when he demanded the complete withdrawal of U.S. forces by the end of 1970. According to Kennedy, Nixon's policies were synonymous with "war and war and more war." George McGovern went one step further than Kennedy. Praising the protests as the highest patriotism, McGovern demanded the immediate withdrawal of American forces from Vietnam.[15]

Nixon held a news conference on the day of the protests to explain why the moratorium would not affect his Vietnam policy:

> If a President—any President—allowed his course to be set by those who demonstrate, he would betray the trust of all the rest. Whatever the issue, to allow government policy to be made in the streets would destroy the democratic process. It would give the decision, not to the majority, and not to those with the strongest arguments, but to those with the loudest voices.[16]

In response to the ongoing protest movement, Nixon delivered the November 3, 1969, television address, which we have already discussed in detail. We recall that Nixon was convinced, after making this speech, that he had the support of the American people for his Vietnam policies. Nixon, however, has recounted in his *Memoirs* how his family was livid with anger when they heard the reaction of television commentators. Then and there he decided "to take on the TV network news organizations for their biased and distorted 'instant analysis' and coverage."[17] His speechwriter, Pat Buchanan, urged a direct attack on the network commentators, and the two of them wrote the speech that Spiro Agnew delivered, in which he "tore into the unaccountable power in the hands of the 'unelected elite' of network newsmen."[18]

Thousands of letters and telegrams poured into the White House in support of Agnew's speech. Frank Stanton, president of CBS, however, called it "an unprecedented attempt by the Vice President of the United States to intimidate a news medium which depends for its existence upon government licenses." George McGovern said, "I feel that the speech was perhaps the most frightening single statement ever to come from a high government official in my public career." In support of President Nixon, Gerald Ford said the media should be called to account if they distorted the news: "I don't know why they should have a halo over their heads."[19]

Agnew's speech was carefully timed to coincide with a second moratorium scheduled for November 15. The protesters mustered a respectable showing but achieved little in terms of challenging the Nixon administration on Vietnam. In San Francisco, a crowd of 125,000 yelled "Peace!" for several hours. In Washington, nearly 250,000 demonstrators gathered for a forty-hour "march against death." Throughout the day, they walked in single file, carrying placards bearing the name either of a dead soldier or of a devastated village in Vietnam. Thousands shouted their antiwar message, while

President Nixon remained in the White House and watched football games on television.

Other rallies in the nation's capital supplemented the initial demonstration, but the crowds were too diversified to accomplish lasting results. According to *U.S. News and World Report,* the demonstrations in Washington included "moderates, liberals, pacifists, students, teachers, clergymen, radicals and Communists . . . united only by their opposition to the war."[20] When the second Vietnam Moratorium ended in November, each dissenting group went back to pursue its own special interests.

At the end of 1969, it looked as if Nixon had defeated his antiwar opponents. The protest movement had grown in numbers during the fall, but the President had been able to nullify much of its impact by clever propaganda and by stinging counterattacks. Before the end of the year, Nixon gained added support from right-wing congressmen, who published a study of the peace movement claiming that it was dominated by Communists.[21]

Encouraged by the continued silence of the majority, Nixon and Kissinger began to carry out their plans for an escalation of the war. In December the President asked Congress for $20.7 billion in additional appropriations for the Pentagon, which Congress approved in routine fashion. "No major weapon has been left out of this bill," Senator John Stennis announced proudly.[22]

In contrast, the Vietnam Moratorium produced deep frustration among the thousands of individuals who hoped to induce the administration to seek peace. That frustration was tragically exemplified by Craig Badiali and Joan Fox, both seventeen years old, in Blackwood, New Jersey. They returned home after the Vietnam Moratorium deeply disturbed about the suffering in Vietnam. After writing notes to parents and friends, Craig and Joan committed suicide, in the name of peace. One of the notes read:

> Why? Because we see that people just won't do and say what they feel, and you can't just tell someone to. It seems that people are only touched by death and maybe people will be touched enough to look into their lives. And if just one person is touched enough to do something constructive and peaceful with their life, then maybe our death was worth it.
> Why?—because we love our fellow man enough to sacrifice our lives so that they will try to find the ecstasy in just being alive.

Afterwards, a Blackwood teacher concluded:

> [Each set of parents] wanted to hide the tragedy in a closet and forget about it. To them, Joan and Craig had done a foul and debasing thing in protesting the war. . . . The people in this town simply could not face the fact that otherwise normal kids would choose to die for such things as peace and brotherhood. When they couldn't come up with an explanation that the kids were sick or crazy or aberrant, they just went and shut themselves off from it.

A local minister called the suicides "an evil deed" and likened the teenagers' plea for peace to the actions of those who would "surrender this country to the Communists."[23]

On Christmas Day 1969, a number of American "refugees" held a "Christmas Dinner in Peace" in Montreal, Canada. Together with their families, they sang antiwar songs and hung their military dog tags from a special Christmas tree. Representing 100,000 exiles living in Canada alone, the Montreal group prayed for a speedy end to Nixon's war in Vietnam.[24]

During the winter and spring of 1970, scattered demonstrations in Canada and the United States made a few headlines, but for the most part the peace movement remained fragmented and immobile.[25] In Carbondale, Illinois, antiwar leaders organized a series of demonstrations against Southern Illinois University's Center for Vietnamese Studies. Funded by a grant from the AID, the center had become a symbol of the Vietnam War. Not only did the center serve as a mouthpiece for White House policy, it also reminded students of how the government had infiltrated college campuses. "There it stood, ugly and offensive, a focus for our sense of outrage, a destination for our marches and demonstrations."[26]

Other protests took place on campuses and in the streets, as student leaders organized a new wave of demonstrations against the war. Though not as large as the rallies in the fall of 1969, protest marches occurred in Los Angeles, Atlanta, Houston, Washington, and Detroit. Three violent demonstrations took place in mid-April 1970. In Massachusetts, 76,000 people converged on Boston Common, where, under the influence of radicals, the crowd rioted and a night of violence followed. In California, 4,000 activists executed a mock assault on the Berkeley ROTC building and then went on a destructive rampage for two days. In Ohio, students demanding the abolition of ROTC at Ohio State University fought with police for six hours, before Governor Rhodes finally called in the National Guard and imposed a strict curfew.[27]

Then, on April 30, 1970, Nixon sent U.S. forces into Cambodia. His announcement galvanized the antiwar movement into greater action. *Newsweek* wrote:

> The war-weary American public had consoled itself for months with the prospect of a gradual U.S. disengagement from the war and many Americans heard the President's announcement with shock and dismay. Within hours of his TV address, campuses from California to Maryland were rocked by demonstrations and violence and the once-moribund peace movement sprang back to life.[28]

The demonstrations that followed Nixon's speech and his subsequent comments were intense and widespread. The morning after his TV address, Nixon made several remarks, overheard by reporters, about student "bums . . . blowing up campuses" while our soldiers in Vietnam "stand tall."[29] Without doubt, the publicity surrounding this statement added fuel to the fires of dissent and helped spark the nationwide outcry against Nixon's invasion of Cambodia.

Thousands descended upon Washington for a week of antiwar rallies and protest marches. Campuses at the University of Maryland, at Ohio State, and at Stanford exploded with violence. Confrontations led to skirmishes with police, which resulted in beatings and arrests. The National Student Association called for Nixon's impeachment; eleven Eastern university newspapers called for a nationwide campus strike; and 1,200 members of the Lawyers Committee for More Effective Action to End the War lobbied Congress for a cutoff of funds for the Vietnam War.

At Princeton University, thousands of students assembled in an auditorium, seething with anger. The student leaders, calming the anger, expressed what they believed to be the most effective way to produce a solution to the Vietnam problem. They asked students to to participate fully in the political process and to elect leaders more likely to pursue the path of peace. The students accepted what became known as the "Princeton Doctrine."[30]

Although Nixon bore the brunt of the protest, Henry Kissinger did not escape the scorn of opponents of the war. A group of Harvard professors traveled to Washington in early May and confronted their former colleague. In their opinion, the decision to invade Cambodia was "incomprehensible . . . disastrous . . . dreadful . . . more horrible than anything done by LBJ." One professor bluntly stated that "somebody [forgot] to tell the President that Cambodia was a country; he acted as if he didn't know this."[31] Another professor summed up the futility of their efforts:

> It's one of those problems when you look out of the window and you see a monster. And you turn to the guy standing next to you at the very same window and say, "Look, there's a monster!" He looks out the window and doesn't see the monster at all. How do you explain to him that there really is a monster?[32]

The tension reached a fever pitch after May 4, 1970. On that day National Guardsmen, called out at Kent State University after four days of demonstrations and rioting, shot and killed four youths who protested the war; nine others were wounded. A governmental commission concluded that the events at Kent State were "unnecessary, unwarranted and inexcusable."[33] Looking back, Nixon wrote: "Those few days after Kent State were among the darkest of my presidency. I felt utterly dejected when I read that the father of one of the dead girls had told a reporter, 'My child was not a bum.' "[34]

The Kent State deaths, followed by the equally shocking killing of students at Jackson State College in Mississippi, unleashed a nationwide protest in the second week of May 1970. Four hundred college campuses went on strike and were joined, at least in spirit, by 500 others. The New Mobilization Committee scheduled antiwar rallies across the country, and the Student Mobilization Committee called for "immediate massive protests, . . . rallies, teach-ins, seminars and other actions . . . to show the opposition of the American people to Nixon's war policies."[35] Within a few days, thousands of angry demonstrators descended on the nation's capital once again. Kissinger has described the scene vividly:

> Washington took on the character of a besieged city. A pinnacle of mass public protest was reached by May 9 when a crowd estimated at between 75,000 and 100,000 demonstrated on a hot Saturday afternoon on the Ellipse, the park to the South of the White House. . . . A ring of sixty buses was used to shield the grounds of the President's home. After May 9, thousands more students, often led by their faculty, [arrived in Washington] to denounce "escalation" and the "folly" of their government.[36]

Despite the growing protest in the streets, Congress was still hesitant to challenge the President. As Senator Fulbright concluded: "Active, organized dissent is [still] the only reliable restraint we have on a leadership which seems bent upon a disastrous course in Indochina."[37] To divert people's minds from Vietnam, the President tried a variety of means. For example, the Justice Department tried Huey Newton of the Black Panthers three times for terrorism, but a jury rejected the trumped-up charges on each occasion. In Chicago, the government battered away at the Chicago Seven for four months before another jury finally dropped conspiracy charges against the defendants. In another case, the FBI accused Father Philip Berrigan and six others of plotting to kidnap Henry Kissinger, but the jury voted to release all seven defendants.

Clearly, Nixon also attempted to shift the blame for the continuing war in Vietnam to his internal opponents, who, he charged, encouraged the enemy by their actions. He also hoped that, by ordering Attorney General Mitchell to publicize an imagined threat to internal security, he could insure that his party could avoid the war issue during the midterm elections in 1970. While the Justice Department pressured the courts to convict domestic radicals, Nixon campaigned heavily against congressional doves and other political leaders who posed a threat to the administration.

All of these diversion tactics could not minimize the intense opposition to Nixon's war. There came a time when certain legislators on Capitol Hill began to attempt to restrict the war-making powers of the President. Still, despite the growing protest in the streets, Congress was hesitant to challenge the President.[38]

President Nixon seemed unmoved and undeterred. In response to a reporter, he noted:

> They are trying to say that they want peace. They are trying to say that they want to stop the killing. They are trying to say that they want to end the draft. They are trying to say that we ought to get out of Vietnam. I agree with everything that they are trying to accomplish. I believe, however, that the decisions that I have made, and particularly this last terribly difficult decision of going into . . . [Cambodia]—I believe that that decision will serve that purpose, because you can be sure that everything that I stand for is what they want. [!][39]

He encouraged Vice President Agnew when the latter claimed that most protestors were just "out on a typical spring lark." He praised

Peter Brennan and his construction workers when they assaulted a protest march in New York City. He publicized the outpouring of lower-middle-class resentment toward students, especially one statement which read: "If the troublemaking students have no better sense than to conduct themselves as they do, . . . they justly deserve the consequences that they bring upon themselves, even if this does unfortunately result in death." Finally, the President seized upon every incident of radical violence, like the explosion at the U.S. Army Mathematics Research Center on the University of Wisconsin campus, and suggested that today's protesters were tomorrow's bombers. These tactics, coupled with the use of illegal surveillance, carried Nixon and Kissinger through the summer of 1970.[40]

The revolt within the U.S. armed services was one of the most important and little known aspects of the antiwar movement. As the war continued in Vietnam, growing numbers of GIs refused to support policies which they believed were immoral and unjust. Some of the GIs who had fought in Vietnam refused to do so again. At home, on several military bases, dissatisfied GIs organized antiwar coffeehouses and underground newspapers.

The GI protest was led by certain seasoned veterans who had been to Vietnam. In their opinion, the issues were much the same as those dealt with by the Nuremberg War Crime Trials after the Second World War: crimes against humanity, the strict accountability of all participants for orders given or actions taken, and the right and duty of individual soldiers to disobey orders they felt violated a moral code of conduct.[41]

Before 1970, the GI protest movement lacked coordination, and instances of unrest had been fragmented. In March 1969, for example, dissident soldiers at Fort Jackson, South Carolina, gathered signatures on a petition and held an informal debate on the morality of the Vietnam War. After the base commander warned of possible retaliation, military police arrested and court-martialed eight soldiers. According to *Newsweek*, the court-martial represented an attempt by the Pentagon to quash the "rising tide of antiwar, antimilitary dissent within the armed forces."[42] In June, at Fort Dix, New Jersey, thirty-eight stockade prisoners rioted to draw attention to the harsh military justice facing all dissidents. Antiwar GIs, together with protest groups from around the country—in particular the SDS, the Quakers, the Black Panthers, Clergy and Laymen Against Viet-

nam, and the Student Mobilization Committee—converged at Fort
Dix on October 12 to demonstrate against the military establishment.
They captured the news headlines by invading the Fort Dix com-
pound.[43]

During the October 1969 Vietnam Moratorium, soldiers at Fort
Bragg, North Carolina, marched in a demonstration, while GIs at
Fort Sam Houston, Texas, defied an order which forbade a mass
meeting to discuss the war and met in downtown San Antonio. A
dynamic new group, GI's for Peace, protested on Veterans Day,
marched in numerous rallies, and published a newspaper called
Gigline.[44]

By the spring of 1970, the number of antiwar GI organizations had
multiplied, and dissent within the armed services had grown dramatically. When Nixon invaded Cambodia on April 30, GI representatives met with leaders of the New Mobilization Committee and
formed a GI Task Force within the civilian antiwar movement. The
Task Force immediately set out to organize and plan for nationwide
demonstrations at military bases, on May 16, 1970. As a result, despite warnings from the Pentagon, GIs staged seventeen rallies at
army, air force, and navy bases, forcing cancellation of the traditional
Armed Forces Day. David Cortright, an expert on military dissent,
analyzed the results of the protest:

> The events of Armed Forces Day not only demonstrated widespread
> antiwar sentiment within the ranks but sparked continuing political
> activity at many bases. . . . Just as importantly, the May 16 actions had
> great impact on the civilian community. The spectacle of simultaneous
> soldier demonstrations . . . aroused renewed appreciation of the poten-
> tial of G.I. resistance. As Abbie Hoffman quipped to the crowd at Fort
> Meade: "Behind every G.I. haircut lies a Samson."[45]

This protest became a catalyst for a full reexamination of the military system. What GI groups found was disturbing. More than 7,000
prisoners languished in army stockades, while racism, racial violence, inequities in the draft system, and official sabotage of collective bargaining drives persisted.[46] As a result, GIs United Against the
War in Vietnam published a "Statement of Aims" in late 1970:

> For the past decade our country has been involved in a long, drawn-out,
> costly and tragic war in Vietnam. Most Americans do not support this
> war—increasing numbers are demonstrating their opposition, includ-

ing active duty G.I.'s. . . . We, as G.I.'s, are forced to suffer most of all in the Vietnam fiasco. Many of us were drafted into the Army against our will—nearly all of us are kept in its grasp against our will—all in order to carry out this illegal, immoral and unjust war.[47]

In addition to the GI war resisters, the Vietnam Veterans Against the War group emerged. Formed during a peace march in 1967, the VVAW had grown slowly during the transition from Johnson to Nixon. In February 1971, it received growing publicity when 150 antiwar veterans met in Detroit and conducted hearings on Vietnam war atrocities. The Detroit gathering, known as the Winter Soldier Investigation, produced damning testimony. For three days, the veterans reported "acts of violence which they had either committed or witnessed during their tours in Vietnam." As VVAW leader John Kerry wrote, "These veterans came together in Detroit to tell Americans what their country was really doing in Vietnam."[48]

Yet, in the midst of the Winter Soldier Investigation, President Nixon ordered the invasion of Laos. As Kissinger recalled:

> That dormant beast of public protest—our nightmare, our challenge . . . —burst forth again. When objectives are shared, the domestic debate can address tactics. . . . But when there is no agreement on fundamental premises, when the challenge is not only to perception but to motive, then differences take on the character of a civil war.[49]

Both the press and the Congress reacted sharply to the invasion of Laos. The *Milwaukee Journal,* for example, declared that "the United States can no longer stand the internal frustrations and disruptions that the bloody, tragic and immoral war is costing."[50] On Capitol Hill, no fewer than seventeen resolutions were introduced in the next five months to limit, restrict, or end presidential authority to fight the Vietnam War.[51] The most important challenge came from Senator Mike Mansfield's resolution that stated:

> the U.S. should "terminate at the earliest practicable date all military operations" in Indochina and undertake [to provide for the] "prompt and orderly withdrawal" of all U.S. forces not more than nine months after [the bill's] enactment subject to the release of American POW's.[52]

Nixon, with conservative support, was able to defeat this and other resolutions by the Congress. As J. William Fulbright concluded:

The current restraints imposed by Congress are utterly insufficient to the task. All they really do is to provide the Administration with an excuse for doing anything and everything that is not explicitly forbidden—and, as we have seen, all it takes to transfer some contemplated military action from the prohibited category to the permissible is a certain agility in semantics and an extraordinary contempt for the Constitutional authority of Congress.[53]

In the streets, the antiwar movement was determined to show Nixon and Kissinger that opposition to the Laos invasion was just as intense as opposition to the invasion of Cambodia. As a result, Vietnam Veterans Against the War led a new wave of demonstrations in April–May 1971. On April 18, over 2,000 veterans converged on Washington to begin a week-long demonstration called Operation Dewey Canyon III. Unofficially, the group advertised its protest as "a limited incursion into the country of Congress." Wearing fatigues and field jackets, the veterans, some of them missing arms and legs, marched to Arlington Cemetery to honor the war dead and then went on to the Capitol with a list of demands. Hundreds of protesters talked for hours with members of Congress; 110 were arrested when they blocked the entrance to the Supreme Court; many more joined in a candlelight march around the White House. The most dramatic moment of all occurred when the veterans threw all of their Vietnam medals onto the steps of the Capitol in a supreme gesture of contempt.[54]

Inside the chamber of the Senate Foreign Relations Committee, John Kerry of the VVAW testified eloquently against the war and against the draft:

We wish that a merciful God could wipe away our own memories of that service as easily as this Administration has wiped away their memories of us. But all that they have done . . . by this denial is to make more clear than ever our own determination to undertake one last mission— to search out and destroy the last vestige of this barbaric war, to pacify our own hearts, to conquer the hate and fear that have driven this country these last ten years and more, so when thirty years from now our brothers go down the street without a leg, without an arm, or a face, and small boys ask why, we will be able to say "Vietnam" and not mean . . . a filthy obscene memory, but mean instead the place where America finally turned and where soldiers like us helped in the turning.[55]

Dewey Canyon III was only the beginning of a month-long spree of demonstrations and protests against Nixon's war in Vietnam. In some respects, it was the last hurrah of the antiwar movement. On April 23, the Concerned Officers Movement held a peace memorial in Washington's National Cathedral and 700 GI protesters attended. On April 24, a huge crowd of over 300,000 people marched through the streets of Washington, led by 500 GIs and members of Vietnam Veterans Against the War. One week later, 200,000 antiwar forces gathered for a May Day campaign of civil disobedience. The protest groups threatened, as one banner read, to "Stop the Government or Stop the War." The participants planned to clog all federal buildings with a sit-down strike and to block all roads and bridges into the city. As the May Day strike began, the authorities moved in and illegally arrested 12,000 protesters during the next three days. In the end, police pressure took its toll. By mid-May, most of the demonstrators left for home.[56]

The White House adopted a siege mentality and lashed out against its critics. The President believed that North Vietnamese Communists had influenced the May Day protests, while Kissinger accused the demonstrators of trying to discredit their own government. Both ignored a Gallup Poll which revealed that 61 percent of Americans now felt the war was a mistake.[57]

In June 1971 a different type of "dissent" appeared. On June 13 a portion of the "Pentagon Papers" was published in the *New York Times*. As we have already recalled, Secretary of Defense McNamara had commissioned a research project during the Johnson administration known as a "History of U.S. Decision-Making Process on Vietnam Policy." This study included 1.5 million words of official analysis and 1 million words of secret documents, covering the period 1945 to 1968. The report had failed to influence the Johnson administration, and it does not appear that it had any effect on the decision-making in the new Nixon administration since it continued to lie in secret Pentagon archives. Robert McNamara had vainly endeavored to have this report declassified, but now it was leaked and published, and for the first time the American people had an opportunity to become apprised of its content.

The Pentagon Papers disclosed the nature of the U.S. secret involvement in Vietnam, the errors that caused the United States to enter the Vietnam struggle, the weaknesses and the stupidity of decision-making during the entire period, the escalation of the U.S. in-

volvement in the Vietnam War, and the steady stream of propaganda
that had been issued to deceive the American people.

The man responsible for these shattering revelations was Daniel
Ellsberg, who had been a RAND analyst and a consultant to both
President Johnson and Henry Kissinger. After witnessing the terrible air war, the failure of the Vietnamization policy, and the prevailing climate of corruption in Vietnam, Ellsberg became an opponent
of the war. He obtained a copy of the report and turned it over to the
Times.[58]

The White House reacted predictably. Kissinger accused Secretaries Laird and Rogers of leaking top-secret information. The President moved quickly to block publication of the documents, claiming
that "the national defense interest of the United States and the nation's security" would suffer "immediate and irreparable harm." Under orders from Nixon, the Justice Department won a court order
barring further release of the papers, but the *Times* challenged the
court order before the Supreme Court and won.[59] It resumed publication of the Pentagon Papers at the end of June 1971.

Though the Pentagon Papers, written in 1968, naturally made no
reference to the Nixon administration, both Nixon and Kissinger
viewed their publication as a direct threat to themselves. Clearly,
they did not want public debate about the reasons why the United
States entered Vietnam. In addition, they worried lest Ellsberg's
actions encourage others to leak information even more damaging.
Therefore, Nixon ordered domestic adviser John Ehrlichman to set
up a special investigation unit, known as the "plumbers." The White
House recruited former CIA operative E. Howard Hunt and retired
FBI agent G. Gordon Liddy to head the team. The plumbers' first
assignment was to dig up dirt about Daniel Ellsberg. In September
they burglarized the office of Ellsberg's psychiatrist, setting off the
train of events leading to the Watergate affair. In order to make an
example of Ellsberg,

> the government charged him [not only] with conspiracy and the theft of
> official documents, but also with espionage, in a new interpretation of
> that offense which made it clear that the administration regarded the
> American press as an enemy power.[60]

The charges did not hold up in court, but the message was clear:

Anyone challenging Nixon's conduct did so at his or her personal peril.

The antiwar movement had vainly attempted during the Johnson administration and Nixon's first four years to halt the crescendo of death and destruction. Those who attempted to halt it through the political process also failed. Perhaps the political process itself failed because it had not addressed the central issues sufficiently. Certainly, Congress failed to check the executive branch. Those who protested grew tired and disillusioned, and they were unable to muster further major protests, except in isolated instances. During the crisis of May 1972, when Nixon and Kissinger mined the harbors of North Vietnam, demonstrators marched in two dozen cities and on many college campuses. Thirty thousand rallied in New York City shouting "Out now!" Leaders in the arts and sciences went to jail after an end-the-war vigil at the Capitol. A group of Ivy League university presidents assailed Kissinger in Washington. A news writer declared, "Nixon has lost touch with the real world," but the demonstrations of May 1972 were not, as one observer noted, "the headline-seizing, trauma-causing, politically polarizing occasions some of their predecessors had been in the earlier years."[61]

Seven months later, during the Christmas bombing campaign against Hanoi and Haiphong, the administration weathered another outburst of criticism. News headlines read: "New Madness in Vietnam"; "The Rain of Death Continues"; "Terror Bombing in the Name of Peace"; and "Beyond All Reason." Members of Congress expressed their outrage, while antiwar activists echoed the sentiments of Jerry Gordon, coordinator of the National Peace Action Coalition:

> The American people have been lied to once again. Instead of peace being at hand, there is intensified war. Instead of the slaughter in Vietnam ending, it has escalated.[62]

Finally, during Nixon's second inaugural in January 1973, a demonstration took place beside the Washington Monument. Seventy-five thousand protesters, "moved by habit and disgust," gathered to honor everyone who had struggled for peace during the past ten years.[63] As Nixon raised his hands and gave the victory sign, the demonstrators reminded their listeners that the same man was being sworn in to the same office as the same war went on.

:15

THE PEKING SUMMIT
February 21–28, 1972

As Richard Nixon recalls:

> At 7:30 on the evening of July 15, 1971, I spoke to the nation from a television studio in Burbank, California. I talked for only three and a half minutes but my words produced one of the greatest diplomatic surprises of the century. . . . "Premier Chou En-lai and Dr. Henry Kissinger, President Nixon's Assistant for National Security Affairs, held talks in Peking from July 9 to 11, 1971. Knowing of President Nixon's expressed desire to visit the People's Republic of China, Premier Chou En-lai, on behalf of the Government of the People's Republic of China, has extended an invitation to President Nixon to visit China at an appropriate date before May 1972. President Nixon has accepted the invitation with pleasure. The meeting between the leaders of China and the United States is to seek the normalization of relations between the two countries and also to exchange views on questions of concern to the two sides."[1]

There was ample reason to be surprised and shocked when Cold Warrior Richard Nixon journeyed, hat in hand, to visit his archenemy, Mao Tse-tung. Nixon had reiterated time and time again that China was the United States's ultimate enemy in Indochina. Yet given the nature of American politics, perhaps only a Richard Nixon could travel to Peking seeking reconciliation with the People's Republic of China. Anyone else would have been accused of being soft on Communism.

The reaction to Nixon's upcoming summit was highly favorable as evidenced by Max Lerner's comment: "The politics of surprise leads through the Gates of Astonishment into the Kingdom of Hope."[2] Even superhawk and Cold Warrior Senator John Stennis said, "The President has made a good move; now it's up to him to follow through and I'm going to back him up."[3]

How did it happen, then, that when Richard Nixon became President in 1969, with a "plan to end the war," he did not immediately undertake to make this identical journey? Why did Nixon wait until February of 1972 to undertake this summit conference with the leadership of the People's Republic of China? Had he made this journey when he first became President, he might have had the opportunity to end the Vietnam War then and there, and saved millions of lives, without the tragic consequences of his continuing the war in order to achieve victory.

There is no easy answer to these questions. In order to understand why this had not happened previously, let us briefly look backward and recount the nature of the U.S. relationship with China, and how Richard Nixon had reacted to China, prior to this summit conference.

Prior to 1971, when Nixon announced his intention to go to Peking, the United States was still supporting Chiang, a petty dictator, marooned on a tiny island with the delusion that he and his aging generals could somehow yet conquer the People's Republic of China. And the United States of course had been engaged in a war in Vietnam and Southeast Asia, secretly and openly, for over twenty years. As we have pointed out, this war was undertaken primarily because of the fear of the United States that it was necessary to draw the line in order to stop Chinese, as well as Russian, aggression.

For a quarter of a century, the United States had been convinced that it must contain China's potential for military adventurism and to prevent its becoming a successful, powerful nation. The United States had given no diplomatic recognition to China and banned all trade, travel, or commercial dealings of any kind with China, fearing that by doing so it would assist a potential enemy. When Lyndon Johnson became President, he set out to prevent the "slant-eyed Communist bastards" from North Vietnam, the puppets of the Chinese, from taking over all of Vietnam.

Richard Nixon had always supported all these U.S. policies. In his opinion, China was ruled by "ruthless disciplined ideologues" who had seized power when America's cowardly containment policy had lost the mainland to Communism. During the Johnson administration, Nixon ranted against China's aggressive tendencies and the threat posed by Mao's regime. He reiterated in numerous speeches that the Vietnam War was "the cork in the bottle of Chinese expansion in Asia," vital not only to defend South Vietnamese freedom but also to halt Peking's indirect aggression. If the United States wanted to win the war, Nixon maintained, it should escalate and thereby quarantine the war, even though a decision to destroy enemy supply lines might infuriate China. As Nixon said, prior to his startling election victory in 1968:

> There are risks, yes. But the risks of waiting are much greater. This becomes apparent when we look ahead and realize that if South Vietnam is lost, and Southeast Asia is lost, and the Pacific becomes a Red [Chinese] Sea, we could be confronted with a world war where the odds against us would be far greater.[4]

When Richard Nixon became President, he publicly and officially assumed an attitude toward China that might assist him in accomplishing his ultimate objectives. This resulted in schizophrenic announcements that alternated between conciliatory gestures and Cold War rhetoric. In his inauguration address, Nixon sent an indirect message to Peking. "Let all nations know," the new President said, "that during this administration our lines of communication will be open. We seek an open world—open to ideas, open to the exchange of goods and people—a world in which no people, great or small, will live in angry isolation." Yet, only seven days later, during his first news conference, Nixon complained of Chinese aggressiveness. "Until some changes occur on their side," he concluded, "I see no immediate prospect of any change in our [China] policy."[5]

In February 1969 the President first instructed Kissinger to encourage the rumor that Washington was exploring possibilities of rapprochement with the Chinese, and then ordered the Departments of State and Defense to begin a review of U.S. China policy. Nixon also expressed a desire to communicate with China during a state visit to France at the end of February. Yet on his return to the White House, the President cited China as the primary target of the Pentagon's new "Safeguard" antiballistic missile program:

> The Chinese threat against our population . . . cannot be ignored. By approving this [Safeguard] system, it is possible to reduce U.S. fatalities to a minimal level in the event of a Chinese nuclear attack in the 1970's. . . . I would imagine that the Soviet Union would be just as reluctant as we would be to leave their country naked against a potential Chinese Communist threat.[6]

Not surprisingly, Peking remained wary of U.S. intentions, though events on China's northern border soon made Chinese leaders more anxious than before to develop friendly relations with Washington.

During March–May of 1969, heavy fighting broke out between Chinese and Soviet forces along the Ussuri River in northeast China and along the frontier in Sinkiang province. Each side accused the other of aggression and immediately braced for an all-out assault, but the border incidents did not precipitate a general war, only an intensification of propaganda attacks. Realizing that Russia was as much a threat to its security as the United States, Peking was prepared to be responsive to U.S. overtures during the coming months.

Nixon now saw the possibility of driving a wedge between China, Russia, and Vietnam, and believed this was a propitious time to cultivate the China option so that later he might obtain China's assistance in procuring a favorable treaty with the Vietnamese. On June 26, 1969, Nixon decided to modify some of the trade controls against China. This was the beginning of concessions to induce China to abandon Vietnam. Thereupon, Nixon asked Pakistan President Yahya Khan and Romanian President Nicolae Ceausescu to convey his desire for diplomatic contact to the Chinese.[7]

Like adding chips in a poker game, the White House continued to send signals to Peking throughout the rest of 1969. In July, Nixon authorized U.S. passports for travel to China. In August, Kissinger directed U.S. Ambassador Walter Stoessel in Warsaw to approach his Chinese counterpart and reveal Washington's interest in serious talks about normalizing relations. Then Nixon modified America's twenty-year-old naval patrol in the Taiwan Straits. No longer would two U.S. destroyers be on constant alert to protect the island fortress of Chiang Kai-shek.

China reacted to these gestures, and in December, President Yahya Khan reported that Chou En-lai had agreed to resume ambassadorial talks in Warsaw.[8] In a statement on China in his year-end press briefing, Kissinger emphasized that negotiations could not be one-sided. But he went on to state that Peking's position in Asia was of major importance to the United States:

> The Chinese people are obviously a great people. . . . They will influence international affairs whatever we intend to do. . . . And their policy, for good or ill, will determine the possibilities for peace and progress. . . . They will make their decisions on the basis of their conceptions of their needs, and of their ideology. But to the degree that their actions can be influenced by ours, we are prepared to engage in a dialogue with them.[9]

On January 20, 1970, Ambassador Stoessel met in Warsaw with Lei Yang of the Chinese Embassy. Both diplomats made startling proposals. Stoessel declared that the United States "would be prepared to consider sending a representative to Peking for direct discussions with your officials." Lei Yang followed with an identical suggestion.[10]

At the next Warsaw meeting, Lei Yang formally accepted Nixon's offer to send an emissary to Peking. To dramatize the apparent breakthrough, Chou En-lai sent a message to Nixon and Kissinger through Yahya Khan. Peking no longer feared a U.S.-Soviet double-cross; in fact, Chou hastened to add, barring a sudden expansion of the fighting in Vietnam, "A war between China and the U.S. is seen now as a very remote possibility."[11] The White House took further steps in March to ease travel and trade restrictions.

Yet all this time, Nixon left no stone unturned in his attempt to win a military victory. He and Kissinger therefore risked the entire China initiative by invading Cambodia on April 30, 1970. As soon as U.S. and South Vietnamese forces crashed across the border into neutral Cambodia, China canceled the Warsaw talks and severed the fragile diplomatic channels that had opened. Radio Peking accused Washington of a flagrant provocation in Southeast Asia, and Chairman Mao Tse-tung issued a declaration entitled "People of the World, Unite and Defeat the U.S. Aggressors and All Their Running Dogs."[12]

Nixon's immediate response was to order elements of the Seventh Fleet back into the Taiwan Straits. "Stuff that will look belligerent," Nixon demanded. "I want [the Chinese] to know we are not playing this chicken game. . . . There's no recourse. I want them there within 24 hours."[13] But the order was never implemented.

In October 1970, when the White House realized its invasion of Cambodia had failed to produce military victory, Nixon returned to the China option. In the October 5 issue of *Time*, Nixon was quoted as saying, "If there is anything I want to do before I die, it is to go to China. If I don't, I want my children to." Three weeks later, during the United Nations' Twenty-fifth anniversary celebration, Nixon asked President Yahya Khan of Pakistan to make contact again with China and revive the idea of sending a U.S. emissary to Peking. Then, at a state dinner for Romanian President Ceausescu on October 26, Nixon toasted the People's Republic of China. It was the first time an American President had referred to mainland China by its official name.[14]

Soon after sending these signals, the Nixon administration decided to continue to block Peking's admission to the United Nations, but even this cornerstone of American policy underwent careful scrutiny by the President. On November 22, 1970, Nixon dictated the following memo for Kissinger:

> On a very confidential basis, I would like for you to have prepared in your staff—without any notice to people who might leak—a study of where we are to go with regard to the admission of Red China to the UN. It seems to me that the time is approaching sooner than we might think when we will not have the votes to block admission. . . . The question we really need an answer to is how we can develop a position in which we can keep our commitments to Taiwan and yet will not be rolled by those who favor admission of Red China.[15]

Despite China's disappointment at the United Nations, Chou En-lai responded favorably to the message delivered by President Yahya Khan. On December 9, 1970, the Pakistani ambassador in Washington reported to Kissinger that Chou wanted to reopen communication with Washington. Chou was prepared to invite "a special envoy of President Nixon's" to Peking to discuss the Taiwan situation. Nixon gave tentative approval to the idea of a visit but suggested that talks encompass "the broad range of issues which lie between the People's Republic of China and the United States, including the issue of Taiwan."[16]

While Nixon and Kissinger waited for an official Chinese invitation, two additional signals were received in Washington. First, Mao Tse-tung told American journalist Edgar Snow that he "would be happy to talk with [Nixon], either as a tourist or as President."[17] Then the Romanian ambassador in Washington handed Kissinger a message from Chou En-lai hinting that President Nixon himself would be welcome in Peking. For the first time, China's leaders had broached the possibility of a presidential visit to Peking.[18]

Nixon, however, soon risked his projected trip to Peking by instigating another major escalation of the conflict. On February 8, 1971, he sent South Vietnamese invaders into Laos. The southern Chinese army went on alert, and the *People's Daily* newspaper denounced Nixon's war policy. "By spreading the flames of war to the door of China," it wrote, "U.S. imperialism is on a course posing a grave menace to China. . . . Nixon has indeed fully laid bare his ferocious features, and reached the zenith in arrogance."[19] Though the invasion of Laos failed, Nixon correctly saw that the Chinese were now interested in a great many other issues than the war in Vietnam. They might protest in public, but henceforth, in private, the discussions between Peking and Washington were to continue without interruption.

On February 25, 1971, President Nixon submitted to Congress his second annual Foreign Policy Report. In the section dealing with China, Nixon reiterated his administration's desire for improved relations with the People's Republic of China. "In the coming year," he promised, "I will carefully examine what further steps we might take to create broader opportunities for contacts between the Chinese and American people. . . . What we can do, we will."[20] Less than a month later, the White House ended. all restrictions on U.S. passports for travel to China, and Kissinger proposed another ambassadorial meeting in Warsaw.

The next move was up to Chou En-lai. It came in an unusual form: "ping-pong diplomacy." In April, Chinese officials invited the U.S. table-tennis team touring Japan to visit China. Nixon immediately authorized acceptance of the invitation. Nixon then made another major concession and ordered an end to the twenty-year-old trade embargo with China, stating that some day soon he would like to go to China. Ending the isolation of mainland China, said Nixon, would remain a major goal of his administration.[21]

The long-awaited breakthrough occurred on April 27, 1971. Pakistani Ambassador Hilaly delivered to Kissinger an urgent message from Chou En-lai. The key passage read:

> The Chinese Govt reaffirms its willingness to receive publicly in Peking a special envoy of the President of the U.S. (for instance, Mr. Kissinger) or the U.S. Secy of State or even the President of the U.S. himself for a direct meeting and discussions.[22]

Nixon and Kissinger then decided to suggest a presidential summit in Peking. In advance of Nixon's visit, however, Kissinger would undertake a secret mission to China to prepare an agenda and begin an exchange of views on all subjects of mutual interest. On June 2, 1971, Chou En-lai formally accepted the American proposals.

When Kissinger's plane departed, on July 1, 1971, his journey was designated with the code name "Polo," a reference to Marco Polo, the thirteenth-century Venetian traveler to China. He first stopped in South Vietnam and India before landing in Pakistan on July 8. There he complained of a stomachache and apparently retired to the mountain retreat of President Yahya Khan. In reality, Kissinger slipped aboard a Pakistani jet and flew to Peking. For the next two and a half days, Kissinger held a series of meetings with Chou En-lai and other high-ranking Chinese officials. Kissinger remembers Chou as "one of the two or three most impressive men I have ever met. Urbane, infinitely patient, extraordinarily intelligent, subtle, he moved through our discussions with an easy grace that penetrated to the essence of our new relationship."[23]

Vietnam was undoubtedly central to these early negotiations. On the eve of Polo, Nixon ordered B-52 strikes against North Vietnam, signaling a hard-line stance during the upcoming visit. If China wanted action on Taiwan, Nixon was saying, it would have to pressure Hanoi into accepting an American settlement. On this point, however, Kissinger had met his diplomatic match, as Tad Szulc relates:

> If Kissinger ran into foul diplomatic weather in Peking, it was over the Vietnam War, a topic he discussed fully with Chou. . . . Kissinger sought some commitment from Chou, most delicately, for Chinese assistance in his efforts to negotiate a peace settlement. Chou, just as delicately, sidestepped the suggestion.[24]

In the end, both sides exchanged views on all outstanding issues and agreed on early 1972 as the target date for a Nixon-Mao-Chou summit. Upon leaving Peking, Kissinger cabled a single code word, "Eureka," back to the White House to signify that a presidential visit had been arranged. After completing his trip, Kissinger wrote to Nixon:

> We have laid the groundwork for you and Mao to turn a page in history. But we should have no illusions about the future. Profound differences and years of isolation yawn between us and the Chinese. They will be tough before and during the summit on the question of Taiwan and other major issues. And they will prove implacable foes if our relations turn sour.[25]

Before this visit could take place, a major hurdle needed to be overcome. The People's Republic of China demanded that Chiang

Kai-shek's Nationalist China be expelled from the United Nations and that the United States withdraw its diplomatic recognition of Taiwan and cancel its military treaties with it. All this would be hard for many of Nixon's conservative supporters to swallow.

In public, therefore, the White House instructed UN Ambassador George Bush to defend Chiang Kai-shek's seat at all costs. Behind the scenes, however, Nixon and Kissinger actually worked to undermine Chiang's position. Chou En-lai had demanded resolution of the UN issue before he would agree to a specific date for Nixon's visit. "It [was not] easy for me," Nixon remembers, "to take a position that would be so disappointing to our old friend and loyal ally, Chiang. . . . In this case, however, I felt that the national security interests of the United States lay in developing our relations with [Peking]."[26]

Before the UN General Assembly voted on the China question, Kissinger returned to Peking to finalize plans for Nixon's visit. Kissinger and Chou En-lai then drafted most of what became the Shanghai Communiqué, the document Nixon and Chou would sign to end the upcoming summit. In this document, China reaffirmed its claim to be the sole legitimate government of China, while the United States settled for a vague statement of policy which read:

> The United States acknowledges that all Chinese on either side of the Taiwan Strait maintain there is but one China and that Taiwan is a part of China. The United States government does not challenge that position. It reaffirms its interest in a peaceful settlement of the Taiwan question by the Chinese themselves.[27]

Both sides agreed to emphasize not only common ground but also the vast difference of opinion on such issues as Taiwan and Vietnam. On October 25, before Kissinger left Peking, the UN General Assembly voted as expected to expel Taiwan and admit mainland China.[28] Now Nixon had complied with the most important of China's demands. The summit was officially set for February 21, 1972.

The White House waited until November 29, 1971, to announce the agreed date of Nixon's visit to Peking. In the meantime, furious planning and preparation took place on opposite sides of the globe. The mood in Washington has been described as euphoric, most likely because Nixon expected to win Chinese assistance in ending the Vietnam War. After three years of stalemate, escalation, and military setback, Nixon and Kissinger finally chose to play the "China card," which, if successful, would soon allow the United States to wriggle out of Vietnam.

The timing of the move was important. By early 1972 it was apparent that military victory in Vietnam was becoming more unlikely. Likewise, a negotiated settlement favorable to General Thieu and the Saigon government was also highly unlikely, in spite of secret U.S. promises and last-minute escalations. While in China, therefore, Nixon would try to persuade Mao and Chou to pressure Hanoi into a quick settlement of the war. In addition, the China summit would have a similar, if indirect, influence on Russian leaders, who were suspicious of Sino-American relations to begin with. Undoubtedly, during the proposed Moscow summit, later in 1972, Nixon would have more leverage in asking for increased Russian pressure on Hanoi. Finally, the spectacle of an American President visiting mainland China during an election year would be sure to create a public-relations tidal wave which, in turn, would overwhelm the unresolved Vietnam problem and sweep Nixon headlong into another term as President.

As the President and his advisers realized, the timing of the China initiative was perfect. Chou En-lai had emphasized, however, that prior to the summit, neither side should publicly discuss the Vietnam War, and the White House agreed. China was concerned about the effects of such a disclosure on North Vietnam. As Kissinger explained to Congressman Gerald Ford:

> Hanoi's leaders are perplexed about the international situation. With their natural Vietnamese suspiciousness and their Communist paranoia, they are deeply troubled about what is going on between the U.S. and China. There's nothing the Chinese can tell them that will convince Hanoi that no double-cross is in the offing. They have fought 25 years, and now they see great things happening around them, great decisions are being made and they fear they may be left out.[29]

If Washington or Peking admitted that Vietnam was one of the reasons for Nixon's visit, then Hanoi, it was felt, would immediately move closer to Moscow and Chinese pressure would become ineffective. As a result, Chou insisted on a "public silence" regarding the Vietnam War, and Nixon very carefully informed key newsmen and congressional leaders of this arrangement. On the surface, Vietnam would *not* be the reason for his trip. "Under no circumstances,"

Nixon told Fulbright, "should you say that we say the trip to Peking will help in Vietnam. That's verbatim, we're not saying it."[30]

While Nixon and Kissinger pored over briefing books and plotted negotiating strategy, General Alexander Haig and an advance technical team arrived in Peking to coordinate security, communications, and television coverage of Nixon's visit. The White House realized the TV potential of Nixon's meetings with Mao and Chou, not to mention the lavish banquets planned by the Chinese or the sightseeing excursions scheduled for the President and First Lady. The advertising genius of the Nixon administration would see to it that millions of Americans, watching via satellite on prime time, would have no idea how desperate Nixon and Kissinger were to appease the Chinese and improve their position in Vietnam. As far as the American public was concerned, the China summit would be Nixon's finest hour.[31]

On the morning of February 21, 1972, *The Spirit of '76* touched down in Peking. There, in the bitter cold, Chou En-lai stood waiting to greet the presidential party. Both Nixon and Kissinger were aware that John Foster Dulles's refusal to shake hands with Chou at the 1954 Geneva Conference had insulted the Chinese leader deeply. Nixon immediately seized Chou's hand after stepping onto the airport runway. Both sides understood the symbolic nature of this initial handshake; to Nixon, it marked the point at which "one era ended and another began." When the austere reception drew to a close, Chou escorted the President to a special government guesthouse outside Peking.

Around 2:30 that afternoon, Chou informed Kissinger that Chairman Mao Tse-tung would like to see the President. Without bothering to include Secretary of State Rogers, Nixon and Kissinger rushed to Mao's residence in the Imperial City, where the first substantive meeting of the summit took place. "Our common old friend, Generalissimo Chiang Kai-shek, doesn't approve of this," Mao joked. "He calls us Communist bandits." Nixon replied that the changing world situation had brought them together at this opportune moment.[32]

For the next hour, Nixon and Mao exchanged views and discussed the major problems confronting both countries. Nixon emphasized the threat of Soviet aggression and the need for security throughout Asia. What Mao wanted most of all was assurances from Nixon that the United States was winding down the war in Vietnam. Nixon promptly gave these assurances. Near the end of the session, Mao winked and told the President not to fret about Chinese propaganda. "I think that, generally speaking, people like me sound like a lot of big cannons. That is, things like 'the whole world should unite and defeat imperialism, revisionism, and all reactionaries, and establish socialism.'" Very subtly, it seemed, Mao had made the point that age-old rhetoric should not keep China and the United States apart.[33]

Following the unscheduled meeting with Mao, Nixon returned to the Great Hall of the People for the first of four plenary sessions with Chou. These were generally held in the afternoons, following much publicized sight-seeing trips to the Great Wall, the Summer Palace, and other attractions. The most important meeting occurred on February 22, when Nixon and Chou discussed Vietnam, Taiwan, and the balance of power in Asia. The President startled his host by advocating a permanent U.S. military presence in the Pacific to be aimed at the Soviet Union, not China. Consequently, said Nixon, if Peking would assist in reducing "tensions in the area" (i.e., Vietnam), Nixon saw no reason why U.S. forces on Taiwan might not be removed. The President's message was clear: America was quite prepared to compromise Taiwan for a settlement in Vietnam.[34]

Chou En-lai was equally forceful in presenting China's view of the world situation. Peking had no aggressive designs against its neighbors, Chou assured Nixon. His government fully expected to "liberate" Taiwan at some future date, but resolution of this "internal affair" would be accomplished peacefully. In the long run, Chou agreed, the issue of Soviet expansionism would be paramount in Chinese minds. He insisted, however,

> the most pressing question now is Indochina, where the whole world is watching. . . . Our position is that so long as you are continuing your Vietnamization, Laosization, and Cambodianization policy, and as long as they continue fighting, we can do nothing but to continue to support them.[35]

Interrupting Chou, Nixon countered with a message to be passed along to Hanoi:

> Let me cut away the eight points, the five points, and the thirteen points and all the other points and come right down to what our offer really is. If I were sitting across the table from whoever is the leader of North Vietnam and we could negotiate a cease-fire and the return of our pris-

oners, then all Americans would be withdrawn from Vietnam six
months from that day.[36]

Nixon, in effect, was suggesting that China pressure Hanoi to accept
U.S. peace terms, and that the President wanted Peking to help him
negotiate favorable peace terms with Vietnam. It was ironic that
while President Nixon, Mao Tse-tung, and Chou En-lai were indulg-
ing in lavish banquets in Peking, U.S. troops were fighting in Indochina, thousands of tons of bombs were destroying South Vietnamese villages as well as North Vietnamese areas, and thousands of
Southeast Asians continued to die. Hundreds of U.S. planes were
being shot down by Chinese antiaircraft gunners. During this period
of heavy bombing, over 300,000 Chinese gunners were being rotated
to man these modern Russian-supplied antiaircraft weapons.[37]

Nixon and Kissinger left China on February 28. Nixon said in his
final toast in Peking: "We have been here a week. This was the week
that changed the world." The people of the United States, with few
exceptions, applauded the President's mission. Press reaction was
favorable, even congratulatory. Only a few commentators and individuals were critical, mainly because they felt Nixon had betrayed
Taiwan.[38]

Five days after Nixon left Peking, Chou En-lai went to Hanoi. He
assured the Vietnamese that he had not sold them down the river
during the Peking Summit. Shortly after he left, Hanoi began its
spring offensive and for the first time invaded South Vietnam with its
own conventional forces, inflicting a severe defeat upon Thieu's
forces. Nixon had failed to end the Vietnam War, but the Peking
Summit laid the groundwork for the subsequent U.S. rapprochement
with the People's Republic of China. It was to be America's only
"reward" for having lost the Vietnam War.

Epilogue

What follows digresses slightly from the story of Richard Nixon's
summit meeting in Peking. The author believes, however, that what
follows has historic importance. We will paraphrase and describe in
the language of Richard Nixon facts that have been believed for more
than a quarter of a century by foreign policy experts and China

scholars with whom the author has had intimate contact during this entire period. They are written by a former President who believed almost the opposite prior to his summit trip to China. These beliefs helped trigger and sustain the devastating Vietnamese war.

Richard Nixon remains a leading proponent of conducting a war, this time against Russian Communism, until total victory is achieved. At the same time he almost conclusively proves the fallaciousness of the U.S. Vietnam War and the U.S. Cold War against China. Nixon first establishes a principle that seems directly contrary to his World War III utterances to the effect that conflict and controversy might better be resolved by negotiation and understanding rather than military buildups and confrontations, when he later writes:

> . . . Therefore, as policies changed and interests shifted, hostility could more readily be replaced by respect, cordiality, even friendship.
>
> To a considerable extent, this happened in my own dealings with China's leaders. We began our talks with no illusions about our philosophical differences, and with no effort to conceal or paper them over. But we were cordial. We were respectful. And, in exploring together both our common interests and our divergent interests, we developed a high degree of trust and a considerable personal rapport. . . .[39]

Nixon's statements now seem to indicate that it should have been possible to accomplish the peace and rapprochement that China always wanted with the United States:

> China turned toward the United States because it saw itself surrounded by potentially hostile forces. To the north—the direction from which, historically, the "barbarian" invasions had come—stood the Soviet Union. . . . To the south was India. . . .
>
> To the northeast, China saw Japan. . . . Though our system was opposed to theirs, our interests were opposed to those of the Soviet Union, the neighbor that posed the most serious and most immediate threat to China itself. So the Chinese had reason to want better relations with us.[40]

Nixon's recognition of the need for changing policies and personal diplomatic negotiations and understanding, which finally resulted in the China rapprochement, is highly significant, particularly in the light of the military—no substitute for victory—stance that he pursued in the Vietnam War and still advocates:

The hostilities that existed between China and the United States in the 1949–1972 period were the result of politics, not of personality; they stemmed from a clash of national interests, not a clash of national cultures. Therefore, as policies changed and interests shifted, hostility could more readily be replaced by respect, cordiality, even friendship.[41]

Richard Nixon today seems to have largely admitted the failure of the U.S. Cold War against Communist China. When China became a Communist state, the United States set out to prevent China's development as a great power. The United States supported Chiang in his vow to reconquer China and depose its Communist leaders. It also denied China any assistance, prohibited trade, commerce, travel, or practically any relationship that might assist China. As Nixon points out, the Cold War lasted from 1949 to 1972, but he now observed that China had its own internal problems and needs, which were far more important than its so-called desire to engage in military conquest or adventure.

Nixon points out that China has "a billion people, most of them living almost as their ancestors did centuries ago," but they are in a rush to catch up economically and to become a great industrial power. He then makes a major comparison between China and modern Japan, pointing out that today perhaps Japan is the world's second greatest industrial power, but that China has nine times the population of Japan and an incomparably greater wealth of natural resources. He further points out that the Chinese people have proven themselves as competent as the Japanese. It appears to Nixon that some day China will become an even greater industrial and military power than Japan.[42] Reversing all previous U.S. theories, Nixon now says:

It is in our interest to have a strong China, because a weak China invites aggression and increases the danger of war. We and our European allies should do what is necessary to see that China acquires the military strength necessary to provide for its defense.[43]

Nixon's current appraisal is little different from what many observers believe has always been the real focus of the foreign policy of the People's Republic of China, and which may also pertain to the Soviet Union:

When I last visited China in 1979 the focus of its leaders' foreign policy concerns was on security, not expansion; they were interested in internal development, not foreign adventure. But they were deeply, intensely concerned with the Soviet threat and with whether the U.S. response to it would be adequate. The remarkably sophisticated global view they displayed was not that of the empire builder seeking worlds to conquer, but rather that of the world statesman seeking to maintain a global balance of power so that other nations as well as his own can be secure. If this view prevails into the next century, then China may indeed be "a great and progressing nation" and a powerful force for peace in the world. If we show that we are strong and reliable partners in maintaining security, there will be a better chance that that view will prevail.[44]

The rapprochement with the People's Republic made possible by the Nixon/Chou summit has become a fact of life. On January 1, 1979, full diplomatic relations were established with the People's Republic of China and on January 29, 1979, Deputy Prime Minister Teng Hsiao-P'ing visited Washington. U.S. diplomatic and military ties with the Nationalist Chinese regime in Taiwan were also severed.

President Nixon meets with advisers on Vietnam in White House Cabinet Room, September 1969. *Left to right:* Presidential Assistant Henry Kissinger, Attorney General John Mitchell, Vice President Spiro Agnew, Pacific Commander-in-Chief Adm. John S. McCain, U.S. Commander in Vietnam Gen. Creighton Abrams, CIA Director Richard Helms, Philip Habib of the Paris negotiating team, U.S. Ambassador to Vietnam Ellsworth Bunker, Secretary of State William Rogers, of the Joint Chiefs of Staff. *Wide World Photos.*

For the first time in the Vietnam War, giant U.S. B-52 bombers hit fuel dumps and supply areas around the North Vietnamese port of Haiphong, April 1972. (In this file photo, B-52 bombers are shown in action over South Vietnam in 1966.) *United Press International Photo.*

Residential quarter in Haiphong following bombing by U.S. B-52s; the small "pond" is a bomb crater, July 1972. *United Press International Photo.*

Nixon and Kissinger toast the Russians after signing the SALT agreement, with the smiling approval of Secretary of State William Rogers and Soviet Premier Leonid Brezhnev, May 26, 1972. *United Press International Photo.*

President and Mrs. Nixon and Premier Chou En-lai review troops as Nixon leaves Peking, February 26, 1972. *Wide World Photos.*

Nixon and Chou En-lai toast each other during the final Peking Summit banquet in Shanghai, February 28, 1972. *Wide World Photos.*

The United States and Vietnam sign agreement in Paris to end Vietnam War, January 27, 1973. *Wide World Photos.*

Ambassador Graham Martin talks to newsmen shortly after evacuation of Saigon, May 2, 1975. "If we had kept our commitments," said Martin, "we wouldn't have had to evacuate." *United Press International Photo.*

Vietnamese try to scale U.S. Embassy wall in desperate attempts to get aboard the evacuation flights, May 1, 1975. *Wide World Photos.*

A South Vietnamese youngster runs through a sea of empty soft drink and beer cans along the main road leading out of Saigon, a vestige of the American presence in South Vietnam, April 1973. *Wide World Photos*.

:16

THE MOSCOW SUMMIT
May 20–29, 1972

After President Nixon announced on television that he intended to break the China barrier and visit Peking, he also wrote a letter to Leonid Brezhnev, the Russian leader, urging concrete solutions for remaining problems like Vietnam. Five days later, on August 10, 1971, the Kremlin issued a formal invitation for the President to visit Moscow in 1972. Nixon then went on national television on October 12, 1971, to announce that a summit at Moscow would take place on May 22, 1972.[1]

This announcement had been long in coming. President Nixon had resisted a summit unless Russia would stop assisting the Vietnamese. Nixon had met Anatoly Dobrynin, Soviet ambassador to the United States, for the first time on February 17, 1969. Dobrynin presented his government's views on U.S.-Soviet relations, and as Kissinger writes, "he [even] hinted at the possibility of a summit meeting." Nixon responded with tough talk about the "fundamental differences that exist between us." A summit was out of the question, he concluded, unless Moscow was prepared to "defuse critical political situations like the Middle East and Vietnam and Berlin."[2]

Following the meeting, Kissinger wrote to the President:

> I think the current Soviet . . . interest in negotiations, especially on arms control . . . stems in large measure from their uncertainty about the plans of this Administration. . . . [I think] we should seek to utilize this interest . . . to induce them to come to grips with the real sources of tension, notably . . . Vietnam.[3]

In the months ahead, Nixon and Kissinger increased diplomatic pressure on Moscow, hoping to force the Kremlin to cooperate on

Vietnam. More than ten times in 1969 alone, Kissinger asked Dobrynin for Soviet help in ending the war. At one point, he even intimated that "while we might talk about progress in other areas, a settlement in Vietnam was the key to everything." In September, Kissinger stressed that Moscow, by its failure to apply pressure on Hanoi, had practically sabotaged U.S.-Soviet relations. Nixon added that "as far as Vietnam is concerned, the train has just left the station and is now headed down the track."[4]

Moscow, however, wanted détente, arms limitation under SALT, normal trade relationships, an end to the war in Vietnam on terms satisfactory to Hanoi, and improved relations with the United States. It was apparent to the Russians that Nixon, however, was escalating the air war in Vietnam and was attempting to force Moscow to use its influence to compel Hanoi to enter into a treaty on Nixon's terms.

Dobrynin reiterated, time and again, that Soviet influence on Hanoi was limited. On October 20, 1969, two years before Nixon announced the projected summit for 1972, Dobrynin confronted Nixon in the Oval Office and expressed his government's dissatisfaction with U.S.-Soviet relations as well as with U.S. escalation in Vietnam, which he labeled as "extremely dangerous." His candid remarks touched a raw nerve in the President, who immediately launched into a tirade about Soviet intransigence around the world. On Vietnam, Nixon proclaimed:

> You may think that you can break me. You may believe that the American domestic situation is unmanageable. Or you may think that the war in Vietnam costs the Soviet Union only a small amount of money while it costs us a great many lives. I do not propose to argue with this kind of assessment. On the other hand, Mr. Ambassador, I want you to understand that the Soviet Union is going to be stuck with me for the next three years and three months, and during all that time I will keep in mind what is being done right now, today. If the Soviet Union will not help us get peace, then we will have to pursue our own methods for bringing the war to an end. We cannot allow a talk-fight strategy to continue without taking action.[5]

Undaunted, Dobrynin again approached Kissinger in January 1970 asking about a rumor that Nixon was interested in a summit. "Following our established policy," Kissinger has written, "I threw cold water on the idea." On April 7, 1970, however, Kissinger told Dobrynin that a summit might be possible if a "major breakthrough" occurred on SALT or on Vietnam. All of this might have been a normal

Nixon deception tactic. On April 30, 1970, the United States invaded Cambodia. In early June, Nixon declared his willingness to "let bygones be bygones" between the United States and Russia. By then the Cambodian invasion had proved a failure. On October 22, 1970, Soviet Foreign Minister Gromyko visited Washington for an exchange of views with Nixon and Kissinger. Gromyko condemned the Cambodian invasion but nevertheless reaffirmed Soviet interest in a summit. Nixon pressed for an immediate announcement, hoping to capitalize on a summit breakthrough before the 1970 midterm elections, but Moscow refused to participate in the ploy.

Following the meeting between Nixon and Gromyko, Dobrynin cautiously sounded out Kissinger again about the possibility of a summit. The Russians appeared willing, but in February 1971 the U.S.-sponsored invasion of Laos occurred. Moscow condemned the U.S. escalation and the havoc it continued to wreak on U.S.-Soviet relations. Russia announced that talk of a summit now was premature.[6]

After Cambodia and Laos, the White House no longer felt confident of military victory in Vietnam. Optimism turned to desperation, and the administration's attitude toward both the China and the Russia summit changed dramatically. It became imperative, from Nixon's point of view, that he travel to Peking and Moscow seeking assistance in ending the Vietnam conflict. Once this realization hit home, the main roadblocks in the way of a Russian summit were broken, and several negotiating breakthroughs occurred.

On May 20, 1971, President Nixon announced that Russia and the United States had reached a major understanding on SALT. Moscow had agreed to freeze production of offensive weapons while the two sides worked out an agreement limiting defensive ABM systems. This breakthrough, seemingly minor in nature, led directly to the final SALT pact approved in 1972. Stalled negotiations on Berlin were renewed and an agreement was entered into that reduced tensions in the divided city. After the Peking summit was announced, it appeared, by October of 1971, that a Moscow summit could now be held, but for some inexplicable reason, this Moscow summit was scheduled for May 22, 1972—seven long months away.[7]

During these months the devastating war in Vietnam went on. Tens of thousands of Vietnamese continued to die and their lands were devastated as a result of the massive technological air war.

Hanoi no doubt watched with fear and trepidation Nixon's cordial meetings with Mao and Chou En-lai in Peking and was no doubt concerned about the upcoming Moscow summit. The Vietnamese could not be sure, despite the massive assistance it had received from both China and Russia, that either China's or Russia's national interests might not transcend Vietnam's. Neither North Vietnam nor the National Liberation Front in the South had any intention of having their ultimate fate determined in either Peking or Moscow.

In order to make this point perfectly clear, Hanoi now decided to undertake a powerful spring offensive and to commit its conventional forces to this battle. Hanoi's forces pushed across the DMZ on March 30, 1972, and quickly destroyed an entire ARVN division. Scores of ARVN soldiers and many officers simply defected as the North Vietnamese approached Quang Tri City, the important capital of Quang Tri province.[8] Later in April, after Quang Tri City fell to the North Vietnamese, Saigon's elite Ranger Division fled in panic, leaving behind their tanks, guns, and artillery. American advisers barely escaped with their helicopters. One historian has written of ARVN's conduct in the retreat that followed:

> Reaching Hue, the ARVN troops became a drunken mob, wrecking and looting shops and raping women. The Marines and Rangers beat up and sometimes even killed soldiers of the hapless 3rd Division. Stalls in the U.S.-financed central market were looted and then the whole market was set afire. The next morning, tens of thousands of people, including Saigon government civil servants, began jamming the road south toward Danang.[9]

The push across the DMZ was not the only action that April. To the northwest of Saigon, North Vietnamese units entered Binh Long province and surrounded the district capital. Within a week, Hanoi's forces "inflicted heavy casualties on the ARVN Fifth Division, which fell back, again leaving large numbers of tanks and guns."[10]

Another area of fighting was Pleiku in the Central Highlands, where the North Vietnamese attacked several ARVN bases. After cutting the roads and forcing the South Vietnamese to abandon their early positions, the North Vietnamese quickly captured the headquarters of ARVN's Twenty-second division; "the 22nd division's troops 'got scared and ran'. . . . when the PLAF [North Vietnamese] attacked at night with tanks." They encircled town after town during April and May, and after the ARVN abandoned Kontum on April 26,

U.S. planes and South Korean troops rushed in to prevent a total collapse.

The final battlefield in Hanoi's spring offensive of 1972 was Binh Dinh province along the Gulf of Tonkin. As the North Vietnamese approached the town of Hoai An, the soldiers of ARVN abandoned their weapons, took off their uniforms, and fled, allowing the North Vietnamese to march in unopposed. Forty percent of another ARVN regiment ran away as well, while 8,000 local militiamen simply joined the North Vietnamese offensive. By the first of May, Hanoi's army controlled most of the province with little opposition.

The ARVN lost 70,000 troops between late March and June 1972, many more when the counterattacks began, and nearly 20,000 due to desertion. The casualty figures for North Vietnam's army were much less even by Pentagon accounts, while Hanoi ousted the ARVN from thousands of villages and hamlets. With Saigon's influence partially out of the way, the National Liberation Front was also able to resume its activities among the peasants.[11] In addition, Vietcong guerrillas freed thousands of peasants from Thieu's resettlement camps and dealt a mortal blow to the government's pacification program.

The North Vietnamese did not press their advantage. They had accomplished their objectives: Both they and the National Liberation Front controlled a great share of the land and people in South Vietnam; they had proven that Vietnamization was a failure and that they could not be controlled by any foreign power. The North did not deem it necessary to annihilate the ARVN, and they did not wish to alienate the South Vietnamese peasants for whom they were also fighting. They now wished to force the United States to conduct serious negotiations.

Nixon recounted that he was sitting in the Oval Office talking to Kissinger when a staff member sent in a note telling them that "the North Vietnamese had attacked across the DMZ."[12] Both Nixon and Kissinger reacted violently to this invasion. Kissinger assumed a new role as a war leader, acting like a man possessed. He assisted in directing the B-52 bombings so as to send signals to Hanoi, Peking, and Moscow. In addition to his role as a diplomat, he now became a warrior. Kissinger, leaning over huge maps of the battle area, moved fleets across the Pacific and shouted orders to admirals and generals.[13]

Nixon was highly perturbed. He had just completed what seemed

262 : Richard Milhous Nixon's Vietnam War

to be a highly successful summit in Peking, and was preparing for another one in Moscow, only to be confronted with a devastating escalation of the war by the North Vietnamese which might lead to a crushing defeat not only of the South Vietnamese but also of the remaining U.S. forces in Vietnam. Nixon noted that if the North Vietnamese armies were able to join with the Vietcong, rout the South Vietnamese forces, and capture Saigon, the war would be lost and the remaining 69,000 American troops would be in serious danger. Kissinger comforted the President by remarking that even if the United States had to pull out in the face of an enemy victory, people would still give Nixon credit for an honorable winding down of the war, and that everyone would be so glad the war was over that the situation would not be impossible to handle. Both Haldeman and Kissinger assured Nixon that even if he lost the war he could survive politically.

For Nixon defeat was not an option. He decided to make this battle an all-out test of how America was able to respond, to pull out all stops and to go for broke in order to show North Vietnam, as well as the Soviet Union, that the United States would only negotiate from a position of strength. As North Vietnamese tanks rumbled into South Vietnam on four fronts, the administration quickly launched one of the heaviest military buildups since World War II. Under the code name "Linebacker," the White House escalated the war to the fullest extent possible, sending fifty ships into the Gulf of Tonkin. Of these fifty ships, six were aircraft carriers, fully loaded with fighter-bombers. In addition, the Pentagon announced that 10 to 20 additional B-52s were in flight to Thailand, pushing the total number of planes at Thai bases to 53 B-52s and 224 fighter bombers. On Guam, new arrivals increased the arsenal of B-52s to 100.[14]

By the end of April, over 1,000 American warplanes were poised and ready. The U.S. strike force flew into action within days of the initial North Vietnamese push. Nixon had no qualms about bombing South Vietnam; U.S. bombers blasted away as if all South Vietnamese villages had become a free-fire zone. Especially in the Mekong Delta, Nixon unleashed the B-52s day after day, each plane loaded down with thirty tons of bombs. "The result of this, the heaviest use of B-52s in the heavily populated Delta of the entire war, was a massive increase in death and injury to innocent civilians, as the bombs fell on their fields and around their homes."[15]

There were other options that Nixon had hinted might take place: Planes might attack the dikes in North Vietnam, thereby flooding large areas of the country and killing untold numbers of civilians. The South Vietnamese might undertake an invasion of North Vietnam directed by the United States and aided by U.S. air power. A naval blockade of North Vietnamese ports might be undertaken. The primary option that was considered, however, was the mining of the ports of North Vietnam to prevent the further inflow of supplies.[16]

On May 1, Brezhnev wrote Nixon a letter warning against any actions that "might hurt the chance of a successful summit." Nixon's advisers were concerned that if the United States mined the Vietnamese ports, the summit might be canceled. Nixon consulted John Connally, who said: "Most important, the President must not lose the war! And he should not cancel the summit."[17] Nixon then said, "The summit isn't worth a damn if the price for it is losing in Vietnam."[18]

Having decided to mine and blockade the North Vietnamese harbors, Nixon went to Camp David to prepare a speech announcing his decision. He invited Ambassador Dobrynin to the White House to listen to it and sent a letter to Brezhnev stating his reasons for the blockade. He promised to join with the Russians for a "statesmanlike effort . . . to bring about a peace that humiliates neither side and serves the interests of all the people involved." Nixon then held an emergency meeting of the National Security Council on May 8, 1972, and issued an executive order to the Pentagon to seal North Vietnam's ports with high-explosive mines. The die had been cast.[19]

That night the President explained to the American people that Hanoi's offensive in South Vietnam "gravely threatened" American lives and that "there is only one way to stop the killing." The United States had decided to "keep the weapons of war out of the hands of the international outlaws of North Vietnam."[20]

Nixon, fearing a total collapse of the South, was now ready to renew the all-out war against the North and to launch B-52 attacks on North Vietnam. It was the first time that these huge bombers had flown missions over the North since 1967. The President was also ready to begin another drastic escalation of the war, by launching unrestricted B-52 raids against Hanoi and the port of Haiphong. Secretaries Laird and Rogers opposed these raids, fearing that they would cause the cancellation of the Moscow summit. Kissinger urged

Nixon to proceed, contending that America's honor was at stake. Nixon agreed. The raids against Hanoi and Haiphong, code-named Freedom Porch Bravo, were carried out as scheduled on April 15–16, causing extensive damage and loss of life for the people of North Vietnam.[21]

During these B-52 attacks the bombers inadvertently struck four unarmed merchant ships flying the Russian flag. Moscow's reaction was in sharp contrast to the reaction of Lyndon Johnson and the U.S. Congress during the alleged firing upon American vessels at Tonkin Gulf. Had Russia reacted in the same way, World War III might have become a reality. Instead, Soviet leader Leonid Brezhnev held an emergency meeting of the high-level Russian Politburo, but no immediate action was taken.[22]

Within a day the U.S. aircraft had not only machine-gunned two Soviet ships, but also had placed enough mines in Haiphong Harbor to prevent navigation there during the ensuing year. A total of thirty-six vessels from different countries were trapped in the harbor and subject to air attacks by American bombers. It appears that this blockade of the Haiphong Harbor did not shut off the flow of supplies into North Vietnam as Nixon and Kissinger had hoped, in view of the fact that North Vietnam was receiving an estimated 90 percent of its supplies by means of overland rail shipments. In addition, the mining had a worldwide negative effect as nations almost universally condemned it as an open act of war that endangered world peace.[23]

Likewise, as a consequence of these actions, the North Vietnamese on April 15, 1972, canceled a resumption of the Paris peace talks that were to have taken place on April 25. This was the meeting which the Soviets had noted might result in the United States reaching an agreement with the North Vietnamese. Nixon then told Kissinger to cancel the presummit meeting where he was scheduled to arrange the Moscow summit. Nixon told Kissinger the only reason he or Kissinger should go to Moscow was to discuss Vietnam. Kissinger disagreed and believed that Nixon should go to Moscow in any event. This created a crisis atmosphere. Nixon threatened to withdraw as a candidate for President in the next election in view of what was transpiring, and suggested that perhaps Rockefeller, Reagan, or Connally should take his place. After an "emotional" meeting with Kissinger, Nixon agreed that Kissinger might go to Moscow in the latter part of April.

In my conversations with Kissinger, and in the instructions I sent him in Moscow, I stressed that I wanted him to make Vietnam the first order of business and to refuse to discuss anything that the Soviets wanted . . . until they specifically committed themselves to help end the war.[24]

Kissinger went to Moscow but Brezhnev refused to put any pressure on Hanoi to force a final settlement. Upon Kissinger's return, on April 26, 1972, Nixon delivered a memo to Kissinger in which he again threatened to cancel the summit "unless we get a firm commitment from the Russians to announce a joint agreement at the summit to use our influence to end the war prior to May 15."[25] Meanwhile, the canceled Paris peace talks were rescheduled for May 2. On May 1, as Kissinger was preparing to leave for Paris, he received a cable from General Abrams, which he immediately brought to the Oval Office as Nixon was meeting with Haldeman. He informed Nixon that Quang Tri had fallen and that it appeared that Hue might be next and that its loss would be a serious blow. Nixon writes:

What else does he say, I asked. Kissinger cleared his throat uncomfortably and said: "He feels that he has to report that it is quite possible that the South Vietnamese have lost their will to fight, or to band together, and that the whole thing may then be lost." I could hardly believe what I had heard. I took the cable and read it for myself. "How could this have happened?" I asked. . . .[26]

Despite the defeat of South Vietnamese forces by North Vietnam; despite the bombing of Russian ships in Haiphong Harbor; despite the fact that Brezhnev would not promise to "take Nixon off the hook" and procure a peace treaty in Vietnam primarily on Nixon's terms; and contrary to most observers in Washington, who could not believe that the Russians would be willing to receive Nixon in Moscow after these and other provocations, the Moscow summit was as long last about to take place. The Russians were realists. As we have pointed out, they had always wanted détente; they had never wanted the Vietnam War; they had watched with astonishment and dismay Nixon's warm reaction to the Chinese embrace in Peking; they knew that a Chinese-U.S. rapprochement could have dangerous consequences for them. They therefore decided to hold this summit conference regardless of everything that had happened. Perhaps at this summit they might still make some advantageous agreements with Richard Nixon as China had already done. On May 11, 1972,

Brezhnev announced that the upcoming summit meeting with Nixon would be held on schedule.

On May 20, 1972, *Air Force One* left Washington on the way to Moscow. In transit, Kissinger said exuberantly to Nixon: "This has to be one of the great diplomatic coups of all times! Three weeks ago everyone predicted it would be called off, and today we're on our way."[27] On the day of his arrival, Nixon met privately with Brezhnev at his Kremlin office. "Brezhnev's tone was cordial, but his words were blunt. It had not been easy for him to carry off the summit after Nixon's recent actions in Vietnam," but he had done so because of the "overriding importance of improving Soviet-American relations and reaching agreement on [many] serious issues." He then expressed the desire to establish a friendly personal relationship with Nixon. Nixon responded that major differences are usually overcome at the top level; if you left them to the bureaucrats, there would never be progress. Brezhnev warmly agreed.[28]

A lavish dinner was held that evening in the splendid Hall of the Grand Kremlin Palace. Nixon's toast was almost an ironical antithesis of his actions prior to the summit:

> We should recognize that great nuclear powers have a solemn responsibility to exercise restraint in any crisis, and to take positive action to avert direct confrontation.
>
> With great power goes great responsibility. It is precisely when power is not accompanied by responsibility that the peace is threatened. Let our power always be used to keep the peace, never to break it.[29]

The first official plenary session was held the next day in St. Catherine's Hall, a large ornately gilded room. Kissinger reports that Nixon was flanked by Secretary of State Rogers and himself with a full complement of White House and State Department aides, "guaranteeing that Nixon would say nothing significant."[30] Representing the Soviets were Kosygin, Podgorny, Gromyko, and Dobrynin. Nixon began by saying:

> "I would like to say something that my Soviet friends may be too polite to say," I began. "I know that my reputation is one of being a very hard-line, cold-war-oriented, anticommunist."
>
> Kosygin said dryly, "I had heard this sometime back."

"It is true that I have a strong belief in our system," I continued, "but at the same time I respect those who believe just as strongly in their own systems. There must be room in this world for two great nations with different systems to live together and work together. We cannot do this, however, by mushy sentimentality or by glossing over differences which exist."[31]

The session was devoted to trying to iron out three remaining technical issues that stood in the way of the final approval of SALT I: (1) the distance between the two ABM sites, permitted by the treaty; (2) what increases in size or volume, if any, of existing ICBMs and ICBM silos should be permitted; and (3) what silos were to be counted.[32]

The most important meeting, however, took place the following evening. Kissinger writes that the confrontation began when Brezhnev "kidnapped the President of the United States." He relates how Brezhnev invited Nixon to dinner with only the top-level Soviet leadership, the dinner to be held at a "dacha," a guest house on the Moscow River. Nixon and Brezhnev arrived at the dacha after a mad forty-five-minute dash first by limousine and then by hydrofoil. Kissinger and Nixon's Secret Service followed Nixon and Brezhnev frantically, almost losing sight of them from time to time. Nixon's security teams were not only frantic, but greatly concerned. Brezhnev, however, was in high spirits when everyone arrived at the dacha.

Finally, Nixon and the top Soviet leadership team faced each other across an oval table to discuss the Vietnam issue. Nixon summarized the U.S. position: He had not chosen this moment for his recent escalation of the war, but once Hanoi began its spring offensive, aided by Russian equipment, the United States had to react as it did. Nixon then stated that the United States would not reconsider its present policies unless Hanoi indicated new flexibility in its negotiating stance, and insisted that Moscow use its influence to force Hanoi to reconsider its position. "As for us," said Nixon, "we were determined to bring the war to a conclusion, preferably by negotiation, if necessary by military means."

When Brezhnev responded, the "easy camaraderie vanished," and the tone was firm and unyielding. He castigated the United States not only for the "cruel bombing" but for the whole history of the U.S. Vietnam involvement, which he said was designed to embarrass the

Soviet Union. Military actions were not necessary to end the war; Hanoi was eager to negotiate; and all the United States needed to do was to get rid of Thieu and accept Hanoi's "reasonable" political program and peace could be achieved. Brezhnev concluded by criticizing Chinese foreign policy and the Shanghai Communiqué.

It was now Kosygin's turn to assail America's Vietnam policy. He did so unemotionally and in an analytical manner. He noted his original conversations with Lyndon Johnson, who had boasted of a potential victory in Vietnam and then failed to achieve it. Kosygin warned Nixon that the same fate could befall him. He was bitter about the U.S.-inflicted damage to Soviet ships and the loss of Soviet lives in Haiphong Harbor. He then made the toughest statement of the summit when he said that Hanoi might reconsider its previous refusal to permit forces of other countries (Russia) to fight on its side.[33] Nixon, reacting strongly to this statement, remarked that

> this was going too far. For the first time I spoke. "That threat doesn't frighten us a bit," I said, "but go ahead and make it."
>
> "Don't think you are right in thinking what we say is a threat and what you say is not a threat," Kosygin replied coldly. He said, "This is an *analysis* of what may happen, and that is much more serious than a threat."[34]

If the United States would get rid of Thieu, Kosygin suggested, another Moscow summit would be a logical place to work out terms Hanoi would accept.

Soviet President Podgorny concluded the Soviet presentation. He reaffirmed the Russian fear of China, noting that he had been in Hanoi when he learned of Kissinger's secret trip to China the previous summer, and thus was able to reassure the North Vietnamese that Nixon would also visit Moscow. Podgorny seconded the conclusion of his colleagues, in bellicose tones, that the war in Vietnam was "unlawful" and "sheer aggression." Meanwhile, Brezhnev paced the floor. Nixon's own version of how the meeting was concluded follows:

> After about twenty minutes, Podgorny suddenly stopped and Brezhnev said a few more words. Then there was silence in the room. By this time it was almost eleven o'clock. I felt that before I could let this conversation end, I had to let them know exactly where I stood.

I pointed out that I had withdrawn over 500,000 men from Vietnam. I had shown the greatest restraint when the North Vietnamese began their massive buildup in March, because I did not want anything to affect the summit. But when the North Vietnamese actually invaded South Vietnam, I had no choice but to react strongly.

"The General Secretary remarked earlier that some people may have wondered whether the action I took last month was because of irritation," I said. "If that were the case, I would be a very dangerous man in the position I am in. But that is not the case. On the contrary, my decision was taken in cold objectivity. That is the way I always act, having in mind the consequences and the risks.

"Our people want peace. I want it too. But I want the Soviet leaders to know how seriously I view this threat of new North Vietnamese escalation. One of our great Civil War generals, General Sherman, said, 'War is hell.' No people knows this better than the Soviet people. And since this new offensive began, 30,000 South Vietnamese civilians, men, women, and children, have been killed by the North Vietnamese using Soviet equipment.

"I would not for one moment suggest that the leaders of the Soviet Union wanted this to happen. What I am simply suggesting is that our goal is the same as yours. We are not trying to impose a settlement or a government on anybody."

They listened intently to what I said, but none of them made an attempt to respond.

With that we went upstairs, where a lavish dinner was waiting for us. . . .[35]

This was the last meeting attended by all the principals where there was any major discussion of the Vietnam problem. If the United States had come primarily to procure Russian assistance to end the Vietnam War, the summit was a failure.

Nixon and Kissinger, however, now pushed on to obtain a SALT I agreement, stating for the public record, that this was the important reason for the summit. After the dacha meeting, Kissinger visited Nixon at 1:00 A.M. and informed him that "the Pentagon was almost in open rebellion and the Joint Chiefs were backing away from the SALT position." Nixon replied that he intended to make a SALT agreement on his terms regardless of the Pentagon position.

The next day the Politburo agreed to all of Nixon's terms for the signing of the SALT agreement. At 11:00 that night in the Kremlin, Brezhnev and Nixon, notwithstanding their failure to agree on Vietnam, signed the ABM treaty and the Interim Offensive Agreement, and proclaimed it a historic achievement.[36]

The following day Nixon flew to Leningrad to visit the cemetery and the museum which depicts the death of millions of Leningrad's people during the World War II siege, a grim reminder of the Russians' inordinate fear of being attacked. While at the museum, Nixon read the diary of Tanya, who had watched her family die, one by one, until she too was found dead.

Nixon then flew back to Moscow and spoke on Russian television of the danger of an unchecked arms race, emphasizing America's desire for peace. He ended with the story of Tanya, bringing tears to Brezhnev's eyes, who then, to Nixon's surprise, asked: "Would you like to have one of our highest officials go to the Democratic Republic of Vietnam in the interests of peace?" Nixon said that such a visit might make a major contribution toward ending the war, and while it was taking place he would suspend the bombing of Hanoi.[37]

The Moscow summit ended on May 29. Nixon boarded *Air Force One*, stopped en route in Tehran to visit the Shah of Iran, and then on to Washington to address a joint session of Congress and to receive the accolades of the American people, who had watched on television every phase of his sensational journey. The protest movement and opposition to the Vietnam War were stilled. The Democratic presidential campaign was ignored, and Richard Nixon—despite Watergate and despite Vietnam—coasted to an easy victory over the Democratic candidate George McGovern.

Fulfilling Brezhnev's promise, President Podgorny went to Hanoi in July of 1972. Nevertheless, the war continued with unabated fury into 1973.

:17

BOMBING—CAMPAIGNING—
NEGOTIATING
June–November 1972

This election story begins when Nixon returned to Washington from the USSR on June 1, 1972. He turned at once to his major concern: the fall elections. His renomination by the Republican Party was not in any real doubt, but he was apprehensive about the campaign the Democrats would mount against him. His victory in the presidential election of 1968 had imposed on him the mandate of making peace in Vietnam. To that end he had publicized a "peace plan," had flown to Moscow and Peking and made speeches about a new era of friendship:

> Everywhere new hopes are rising for a world no longer shadowed by fear and want and war, and as Americans we can be proud that we now have an historic opportunity to play a great role in helping to achieve man's oldest dream—a world in which all nations can enjoy the blessings of peace.[1]

Yet, Richard Nixon had not brought peace.

In the fourth year of Nixon's presidency, in 1972, the fighting continued. Most of the U.S. ground troops had been withdrawn, but the ARVN stepped up its counterattacks against enemy positions in the wake of the North Vietnamese spring offensive. For months, the army of General Thieu, supported by the United States, tried to dislodge the North Vietnamese. From late June to mid-September, Thieu's army inched closer to the previously captured Quang Tri City. Nixon argued that this was a sign that Vietnamization was working, but the reverse was true, since American bombs accompanied Thieu's forces each step of the way. The United States provided what was probably the largest concentration of firepower so far in the war, including shelling from seventeen U.S. cruisers and destroyers, and bombing by B-52s. Still the ARVN could not defeat the North Vietnamese. To solve the problem, Thieu declared the entire area from Quang Tri north to the DMZ a free-fire zone.[2] Once again, U.S. bombers saturated an entire province of South Vietnam.

The air war thus continued to be a way of life for millions of peasants in Indochina. U.S. planes flew thousands of sorties during the summer of 1972 in a last-ditch effort to perfect the laser-controlled "smart bombs."[3] Hanoi charged that many of these bombs were falling on the system of dikes along the Red River. These dikes held back the waters of North Vietnam's most important river, protecting millions of people from flooding. Nixon at first called the accusations inaccurate, but when pictures of extensive damage to the dikes appeared in the press, the President revised his position somewhat, claiming that the air force "has used great restraint in its bombing policy. . . . We have had orders out not to hit dikes."[4] Nixon concluded that Hanoi's version of the dike controversy was a total fabrication. But eyewitness reports confirmed extensive bomb damage; if the United States was not bombing the dikes deliberately, it was clear that no special effort was being made to avoid hitting them. By August 1972, U.S. bombs had damaged fifty-eight dikes, but the system held together.[5]

In attempting to quiet the criticism of the dike bombing, Nixon compared his situation to that of Eisenhower in World War II. Eisenhower had decided to bomb the cities of Germany because "the height of immorality would [have been] to allow Hitler to rule Europe."[6] Nixon faced a similar dilemma:

> We are not using the great power that could finish off North Vietnam in an afternoon, and we will not. But it would be the height of immorality for the United States at this point to leave Vietnam, and in leaving, to turn over to the North Vietnamese the fate of 17 million South Vietnamese.[7]

There was a further point:

> Those who say "End the war" really should name their resolution "Prolong the war." They should name it "Prolong the war," not because they deliberately want to. They want to end the war just as I do, but we have to face this fact: We have only one President at a time, as I said in 1968.[8]

As the dike controversy died down, the President and the Pentagon turned their attention again to the business at hand—wearing down the enemy by round-the-clock bombardment. Somehow, the impersonal nature of the air war generated fewer headlines than the search-and-destroy missions and battleground casualties.

> The B-52s, chauffered by skilled young technicians, went out in waves over both North and South Vietnam, blowing huge craters in the terrain below. From heights of 30,000 to 50,000 feet the air strikes came without warning. The big machines fixed their targets by radar and dropped their bombs without seeing where they fell. In the long, slow flight from Guam the crews ate T.V. dinners and blueberry pies from the commissary, warmed up in galley ovens. The six men of a B-52 crew, remote from the reality of the war, acted as an extension of the computer which governed their plane. They constituted the most detached and impersonal operation in the history of warfare. The triumph of technology was complete.[9]

The total tonnage of bombs dropped by 1972, largely by B-52s, exceeded 800,000 tons by the time of the November election.[10] Calculations showed that by the spring of 1972, for each minute Nixon had been in office, one ton of bombs had fallen somewhere in Indochina.[11]

But Nixon could not be certain that the American voters would view the bombing with the same detachment. He attempted, therefore, to camouflage the real state of affairs; he had learned that what the President *appeared* to be doing was at least as important as his actual deeds. Moreover, he could be seen actively pursuing what appeared to be a genuine search for peace. From the early months of 1972, Nixon had saturated the air waves with his presence as a great leader. His trips to China and Russia were conducted in such a way as to become masterpieces of public relations. While Nixon traveled the globe, conferring about momentous events with Mao, Chou, Brezhnev, and Kosygin, at home his Democratic rivals squabbled with one another.

At the same time, Nixon faced a domestic crisis—the Watergate scandal. This story is well known, but we will recap it here briefly because what happened over Watergate ultimately had a major influence in the decisions that finally ended the Vietnam War. In June 1972 a group of five men illegally entered the headquarters of the Democratic National Committee, located in the Watergate apartment complex in Washington, D.C. While attempting to plant electronic bugs, the group was discovered and arrested.

At the time, no one knew that the burglars were part of the Plumbers unit, formed by White House officials to plug new leaks and to conduct clandestine surveillance. No one knew that the five suspects were working for the Committee to Re-elect the President and that Nixon aides had authorized an entire campaign of dirty tricks and criminal activity. Only when *Washington Post* reporters Bob Woodward and Carl Bernstein began to investigate the bizarre events at the Watergate did the public begin to ask questions. Soon, the reporters were able to connect the break-in with strange goings-on at the Nixon White House. Without a doubt, the persistence of America's free press threatened the President and his staff.

It is a moot point if Nixon actually ordered the Watergate break-in or if he even knew about it beforehand. But by encouraging the Plumbers on previous occasions, he had shown his affinity for this type of conduct and led his campaign workers to believe that he approved of illegal, clandestine operations against political opponents. Therefore, in June 1972 the Plumbers who broke into the Watergate were the spark that could very easily ignite a powder keg of crime and scandal. Nixon worked furiously to cover up the story, and only bits and pieces about the Watergate incident emerged in the summer of 1972.[12] For the remainder of the year, Nixon was able to stifle the investigation and shield his drive for reelection.

George McGovern, the leading Democratic candidate, accused Nixon of indirect responsibility for Watergate, but the public refused to associate the President of the United States with something termed "a third-rate burglary." When on September 15, 1972, Watergate indictments were handed down against E. Howard Hunt, Gordon Liddy, and the five men arrested in the Watergate building, most of the country felt the incident was closed. So with Watergate under control, Richard Nixon accepted the nomination of the Republican Party in the summer of 1972.

Nevertheless, Nixon still worried about the fall campaign, in which the Democrats were sure to raise the issue of the war and his unfulfilled promise to obtain peace in Vietnam. Therefore, Nixon dispatched Kissinger to reopen the peace talks with the North Vietnamese. He went back to Paris in July with a negotiating position that had changed little since the suspension of the secret talks in the spring. At the same time, Nixon was also considering a plan to invade North Vietnam with ARVN ground units backed by U.S. air support.[13]

Kissinger and Le Duc Tho discussed the entire range of issues: a cease-fire, complete withdrawal of U.S. military personnel, the return of all prisoners of war, and a coalition government that would represent all South Vietnamese political beliefs. When the dust had cleared, the issue of what to do with General Thieu remained the principal obstacle to peace.[14] The North Vietnamese proposed a three-party coalition that would include Thieu's party but, specifically, not Thieu himself. The United States would not compromise its support of Thieu. After eight long years and thousands of American deaths, the struggle in Vietnam had apparently become that of defending Thieu.[15]

Despite the deadlock in the negotiations, both sides agreed to meet again in September 1972. To prepare for the next sessions, Kissinger traveled to Saigon for talks with General Thieu. Nixon's adviser explained the problems of negotiating in an election year and then tested a new idea: a commission to oversee new elections for South Vietnam. If Thieu had no objections, Kissinger felt sure that U.S. firepower would force Hanoi to go along. In the meantime, Kissinger promised, the United States would build up Saigon's military strength, and, after the U.S. presidential election, Nixon would not hesitate to bring North Vietnam to its knees in order to maintain Thieu in power.[16] True compromise did not appear to be a part of the Nixon strategy.

The North Vietnamese, however, decided to make a major concession to break the deadlock. Both Peking, on July 20, and Moscow, on September 26, had used or were to use persuasion to get their allies in both North and South Vietnam to drop the demand that Thieu step down.[17] On September 11, the Vietcong called for a government of national concord, one that would reflect the reality of two administrations and two armies. If the United States would help to establish a National Council of Reconciliation and Concord and make this body responsible for carrying out the final peace agreement, then Hanoi would officially drop its opposition to General Thieu.[18] In other words, Thieu could stay in power provided there were safeguards to guarantee new and fair elections. It seems that North Vietnam had come to understand what Russia and China already knew, that without the United States to protect its client regime in Saigon, the Thieu government would inevitably collapse and Vietnam might finally be united.

Meanwhile, Nixon continued to campaign as a statesman and

peacemaker. He told the public that "if we can make the right kind of settlement before the elections, we will make it. If we cannot, we are not going to make the wrong kind of settlement before the elections." We will do everything in our power, Nixon said, "to convince [North Vietnam] that waiting until after the election is not good strategy."[19] The public statements ignored the Vietcong concessions and placed the blame for the continuation of the war on North Vietnam.[20] The President and Henry Kissinger still hoped that Hanoi would capitulate and accept Washington's terms.

In the light of everything that had happened, the weakness of Nixon's political opposition seems incredible. Despite years of administration promises, the war dragged on. Instead of ending the war, Nixon had escalated the U.S. involvement to new heights. The invasions of Cambodia and Laos and the massive bombing war throughout Southeast Asia caused many citizens to believe that Nixon was following a bankrupt policy in Vietnam. As Theodore White has written:

> The American appetite for war had long since been sated in Vietnam. From faculty club to student union, from bar to parlor, from Wall Street to Main Street, all wanted out of Vietnam.[21]

The Democrats nevertheless had trouble mounting a strong campaign against Nixon. The beleaguered Edmund Muskie, George Wallace, victim of an assassination attempt, Senator Henry Jackson, and John Lindsay fell by the wayside. The only candidate Nixon really feared—Edward Kennedy—chose not to enter the race. Finally, Hubert Humphrey battled George McGovern for the nomination, while Nixon rejoiced at the prospect of a victory for McGovern: "To me his steady climb was as welcome to watch as it was almost unbelievable to behold."[22]

The Democrats offered the American people a peace candidate. But McGovern ran an inept campaign and lost the initiative regarding the Vietnam question. Theodore White has described Nixon's shrewd efforts to counteract McGovern:

> His [McGovern's] first issue was peace. . . . McGovern was for accords with China, Russia, with the whole communist world. But so, too, of course was Nixon—and from February (when Nixon went to Peking just before the New Hampshire primary) until May (when the President went to Moscow just before the California primary) all the while that

McGovern preached accommodation, live and let live with Communism, there on the tube of the television, was the President of the U.S.
practicing what McGovern preached.[23]

Having built up a huge lead in the polls, the President decided to
stay above the battle as much as possible. He recruited surrogate
campaigners who appeared on the President's behalf and who defended his record.[24] McGovern tried to attack Nixon on Watergate,
but to no avail. He tried to attack Nixon on corruption but gained
little advantage. He even proposed dramatic economic solutions (the
$1,000 tax rebate to everyone), but these were quickly discredited.
Columnist Art Buchwald remarked that "if Nixon resembled a used
car salesman, McGovern looked like one of his customers."[25] Even
LBJ stated that "the McGovern people are going to defeat themselves."[26]

Still, Nixon realized that Vietnam was a volatile, uncertain element in his campaign, one which could explode against him at any
time. There had been isolated incidents of protest throughout the
spring and summer of 1972. During May, when the United States
mined the harbors of North Vietnam, demonstrators marched in two
dozen cities and on many college campuses. Thirty thousand rallied
in New York City shouting "Out now!" Leaders in the arts and sciences went to jail after an end-the-war vigil at the Capitol. A group of
Ivy League university presidents assailed Kissinger in Washington.
A news writer declared, "Nixon has lost touch with the real world."[27]
During the Republican National Convention in Miami in August,
Ron Kovic, a disabled Vietnam veteran, interrupted Nixon's acceptance speech and shouted, "Stop the bombing! Stop the war! Stop the
bombing! Stop the war!"[28] Even though the Democrats had failed to
capitalize on it, antiwar feeling was still in evidence as Kissinger
continued to negotiate with the North Vietnamese.

On October 8, 1972, Kissinger met Le Duc Tho at a French villa on
the outskirts of Paris. The North Vietnamese delegation surprised
the Americans by presenting a nine-point draft agreement to serve as
the basis for negotiations. The document went beyond the lists of
demands each side had exchanged for almost five years. It called for
an immediate cease-fire-in-place in Vietnam within twenty-four
hours of the signing of the agreement, a full U.S. withdrawal within
sixty days of the agreement, and a coalition government, thus recognizing Thieu's position in Saigon, and it proposed new elections

under the direction of a broad National Council of Reconciliation and Concord.[29] Simply put, the North Vietnamese document provided a "step-by-step [reunification of Vietnam] through peaceful means."[30]

Kissinger met with Le Duc Tho for three more days in October. He demanded certain changes in the text. Washington especially wanted to quash any notion that Saigon would be required to release its Vietnamese civilian prisoners when Hanoi released the American POWs. Hanoi accepted this revision in the text and prodded Washington to finalize the negotiations. Le Duc Tho even suggested a timetable for signing the agreement and announcing the end of the war. Kissinger replied that he would first have to confer with President Nixon. It was possible that the war would be over by October 30, 1972.[31]

Le Duc Tho returned home believing that he had a commitment from Kissinger that Thieu would not have a veto over the settlement. The end was in sight, or so it seemed. The long and bloody war and the equally bloody road to peace had apparently run their course. Unfortunately, as Porter has written:

> the last steps of the road [to peace would indeed] be blocked by yet another resurgence of the very concern for the survival of the U.S. client regime in Saigon which had blocked agreement for four years in Paris. For when the terms of the agreement collided with the interests of the Thieu regime, Nixon was willing to jettison the October compromise and thus imperil the whole agreement.[32]

Shortly after Kissinger's return from Paris, the Nixon administration began to back away from the October draft agreement. General Haig and William Sullivan, both working closely with Kissinger, suggested that Hanoi's draft did not adequately protect U.S. interests.[33] Then from the Pentagon came word that Operation Enhance, code name for the latest shipment of arms and supplies to the Thieu regime, would not be completed by the end of October. Another factor for Nixon to consider was General Thieu himself. The Saigon dictator, quite aware that an agreement meant the evacuation from Vietnam of the United States, announced that he would neither make concessions to Hanoi, nor recognize any made by Washington. Understandably, Thieu was attempting to solidify his position and to convince the United States to continue to support South Vietnam.

His speeches in the fall of 1972 were more threatening toward North Vietnam than ever before, his policies in the South more brutal and corrupt.[34] By acting out his role as the helpless victim of aggression, Thieu in effect dared Nixon to sign an agreement with Hanoi. It was a wild gamble that paid off, at least for the time being.

By the time the end of the reelection campaign was in sight, Nixon felt his position was strong enough not to require the actual signing of the peace treaty. Simply by negotiating on the peace proposals, Nixon had forced McGovern into the difficult position of advocating extreme solutions. The day that Kissinger arrived in Paris, McGovern went on national television and told the American people that if he were elected President he would stop all bombing of North Vietnam, withdraw all U.S. troops from Vietnam, stop all aid to South Vietnam, and ask for nothing in return—not even the release of American prisoners of war. This speech was McGovern's ultimate gamble, but again he had misjudged the national mood. The American public wanted peace, but not surrender, and the Republicans immediately branded McGovern as the "architect of surrender." The President announced that his negotiations would bring peace with honor. McGovern's position was represented as running away in disgrace.[35]

Once he had decided that he did not need to sign the peace treaty in order to win the election, Nixon faced the problem of not making that fact clear to Hanoi. Both the enemy and the American public had to be deceived until the election was over. Then Nixon could once more step up the bombing to try to force Hanoi into a surrender rather than a settlement. The important thing was to delay further negotiations while giving the appearance that Washington wanted to conclude and implement an agreement on schedule. Kissinger flew back to Paris and demanded several additional changes in the draft agreement. When North Vietnam agreed to the changes, the President sent a secret message to Hanoi which stated, according to the North Vietnamese: "The United States side appreciates the good will and serious attitude of [North Vietnam]. The text of the agreement can now be considered complete." Yet the secret message also asked that the timetable for signing the document be delayed by two days because "complex questions" remained to be solved.[36]

Kissinger traveled to Saigon on October 18, 1972, knowing full well that Thieu would try to slam the door in Washington's face.

Thieu reacted to the draft agreement with undisguised fury. His attitude was described as that of a "trapped tiger."[37] The South Vietnamese dictator listed twenty-six revisions that he wanted to see included in the October agreement. At the top of the list were three major changes: There could be no National Council of Reconciliation and Concord alongside his own government; North Vietnamese military forces must withdraw from South Vietnam, and the DMZ would have to become a true border separating North and South. From October 18 to 23, Kissinger negotiated with Thieu—but Washington's puppet had suddenly cut his strings. Saigon used what several observers have called "the power of its own weakness" to stall efforts to end the war.[38] Thieu continued to gamble that Nixon would not desert America's client state.

Thieu had a basis for his position. Whereas Kissinger promised Saigon only a fighting chance, and millions of dollars in arms and supplies to carry on after U.S. withdrawal, Nixon had already decided to allow Saigon the appearance of veto power over the entire agreement.[39] As one administration source revealed, "We were not prepared to lower the boom on Thieu in October."[40] "We never intended to wrap this up by election day," stated a White House official.[41] So Kissinger's mission to Saigon was not, after all, designed to persuade Thieu to go along with the agreement. He merely wanted to collect Thieu's objections before going back to Paris and demanding more concessions. In the eyes of the North Vietnamese, it was a dirty trick, made worse by Nixon's constant reassurance that all was well. Porter has concluded that these facts brought

> into sharper focus what the administration's own account has tried to obscure: that it was not Thieu who sabotaged the October agreement and derailed the scheduled signing, but Nixon, who judged that the terms and timing of the agreement were too unfavorable to his Saigon client state. Thieu's opposition to the agreement . . . [therefore] was not the cause but [merely] the occasion for delaying the signature.[42]

When the United States finally told Hanoi's negotiators that an agreement would be delayed, North Vietnam reacted angrily and released to the press their version of the events: Washington had made an oral agreement and then backed off from the negotiations. This accusation of bad faith was released on October 26, but Nixon and Kissinger reacted quickly, outmaneuvered Hanoi, and stole the headlines.[43] On the heels of North Vietnam's disclosure, Kissinger held a news conference of his own and announced:

> Ladies and gentlemen, we have now heard from both Vietnams and it is obvious that the war that has been raging for ten years is drawing to a conclusion. . . .
>
> We believe that *peace is at hand.* We believe that an agreement is within sight. . . . Peace is within reach in a matter of weeks, or less, depending on when the [next] meeting takes place.[44]

These words fired the imagination of the press and the public. Few bothered to put Kissinger's speech in perspective. Few seemed to hear the warning at the end of the news conference: "We will not be stampeded into an agreement until its provisions are right." A continuation of the war seemed likely, as Nixon reverted in the peace negotiations to the former unhurried pace.[45] By early November, the President no longer talked of peace and withdrawal. Instead, he openly criticized what he saw as arbitrary deadlines imposed by the other side. In addition, Nixon warned that central points in the negotiations remained unsolved. The implications of Nixon's hard line seemed to go unnoticed in a country caught up in election fever.[46] Nixon and Kissinger were obviously working on a new strategy, to take effect when the United States could once again threaten North Vietnam with an air war. In other words, the administration was laying the foundation for a whole new phase of war and diplomacy—after the elections.[47]

In fact, Nixon did not even bother to wait until after the election to attempt to wring more concessions out of the North Vietnamese. On November 2, 1972, Nixon ordered heavier B-52 raids in the North. In his own words, "The plan now was to exert increasing pressure on Hanoi by beginning the bombing near the DMZ and then moving it slightly farther north each day."[48] The American people had no idea that Nixon intended to punish Hanoi severely in a last effort to win military victory as a preface to his version of a peace. For the third time in eight years, the American people were duped: Peace was not at hand; rather, a savage round of escalation was about to begin in Vietnam.

PART FOUR:

THE VIETNAM DISASTER

:18

THE PARIS PEACE AGREEMENT
January 1973

Now that Nixon had announced that "peace is at hand," he pursued his plan to achieve total victory by the most savage aerial attack on North Vietnam of the entire war, in an effort to force Hanoi to surrender. Kissinger agreed to meet with Le Duc Tho again on November 20, after the election was over. In the meantime, the United States concentrated on supplying Saigon with every available weapon. The United States sent General Thieu a huge supply of tanks, helicopters, bombers, and fighter aircraft. The delivery of weapons, all soon to be lost to the North Vietnamese, cost this country several billion dollars and weakened our other bases around the world.[1] South Vietnam, meanwhile, emerged "with the fourth largest air force in the world—more than 2,000 aircraft—even though its pilots had not yet been checked out to fly some of the more sophisticated planes."[2]

North Vietnam watched in amazement as U.S. cargo planes and ships unloaded equipment that General Thieu could use to continue the war. Operation Enhance Plus was open-ended. The Nixon administration was trying to squeeze its entire military aid program for South Vietnam for the coming year into a matter of weeks, before any peace agreement was reached.

Enhance Plus was crucial to the Nixon-Kissinger strategy for ending the war on America's terms. They felt confident that such pressure would strengthen their negotiating position and force Hanoi to yield to their terms. From Nixon's point of view, Enhance Plus served two purposes. The program bolstered the Saigon regime and made Thieu more amenable to an eventual peace treaty. The President sent General Haig to Saigon to supervise the delivery. Haig warned Thieu that the time would come when the United States would be forced to leave Vietnam and that he should cooperate with the White House.[3] He made it plain that the South Vietnamese leader should concentrate on how to survive after the United States left Vietnam.[4]

Project Enhance Plus had the additional objective of showing Thieu that the United States meant to stand behind him. To emphasize this point, President Nixon ordered new air strikes against North Vietnam just as Enhance Plus began. North Vietnam accused Nixon of "strengthening the Nguyen Van Thieu clique to prepare for new aggressions,"[5] but Le Duc Tho did return to Paris for another meeting with Kissinger. At that meeting, Le Duc Tho issued the following statement:

> If the U.S. protracts the negotiations, delays the conclusion of the agreement, and continues the war, the Vietnamese will have no other way than to resolutely carry on their fight until genuine independence, freedom and peace are achieved.[6]

The United States responded by introducing new demands that reopened issues already agreed upon in October 1972. Kissinger now asked that the DMZ be recognized as a provisional boundary, that North Vietnam withdraw some troops from the South, and that Hanoi give further recognition of the sovereignty of South Vietnam. Kissinger also outlined some of Thieu's objections. Le Duc Tho conceded some minor points but refused to discuss fundamental changes in the agreement. When Washington introduced further new demands on November 25, the North Vietnamese asked for a recess.[7] The two sides appeared deadlocked once again.

As Kissinger left Paris, he threatened that the war would be intensified unless Hanoi yielded. In one cable to Kissinger, Nixon said:

> If they were surprised that the President would take the strong action he did prior to the Moscow summit and prior to the election they will find now, with the election behind us, he will take whatever actions he considers necessary to protect the U.S. interest.[8]

Nixon then made a secret commitment to Thieu that if the North Vietnamese in any way breached the projected agreement, the United States would come to Saigon's rescue. "You have my absolute assurance," Nixon wrote, "that if Hanoi fails to abide by the terms of the agreement it is my intention to take swift and severe retaliatory action."[9] The President assured his inner circle that he intended to keep this secret commitment. He also directed the Pentagon to finish work on a special plan to carry out the commitment, should it become necessary, known as "Organizational Changes in Southeast Asia." This plan outlined how the United States could stay involved in Vietnam: After a settlement was reached, the U.S. military command in Saigon would be replaced by an American Defense Attaché Office (DAO), which would carry out many of the same functions.

The DAO would coordinate "in-country" military operations, control "U.S. air surveillance," direct security measures for the ARVN, and set up a network to provide intelligence reports in South Vietnam and "adjacent territories." In addition, the DAO would "participate in the planning for resurgence, . . . reintroduction and employment of [tactical air operations] . . . to include strike planning."[10] This plan established the fact that despite anything the peace agreement might say about American withdrawal from Vietnam, the U.S. military intended to stay and prepare for the eventuality of a new air war, using the B-52s based in Thailand on a twenty-four-hour-a-day alert basis.[11]

Kissinger and Le Duc Tho resumed their discussions the first week of December 1972 in Paris. The two representatives hashed through all the issues again, but neither side retreated from its respective position. Kissinger held firm on the major changes that both Nixon and Thieu wanted in the October agreement, and threatened North Vietnam with further bombing attacks if Hanoi did not concede. Tho, for his part, hoping to force Kissinger to negotiate more realistically, started drawing back on some of the concessions Hanoi had already made. In particular, the North Vietnamese representative hinted that the release of political prisoners held by Thieu might have to coincide with the release of the American POWs.

Kissinger refused to compromise and the talks broke down again on December 13, 1972. Kissinger returned to Washington and met with Nixon the next day. They decided to issue an ultimatum to Hanoi: Yield to U.S. demands within three days or face a bombing campaign. Moving quickly, Kissinger explained the situation to Admiral Moorer of the Joint Chiefs and asked how many B-52s were available for an attack on North Vietnam. The answer apparently satisfied the White House, for when the arbitrary deadline ran out on

December 17, Nixon immediately ordered the greatest air attacks of the war against Hanoi and Haiphong.[12]

To justify the bombing, Kissinger told the American people that North Vietnam was at fault and had sabotaged the talks in Paris. He said that Hanoi had introduced "one frivolous issue after another" as part of a great "charade," and each time "a settlement was . . . within our reach, [it] was always pulled just beyond our reach."[13] Kissinger was simply following President Nixon's instructions:

> We must cast this if we possibly can in the light that the North Vietnamese rather than we were responsible for the breakdown in negotiations; and then we should talk in as low-key a manner as possible, and act as strongly as possible without making a big to-do about the fact that we were stepping up the bombing and in effect resuming the war. . . .[14]

Alexander Haig made it plain that: "This man [Nixon] is going to stand tall and resume the bombing and put those B-52 mothers in there and show 'em we mean business."[15]

For the next twelve days, from December 18 to December 30, the United States bombed Hanoi and Haiphong with more ferocity than at any time in the history of the Vietnam War, dropping over 35,000 tons of bombs in the middle of North Vietnam's two major urban centers.[16] Nixon and the Pentagon unleashed two hundred B-52s; the giant stratofortresses flew in groups of three, carrying 500- and 750-pound bombs, which, when dropped, literally engulfed rectangular areas, one mile long and one-half mile wide, of the city.[17] The military expected that population centers as well as military targets would be wiped out, and in most cases the target areas emerged as heaping mounds of rubble. The rubble represented the Pentagon's admitted goal—"crippling the daily life of Hanoi and Haiphong and destroying North Vietnam's ability to support forces in South Vietnam."[18]

The Christmas bombings of 1972 caused massive destruction and suffering. More than 2,000 civilians died in Hanoi alone.[19] Entire neighborhoods were obliterated, transportation facilities completely destroyed, and important hospitals devastated. The Bach Mai hospital, Hanoi's most up-to-date medical facility, with over 900 beds, was left in ruins. Foreign reporters described fifty-foot craters and uprooted trees in the very heart of Hanoi.[20]

President Nixon told one columnist that he ordered the bombings because "the Russians and Chinese might think they were dealing with a madman and so had better force North Vietnam into a settlement before the world was consumed by a larger war."[21] Many people agreed that only a madman could have ordered the kind of destruction carried out by the B-52s on civilian population centers.

In fact, when the Christmas bombings were over, the United States had actually lost ground in the effort to end the war on its terms. Nixon had underestimated the determination of the North Vietnamese people. The attack against Hanoi had been anticipated; many important offices and many of the people had been moved out into the countryside, where the air attacks were less intense. The President also underestimated the skill of the North Vietnamese defense forces. The B-52s came under steady fire from North Vietnam's SAM missiles. Between thirty-three and thirty-five of them, carrying almost 100 U.S. airmen, went down in twelve days. The official figure of only fifteen planes lost was almost certainly in error. The new-found accuracy of North Vietnam's gunners shocked the Pentagon, so much so that by the end of December the Joint Chiefs strongly urged an end to the bombings.[22]

Finally, Nixon underestimated his critics at home and around the world, who condemned the Christmas bombings as "war by tantrum" or "Stone Age strategy." From the Pope's outcry against the "harsh . . . war actions" to the British view that here was "a man blinded by fury or incapable of seeing the consequences of what he is doing," outrage was the standard response. The *Washington Post* described Nixon's air blitz under the headline "TERROR BOMBING IN THE NAME OF PEACE," while other sources of world opinion agreed with Leonid Brezhnev's judgment, politically inspired or not, that Nixon's decision to level Hanoi was nothing more than barbaric.[23]

The White House announced on December 30 that Henry Kissinger and Le Duc Tho would hold their next meeting in Paris on January 8, 1973. In light of the subsequent agreement, many people have assumed that the Christmas air raids were responsible for ending the war. But the truth is that Nixon's last brutal fling achieved little or nothing for the United States. The agreement worked out in January 1973 differed little from the one reached the previous October.

> Nixon's bargaining hand [at the Paris peace talks] had been greatly weakened. His last major bargaining chip had been used to no avail, and now his administration was under even more intense pressure than before to reach agreement without delay. . . .

Later the Administration would do its best to persuade the U.S. public that the bombing had made the North Vietnamese more cooperative at the peace table. A Gallup poll taken some weeks later showed that 57 percent of those polled believed that the Christmas bombing had contributed to the peace settlement.

In an ironic way, it was true; by its political and military failure the bombing of Hanoi and Haiphong made the Paris agreement possible. For it forced Nixon and Kissinger to accept the very terms which they had rejected in October, November and December. While the threat of massive bombing had seemed to give Nixon leverage over the North Vietnamese, the battle of Hanoi showed how apparent strength could be transformed into diplomatic weakness.[24]

More than once Henry Kissinger had bragged that, if worse came to worse, he could "reduce Le Duc Tho to tears" with America's B-52s.[25] When Kissinger arrived at the January peace talks, Tho greeted him with the icy comment, "I am a personal victim of yours," as if the North Vietnamese representative had heard of Kissinger's boasts. After a stormy first day, the two sides got down to business on January 9 and finally worked out a peace agreement by January 13, 1973.[26] The United States had clearly yielded in its demands. For example, Kissinger agreed to allow migration and movement across the DMZ, thus recognizing the temporary nature of the dividing line. The United States also agreed to upgrade the National Council of Reconciliation and Concord, allowing it to stand alongside Thieu's government; the council would be responsible for future elections. Indirectly, Kissinger even gave in to Hanoi on the issue of recognizing the Vietcong. One of the two peace documents was signed by representatives of the Vietcong. The United States agreed that the National Liberation Front would share power with the Thieu government in a divided South Vietnam.[27] According to the Kalb brothers:

> Nixon got the prisoners back, Tho got the Americans out, Thieu got to keep his hold on power, and the PRG [Vietcong government] got a degree of political legitimacy in South Vietnam. Everybody got something, but nobody got everything.[28]

There was no guarantee that the Thieu regime would survive after the United States finally withdrew from South Vietnam. Despite their secret commitment to Thieu, both Nixon and Kissinger must have known that South Vietnam's future was bleak. The United

States could bolster Thieu's regime, escalate the war until the very end, and even, if necessary, work to subvert the final agreement, but Kissinger himself admitted, "The most that could be salvaged from the U.S. involvement in Vietnam was a 'decent interval' between an American pullout and the possibility of a Communist takeover."[29] The United States had become involved in the war to save South Vietnam from Communism; the terms of the peace agreement did not safeguard that goal.

The chief provisions of the Paris agreement signed on January 27, 1973, were:[30]

1. A cease-fire in place throughout all of Vietnam, and an end to all ground, air, and naval combat operations. This important provision tacitly recognized the right of North Vietnam to retain the bulk of its military forces in South Vietnam. No withdrawal of North Vietnamese troops from the South was required.

2. A complete withdrawal of U.S. military forces within sixty days (including all advisers and technicians), the removal of U.S. war materiel, and the dismantling of all U.S. bases.

3. A return of all military prisoners of war from both sides within sixty days.

4. A prohibition against sending new military personnel (including advisers, technicians, or police) into South Vietnam, and a prohibition against sending new war materiel into South Vietnam. Both sides were permitted to replace weapons and war materiel that had been destroyed, damaged, worn out, or used up—but only on a one-for-one replacement basis. No new types of weapons could be introduced.

5. A three-party Council of National Reconciliation and Concord would be established. The Council would include representatives from Thieu's government, from the National Liberation Front, and from the neutralist factions. Its job would be to organize and help supervise free, democratic elections in South Vietnam. Thieu's government and the NLF would hold two-party conferences to work out the initial arrangements. Until the elections, all people in South Vietnam would have personal freedom, freedom of speech, freedom of the press, freedom of meetings, organization, and political activity, and freedom of movement and residence.

6. A new International Commission for Control and Supervision (ICCS) would be formed to supervise the cease-fire, the withdrawal

of U.S. forces and the dismantling of U.S. bases, and the return of POWs. The ICCS could only investigate and report violations; it would have no authority to punish violations.

7. A Joint Military Commission made up of representatives from the United States, Thieu's government, the NLF, and North Vietnam would be formed in Saigon (with branches throughout the country) to enforce the Paris agreements.

8. All foreign countries would end all military activities in Laos and Cambodia as soon as possible. Then all foreign military forces were to be withdrawn.

9. The United States would discuss reconstruction aid with North Vietnam. The terms of this provision were very vague in the public document, but several sources allege that Kissinger promised huge amounts of U.S. aid to North Vietnam.

The terms of the treaty showed that the last three months of the war, from October 1972 to January 1973, were totally meaningless, a futile propaganda exercise. From a broader perspective, the final four years of the war gained nothing and meant nothing. All those months of fighting caused indescribable suffering in the United States and in Vietnam.

A "peace treaty" had been agreed upon, but as time passed it became apparent that neither party signed it in good faith. Enhance Plus and the establishment of the DAO evidenced Nixon's determination to bolster the Thieu regime. A U.S. military presence was maintained in South Vietnam by simply replacing military personnel with large numbers of U.S. "military civilians"—soldiers without uniforms.

> The U.S. intended to bring in a large force of civilians to other jobs previously done by the U.S. military personnel. . . . The thinly disguised military personnel . . . included both persons hired directly by the U.S. and those employed by the 23 corporations [under] government contract in Vietnam. . . . Several thousand of these military technicians, many of them recruited directly from the military and officially "retired" for the purpose, entered Vietnam as the last American troops were being withdrawn.[31]

Nixon did not deactivate the U.S. Air Force headquarters in Saigon, as required in the agreement; instead, he moved it a few hundred miles northwest to the Nakhom Phanom Royal Thai Air Base in Thailand. There the Seventh Air Force remained poised on the Thai border, ready at a moment's notice to send U.S. jet bombers back into action in Indochina. Instead of returning home when they left Vietnam, many aircraft squadrons were simply reassigned to one of the six huge U.S. air bases in Thailand, armed and ready for future action. Diplomatically, Nixon zeroed in on the International Commission for Control and Supervision (ICCS), which was to consist of representatives from three neutral countries. He insured that Canada was a member of the ICCS so as to have a friendly voice on the commission. After weeks of intense pressure, the reluctant Canadians finally bowed to Nixon's demand and accepted membership on the ICCS.[32]

President Nixon openly hinted that he had no intention of supporting other provisions of the peace agreement. On January 23, 1973, four days before the signing ceremony, Nixon announced that the United States would not support free elections, and proclaimed that the United States would "continue to recognize the Government of South Vietnam as the sole legitimate government in South Vietnam."[33]

Nixon's determination to nullify aspects of the peace agreement encouraged General Thieu to do the same. In the closing days of the war, both the ARVN and their North Vietnamese/Vietcong adversaries occupied hundreds of villages in disputed territory. When the cease-fire went into effect, both sides were to remain in place. But General Thieu did not abide by this provision. For the next several months, in complete violation of the treaty, he unleashed the South Vietnamese armed forces against hundreds of disputed villages, using both aircraft and artillery against his own people. Within the first few months of 1973, the forces of General Thieu had driven the Communists out of hundreds of towns and villages under their control at the time of the cease-fire.

Thieu also conducted a terribly harsh—and illegal—campaign of terror against internal enemies and political opponents in South Vietnam. Although the peace treaty specifically guaranteed the freedoms of speech and assembly, as well as the freedoms of movement and residence, General Thieu undertook severe policies against his enemies.

Thieu issued new orders to his police and military forces: shoot to kill [all] those who "urge the people to demonstrate, and those who cause disorder or invite others to follow communism"; shoot anyone who deserts; arrest and detain neutralists [and people] who "incite the people to create disorder and confusion, or to leave those areas controlled by the government in order to go into communist controlled zones." . . .[34]

Nowhere was Thieu's determination to ignore certain unacceptable terms of the peace agreement more evident than during the negotiations to set up a National Council of Reconciliation and Concord. The council's task was to organize free elections, an event Thieu could not permit to take place. Talks between Saigon and the NLF to set up the council began on March 19, 1973, outside Paris. Before discussing any of the issues, Thieu demanded that the North Vietnamese withdraw all of their military personnel from South Vietnam. This demand was directly counter to the peace agreement, with its cease-fire in place, which permitted the North Vietnamese to remain in South Vietnam, and in any case the NLF had no authority even to discuss issues affecting the North Vietnamese. General Thieu obviously knew this, but he had no intention of ever agreeing to the formation of a National Council of Reconciliation and Concord as required by the Paris agreement. After four fruitless months, the talks broke up on July 23, 1973.

Another of General Thieu's plans to subvert the peace, apparently with America's blessing, was to destroy the effectiveness of the chief enforcing agent, provided for in the peace agreement—the Joint Military Commission made up of representatives of the United States, North Vietnam, the NLF, and the Saigon government. The JMC was responsible for insuring full implementation of the cease-fire, the American withdrawal, the exchange of prisoners, and the temporary division of South Vietnam into Communist and non-Communist zones.

When the North Vietnamese officials arrived in Saigon to begin work on the JMC, Thieu harassed the group and isolated its members. The North Vietnamese became virtual prisoners in a compound at Tan Son Nhut air base. Their treatment was so harsh that the Hanoi government threatened to stop releasing American prisoners of war. Only then did the United States bring pressure on Thieu to improve the situation.

The NLF delegates to the Joint Military Commission suffered even greater harm at Thieu's hands. They were scheduled to be picked up at various villages and jungle encampments by government aircraft or trucks and then escorted to JMC headquarters in Saigon. When the NLF delegates informed Thieu's government where they were to be picked up, Thieu ordered his military forces to bomb and shell those areas. Naturally, because of these armed attacks, this treachery, very few NLF members ever joined the JMC. In the end, General Thieu's continual harassment and obstructionism completely nullified the Joint Military Commission.[35]

By the summer of 1973, Thieu had done everything in his power to keep the Paris agreement from being fully implemented. It is apparent that only Nixon's promise that the United States would intervene to support him, and cash payments, had induced the South Vietnamese leader to cooperate. Thieu continued to hang on to his letters from Nixon, the latest dated January 15, 1973, in which the President promised to respond with full force if necessary to preserve the Saigon regime.[36]

The North Vietnamese had no greater interest than Thieu in the final implementation of the Paris accords. They had supreme confidence that after a decent interval had elapsed, they would ultimately be victorious. In the meantime, they simply went through the motions of complying with the Paris agreement. The State Department at one time issued a white paper outlining all of the North Vietnamese actions in violation of the treaty. Many of these were true.

The apparent patience and restraint of North Vietnam appeared to be deeply frustrating to President Nixon. He was still totally committed to the concept of winning in Southeast Asia. Under the pressure of Watergate, he attempted to focus the attention of Congress and the American people again on the Vietnam problem and to prepare them for the necessity of resuming the war when the time came that he would need to fulfill his secret promise to Thieu. He thus emphasized North Vietnamese cease-fire violations, allegations, for example, that North Vietnam had not withdrawn completely from Cambodia and Laos. The Paris agreement had not set any specific time limit for their withdrawal, so Nixon was almost certainly correct that there were still some North Vietnamese in those countries after the cease-fire. Without giving the North Vietnamese a reasonable time to withdraw their remaining forces, Nixon ordered U.S. bombers to attack. By the end of the month of February, the Seventh Air Force was flying over sixty B-52 missions per day against Cambodian targets.[37]

These aircraft, flying out of Thailand, came under the authority of the new air force headquarters at Nakhom Phanom Air Field on the Thai border.

Nixon also continued to maintain the massive U.S. supply program to Saigon. After January 1973 the White House actually increased the amounts of aid to General Thieu, and allowed South Vietnam to take over all U.S. bases intact, contrary to the peace agreement. Hanoi responded with a modest resupply program of its own. The North Vietnamese built a paved road to the South and sent in food and logistical supplies, but the Pentagon discovered through its reconnaissance that relatively little military equipment came down Hanoi's road into South Vietnam after the cease-fire. Nevertheless, on March 15, Nixon threatened for the first time to take unilateral action if necessary to force North Vietnam to stop their "infiltration" into the South.[38] Nixon then resumed aerial reconnaissance flights over North Vietnam in April 1973. In the past, reconnaissance flights had usually signaled the resumption of full-scale bombing against the North.

About ten days after the Paris agreement was signed, Kissinger flew to North Vietnam for talks on war reconstruction aid as required by the accords. The two sides agreed that, in mid-March, Washington and Hanoi would begin negotiations in Paris. These talks moved along so smoothly that by March 27 most of the problems were solved,[39] but in April 1973 Nixon called a halt to the talks and publicly threatened North Vietnam with renewed bombing.

Before these bombing threats could be put to the test, however, the presidential house of Watergate cards, so carefully built over the past ten months, began to fall down upon Nixon's head. On April 30, 1973, Nixon was forced to announce the resignations of his two top aides, H. R. Haldeman and John Erlichman, his attorney general, Richard Kleindienst, and his legal counsel, John Dean. From that day onward Nixon was unable to maintain effective control over his foreign policy.

Nixon's power began to ebb like the tide. Only a few weeks earlier, he had summoned General Thieu to San Clemente and instructed him to continue the pretense of negotiating with the Communists, largely to quiet his critics in Congress and the press. Thieu's continued cooperation was bought at the cost of new economic aid and a promise that North Vietnam would be subject to massive and brutal retaliation if it broke any of the agreements.[40]

The end was drawing near. Only four days after Nixon was forced to fire Haldeman, Erlichman, Kleindienst, and Dean on April 30, the House Democrats voted to cut off funds for the bombing of Cambodia. On May 19, 1973, the full House voted likewise. Still Nixon persisted. The cut-off would not become law until the Senate passed the measure. Meanwhile, Nixon continued to pound Cambodia day after day.

Nixon's final attempt to somehow achieve victory in Vietnam came the following month when Brezhnev visited the United States. Nixon entertained Brezhnev at San Clemente, where he again tried in vain to enlist Russia's support in forcing North Vietnam to accept U.S. terms.[41] On the last day of Brezhnev's visit, the U.S. House of Representatives agreed to a Senate bill calling for an immediate cut-off of all funds for U.S. bombing in Cambodia. Although Nixon vetoed the bill, he was a beaten man. Reluctantly, he agreed to stop all U.S. bombing in Indochina on August 15, 1973.

An era of direct U.S. military involvement in Indochina ended when the last bomber to strike Cambodia returned to its base in Thailand. For almost thirty years the United States had been involved in Southeast Asia. For four and a half years, Richard Nixon had fought a deadly war in Southeast Asia to achieve total victory. At long last Congress finally put an end to the war, which fact Nixon continues to lament:

> The war in Vietnam was not lost on the battlefields of Vietnam. It was lost in the halls of Congress, in the boardrooms of corporations, in the executive suites of foundations, and in the editorial rooms of great newspapers and television networks. It was lost in the salons of Georgetown, the drawing rooms of the "beautiful people" in New York, and the classrooms of great universities. The class that provided the strong leadership that made victory possible in World War I and World War II failed America in one of the crucial battles of World War III— Vietnam.[42]

FINAL COUNTDOWN
January 27, 1973–April 30, 1975

Neither the peace agreement nor the end to U.S. bombing brought peace to Southeast Asia. Real peace was impossible so long as the United States supported General Thieu.

> The Paris Agreement could not end the war because Thieu had been assured by the Nixon Administration that he would get full U.S. backing for a policy of avoiding political accommodation and continuing the military offensive.[1]

Nixon's power to act was now limited, but he remained absolutely committed to General Thieu. He no longer had the power to carry out these commitments openly, so he tried to fulfill them indirectly. One way was to permit Thieu to violate the provisions of the peace treaty. An incident might be provoked that would convince Congress and the American public to send U.S. troops back into Vietnam.

In July and August 1973, ARVN units launched several large-scale military operations, including a major thrust into Binh Dinh province. Infantry and ranger battalions pushed the Vietcong out of a rich agricultural area and then seized all of the rice fields and rice supplies.[2] At the same time, Thieu's air force struck at the Cambodian border and deep into the populated delta regions south of Saigon. Following these raids, the ARVN attacked North Vietnamese outposts which had been guaranteed under the Paris agreement and seized more than 700 villages and hamlets.[3]

In early October, sporadic ground action by the ARVN gave way to concentrated bombing raids by Saigon's air force. Tay Ninh province along the Cambodian border suffered the most from Thieu's air war. Hundreds of planes attacked strategic crossroads and entry points through which supplies came to North Vietnamese units, as more civilians lost their homes, their crops, and their lives. American troops were gone, but the previous U.S. pattern of air strikes and the search-and-destroy missions continued. The ARVN pushed into Quang Duc province, also along the Cambodian border, and fought pitched battles against several Vietcong units. Using U.S. artillery and armored vehicles, Thieu's army held its own. The ARVN appeared to have found new life.[4]

Thieu also showed himself an apt pupil of U.S. propaganda techniques. He called his own extensive military operations preemptive attacks, justifying them by saying that unless South Vietnam struck first, Hanoi and the Vietcong were sure to seize all disputed territory. By October, Thieu was spreading rumors that North Vietnam planned to launch a general offensive. To meet the so-called challenge, ARVN's Twenty-fifth Division assaulted a North Vietnamese camp in Tay Ninh province, suffering numerous casualties, and then overran a rubber plantation that was clearly located in VC territory. All the while, the Saigon government continued to accuse North Vietnam of violating the cease-fire.[5] United States intelligence analysts conceded privately that there was little evidence for such accusations.

Despite Thieu's provocations, the North Vietnamese continued to exercise restraint. By the end of October 1973, however, the Politburo in Hanoi had decided to strike back in response to Saigon's actions, but only on a limited scale.[6]

> According to U.S. intelligence sources . . . the directives [from Hanoi stated] that the purpose of such counter-attacks was still limited to punishing Saigon's cease-fire violations and that they must not cause the breakdown of the cease-fire itself.[7]

Hanoi clearly preferred to avoid aggressive moves in South Vietnam. Yet Saigon seized upon every Vietcong operation, however minor, as if the dreaded general offensive had begun. In fact, North Vietnamese forces only attacked ARVN bases illegally built in territory granted to North Vietnam by the peace agreement.[8]

Thieu's campaign became more and more reckless, more and more obviously provocative. There was good reason for this. He needed desperately to utilize Nixon's secret promises as soon as possible. Behind all the blustering and military pomp, he knew his own situation was unstable. South Vietnam's economy, supported for years by the American taxpayer, was practically bankrupt now that U.S. troops were gone. Politically, support for his government was eroding rapidly; militarily, he knew the ARVN alone would be no match for the North Vietnamese when they finally decided that a decent interval had passed and they could take direct action. Finally, Thieu was aware that Nixon was locked in combat with a hostile Congress on the issue of Watergate.

> Thieu saw the distinct possibility that both the pledge of U.S. air support and plentiful military and economic aid might disappear within a relatively short time. Thieu, who felt that Saigon faced a military showdown with the Communists eventually in any case, wanted it to come as soon as possible.[9]

Thieu and the American Embassy in Saigon worked out a strategy to make the best of this difficult situation. Officials from Washington and Saigon would try to convince the American Congress to vote greater and greater aid packages for General Thieu. At the same time, Saigon would try to provoke North Vietnam into launching a new war. With this "incident" Thieu tried to reenact LBJ's Tonkin Gulf strategy.

Meanwhile, the U.S. ambassador to Saigon, Ellsworth Bunker, who had resigned his post after the American withdrawal was complete, had been replaced by Graham Martin. The new ambassador was a "perfect extension of the Nixon White House."[9a] "A super American patriot," claimed one associate. "He didn't give a goddamn about the Vietnamese. All he cared about was the United States." Martin, who hated Communism with a fervent passion, was "the next best thing to a B-52." Another official remembered that

> to him there was nothing so loathsome as being a Communist. His attitudes were formed at a time when Communism was the nemesis of all that was good, and Vietnam was a psychological battleground for him.[10]

An admirer of Henry Kissinger, a willing surrogate of Richard Nixon, and committed to Thieu, Martin brought to his new post a crusading spirit and a wealth of experience in the areas of secret intelligence, propaganda, and power politics. Martin was the perfect man to stand behind Thieu and implement Nixon's policy.

General John Murray, assisting the new ambassador, ran the Defense Attaché Office (DAO), which, in apparent violation of the peace treaty, was America's military headquarters in Saigon. Murray advised ARVN leaders and sometimes directed South Vietnamese military operations. The DAO was an integral part of Nixon's secret commitment to General Thieu. From the DAO approximately fifty American military officers, disguised as civilian workers, concentrated on the miliary aspects of the situation. Murray coordinated military aid, researched ways to bring U.S. forces back into the struggle, and maintained permanent contact with the U.S. air command in Thailand, home for 50,000 American soldiers and hundreds of fighter-bombers.[11] Murray also kept in touch with Thomas Polgar, station chief of the CIA in South Vietnam.

With the U.S. Army gone, the CIA network had once again become very influential. CIA intelligence activities from 1973 to 1975 were remarkably similar to those of 1963–64. Furthermore, just as Colonel Lansdale and William Colby had used propaganda and false information to justify their covert activities, so the new faces in the CIA excelled at propaganda and misleading reports. No matter how harmless North Vietnam's intentions seemed to be in 1973 and 1974, Station Chief Polgar consistently overruled cautious analysts, choosing instead to sound the alarm. Polgar and General Murray were right in line with Ambassador Martin. As a result, a steady stream of rumors and alarmist reports were sent to Washington to badger Congress for more aid.[12]

Private business interests did their share too. For example, Northrop Aviation Company helped ram a new and more expensive jet fighter through the Congress and into Saigon's air force. Senator James Pearson of Kansas worked actively as Northrop's advocate, ignoring the fact that supplying Saigon with new planes was yet another U.S. violation of the Paris peace agreement.[13]

General Thieu, his confidence bolstered by increased U.S. aid, announced in November 1973 that the Third Indochina War had begun. Saigon's air force promptly bombed the South Vietnamese town of Loc Ninh, held by the North's forces, demolishing a hospital and killing more than a hundred civilians. The air raids became more numerous in late November and December.[14] With the bombing strikes came harsher warnings from Saigon that soon the ARVN would launch operations deep into North Vietnamese sanctuaries. Thieu ended the year with new orders to attack enemy territory and with a prophetic statement: "As far as the armed forces are concerned, I can tell you the war has restarted."[15]

Thieu's aggressive attitude posed a problem for Hanoi's leaders, who were still determined to keep the war from escalating, if only for tactical purposes. It is apparent that Thieu was in a bind and needed to act promptly to save himself, but time was on the side of Hanoi, who could afford to wait for the most apropos moment before abrogating its agreements under the treaty. When Kissinger suggested a secret meeting with Le Duc Tho to discuss the situation in Cambodia, Hanoi seized the opportunity to criticize U.S. and South Vietnamese cease-fire violations.[16] Each side said that the other had called the meeting. During the discussions on December 20, Tho made no commitments and listened while Kissinger argued for continued North Vietnamese restraint, on the grounds that Thieu, with his billions of dollars worth of American weapons, was unbeatable.[17]

The continued fighting in Vietnam was at that moment particularly embarrassing for Kissinger personally. Only ten days before this Paris meeting, Kissinger had received the Nobel Peace Prize for his efforts to end the war in Vietnam. Le Duc Tho had been declared co-recipient, but Hanoi's representative angrily refused to attend the awards ceremony. "When the Paris agreement on Vietnam is respected," he explained in a realistic appraisal of the situation, "when guns are silenced, and peace is really restored in South Vietnam, I will consider the acceptance of this prize."[18]

As the year drew to a close, the State Department released a bulletin that accused North Vietnam of continual and obvious violations of the cease-fire. Unquestionably, the North Vietnamese violated the treaty, but in fact Thieu made every effort to induce these violations in order to gain more support from the United States. The State Department bulletin read:

> Communist violations of the Paris Accords . . . have reached a dangerously high level. The build-up in men and arms of North Vietnamese forces in South Vietnam gives the Communists a capability for offensive action greater than that deployed before their spring 1972 offensive. The United States Government intends by every possible means to deter Hanoi from continuing on its present course. One of our efforts must be to bring to bear on Hanoi the pressure of external public opinion and to encourage other governments to exert a restraining influence on North Vietnam.

> The fighting continues. Ceasefire violations are numerous, and in the past two months they have become more serious and blatant. None of

the bodies established to implement the cease-fire has functioned effectively because the Communists have failed to facilitate the work of
these peace-keeping mechanisms. . . . Further the ICCS has been
crippled in its supervisory role because of persistent obstructionism on
the part of its Communist members, Poland and Hungary.

There has been no progress toward a political settlement. North Vietnam remains determined to gain power in the South, by military means
if necessary; and the South Vietnamese remain determined to prevent
this. Communist efforts to win greater support from the South Vietnamese people have failed dismally. The current level of hostilities initiated by the Communists may reflect their conclusion that they have no
chance to win a political contest in South Vietnam and that the military
route represents their only hope of gaining control of the South. . . .
Since January 27, over 70,000 fighting men have moved illegally into
the South, bringing total Communist combat strength to between
180,000 and 190,000. This infiltration has recently been increased back
up to wartime levels. . . . While committing major violations of the
Agreement, the Communists have unleashed a massive propaganda
barrage claiming alleged U.S. and GVN [South Vietnamese] ceasefire
violations. Hanoi has sought to pin the blame for the deteriorating military situation on U.S. encouragement of and assistance to GVN. . . .[19]

As 1974 opened, the major issue for President Nixon was how far it
was possible to go politically in support of Thieu's military operations and policies. In addition to the renewed fighting, there had
been, for example, no progress toward the formation of a National
Council of Reconciliation and Concord, and no attempt to organize
general elections. As the weeks passed by, President Nixon spoke
less and less about the terms of the Paris agreement and the need for
peace. His main concern was making sure that South Vietnam got all
the aid it needed. In his memoirs, the President tried to justify his
devotion to General Thieu by stating that "the North Vietnamese
were clearly preparing a new offensive in Cambodia and South Vietnam, aimed at testing our willingness and ability to enforce the Paris
agreement."[20]

Administration efforts to squeeze extra funds out of the Congress
were eagerly led by Graham Martin. Assuming that a cease-fire in
Cambodia would free millions of dollars of aid for use in South
Vietnam, he suggested that Kissinger compromise with Prince Siha-
nouk. But Kissinger's mind was closed. As he told John Gunther
Dean, the ambassador in Phnom Penh, "I don't want to hear about
Laos-type compromises."[21] Martin then began to look for other ways
to achieve his goals.

Martin first clamped down on leaks in the American embassy and among CIA analysts to insure that Washington and the American people heard the story he wanted them to hear.[21a] The ambassador was especially harsh on journalists who tried to report U.S. violations of the Paris agreement, or who cast doubt on the prediction that North Vietnam was planning a general offensive. They were "mouthpieces of Hanoi," Martin said,

> whose emotional involvement in a North Vietnamese victory is transparently clear and whose reporting, features and editorials combine to present gross and blatant distortions to the public.[22]

At the same time, the ambassador openly insulted antiwar congressmen such as Edward Kennedy and antiwar religious figures such as the Reverend William Webber. A favorite technique was to publish the pictures of dead Vietnamese children and then to blame their deaths on the encouragement U.S. antiwar leaders supposedly gave to the enemy. Most notorious of all Martin's schemes, however, was an unsuccessful attempt to lobby Congress for more aid. Martin even offered to finance the project, but the South Vietnamese officials he contacted were too greedy and corrupt to be able to make a decision about who should handle the funds. Although Martin's propaganda alienated many congressmen, it was intended to lay the necessary groundwork for another battle over appropriations.[23]

The crucial congressional vote occurred on April 3, 1974. The Senate Armed Services Committee decided not to increase the current Vietnam aid budget and to cut the existing aid package, which went below $1 billion for the first time in ten years. Although many people felt $1 billion was still far too much money to squander in South Vietnam, the Nixon administration reacted as if the budget cut had created a new crisis in U.S. foreign policy. The Defense Attaché Office in Saigon informed the Pentagon that the amount approved by Congress had in fact already been spent in an effort to get the ARVN ready for a new offensive in 1974. The Joint Chiefs offered to transfer to South Vietnam funds approved for other purposes, but Congress intervened with a terse reminder: "It cannot be emphasized too strongly that the statutory ceiling . . . enacted in fiscal year 1974 remains unaltered and shall not be circumvented by accounting adjustments."[24]

At this point, President Nixon entered the debate with a special request for another $940 million, supposedly "to assist South Vietnam, Cambodia, and Laos in their efforts to shift their economies from war to peace and to accelerate the reconstitution of their societies."[25] But Congress no longer believed the chief executive's promises; members doubted that a new appropriation would go toward rebuilding Southeast Asia. They told Nixon that if he wanted them to believe that a real threat of a Communist takeover actually existed, the administration would have to do a better job of proving its case.

General Thieu stepped into the breach, determined to provide Nixon with just such proof—real or manufactured. Throughout one period of the debate, Thieu had remained confident that Nixon would be able to keep his promise of additional aid; he "was still convinced that Americans would come to his assistance with bombers if necessary."[26] When the vote to cut the aid to Vietnam finally came, Thieu was dumbfounded—and in deep trouble. So he decided to take matters into his own hands, using the weapons he knew best.

His new ploy was the logical culmination of several months of offensive actions. Two months earlier, in February 1974, Thieu had ordered several attacks into territory held by the North Vietnamese. Alleging Communist violations of the cease-fire, he sent the ARVN into Quang Ngai province along the eastern coast, an area controlled by the Vietcong since 1964. The army's push into Quang Ngai "involved building many new military posts, relocating the population, . . . burning the old villages, and police operations to arrest and detain suspected Communist cadres." At the same time, two ARVN divisions invaded the area west of Saigon known as the Iron Triangle, and other divisions attacked North Vietnamese bases in the northern delta. These raids had two main goals: to seize as much land as possible and to provoke North Vietnam into a large-scale counterattack. By April 1974 Thieu had achieved partial success with the first goal, but had failed to force Hanoi out of its defensive posture.[27] Thus, when the U.S. Congress cut South Vietnam's aid, Thieu decided on a dramatic act to show that Hanoi was planning an offensive.

On April 11, Thieu quietly ordered the evacuation of Tong Le Chan, an outpost manned by several hundred ARVN soldiers. The North Vietnamese, fully aware of the evacuation, moved into Tong Le Chan unopposed after the ARVN had slipped away into the bush.

The next day Saigon unleashed a barrage of propaganda claiming that the Communists had launched a massive ground attack and had overrun the base.[28] Complaining that Hanoi had destroyed the significance of the Paris agreement, General Thieu ordered his representative to walk out of the ongoing political talks in Paris. He also forced a breakdown of the Joint Military Commission's activities inside South Vietnam, as it struggled to monitor the cease-fire. In all these actions, Thieu found willing accomplices both in Saigon and Washington. Martin used the Tong Le Chan incident to influence Congress, and Kissinger accused North Vietnam of aggression.[29]

But Thieu's ploy failed. North Vietnam refused to fall into the trap and did not take any additional action in the area. In the United States, Congress remained skeptical. Its members knew that the nation was strongly opposed to any further involvement in Southeast Asia. They no longer believed the claims of either Thieu or Nixon, and they stood firm, continuing to reject requests for additional aid. Even the aid appropriation for 1975 was cut. Martin demanded $1.5 billion to save South Vietnam; he even flew to Washington and spent several months there attacking his critics and arguing Thieu's case. General Murray of the DAO compiled chart after chart to mislead Congress and scare up additional support. But the campaign came to no avail. In July, Congress voted an absolute ceiling of $700 million for expenditures in Vietnam.[30]

Four days after the new aid package became law, Richard Nixon resigned. But Gerald Ford continued to carry out Nixon's Vietnam policies as President. One of Ford's first acts as President was to send a personal letter to Thieu assuring him of continued support. Ford promised adequate economic and military aid and praised the two men who were the legacy of Nixon's administration. "In these important endeavors," Ford wrote, "I shall look to Dr. Kissinger, whom I have asked to remain as my Secretary of State, for guidance and support. He has my fullest confidence, as does Ambassador Martin."[31]

Thus the Vietnam involvement remained an integral part of American strategy and an overriding concern for the U.S. government into 1975. After Ford's letter, there were other official demonstrations of support for General Thieu's regime. Kissinger argued Saigon's case before the Russians in Moscow and the Chinese in Peking. Martin devised new methods for applying pressure on Congress. Polgar and the CIA compiled dozens of reports aimed at developing an alarmist analysis of the threat to South Vietnam. The Pentagon and the DAO continued the steady stream of supplies and weapons to Thieu's army, which had already abandoned to the enemy over $200 million worth of materiel and equipment. General Thieu clamped down even tighter on domestic opposition and prepared his draftees for new search-and-destroy missions.[32]

The Vietnamese Communists, meanwhile, drew their own conclusions from the congressional refusal to vote increased aid to South Vietnam and the Nixon administration's inability to exercise power. The decent interval was about to come to a close.

Increased military action began in the early summer of 1974, when North Vietnamese units engaged Thieu's weary army north of Saigon, reoccupying land granted to Hanoi under the peace agreement. As the summer progressed, the military thrusts increased, and the number of villages controlled by Hanoi and the Vietcong grew. Hanoi's troop strength was modest, about 150,000. Yet it consistently defeated Thieu's million-man army because it was better directed, better supplied, and more popular. By the fall, the North Vietnamese had reestablished the status quo ante in South Vietnam; the Thieu government had given up all the territory it had conquered after the Paris agreement.[33]

Positions hardened further in October. The Revolutionary Government of the Vietcong issued an appeal to public figures and organizations in South Vietnam to work for "an end to U.S. military involvement and interference in South Vietnam, the overthrow of Nguyen Van Thieu and his clique, and the establishment in Saigon of an administration willing to implement the Paris Agreement seriously."[34] The NLF appeared ready to test the ARVN's ability to defend itself and America's determination to stand with Thieu.

At a meeting that same month, the Hanoi Politburo agreed on a plan of action called "Resolution for 1975." With the start of the dry season in December, North Vietnam would begin a series of probing attacks and feints in Military Region 3, which surrounded Saigon, to help them decide what to do next.

Before the Politburo made any additional decisions, a spy on General Thieu's staff sent in a report on Thieu's thinking. According to the spy, Thieu believed that the Communists would attack in Tay Ninh province—near the Cambodian border—and would fight only to the end of the dry season in June. With this new information, the Politburo agreed on their next step. The North Vietnamese would attack and attempt to take the district capital of Phuoc Binh, near Saigon. To take and hold it would be a great psychological defeat for the Thieu regime. More important would be the American reaction. If the United States did not rush to Saigon's aid, it would prove that Hanoi had nothing to fear from the United States and that a general offensive would be in order.[35]

On January 1, 1975, the North Vietnamese began shelling Phuoc Binh. Three days later they attacked in force, and by January 7 Hanoi's flag flew over the city. Although the area was of little military value, the victory had tremendous negative impact on morale in the South. Phuoc Binh was the first district capital to fall to the North Vietnamese since Quang Tri City fell in 1972. More important was American inaction. "The American Government," wrote one eyewitness, "was forced to say publicly . . . that under no circumstances would Americans on the ground, on the sea, or in the air re-enter the Vietnam War."[36] In effect, as Frank Snepp has concluded:

> The Communists' . . . victories in northern MR 3 tipped the political scales in Hanoi toward escalation, for in effect they confirmed that the United States would not intervene to stave off a major defeat for its ally.[37]

Le Duan pressed for bolder military actions and suggested widespread attacks in 1975 to create conditions for a general uprising in 1976, which he believed would be the earliest date for success, hoping, however, that Hanoi might liberate all of South Vietnam before 1976 was over.

The leaders in Hanoi immediately began planning for a major new offensive in South Vietnam. General Van Tien Dung was sent south to command the attack with the authority to pursue the offensive without Hanoi's specific approval. This move would prove decisive in the coming months.

Hanoi continued to keep a close eye on Washington, where Kissinger and Ambassador Martin were trying to carry huge new appropriations for South Vietnam through Congress. If the Ford administration could not send U.S. troops back to Vietnam, Kissinger and Martin wanted Congress to authorize about $5 billion in aid over a five-year period. They also wanted a supplemental appropriation of $300 million for the current fiscal year.[38]

Even with his mentor, Richard Nixon, no longer in control, Henry Kissinger was determined to "carry on." Toward this objective he received full cooperation from Ambassador Martin, whose illusions ultimately created chaos in Saigon. According to Alan Dawson,

> [Martin's] critics charged that the death of his son during the 1968 siege . . . at Khe Sanh had closed his mind to arguments and dissent. He was unable to consider, these men said, a softening in the US line. Martin, it was charged, was so autocratic that he would not consider, would not even read a field report that showed weakness or fallibility in the Saigon forces or government. . . .
>
> Martin chose to ignore advice and predictions like these. His confidence in the corrupt leadership of Vietnam and the Saigon Army remained intact, unshaken by disclosures of incompetence or warnings of disorder.
>
> He became, then, a stifler of criticism, a critic of critics, seemingly ignorant of the malfeasance around him.[39]

Kissinger and Martin lobbied on Capitol Hill, but Congress refused to vote the additional aid for Saigon; instead, they decided to send an investigative delegation. When the delegation arrived in February 1975, Martin's embassy staff and CIA offices attempted, to no avail, to show the visiting congressmen what the aid could accomplish. When the congressional delegation returned to Washington on March 2, Martin felt obliged to return with them.[40]

Martin was therefore out of the country on March 9, when the North Vietnamese attacked Ban Me Thuot, an important city in the central highlands. This attack was the beginning of the end. General Thieu was caught off guard by the offensive. He believed that Hanoi's divisions were stationed around Pleiku, another major city in the highlands to the north of Ban Me Thuot. When the attack at Ban Me Thuot began, General Thieu thought it was just a diversion, so he kept most of his highland forces at Pleiku, awaiting the attack that never came. By the time the ARVN realized the seriousness of the Ban Me Thuot attack, it was too late. The ARVN defenders tried to counterattack, but the attempt failed. Ban Me Thuot fell to the North Vietnamese on March 12.

General Thieu then made a crucial decision which sealed the fate of South Vietnam. Against the advice of his field commanders, Thieu ordered the immediate evacuation of all ARVN forces from the highlands. Since the South Vietnamese did not have enough planes for an airlift, the ARVN formed a truck convoy to evacuate Pleiku and Kontum, the two major cities still controlled by the government. This "convoy of tears," which began on March 16, quickly disintegrated into a chaotic retreat. When residents of the area saw the army leaving, they panicked and also fled, thus clogging the army's escape route. Within two days, the North Vietnamese realized what was happening, and General Dung promptly sent his divisions to cut off the army's retreat. The fleeing ARVN divisions were cut to pieces and eliminated from the war.[41]

General Dung then launched a tank attack against Quang Tri, near the old demilitarized zone. By this time the South Vietnamese troops stationed along the northern defense line had heard of the ARVN's bitter retreat from the highlands. They lost heart quickly and fled before the North Vietnamese forces.

This scenario was to be repeated many times in the coming weeks. At the first threat of attack, the South Vietnamese armed forces retreated, often stripping off their uniforms as they left; when they retreated, groups of civilians also fled in panic. First the troops fled to Hue, the former imperial capital. General Thieu went on national television and vowed to defend Hue, but within a short time, he ordered the military to abandon Hue and retreat further south to Da Nang. More than a quarter of a million civilians and military personnel fled from Hue before even a single enemy soldier entered the city. On March 26, only one week after North Vietnamese tanks attacked Quang Tri, the Vietcong flag appeared atop the citadel in Hue. By this time more than 300,000 refugees were clogging Da Nang, South Vietnam's second largest city, about fifty miles south of Hue.[42]

Da Nang had been the site of the largest American military base in South Vietnam. The base still existed, defended by South Vietnamese Army and Marine divisions, augmented by several squadrons of South Vietnamese fighter-bombers. It should have been a veritable bastion of strength. But it was quickly isolated when the North Vietnamese and Vietcong forces came out of the jungle *south* of Da Nang and drove to the coast, thereby cutting off all ground escape routes. Panic swept the city.

A substantial number of Americans still lived in Da Nang: civilians who worked for U.S. companies; agents employed by the CIA, AID, or other government agencies; and former servicemen who married Vietnamese and chose to live in Vietnam. These people required immediate evacuation. Thousands of Vietnamese who had worked for the Americans over the years had also been promised evacuation. But the American Consulate in Da Nang delayed putting evacuation plans into operation. Ambassador Martin concluded that word of a U.S. evacuation would hurt the morale of the Vietnamese and erode the fighting spirit of the ARVN. So the consulate procrastinated while Da Nang became a nightmare. Law and order completely broke down. ARVN soldiers deserted their units and went on a rampage of looting, drinking, and rape. People mobbed the Da Nang airport and harbor in a desperate attempt to escape.[43]

On March 25, Ambassador Martin returned to Saigon. He immediately ordered one of his political counselors to build a press campaign around several vague reports that the Communists were torturing and mutilating civilians in newly captured areas.[44] While panic swept Da Nang, the embassy compiled atrocity stories.

World Airways finally began flying out small groups of refugees on March 27. Important American and Vietnamese officials fled Da Nang, but almost all the Vietnamese employees of the American Consulate were left behind despite a guarantee of safety. On March 28, Ed Daly, president of World Airways, flew a Boeing 727 into Da Nang, against American advice, to attempt a final rescue of refugees. Upon landing, his plane was mobbed by armed ARVN soldiers who boarded the plane and forced Daly to fly them out. Only one woman and two children managed to get on the plane. When it took off, ARVN soldiers who had been left behind fired their weapons at the last plane to leave Da Nang.

With no more planes available, hundreds of thousands of soldiers and civilians put out to sea in anything that would float. Several U.S. merchant ships stood by to pick up survivors, and a few helicopters ferried refugees from Da Nang Harbor to the ships off shore. After several days, these merchant ships, overloaded with thousands of Vietnamese soldiers and civilians, headed south and disembarked their passengers at the former U.S. air base at Cam Ranh Bay, which itself fell to the North Vietnamese a week later.[45]

The Da Nang catastrophe repeated itself the following week at Nha Trang, a hundred miles further south, and at other smaller towns throughout South Vietnam. The process of disintegration was nearly complete. The gateway to Saigon was wide open. But Hanoi did not immediately press its advantage. After the fall of Nha Trang on April

1, the Revolutionary Government of the Vietcong offered to negotiate with Saigon if only General Thieu would step down. They suggested that Big Minh would be the logical replacement.[46] But Thieu,
with half of South Vietnam still apparently under his control, refused
to consider this option. Instead, Thieu raged at Ambassador Martin
and General Weyand, who had been sent to Saigon by President
Ford to assess the situation. Thieu read them Nixon's letters in
which the former President promised an "immediate and vigorous
reaction by the United States" if South Vietnam came under attack.
Thieu angrily insisted that Nixon and Kissinger had betrayed Saigon
with promises that meant nothing. Martin and Weyand assured
Thieu that this was not so. They actually encouraged him to ignore
the offer of negotiations, to stay in power, and to continue the war.[47]

With tragedy looming on the horizon, the embassy staff in Saigon
attempted to preserve morale by doctoring the news. They,

> fearing contagion, moved quickly to avert [panic]. . . . They advised their
> office chiefs and seconds-in-command to soft-pedal the awful truth of what
> was happening to the north . . . in conversations with their own wives,
> secretaries and subordinates. In addition, Charge d'Affairs Lehmann, still
> operating as chief of mission in Martin's absence, carefully muffled all
> potential sources of "bad news" including "American radio," the English-
> language FM outlet operated and financed by DAO. Every hour one of his
> subordinates would review the taped news "feeds" from the United States,
> editing out anything that might alarm Embassy wives listening at their
> portables alongside the swimming pool. The CIA-controlled *Saigon Post*,
> the capital's only English-language daily, likewise began playing down
> the . . . government setbacks.[48]

On April 3, another major city, Dalat, fell to the advancing North
Vietnamese. The ARVN had intended to fortify a new defense line
centered on Dalat, but as usual Saigon failed to move fast enough.
Hanoi cut the southern defense line and foiled Thieu's plans for a
dramatic stand there. Now the best Thieu could hope for was to hold
on to the area around Saigon and the rich Mekong Delta to the south.
The war "continued to sweep in toward Saigon like an onrushing
tide."[49] Pushed in front of it were thousands of panicky refugees
from Pleiku, Hue, Da Nang, Nha Trang, and Dalat, moving south-
ward toward Saigon. Ambassador Martin, hearing about the panic in
other cities, did not want a similar situation when the retreating
swarm reached Saigon. Therefore, he instructed an embassy official
to

call on the Chief of Saigon's municipal police force [and] to ask him to cordon the city off against both refugees and army stragglers. Reluctantly, the Vietnamese official agreed and on 3 April the city was officially closed to all but legitimate, fully documented residents.[50]

In the wake of this action, Martin received numerous pleas to begin the evacuation of American dependents. Although he rejected the call for a general evacuation, Martin adopted a special evacuation plan, in part because of its propaganda value. Ed Daly approached Martin with an offer from World Airways to airlift out of Saigon several thousand orphans who would probably be left behind once the general evacuation began. Martin decided that the U.S. Embassy, not Daly, would conduct the flights. He "hoped that the spectacle of hundreds of Vietnamese babies being taken under the American wing would generate sympathy for the South Vietnamese cause around the world."[51] The American military officers in the Defense Attaché Office added wives and female employees to the flights, as nurses and baby-sitters.

On April 4, the first group of 243 Vietnamese orphans, accompanied by 44 American wives and female employees, boarded an air force C-5A Galaxy. Tragically, the plane crashed, killing more than 200 orphans and most of the DAO wives and employees. Ambassador Martin resumed "Operation Baby-lift" the next day, and, as the flights continued, the DAO was able to evacuate many nonessential personnel.

While attention focused on "Operation Baby-lift," General Weyand returned to the United States and made his report to President Ford. Weyand and his staff were aware that Kissinger favored new aid appropriations for South Vietnam. Therefore, the general recommended to President Ford that a huge grant of $722 million be authorized for immediate military assistance to Saigon. General Weyand stated, "This money is urgently needed for basic military necessity, to provide an even chance for the survival of the Republic of Vietnam."[52]

The Ford Administration accepted General Weyand's recommendation. As Gareth Porter comments:

> Instead of trying to end the killing as soon as possible by pressing for a change of regime in Saigon, . . . the Ford administration went through the motions of asking for an additional $722 million aid on April 11.[53]

In Saigon, Thieu's support had almost entirely disappeared.[54] The situation looked hopeless after the Vietcong began shelling Saigon's perimeter, but Ambassador Martin still refused to face the facts. When the North Vietnamese attacked Xuan Loc, the last government stronghold north of Saigon, Martin and the DAO fell back on technological solutions and rushed in two new superweapons for General Thieu's army.

The first of these weapons was nicknamed the "Daisy Cutter." It was a huge 15,000-pound bomb that the Americans had used to blast helicopter pads out of the jungle. It exploded several feet above the ground and literally destroyed everything within a large area. The Americans had never used the Daisy Cutters against enemy troops, but the DAO handed these bombs over to the South Vietnamese. The second and much more deadly weapon, also never previously used in Vietnam, was called the CBU-55. It was a huge cluster bomb containing many gas canisters. On impact, the bomb would explode, sending the gas canisters in all directions. Almost immediately, the canisters themselves would explode, creating a huge firestorm in the target area. The chances of surviving a CBU-55 explosion were nil.

In the last week of the war, Saigon's air force dropped several Daisy Cutters with devastating results, but only one CBU-55. It exploded near a North Vietnamese encampment, burning to death approximately 250 enemy soldiers. The Americans gave the South Vietnamese several more CBU-55s, but they never had a chance to use them.[55] Despite these developments, the North Vietnamese surrounded Xuan Loc, isolating the ARVN garrison. General Thieu sent one of two remaining paratroop brigades to rescue the city, but it was ambushed and cut to pieces. After several days of heavy fighting, Hanoi's forces completely overran Xuan Loc.

Practically everyone in Saigon and in Washington considered the war lost, except for General Thieu and Ambassador Martin. When the Cambodian capital of Phnom Penh fell on April 16, Congress forced President Ford to order an accelerated evacuation of Saigon. Still Ambassador Martin urged Thieu to remain in office. He repeated an earlier comment: "There has been no advice from Washington for Thieu to step down."[56] On April 17 the CIA obtained positive information that the North Vietnamese were now driving for a final military victory, but Station Chief Polgar kept this report from Martin.[57] The ambassador, in any case, did not want to see such information.

General Thieu's days, however, were numbered. As Hanoi's forces closed in on Saigon, Colonel Vo Dong Giang, chief delegate of the PRG, held a news conference and demanded that Thieu resign. Furthermore, Giang demanded that all "American military advisors disguised as civilians," as well as Martin and all embassy personnel, leave Vietnam.[58] To emphasize their point, Vietcong guerrillas shelled Bien Hoa airbase, only fifteen miles outside Saigon, forcing the government to transfer all remaining planes to Saigon.

Neutralist pressure also continued to build. Father Tran Tuu Tranh, leader of the Anticorruption Movement, published information to show that Thieu was growing rich at the expense of the people. He charged Thieu with running a drug ring inside South Vietnam, depositing government funds in private Swiss bank accounts, and allegedly accepting a $7 million bribe from Richard Nixon, apparently in exchange for Thieu's signature on the Paris Peace Accords.[59] The resulting scandal, along with Thieu's disastrous military decisions, caused him to lose favor with both neutralist politicians and his confused army leaders.[60]

On April 21, 1975, Thieu resigned, ending a brutal, eight-year dictatorship. In a bitter parting speech, Thieu criticized the United States for compromising with Hanoi in 1973. He also complained that Washington had reneged on its promise to reenter the war and rescue Saigon. Watergate, Thieu concluded, had shattered America's resolve. With that, General Thieu boarded a U.S. plane and flew to Taiwan, never to return home, but able to enjoy the vast riches he had acquired illegally as the strong man of Saigon.[61]

Unfortunately, Thieu's departure did not mean an end to the war. Ambassador Martin obstructed all attempts to elevate the neutralist Big Minh to the presidency. Instead, Martin backed the transfer of power from Thieu to Vice-President Tran Van Huong, a senile official who vowed to continue the hopeless war.

As Huong replaced Thieu, Martin was forced to consider more urgently the mass evacuation of Americans and "high-risk" Vietnamese. On April 21, he authorized the official evacuation of Saigon. For the next ten days, amid the chaos and disaster, the United States tried frantically to airlift as many Americans and Saigon residents as possible.

To understand the enormity of the problem, one must remember that the United States employed thousands of Vietnamese under the auspices of the USIS, the AID program, DAO headquarters, the CIA, and the embassy itself. American personnel employed many Vietnamese in private capacities. Then there were thousands of American pseudocivilians who worked for American companies under contract to the DAO, plus the bona fide American civilians who worked for the various oil companies, Bank of America, Chase Manhattan Bank, and so on. Another large group of Americans consisted of former American servicemen who stayed on for various reasons. There were deserters and there were high-level Vietnamese collaborators, military officers, and politicians. Many of these people and their families had been promised evacuation from Saigon and entry into the United States. Even started a month earlier, a full-scale airlift could not have gotten them all out of the country. Not surprisingly, at this late stage, the evacuation disintegrated into confusion and degenerated into corruption and worse. The North Vietnamese, for the most part, let the planes go.

On April 24, as if to give the Americans time to complete their evacuation, a five-day lull settled over Saigon. During this five-day period, the American airlift continued, with dozens of planes leaving each day. Ambassador Martin urged the aged President Huong to stay in power, but, finally, on April 26, Huong buckled under the pressure and agreed to hand over power to Big Minh. To placate Ambassador Martin, Huong delayed another day while his resignation went before the Saigon parliament. On April 27, the day Big Minh was finally voted into power, the North Vietnamese sent three rockets into Saigon, as if to signal that it was too late. Big Minh ordered all Americans out of the country. The end was near.

On April 28, the day that Big Minh was formally sworn in as president, enemy rockets exploded in the heart of Saigon, while mortars hit Tan Son Nhut, Saigon's airport, killing two U.S. Marines and forcing its closure. Ambassador Martin would not order the final evacuation until he had been driven to Tan Son Nhut and seen that its runways were useless. The only way left to evacuate personnel from Saigon was by helicopter. Although the U.S. Navy was standing by offshore for such an eventuality, the navy had planned on conducting a helicopter lift for only a few thousand at most, not the mass of people still remaining.

Panic spread throughout Saigon. Tens of thousands stormed Tan Son Nhut looking for an escape. U.S. helicopters continued to fly out refugees, but, amidst the chaos, it was difficult to determine who had priority for the flights. Others crowded Saigon harbor desperately bribing, begging, and fighting to get aboard the boats and barges. Additional U.S. Marine guards had to be flown in from the navy ships to keep the mob out of the embassy grounds.

American and Vietnamese employees had been told to congregate at pickup points around the city, where special buses would come and take them to evacuation points. Because of the closing of Tan Son Nhut, however, and because most of the streets were clogged with mobs of frantic people, many individuals scheduled for pickup were never rescued. In that frantic last day, most of the Americans were evacuated, along with several thousand Vietnamese; but many thousands of Vietnamese and even some Americans were left behind. More than 600 people were still inside the embassy compound itself awaiting the promised evacuation. They were all legitimate refugees—embassy employees, Vietnamese military and political officers, the ambassador from South Korea, a general in the South Korean Army, and even one American citizen. In the USIS building, more than 100 Vietnamese employees waited for the rescue bus that never came. Many CIA employees were left behind, and, due to the hasty evacuation, so were many incriminating CIA files and dossiers that identified almost every Vietnamese agent and informer. These files could have been destroyed or burned, but it was too late. In the last-minute rush these incriminating files were left intact.

Shortly after midnight on April 30, 1975, a tired and defeated Ambassador Martin climbed to the roof of the American Embassy and, with the American flag neatly folded under his arm, boarded the last evacuation helicopter from Saigon.[62]

Several hours after Graham Martin flew to safety, dawn broke over a silent Saigon. Except for knots of forgotten people around the American Embassy and a few other erstwhile pickup points, Saigon had the appearance of a ghost city. Early in the morning, a final American helicopter landed atop the American Embassy to retrieve the last of the U.S. Marine guards that had "held the fort" during this last night. Quickly it was gone, and an eerie quiet settled over Saigon. The date was April 30, 1975.

At 10:20 A.M., the voice of South Vietnam's last president, General Duong Van Minh, informed Saigon radio listeners that the war was over. "We are waiting here [in the Presidential Palace] for their representatives to come and discuss an orderly transfer of power."[63]

Suddenly, ARVN soldiers and Saigon policemen appeared on the streets, stripping off their uniforms and changing into civilian clothes. Soon the uniforms, small arms, and other impedimenta of the Saigon army were littering the streets, and the former soldiers and police melted into the back alleys and side streets of Saigon.

Within a short time, an array of flags dotted the buildings formerly occupied by Thieu's government. The flag of the Provisional Revolutionary Government was clearly visible, as well as the flag of North Vietnam. These flags were the handiwork of undercover Communist cadres and Vietcong sympathizers. As of yet there were no North Vietnamese or Vietcong soldiers in the city. The capitulation of Saigon had come too swiftly, it had caught the "enemy" unprepared. Finally, in the late morning, a column of Soviet-made tanks entered the city. It met only light resistance as it moved into the center of town. At noon the lead tank knocked down the gate of Doc Lap Palace and drove into the courtyard. By 12:15, the flag of the Provisional Revolutionary Government had been unfurled over the palace.

Soon, a political commissar arrived at Doc Lap Palace and informed General Minh and his cabinet that they were not prisoners. The PRG official asked Big Minh to make a final surrender broadcast over Saigon Radio. At 2:30 P.M., April 30, General Minh addressed the nation:

> I, General Duong Van Minh, President of the Saigon Government, appeal to the armed forces of the Republic of Vietnam to lay down their arms and surrender unconditionally to the forces of the National Liberation Front. Furthermore, I declare that the Saigon Government is completely dissolved at all levels.[64]

With that, North Vietnamese troops in straw hats, ragged field uniforms, and Ho Chi Minh sandals (cut from old tires) began to enter the city. The populace of Saigon peeked out at them from behind shuttered windows and through cracked doors. When they realized that they were in no immediate danger, individuals cautiously began to emerge. Usually the women and children came out first, then the young people. Soon ARVN soldiers, many still in uniform, were seen streaming back into the city, walking unharmed, often alongside North Vietnamese Army soldiers.

As Terzani relates,

thousands of persons mingled with the soldiers, amid the deafening noise of other tanks arriving in clouds of bluish smoke, I saw nothing but smiles—smiles and waving hands. Running, jumping on a tank, getting a lift from jeeps, I made a tour of the city. In working-class neighborhoods the enthusiasm was overwhelming. . . . I saw an old woman with a typical conical peasant hat throw her arms around a young guerrilla. "Hoa binh, hoa binh!" [Peace, peace] she cried. Men wept, children unfurled flags of the Front. . . . Everywhere lay piles of abandoned uniforms, helmets and military boots.[65]

By evening the city was calm and relaxed. The enemy troops seemed very friendly. Although it was obvious from their accents that most of the soldiers were from North Vietnam, they spoke the same language as the Saigonese and seemed anxious to answer questions. In the evening they camped out in the parks and cooked their own food over open fires.

The wily Saigonese, who had bent with the wind and survived under the French, the Japanese, and the Americans, began to feel already that they just might survive now by bending again, this time with the prevailing and more regimented wind of Communism. The long expected bloodbath did not occur. Instead, on May 1, 1975, one day after the fall of Saigon, and thirty years after Ho Chi Minh had made his bid for Vietnamese independence, Vietnam became a unified nation, and the name of South Vietnam's capital was changed to Ho Chi Minh City.

VIETNAM'S CATASTROPHE

> It developed in boot camp, it developed in [infantry
> training], it developed in staging battalion before we
> went over, and it developed all the time we were in
> Vietnam—we hated these people, we were taught to hate
> these people, they were gooks, slants, dinks, they were
> Orientals, inferior to us, they chewed betel nuts, they
> were ugly, you know, they ate lice out of each other's
> hair, they were not as good as us. And you could not
> trust them. I did not think it was racist then, but I
> certainly do now. We just hated the whole people. They
> were all gooks. We were not taught to just call the
> Vietcong or North Vietnamese Army gooks. [Our]
> instructors, the Vietnam veterans, these people we
> looked up to as like next to God, they always referred to
> all of these people as gooks and we picked it up from
> them. And that's the feeling we had all the way through.
> —*Corporal Kenneth Campbell*[1]

Millions of American GIs, mostly young draftees, came ashore in
South Vietnam unsure about the war or their role in it. Most were
scared and confused about fighting a hidden enemy in the jungles of
South Vietnam, particularly one that moved at night and blended
into the general population.

The professional military, who had the responsibility for training
millions of GIs for a one-year stint of duty in Vietnam, apparently
believed that a very important portion of their training was psychological indoctrination. Basic training became a time of brainwashing,
an effort to turn frightened, confused youngsters into robots or ma-
chines. Draftees were taught to hate the Vietnamese people and to
regard them as subhuman. By twisting fear into hatred, the military

was able to convince most GIs that it was necessary to kill Vietnamese. According to Sergeant Jamie Henry, racism was rampant within the army because the "system" had "institutionalized" it:

> When you go into basic training, you are taught that the Vietnamese are not people. You are taught that they are all gooks. All you hear is gook! gook! gook! . . . The Asian serviceman is the brunt of the same racism because the GIs over there do not distinguish one Asian from another. They are trained so thoroughly that all Asians become the brunt of this racism. You are trained gook-gook-gook and once the military has got the idea implanted in your mind that these people are not human, it makes it a bit easier to kill them. . . . The military doesn't distinguish between North Vietnamese, South Vietnamese, Vietcong, civilians—all of them are gooks, all of them are considered to be sub-human. None of them are any good. And all of them can be killed and most of them are killed.[2]

Most of America's expeditionary army went to Vietnam with the understanding that they would be required to spend only one year there. Almost immediately, the troops were sent into the jungle to hunt out the Vietcong. Commanders explained that Vietcong guerrillas wore black pajamas and lived in the rural areas, especially in the small hamlets and villages of South Vietnam. It was the GI's job, according to their leaders, to destroy the enemy so as to save Saigon, and the United States, from Communism.

The American soldier saw nothing but a sea of Vietnamese faces when he entered the villages in search of Vietcong. GIs had been trained to recognize Vietcong by identifying the black pajamas that they wore. Since most of the common peasants wore black pajamas—and many, particularly the farmers, carried machetes to use in the fields—there was absolutely no way to distinguish between friendly civilians and enemy guerrillas. Drill sergeants had never differentiated between "good gooks" and "bad gooks." With that, many soldiers, while genuinely fearful of losing their own lives, fell into line and began to kill Vietnamese villagers—indiscriminately. That special combination of fear and hatred made it much easier than many expected:

> A feeling of constant fear and tension grows up among GIs in the field, who come to view all Vietnamese—all gooks—with suspicion. The army nurtures this psychology through "troop topics" discussions, which play on racial fears and simplistic anti-communism. . . . The GI develops an aversion to his total environment and his primary concern

becomes to survive his ordeal until he can escape it. . . . The survival concern means . . . that the soldier will be more likely to kill a Vietnamese on the mere suspicion, however faint, that the Vietnamese is armed.[3]

And as Richard Hammer explained:

Pretty soon you get to hate all of these people. You get to fear them. They're all out for your ass one way or another, out to take you for everything you've got. You don't know which ones are your enemies and which ones are your friends. So you begin to think that they're all your enemies. And that all of them are something not quite human, some kind of lower order of creature. You give them names to depersonalize them, to categorize them as you've become convinced they ought to be categorized. They become dinks, and slants, and slopes and gooks, and you begin to say and believe "The only good dink is a dead dink." You echo the comments of our buddies that "one million of them ain't worth one of us. We should blow up all of those slant-eyed bastards."[4]

Inexperienced GIs shot first and asked questions later. Steve Pitkin spoke for other Vietnam veterans when he said, "You're so scared, that you'll shoot anything. You'll look at your enemy, and these people that you're sort of a visitor to—you'll look at them as animals while you are turning yourself into an animal."[5]

Search-and-destroy gave GIs the chance to vent their frustration by brutalizing the simple peasants of South Vietnam. Here is a classic example of the search-and-destroy mentality, recounted by Sergeant Henry:

We moved into a small hamlet, nineteen women and children were rounded up as VC suspects and the Lieutenant that rounded them up called the Captain and asked what should be done with them. The Captain simply repeated the order that came down from the Colonel that morning . . . to kill anything that moves. . . . Two men were leading a young girl, approximately nineteen years old and very pretty, out of a hootch. She had no clothes on so I supposed she had been raped, which was pretty SOP, and she was thrown on the pile of nineteen women and children and five men around the circle opened up on full automatic with M-16s. That was the end of that.[6]

Similarly, United Press International reported another incident where the "kill anything that moves" mentality held sway:

"I got me a VC, man I got at least two of them bastards." The exultant cry followed a ten-second burst of automatic weapons fire yesterday, and the dull crump of a grenade exploding underground. The Marines ordered a Vietnamese corporal to go down into the grenade-blasted hole to pull out their victims. The victims were three children between eleven and fourteen—two boys and a girl. Their bodies were riddled with bullets. . . . "Oh my God!" the young Marine exclaimed. "They're all kids."[7]

Besides the slaughter of children and the abuse of Vietnamese women, U.S. forces destroyed villages and crops on a routine basis. Thomas Heidtman has given a vivid account:

> The nickname of [our] company was the "Burning Fifth Marines." Once, just before my first operation, we had a company formation. Our company commander . . . said that we were going out in the morning. . . . Then he said, "We're going to have a Zippo inspection right now." And I would say approximately two-thirds of the entire company had Zippo lighters. We held them up, lit them, demonstrated that they were filled and would burn, then put them away. He smiled and let it go at that. When we went out, I would say at least 50 percent of the villages we passed through would be burned to the ground. There was no difference between the ones we burned and the ones we didn't burn. It was just that where we had the time, we burned them.[8]

Likewise, Captain Robert Johnson has described search-and-destroy missions which had nothing to do with finding Vietcong. Instead, the Americans ravaged village after village in an attempt to "control" the population. According to Johnson:

> I participated in about thirteen search and destroy operations. On all of these operations we systematically destroyed every bit of rice that we couldn't carry [from] civilian villages. If we couldn't burn the hootches, we would blow them up with dynamite. As I said, we did this on a routine basis. It was part of the policy again to encourage civilian population to move into the detention camps controlled by American and Saigon forces. . . . It became clear to me that the . . . search and destroy tactics where we systematically destroyed villages and routinely bombed the surrounding countryside, it became very clear to me that we were waging war not against any abstract ideology but waging war against the Vietnamese people themselves.[9]

After several years of search-and-destroy missions, the Pentagon and General Westmoreland persuaded Saigon to designate large areas of the country as "free-fire zones." Into these areas, first of all, went the ARVN, led by CIA personnel; together they rounded up and relocated as many peasants as possible out of the area. All who refused to abandon their ancestral homes and move to a concentra-

tion camp—dubbed "New Life Hamlets"—were considered Vietcong sympathizers and were treated harshly. When the fortified
camps were full, Ky and Thieu officially declared the area a free-fire
zone. Almost immediately, the U.S. military moved in and began the
systematic destruction of everything within that sector. It was open
season on Vietnamese villages. Areas falling under the "free-fire"
category were completely and utterly destroyed, the ground black-
ened, the people killed, the villages burned.[10] Free-fire zones represented the village war in all its savagery. Peasants trying to remain
on ancestral lands were simply massacred and then chalked up as
Vietcong guerrillas.

The stories of wanton, senseless violence became more common-
place, as evidenced by the testimony of two Vietnam veterans.

Sergeant Jack Smith:

> The GIs, when they originally get in the country, they feel friendly
> toward the Vietnamese and they toss candy at the kids, but as they
> become hardened to it and kind of embittered against the war, as you
> drive through the ville you take cans of C-rats . . . and you peg 'em at
> the kids! . . . you try to belt them over the head. And one of the fun
> games was that you dropped C-rat cans or candy off the back of your
> truck just so the kids will have time to dash out, grab the candy and get
> run over by the next truck.

Corporal Thomas Heidtman:

> So my squad, myself included, went and put a Zippo lighter to the
> village. Burned it. They were still inside the houses. . . . There was no
> such thing as a friendly Vietnamese. Every Vietnamese was a gook. . . .
> To the Marines there was no such thing as a free fire zone in my outfit.
> Every place was a free fire zone.[11]

There came a time when many GIs literally refused to participate
in this savage killing of civilians. As a result, hundreds, perhaps
thousands, were given dishonorable discharges. Many found escape
in alcohol and drugs. The ultimate solution to this problem was to
turn over the killing to the air force, and finally the air war became a
fact of life in South Vietnam. U.S. bombers made the Vietnamese
countryside an utter hellhole, under the heaviest aerial bombardment in history. By 1968, the U.S. Air Force had dropped twelve tons
of bombs for every square mile in Vietnam—all of Vietnam—and the
B-52s had blasted nearly four million bomb craters in the South

alone. The object of this air war was to destroy areas that Washington and Saigon could not control.[12]

The effects of America's bombing war were more readily apparent to members of the press. In 1965 the *Washington Post* reported that American pilots "are given a square marked on a map and told to hit every hamlet within the area. The pilots know they sometimes are bombing women and children." About the same time, Reuters News Agency reported that "planes bombed a nearby village yesterday killing about forty-five villagers, including thirty-seven school children." These abuses passed by with little commotion, as did a bulletin from Japan outlining three separate U.S. strikes against a nonhostile border village.[13]

Charles Mohr of the *New York Times* created a stir when he investigated the frequent use of napalm against the South Vietnamese people. Mohr revealed the gruesome details of a napalm attack, during which the familiar metal cannisters bounce and "roll" across large strips of land, engulfing everything in flames. Villages, fields, jungles, mountains—no corner of Vietnam escaped the onslaught of U.S. firepower. Wrote Mohr:

> There is a woman who has both arms burned off by napalm and her eyelids so badly burned that she cannot close them. . . . The woman had two of her children killed in the air strike that maimed her. . . . Few Americans appreciate what their nation is doing to South Vietnam with airpower. . . . This is strategic bombing in a friendly allied country. . . . Innocent civilians are dying every day in South Vietnam.[14]

Human flesh was especially sensitive to napalm, and people were burned alive during bombing raids. The slightest hint of a napalm attack sent the villagers of South Vietnam scurrying in all directions. For those who hid in bunkers or in the jungle, napalm meant searing, agonizing death unlike any experience in the war. For those who escaped the raging inferno and ran out into the open, air force gunners made sure no one got very far. The result was total destruction and, more often than not, outright extermination.

Sergeant McCusker, a military reporter, has testified that

> after a US napalm raid on a village there were thirty dead children. . . . None were over fifteen. Some of them were babies. Some looked like they had just been sunburned. . . . Others were just charred with guts hanging out. . . . An officer, a Captain, walked up to me and said,

"Well, Sgt. McCusker. . . . do you see what the VC did to their own people?" And I says, "Captain, I saw our planes drop the napalm." He said, "Well, Sgt. McCusker, you better write that the Vietcong did it."[15]

In its war against South Vietnam's villages, the military introduced gas and chemical warfare as well, both extremely effective against defenseless peasants in the rural areas. The chief gas used in Vietnam was called "CS," which burned its victims badly and, at times, caused death. Dennis Caldwell recounted: "I've seen hootches CS'd to drive people out. . . . When the people were driven out, they were killed."[16] The gas, illegal under international law, was also used in a type of game designed to persecute the villagers. Sergeant Michael Hunter explained the game at the Winter Soldier Hearings:

As far as CS gas—we always used CS. CS is the most powerful gas that can be used that will not kill you. It can create bodily harm if you're close—extremely bad burns. . . . [Gas] was constantly thrown . . . at people walking by and [when] the kids . . . four years old ranging to sixteen years old—came around to . . . beg for food, they were CS'd. And what I mean is they were gassed. This didn't happen just once, it happened constantly. . . . And when we didn't use CS out of the grenade we used CS out of the cannister. . . . [I]f you're hit by it, you can be killed.[17]

The other experimental weapon was a highly toxic chemical spray, or herbicide, known as Agent Orange. As early as 1962, the military was testing the chemical in Vietnam to determine its effectiveness as a "defoliant." U.S. leaders wanted to use Agent Orange to destroy the ground cover which acted as a natural camouflage for the Vietcong and to poison food supplies in South Vietnam.

After much discussion about Agent Orange, Washington gave President Diem enough poison to destroy the crops while, at the same time, the United States began a wholesale spraying of South Vietnam's jungles. The chemical eliminated much of the foliage in the jungle lands, but it also killed livestock, contaminated rice fields, and caused severe illness among the very young and the very old. We know now, ten years after the fact, that the GIs who handled Agent Orange in Vietnam are contracting cancer at an alarming rate. Consider, then, the thousands of potential Vietnamese cancer victims who were sprayed by the United States in Vietnam, and as a result are still dying.[18]

If, by some miracle, the villagers survived all of the above—U.S. air attacks, search-and-destroy missions, the pounding of free-fire zones, gas and chemical poisoning, and the constant pressure to relocate into a refugee camp—they were still totally besieged in South Vietnam. By the late 1960s, the CIA had revamped its own war against the peasants in the countryside. Known as "pacification," the new CIA strategy had the same goal as before—to root out the Vietcong. Agents recruited ARVN units, renamed them "revolutionary development teams," and sent them out into the villages to gather information and intimidate the peasantry.[19]

At the same time, the CIA devised a new program known as Phung Hoang—or "Phoenix"—which had as its goal the outright assassination of Vietcong sympathizers. The Phoenix program started about March 1968 and listed "intelligence-gathering" as its main purpose, but this euphemism fooled no one. Phoenix squads were dispatched into the villages, where they arrested and interrogated "suspicious" peasants. More often than not their methods included torture and execution. If, out of fear, certain villagers tried to flee, Phoenix soldiers killed them on the spot. Figures show that at least 20,000 and quite possibly 50,000 to 100,000 South Vietnamese peasants died as a result of the program.[20] In many instances, American military units followed the example set by the CIA.

At the core of America's village war, though, connecting all other components, was the idea that America would win its struggle in Vietnam if it could kill more Vietcong than it lost in casualties. To make the scheme scientific, the Pentagon invented the term *body count* and began to release two sets of figures each week—U.S. killed in action versus Vietcong killed in action. According to the Committee of Concerned Asian Scholars:

> The idea was that if the U.S. could maintain a kill ratio of at least 10-1, the world would see how effective the American war machine was and would know that we were winning. . . . So the stage was set and the pressure was on. Washington demanded that Westmoreland start producing enemy bodies. Westmoreland passed on the word to all division commanders—Bodies!. . . Units who report the highest body count get lavish commendation from the brass. The soldier who kills the most VC by himself during a certain period often gets a cash award or three days off to visit the seaside resort of Vung Tau or even a five-day R&R to Hong Kong or Hawaii. . . . Such pressure to produce more Vietnamese bodies is bound to lead to frequent murder of peasants who live near the field of action.[21]

The GIs in Vietnam interpreted the constant pressure for a high body count as a license to kill. Sergeant Michael Hunter has testified concerning the policy of the First Cavalry Division:

> A body count is a body count. I mean that's exactly what it says. When the battalion commander calls up and says he wants a body count, if there are men, women, children laying out there, he gets a body count of that many people. And usually we'd count about five bodies and it gets back there and it's usually about twenty-five or fifteen bodies.[22]

By realizing what the military had in mind when orders came down for a big body count, we can begin to understand the context in which William Calley's actions at My Lai were carried out, where several hundred Vietnamese civilians were murdered. Other companies were rewarding their men with "Sat Cong badges" for every "Vietcong" killed. Why should Calley have assumed that his actions would not be praised and rewarded?[23]

When news of the massacre at My Lai appeared in the press, the American people were shocked and amazed. But My Lai was not an aberration, nor was it an isolated incident. From 1965 to 1973 there were hundreds—perhaps thousands—of My Lais all across South Vietnam. More often than not, the harsh methods adopted by Calley's unit were "standard operating procedure" during U.S. search-and-destroy missions.

In the years since America's withdrawal, the Vietnamese people have struggled to rebuild their shattered nation. They have had to deal almost daily with the staggering costs and consequences inflicted by the U.S. war machine. In every province of Vietnam, in every city, village, or hamlet, the scars of war remain highly visible, serving as a constant reminder of lost lives and widespread destruction. These scars will haunt the people of Vietnam for many long and painful years.

In the aftermath of America's Indochina war, researchers and historians have tried to calculate the number of Vietnamese war casualties. There is no agreement as to the exact number of direct and indirect casualties that resulted from the U.S. military intervention in the Vietnam War. In the absence of a Vietnamese census, and with thousands having died before and after the U.S. military presence, informed estimates vary from 5 to 15 million. We have been unable to confirm an exact figure, but it is certain that millions died, in addition to the millions who were killed or died as a result of the wars in Cambodia and Laos. Of the numbers, it is estimated that 80 percent died in South Vietnam; the remaining approximately 20 percent were killed in North Vietnam. The group hit hardest by U.S. bombs and search-and-destroy missions was, of course, the peasantry out in the countryside of South Vietnam, but no group in Vietnam— except for the Saigonese—completely escaped the "punishment" meted out by U.S. firepower. The dead and wounded were "everywhere, just everywhere." Of the millions of casualties, it is estimated that at least 75 percent were civilians. America's war was a war against the people of Vietnam, most of whom had no idea why they bore the brunt of America's fury.[24]

Millions of these casualties died violently during air raids and ground battles. Others died of starvation and disease in dingy refugee camps or along the crowded highways. In addition to the war-inflicted and war-related deaths, the war spawned millions of refugees who survived the upheaval only by willpower and sheer luck. This mass of refugees lost everything—homes, livelihood, their friends, families, and relatives. The war wrenched loose and totally disrupted the traditional Vietnamese life-style, driving hordes of refugees into city ghettos, where crime and exploitation abounded, where food supplies were scarce, and where the rates of disease were high. The refugees, many of whom will suffer inwardly for the rest of their lives, can be counted as "living casualties" of America's Vietnam War.[25]

The casualty figures dramatize the terrible human cost paid by the people of Vietnam, but unfortunately these statistics do not tell the complete story. The Vietnamese also suffered the utter physical destruction of their country. It will take years to undo what U.S. technology did to the land. In South Vietnam alone, U.S. bombs left more than 21 million bomb craters, some thirty to forty feet in diameter and thirty feet deep. Twenty-one million bomb craters in a tiny country whose width averages less than 100 miles![26]

Besides the incredible deformity of millions of giant bomb craters, the people of Vietnam have had to contend with the terrible aftereffects of bomb fragments, herbicides, and napalm. When the war ended, 39 million acres of land in Indochina were infested with some kind of shell fragment. Furthermore, by 1973, nearly one-half of all arable land in South Vietnam had been poisoned by defoliants and herbicides. These chemicals destroyed crops, killed unborn children, and left "ghostly grey trees" that will never again regenerate.[27] The United States dropped six pounds of chemicals for every inhabitant in South Vietnam. As one Vietnamese doctor has written:

> At first [the people] felt sick and had some diarrhea, then they began to feel it hard to breathe and they had low blood pressure; some serious cases had trouble with their optic nerves and went blind. Pregnant women gave birth to stillborn or premature children. Most of the affected cattle died, . . . and river fish floated on the surface of the water, belly up, soon after the chemicals were spread.[28]

To many observers, however, the most atrocious weapon of all was the firebomb napalm. Two statements, both by Americans, help to dramatize the devastation of Vietnam's rural areas. Tom Buckley of *New York Times Magazine* wrote in 1969:

> [You see] bomb craters beyond counting, the dead, gray and black fields, forests that have been defoliated and scorched by napalm, land that has been plowed flat to destroy Vietcong hiding places. And everywhere can be seen the piles of ashes forming the outlines of huts and houses, to show where hamlets once stood.[29]

In 1973, John Young, a U.S. POW who was transported throughout Vietnam by his captors, remembered that everywhere he went, "there was nothing to see but craters and land that was dead, land that looked like oatmeal. There were no birds or trees or people; no rice, no gardens. Nothing moved."[30] This was America's Vietnam War.

In 1981, President Reagan, paying tribute to the millions of Vietnam veterans, said they "fought in the finest tradition of the American military in a war they were not permitted to win."[31]

AMERICA'S TRAGEDY

The catastrophic consequences to Vietnam and Southeast Asia that resulted from America's participation in the Vietnam War continue to haunt the minds and hearts of people everywhere. America's tragedy was as great: not in the number of casualties, but in the catastrophic consequences for the American people. The lives of millions of Americans were shattered; others lost respect for their own government; and governments and people throughout the world lost respect for America.

One of the tragedies was what happened to the men who fought in Vietnam. As the previous chapter demonstrated, thousands of GIs, over a period of almost ten years, were trained and ordered to kill Vietnamese guerrillas. As a side effect, they also killed the men, women, and children who were believed to be supporters of the Vietcong, people whom America was supposedly saving from the clutches of Communism.

Of the total of over 6 million men who served in the armed services during the war era, nearly 3 million were sent to Vietnam, and after their tour of duty became veterans. Tens of thousands returned to the United States, knowing full well what happened there. They returned to an ungrateful America that required them to live under the shadow of the war that America lost. It is estimated that up to 700,000 combat and noncombat veterans continue to be plagued by physical, emotional, social, and educational problems.[1]

Not only thousands of veterans, and thousands who left the country or evaded the draft, became victims, but also those other Americans who are still haunted by this nation's longest and most unwanted war. It continues to be a bad dream and also America's tragedy. Veterans contend that America has failed to share the responsibility and the guilt for what happened in Vietnam. The tragedy is unending to the families and friends of the thousands killed.

For the thousands who were seriously wounded the war goes on and on. For the rest of America, the value of their dollars and savings continues to decline, and there are other equally disastrous consequences.

At the top of the list are the human consequences. Between 1961 and 1974, a total of 57,259 Americans lost their lives in Vietnam. "My God, that's the size of a town," cried playwright Lillian Hellman when she saw the final "body count." Of these, 8,000 were blacks, and almost 27,000 (64 percent) were no older than 21.[2] In 1970, almost 70 percent of the casualties were young draftees:

> The Army assumed a remarkable shape in Vietnam. In most organizations it is the permanent long-standing members who usually take on the most critical tasks; the more transient and less-skilled members are relegated to support roles. But not so in the Army during the Vietnam War. There, the "regulars" did less of the fighting than amateurs who had been pressed into the enterprise against their will.[3]

The Pentagon has estimated that 10,303 Americans died in Vietnam for reasons it calls unrelated to the war effort, including those who died in airplane crashes and vehicle accidents, those who were murdered by other GIs, or took their own lives, or died from drug overdoses.

> If a man's death happened because he ran into the blades of a helicopter, was shot by mistake, fell from a watchtower, sank in a river, was blown up by his own explosives, the Army said, in effect, his death had nothing to do with combat. The implication was that the war was not the reason.[4]

The same was true for the number of nonhostile American deaths attributed to something called "friendly fire." According to government figures, 3,731 Americans serving in Vietnam died under fire from other Americans. These deaths occurred when U.S. planes bombed or strafed U.S. ground units, when artillery gunners mistakenly blasted U.S. patrols, when nervous sentries shot their own men along camp perimeters, and, unfortunately, when GIs killed other soldiers through carelessness or accident.[5]

General Westmoreland, U.S. commander in Vietnam and architect of America's search-and-destroy ground war, speaking before an Associated Press convention, assured his audience that thousands of

soldiers who died in Vietnam would have died anyway back in the
States. Most likely, he exclaimed, upwards of 10,000 would have
died in automobile accidents or of natural causes.[6]

On the other hand, Robert Kennedy, as we have previously noted,
expressed in 1968 his own convictions about the war and about U.S.
casualties:

> Here, while the sun shines, our brave young men are dying in the
> swamps in Southeast Asia. Which of them might have written a poem?
> Which of them might have cured cancer? Which of them might have
> played in a World Series or given us the gift of laughter from a stage or
> helped build a bridge or a university? Which of them would have
> taught a child to read? It is our responsibility to let these men live.[7]

Millions of Vietnam veterans were more fortunate and survived,
but of the approximately 3 million men who served, 303,704 were
wounded during combat. Of these, 153,329 were wounded badly
enough to require long-term hospitalization, whereas the other
150,343 survived their wounds without permanent hospitalization.
VA hospitals have treated thousands of Vietnam veterans who are
now blind, crippled, or paralyzed because of the war. Thousands
more suffered amputations or were partially or totally disabled by
the long and costly war.

Later years claimed further casualties. Years after the war, hundreds of former American servicemen and advisers contracted cancer
as a result of their contact with Agent Orange. The Pentagon now
acknowledges that as many as 20,000 unsuspecting Americans may
have handled Agent Orange in Vietnam.

Nearly 350,000 other veterans, or 15 percent of the total, received
less-than-honorable discharges. Their wounds are invisible, but the
scars they carry are no less permanent. Soldiers who were given a
less-than-honorable discharge might have disobeyed an order, even
an order to charge to their deaths up Hamburger Hill, and as a result
been court-martialed. Others, like 300,000 of their comrades, might
have become hooked on drugs and, scared and frustrated, been
forced to accept a dishonorable discharge. Still others might have
confessed to a chaplain their role in a firefight or talked to a reporter
about war atrocities which, in turn, might have prompted the army to
send them packing with a bad mark on their records. For many veterans, dishonorable discharges virtually guaranteed no job, no credit
and no respect when they finally returned home.[8]

A large number of veterans who saw heavy combat in Vietnam are afflicted with what is called "post-traumatic stress disorder," an emotional reaction that has become known as the "Vietnam Syndrome." Its symptoms—still present ten to fifteen years after the veterans returned from a tour of duty in Vietnam, and almost a decade after America's participation in the war ended—are characterized by guilt, anger, rage, flashbacks to unbelievable happenings, leading to nightmares, depression, and an inability to relate emotionally in a normal manner to the American scene.

The classic case might have been that of Dwight Johnson, who received this nation's highest award for killing Communists in Vietnam. Alexander Kendrick has written of Johnson's tragic story:

> Medals had no transferable value in civilian life. While the anti-war veterans demonstrated in Washington, a tall Negro tried to hold up a neighborhood grocery in Detroit and was fatally wounded, shot five times. His wallet contained a membership card in the Congressional Medal of Honor Society, bearing the name of Dwight Johnson. The medal had been awarded at the White House for Sergeant Johnson's action in the Battle of Dakto. . . . "Skip" Johnson, raised on welfare in a slum neighborhood, had been an altar boy and a Boy Scout. When he returned from Vietnam he, like many other blacks, could not find a job. He also had psychiatric problems—he suffered from nightmares about Vietnam. [Finally] . . . the Army asked him to be a recruiter, for obvious reasons, and he made personal appearances and attended testimonial functions. He married and had a son. Credit was easy to get and when the bills began piling up he wrote a bad check. . . . It was said he still had a "ghetto mentality" and could not adjust to a wider world. His stomach began to give him trouble, he neglected his recruiting job, missed appointments, and after treatment in an Army hospital went AWOL. His case was diagnosed as depression caused by adjustment difficulties, under the general heading of Post-Vietnam Syndrome. He was found to have guilt feelings about his survival in battle. The disclosure of the My Lai massacre . . . further unnerved him but he refused to return to the hospital and his unpaid bills continued to mount. Finally the mortgage on his . . . home was foreclosed and his wife had to undergo an operation. The evening he was killed he had asked to be driven to a friend's house to get another loan; instead, while his companions waited in their car, he went around the corner and entered the grocery with a pistol in his hand. "Skip" Johnson was buried in Arlington National Cemetery with an Army honor squad firing a salute, as was the due of a Medal of Honor winner.[9]

There are of course many other cases of continuing human suffering that make it impossible for veterans to forget the Vietnam War. The case of Michael Gorman illustrates the combined effects of

physical injury and emotional distress. Wounded when his helicopter gun jammed, allowing a Vietcong soldier on the ground to shoot
him at point-blank range, Gorman received treatment from VA hospitals in Massachusetts until he could operate a wheelchair on his own,
at which time he returned to his home town of Clarksburg, Massachusetts and began to rebuild his life. Just how difficult that struggle
has been is revealed in a letter Gorman wrote to George McGovern
after his defeat in the 1972 election:

> I'm a Vietnam veteran. I got shot in that miserable war making Vietnam
> safe from Vietnamese. How the hell can . . . the White House want to
> cut my pension after they were so damn willing to send me there. Mr.
> McGovern I can't work because I can't walk. I'm not very educated and
> I need my pension to survive. . . . Don't I rate something for my sacri-
> fice? A sacrifice I didn't give willingly. I was drafted, I didn't say "send
> me to Nam and get me shot." I'm in bad shape, but friends of mine like
> Bill, . . . he's got brain damage, . . . he can't sleep nights because he
> sees the dead he killed haunting him. That's his gift from Vietnam. [My
> friend] Russ . . . has an arm like a pendulum. It just hangs on his
> shoulder. How can he work? We're just people without college degrees,
> sons of factory workers, we fought that crummy war and got shot up in
> it. Don't let them cut our pensions. They've already cut our dreams and
> hopes.[10]

Thousands of other young Americans became refugees because of
U.S. Vietnam policies. These were all strong-willed individuals who
fell into one of three categories: those who refused induction into the
army, deserters who left the military, and activists living abroad or
underground at home who worked diligently against the war effort.
Members of each category broke the law, but they did so based on
their own conviction that a higher law existed: peace, justice, and
morality. On behalf of this higher law, the U.S. Vietnam "refugees"
opposed the war in Vietnam. The parents of one American deserter
living in Canada said:

> Even if [he] did desert, he said himself that he loved this country. . . .
> He wasn't against all war, just this one. If someone came to attack this
> country, he'd fight for the defense of it. . . . Now that we know, we feel
> a lot better.[11]

Thousands of veterans and Americans did not understand or con-
done the actions of these individuals and called upon the government to administer harsh penalties. But thousands of other Ameri-

cans called upon the government to grant clemency. In the fall of 1974, President Ford, after granting Richard Nixon an outright pardon, also appeared to pardon these refugees. When the program of clemency was revealed, however, it did not consist of a blanket amnesty for the youthful exiles who had opposed the war. Under the Ford plan, up to two years of work in public-service jobs were required before America's refugees could officially return home. To speed up the process, each case of desertion or draft evasion would go before a special clemency board, which would then pass judgment. The ACLU estimated that nearly 750,000 persons could have benefited from a simple decree of amnesty; under the Ford plan, only 137,000 were even eligible, and only 22,000 actually applied. Experts who have made a study of this clemency process contend that "for 80 percent of the Board's applicants, the clemency [was] a cruel hoax."[12]

In 1975, Ramsey Clark, former attorney general, estimated that perhaps as many as 2 million Americans, including all eighteen-year-olds who never registered for the draft, could be considered "in legal jeopardy for war resistance."[13] Obviously, these 2 million citizens were all war casualties in their own special way.

Now, almost a decade after the termination of America's direct involvement in Vietnam, Americans continue to suffer because of what happened there. Others are plagued with feelings of doubt, bitterness, guilt, and a lack of understanding of what Vietnam was all about. They have never been told or taken the time to discover the facts concerning this episode in American history. Knowing these facts can not only serve as a catharsis for them but may also assist them in finding the peace of mind and the justice which they are entitled to receive.

Millions of Americans and their families were fortunate enough to escape the human consequences of the Vietnam War. But hardly anyone has failed to feel the economic consequences. "The bills for the war in Indochina will keep coming in for the next century."[14]

There are wide discrepancies between the estimates of total costs and economic consequences of the war. In any event, the costs are mind-boggling. To understand the concept of even $1 billion, consider the following example: A person born 2,000 years ago, before the birth of Christ, would have to have earned $500,000 a year for 2,000 years in order to have $1 billion today. According to Department of Defense figures, the direct cost of the Vietnam War from fiscal year 1965 through fiscal year 1974 was $141.3 billion. One economist, Robert Warren Stevens, however, estimates the direct costs at $171.5 billion. But this direct cost is only a beginning. Tom Riddell estimates the ultimate cost will amount to $676 billion. This cost is derived by adding together all of the incidental costs to the federal government and to the American economy, direct and indirect, including veterans' benefits, interest payments on the national debt, and estimates of the amount of income lost to the American economy.

On the other hand, Stevens estimates the ultimate dollar cost of the Vietnam War will amount to $925 billion. Other competent economists estimate the cost of the war to be substantially less. Whatever figure you choose to accept, the amount spent was enormous. Furthermore, it was basically wasted, with no beneficial results.[15]

The economic problems caused by the Vietnam War began in 1965, when President Johnson escalated the war in Southeast Asia but refused to raise taxes. Escalation caused a severe strain on the U.S. economy, which had just reached a state of equilibrium. There was no budget deficit in 1964–65; there was no unemployment; prosperity was such that farsighted individuals predicted great progress in the struggle against poverty.

President Nixon did little to solve the economic problems that the war had created. In fact, through his blind determination to succeed on the battlefield, Nixon actually compounded America's economic problems. Under the guise of bringing the boys home, the President simply shifted military spending into other channels. In fact, 1969, the year of Nixon's inauguration speech about a new era of peace, was the most costly year of the entire war. The Pentagon's own figures estimate that $29 billion was spent on Vietnam during 1969. Soon after, Nixon intensified America's air war, at a cost of billions of dollars, and began to funnel massive appropriations into the Vietnamization program. These expenditures continued until the last day of the war.[16]

Congress has made projections as to the cost—present and future—of every war in which the United States has ever been involved. For Korea, Congress estimated the ultimate cost at $164 billion; for World War II, the estimated cost was $664 billion. Vietnam will exceed even World War II as America's most expensive war.

If we compare the price tag for Vietnam to other landmark programs carried out by the government, Vietnam emerges once again as one of the most expensive undertakings in U.S. history. The entire interstate highway system cost $53 billion (as of 1972). The man-on-the-moon space program cost $25 billion; the Great Society program, which competed with the Vietnam War after 1964, cost approximately $200 billion. Using Stevens' estimate, the cost of the war averages out to $32,000 per minute. Or to look at it another way, if the Vietnam War had never happened, the government could have taken that money and, if so desired, given more than $6,400 to every person in the United States.

Even if we use the Pentagon's minimum figure of $140 billion as the total cost of the Vietnam War, it means that the United States spent two and a half times as much money fighting in Vietnam's jungles as it has sent out in economic aid to all the underdeveloped countries of the world in the last twenty-five years. It means that each peak year the United States spent nine times as much as North Vietnam's entire gross national product. It means that America spent nearly $350,000 for every actual Vietcong guerrilla killed in the war. And it means that America's war in Vietnam consumed upwards of 70 percent of all funds appropriated for U.S. national defense between 1967 and 1972.[17]

But this astounding cost is only the tip of the iceberg. In the 1980s, other economic problems triggered by the Vietnam War continue to plague the U.S. economy. All economists agree that LBJ's policy of funding the cost of this war without an increase in taxes had a substantial impact, increasing the rate of inflation. The cancer of inflation that grew to double-digit proportions, especially in the areas of food, housing, energy, and health care, haunts every American.

The American public has also been forced to accept the decline of the U.S. dollar overseas and a totally unbalanced balance-of-payments situation. Not only is it bad for the economy when the United States buys or imports billions of dollars more in the way of goods and services from other countries than it sells or exports to those countries, the balance-of-payments crisis also affects every individual who wants to travel outside the United States. The dollar, weakened by inflation, must now survive the furious buying of gold which has driven gold prices up, while the dollar has plummeted on world markets. The dollar used to be the strongest currency in the world, but Vietnam helped destroy its credibility and insured that the dollar would become another casualty of the long and deadly war.[18]

Finally, the fact remains that when it was all over, the United States found itself less secure and militarily weaker. Friend and foe alike of the Vietnam War admit that the massive expenditure entailed by this struggle substantially weakened every branch of the U.S. military establishment. The present administration has convinced many Americans that it is now necessary to spend additional billions of dollars to bolster U.S. security so that the country will be in a position to defend itself now and in the years to come. As a result of past military expenditures and the need for additional expenditures, the manufacturing productivity of the United States has been hampered. The United States now finds itself almost unable to compete with other nations in the free world who spend their money to increase the standard of living of their people, in contrast with the U.S. preoccupation with military expenditures.

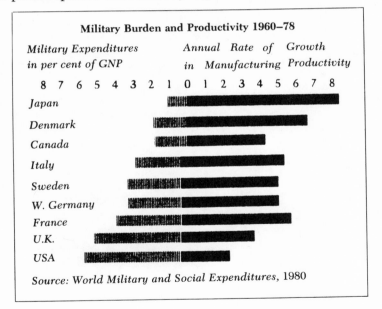

These are just some of the grim realities of the U.S. involvement in Vietnam.

EPILOGUE
A Citizen's Verdict

> Why do men in high office so often act contrary to the
> way that reason points and enlightened self-interest
> suggests? Why does intelligent mental process so often
> seem to be paralyzed? . . . In the case we know
> best—the American engagement in Vietnam—fixed
> notions, preconceptions, wooden-headed thinking, and
> emotions accumulated into a monumental mistake and
> classic humiliation.
> —Barbara W. Tuchman

Vietnam Verdict: A Citizen's History has presented a factual, objective
account of what transpired during the period of the involvement of the
United States in Vietnam. The Epilogue now presents the author's
personal conclusions, with a restatement of certain important facts and
key questions that, in his opinion, require the serious debate and sober
consideration of all citizens of the United States. The first question is:

**Was the Vietnam War the inevitable result of U.S. policies after
World War II? How should the U.S. Vietnam experience, in any
event, affect U.S. foreign policy in the 1980's?**

The war in Vietnam was a direct extension of America's Cold War
policies. The United States sent the Central Intelligence Agency into
Vietnam to contain the spread of Communism, and when the CIA's efforts
failed, President Johnson converted our involvement into a full-fledged
war. Dean Rusk gave the government's official reason for this:

> In Southeast Asia, indirect aggression is not just a threat but an immediate
> danger to vital Free World positions. . . . The Free World must prevent the
> Communists from extending their sway through force. . . . It is not enough to
> contain Communism and try to negotiate specific agreements. The conflict

between the Communists and the Free World is as fundamental as any conflict can be.

The United States lost the war in Vietnam, which has now become a Communist state. Yet the United States continues to pursue the same Communist containment policies elsewhere and endorses the same anti-Communist tactics that failed in Vietnam.

It is the American people rather than their government who have learned from the Vietnam experience. Many Americans today fear that Cold War policy as it was carried out in Vietnam will eventually lead to nuclear war. They are demanding a nuclear freeze, and politicians at all levels of American government are beginning to listen. If popular demand could break the pattern of nuclear escalation, it would surely be a giant step forward.

Yet even a freeze would not eliminate the terrible threat of nuclear holocaust. Everyone in the United States can be killed many times over with the nuclear weapons that already exist. The true road to a more stable international environment would be to combine a nuclear freeze with a freeze on Cold War propaganda. If we could shed the rigidity of Cold War anti-Communism, we could view the world in its great variety and create flexible approaches to world problems.

Some special-interest groups and individuals tell us that we must continue to wage the Cold War and, if necessary, a hot war that we make sure to win next time. In the 1950s when Cold War doctrine was being hammered out, one of its architects said, "If we can sell every useless article known to man in large quantities, we should be able to sell our very fine story in larger quantities." Using all the techniques of modern marketing, the Cold Warriors did succeed in selling us the Cold War.

Here is that lavishly financed story as we have heard it through the years:

> Because of the nature of Communism, the Soviet Union is determined to enslave its own people and its neighbors, and will then proceed to destroy America and enslave the world.
> Because Communists are fanatics willing to pour all their resources into world domination, the Soviets have drawn ahead of us in armaments. Therefore we Americans must devote more and more of our own money to the arms race.
> Because Communism is a super-secret, super-powerful worldwide movement, we must support our own Cold Warriors no matter what they do, even if they lie to us while doing it.

Those Cold Warriors who now control foreign policy in the United States do not appear to recognize the changes that make the 1980s different from the 1950s. It is important that the people of this country examine and debate whether or not in today's world the policies that led to Vietnam should be continued. It is the lives and well-being of the American people that are at stake, and it is imperative that *they* decide whether the trouble caused by the Cold War is still worth the price.

All the formulas of Cold War strategy—subversion, puppet dictatorships, secret war, and, finally, open war—were methodically used in Vietnam. Despite the lives we sacrificed, the billions we spent, and the evil we did, our Vietnam involvement was a foreign policy disaster at every stage.

On balance, the Cold War has been a failure. It has not enabled us to eradicate Communism or destroy the Soviet Union. It has certainly not produced peace. It has led our government to interfere secretly in the affairs of Third World nations, to support and sometimes create corrupt dictatorships, to stockpile arms like a military state, and recklessly to escalate small wars that have nothing to do with us. Despite the incalculable cost of the efforts that the United States has made for decades to curtail Soviet power, the U.S. government now tells its citizens that the Soviet Union exceeds us in military strength and that, despite our own weakened economy, we must spend almost a trillion dollars in an arms race to catch up.

Many other Western nations, however, are convinced that the Soviet Union is no longer a major threat to the world, that the influence of the Soviets has declined, that their economy is in a shambles, that they desperately need peace in order to hold their own empire together, and that Communism has proved itself so ineffective that few want it except underdeveloped nations who have no other source of capital.

In order to end the Vietnam War, the United States ultimately acknowledged that it no longer had a real problem with Communism in the People's Republic of China. President Nixon negotiated a rapprochement with China and its one billion Communist citizens, and this country began the normalization of trade, travel, and other relations with them. In simple logic, why are we still pursuing the Communist containment policy against the Soviet Union? What differentiates Russian Communists from their Chinese counterparts?

It would appear that the Soviet Union has materially altered Stalin's old crusade to colonize the world, because the Soviets found this policy both expensive and counterproductive. They continue, however, to support groups in underdeveloped countries whom they hope will become their friends and whom they claim are trying to overthrow dictators supported by the United States. Certainly the Russians feels the need to counteract U.S. Cold War activities. By now it is difficult to know whether we act because of them or they act because of us and to determine which is the chicken and which the egg in any world trouble spot.

We have pointed out why it is necessary for the American people to discuss the need to curtail Cold Warism as exemplified by Vietnam. There appears to be a reluctance by politicians and political leaders in the public sector to curtail Cold War activities. Why? Who benefits from the Cold War? Pentagon officials who need an enemy in order to increase their appropriations? Defense contractors who spend millions on Cold War propaganda? Politicians who rise to power by manipulating our love of America and fear of foreign interference? Right-wing Cold Warriors who have a phobic fear of Socialism and Communism? In any event, all these groups and many others exert pressure on the President to continue the Cold War.

Even the President seems to enjoy the power that the Cold War gives him. People still believe that only the President can make the decisions necessary to save us from our "enemies." He thus exercises more power over foreign policy than over domestic issues. Successive administrations have inflated this power in pursuing the Cold War, and the public never questioned the military appropriations and the covert and open wars against Communism until late in the Vietnam tragedy. Congress then attempted in some degree to restrict Presidential excesses in foreign affairs. But today the executive branch seems to be making a major effort to remove these restrictions and to intensify the Cold War by spending enormous sums on the arms race.

The next important question and issue that we should discuss and decide is:

In light of the Vietnam experience, should the United States continue to utilize the CIA or other paramilitary groups to support anti-Communist governments?

Billions of U.S. dollars have been spent over the years in arming, supporting, and assisting anti-Communist governments and providing undisclosed funds to the CIA. The CIA was employed in Vietnam, Laos, and Cambodia for many years as a secret force for subversion and paramilitary operations. The CIA, which had been primarily an information-gathering body for the State Department, was transformed into the primary instrument for subversion and sabotage. Its budget and staff were expanded, and it began to report to a special task force accountable to the President. The CIA's new assignment was to give undercover aid to "friendly" (anti-Communist) governments and to undermine groups that might establish socialist regimes. Networks of agents were set up abroad; guerrilla troops were organized in nations where military clout might be helpful.

In the 1950s, U.S. policy makers, fearing Soviet aggressiveness and frustrated by Third World neutrality, decided that high principles do not pay. "If the United States is to survive," said one group of top-level advisers, "long-standing American concepts of 'fair play' must be reconsidered. We must develop effective espionage and counter-espionage services and must learn to subvert, sabotage, and destroy our enemies by more clever, more sophisticated and more effective methods than those used against us."

Over time, using these tactics, the CIA became a shaping force in the internal affairs of many countries—among them Iran, Guatemala, and Cuba. In 1953 the CIA was responsible for overthrowing the Iranian premier Mossadegh and restoring control to the Shah. The CIA helped to oust Guatemala's left-leaning President Arbenz Guzman. CIA efforts to depose Fidel Castro of Cuba led to the unsuccessful Bay of Pigs invasion of 1961 and to an abortive attempt to assassinate him by hiring Mafia killers. "There are no rules in such a game," Cold War policy makers declared. "Hitherto acceptable norms of behavior do not apply."

Nowhere has the CIA been given a bolder opportunity, or more clearly revealed the weaknesses of Cold War policy, than in Vietnam. From around 1954 to 1964 the Agency was the power behind the South Vietnamese government, army, and police force. It also organized an undercover army and air force to fight a secret war in Laos.

Why did the United States and the CIA commit so much of their time and money to Vietnam and Southeast Asia? The United States first supported the French financially in their attempt to recolonize Vietnam. Ho Chi Minh fought and won his war of independence against France. The United States would not support Ho Chi Minh because he was a socialist, and he was forced to accept aid from the Communist bloc.

A peace agreement was finally worked out at Geneva in 1954 by many interested nations, which provided for Vietnam's temporary division into North and South. Elections were scheduled for 1956, and whoever won them was to govern a united Vietnam. Meanwhile Ho Chi Minh ruled North Vietnam. John Foster Dulles, secretary of state under President Eisenhower, refused to accept the agreement. Dulles feared that any free election would result in a landslide for the socialist Ho Chi Minh.

John Foster Dulles and his brother Alan Dulles now began to utilize the CIA in an effort to forestall the holding of elections and the possibility of South Vietnam becoming a Communist state. To achieve this, the U.S. and the CIA policy makers selected Ngo Dinh Diem and set him up as premier of South Vietnam. CIA agents ran the public relations campaign that put Diem into office. They gained control of the South Vietnamese army, bureaucracy, and police for him. They also taught him how to rig elections so that he always won by a large majority in South Vietnam. The United States paid the major cost of the running of Diem's government, and almost the entire cost of the maintenance of his military forces, the ARVN.

With all this help, the United States hoped that Diem would become popular enough to woo the people away from Ho Chi Minh. Instead, Diem turned into a corrupt and ruthless dictator who put his family into office, grew rich from the narcotics trade, and terrorized the Vietnamese. While he expropriated the peasants' land and gave it to his rich friends, his secret police executed thousands of peasants as "Communist sympathizers."

In reaction, the peasants formed a rebel organization, the National Liberation Front, together with a loosely organized guerrilla army known as the Vietcong. Its jungle warfare against Diem's army was successful from the start, both because the Vietcong fought with conviction and because they had increasing support from the mass of South Vietnamese peasants. The ARVN, Diem's forces, were no match for the Vietcong. Most of them had no stomach for fighting their countrymen, whose goals were the reunification of North and South and American withdrawal from Vietnam.

By the time Kennedy became President in 1961, it was clear that the CIA was failing in its monumental effort to sustain a government that the South Vietnamese did not want. Kennedy was persuaded to try and save Diem's regime by sending in 19,000 combat troops, termed "military advisers." But the Vietcong continued to gain territory and the Diem government to lose control of the people. Finally the United States decided to withdraw support from Diem. He was overthrown and assassinated. A week later, John F. Kennedy was also assassinated and Lyndon Johnson became President.

The efforts made by the CIA to implement Cold War policies in Vietnam were obviously counterproductive and unsuccessful. There are indications that despite a current Congressional attempt to curtail their activities, efforts are being made to utilize them or similar agencies to carry on in much the same manner as before. Now that the veil of secrecy that surrounds the CIA has to some extent been lifted, U.S. citizens should determine whether or not they want similar activities to continue.

In the next phase of the U.S. campaign in Southeast Asia, President Lyndon Baines Johnson replaced the covert activities of the CIA with the direct involvement of the U.S. Armed Forces. Thus the next obvious question is:

Should U.S. citizens permit the U.S. government to commit its military forces to implement Cold War policies?

Under President Johnson, the "Cold War" that had turned into a hot war in Vietnam became one of the longest, most expensive, and deadliest wars in our history. Yet it was the only war that the United States has ever lost. The reason many U.S. political leaders now give for our defeat is that the politicians did not let the military win, that political considerations prevented Lyndon Johnson, Richard Nixon, and U.S. forces from pushing on to victory. We need to ask whether this is true. Why was the war lost? And should we try such a war again, next time with more will and more power?

The facts gathered in *Vietnam Verdict* indicate that the war was lost before it started. The United States began losing it during the preceding Cold War years, when the CIA took control of South Vietnam. The CIA's series of puppet dictators lost the support of the peasants, whom the United States was determined to "save" from the clutches of Communism.

Though the Vietnamese peasants wanted only to live peacefully on their farms, the United States sent first the CIA and then the Marines, the Army, the Navy, and the Air Force into their country to fight a phantom enemy, Communism. Our government, however, claimed that the war was caused by a monolithic Communist conspiracy among the Soviet Union, China, and North Vietnam.

If this were true, should we have been fighting a group of peasants in Vietnam? If China was the real enemy, should we have begun the war unless we were prepared to invade the Chinese mainland as well as North Vietnam? And if our other real enemy was the Soviet Union, should we have been prepared to go to war with the Soviets with its potential of a nuclear confrontation? Did all three of these "enemies" want nothing more than to achieve normal relations with the United States?

Consider the facts about the policies of the three countries. In 1946 Ho Chi Minh begged Truman to permit him to establish an independent government without French interference. When Truman refused, Ho turned to the Soviet Union and China for help, although he was always as much afraid of their imperialism as he was of French colonialism.

Then when the United States sent the CIA into South Vietnam to assist

Diem, China supported the revolutionists and the Vietcong with small arms and continuous supplies of food. Russia at first gave North Vietnam reluctant assistance. But as the American involvement escalated and turned into a full-fledged U.S. military operation, both China and Russia materially increased their aid with military supplies and technicians. We did not find evidence that the Russians furnished manpower. As documented in *Vietnam Verdict*, however, Chinese soldiers did man the Russian antiaircraft guns that brought down American planes in the later stages of the war.

When American GIs arrived in Vietnam, they discovered that the enemy they were fighting were the peasants of South Vietnam—an estimated 90 percent of the population. The Vietcong were recruited from the sons and daughters of peasants living in the villages of Vietnam, and in order to kill Vietcong soldiers, it was necessary for Americans to destroy the villages and kill millions of Vietnamese.

While the Vietnamese of all ages were fighting to the death to win freedom against "foreign aggressors," China, with its farms and factories inviolate, could supply Vietnam with food and small arms indefinitely. The Soviet Union likewise could furnish money, antiaircraft guns, and tanks. The result was that China and the U.S.S.R. won a great victory against the United States without losing a man.

In the soiled moral climate of the Vietnam War, U.S. troops fought as well as they could. Millions of young Americans, struggling to save their own lives, learned to hate and kill the men, women, and children whom they had come to save from "Communist aggression."

We have pointed out that in his drive to win the war, President Johnson first inaugurated Operation Rolling Thunder. U.S. jets roared out of bases in Thailand, South Vietnam, and the South China Sea, and by 1968 a minimum of 304,000 missions had been flown and 600,000 tons of bombs had been dropped on North Vietnam. Johnson engineered a four-year round-the-clock bombardment designed to break the will of the North Vietnamese government. At the same time, U.S. planes pounded the South Vietnamese countryside in an attempt to crush the Vietcong. Attacking with canisters of napalm, American jets seared human flesh and scorched villages, farms, and jungle. By the war's end, 21 million craters pocked South Vietnam, a piece of land less than 100 miles long.

In terms of ground forces, by 1968 Johnson had employed more than 540,000 troops. Most of them were draftees with an average age of eighteen, compared with an average age of twenty-eight in World War II. During the Johnson administration, nearly 28,000 U.S. soldiers died, as did millions of Vietnamese.

When Richard Nixon became President, he claimed to have a "secret plan" to end the war. It is now apparent that his plan was to conduct the heaviest bombing campaign in history and thereby force the North Vietnamese to surrender. To reconcile the American people to a stepped-up war, Nixon announced a policy which he called "Vietnamization," in which U.S. troops would be withdrawn gradually and the war turned over to the Vietnamese ARVN. It seems as if Nixon and his advisers must have known by then that the South Vietnamese government could not survive without U.S. military and air support. At first most Americans believed Nixon, although thousands of American soldiers died in 1969 as he initiated the so-called withdrawal of U.S. forces.

Now began the greatest bombardment of all. By 1970–71 the United States had dropped almost 5 million tons of bombs on Vietnam, Cambodia, and Laos—more than double the tonnage dropped in World War II. In the first five months of 1970 alone, 600,000 tons of bombs were dropped in Vietnam—far more than the total amount during the Korean War. Each year thereafter, the tonnage averaged about 1,400,000. B-52 raids alone cost over one million dollars a day. The result was greater destruction than ever inside South Vietnam. Since the military defoliation program had already ruined over 5 million acres of forest land in South Vietnam by the end of 1971, the overall impact of United States action is almost inconceivable.

American citizens must now decide if they remain ready to convert cold wars into additional hot wars as happened in Vietnam. "Citizen" Richard Nixon has not changed his point of view: In *The Real War* he writes:

> The War in Vietnam was not lost on the battlefields of Vietnam. It was lost in the halls of Congress . . . in the editorial rooms of great newspapers and television networks . . . and in the classrooms of great universities. The class that provided the strong leadership that made victory possible in World War I and World War II failed America in one of the crucial battles of World War III—Vietnam.

It is possible to agree with Richard Nixon but for substantially different reasons. The war was lost by our "leaders" and those who condoned the act of sending U.S. military forces into Vietnam to fight a phantom enemy, Communism, because neither these political nor military leaders realized that they were fighting an enemy—most of the South Vietnamese people—which itself was fighting not for Communism but for independence. The war was not lost because the political sector did not permit the military to win. Rather, our political leaders unleashed one of the most deadly wars in history. If Nixon's contention that Vietnam was just *one* of the crucial battles of World War III continues to be supported by U.S. Cold Warriors, the time has come for U.S. citizens to protect their interests and their ultimate security.

Should the U.S. government be permitted to tell its citizens lies in matters pertaining to cold and hot wars? In possession of the facts, should the American people be prevented from discussing and debating these policies?

The President of the United States has been able to usurp the power to make war because most citizens believe that it is necessary to allow him adequate power to protect this nation against the Communist threat. For decades I, too, hated and feared Communism, believing that America was in danger from a Communist takeover and that foreign policy and defense, therefore, must be left to the President and his advisers.

My confidence in having the President protect us changed when I had the opportunity, as civilian co-chairman of a White House Conference on International Cooperation in 1965, to spend a year close to President Johnson and his advisers. What I discovered then shook my belief that only the President, his advisers, and military counterparts know how to protect and defend America. Since then, years of study, travel, and research have strengthened my belief that if we leave the power to "defend" or to make war solely in the hands of the President and his staff, we are in deep trouble.

For LBJ, foreign policy was an exercise in power, and the Cold War was the vehicle that enabled him to rule in the style of a benevolent monarch, that gave him the opportunity to conduct himself as "leader of the free world" with unlimited funds and America's manpower at his disposal.

Thoughtful citizens who would like to debate, discuss, or dissent from a mindless support of the Cold War have often found it inadvisable to do so, particularly after the persecutions of the McCarthy Era. Ordinary Americans who do so are smeared as unpatriotic, and dedicated government and military officials who do so risk their careers.

In this climate, it is easy to understand why it was possible for the Cold War to continue in Vietnam for almost eighteen years and for Lyndon Johnson and Richard Nixon to fight an unpopular "hot" war there for another ten years. But even then they might not have been able to carry it off without using tactics to suppress dissent among U.S. citizens similar to the Cold War tactics used against people in foreign nations.

In order to "sell" its Cold War program to the American people, so that the Presidency would have a free hand in exercising cold and hot war policies, the government engages in an enormous program of "public relations and information," consisting of a barrage of speeches, statements, and press handouts, amounting to the almost continual indoctrination of the American people concerning the evils of Communism. This Cold War rhetoric has varied only slightly down through the years. Its intensity is determined by the need to gain citizen support for political purposes, wars, military appropriations, and to enable the President to have a free hand in foreign policy. After more than a half century of such intermittent incantations and indoctrination, few citizens seem to have questioned the unsupported accusations and the half truths that make Cold Warism an important part of the psyche of the American people.

Lyndon Johnson deceived the American people from the beginning of his Presidency with reference to his Vietnam intentions. His internal planning to escalate the Vietnam involvement was kept secret from the American people. We have previously set forth how President Johnson procured Congressional authority to continue his hitherto secret war by reason of an alleged incident that enabled him to persuade Congress to pass what became known as the Tonkin Gulf Resolution. As Senator Gruening later said:

> Many people don't even know the story of the Tonkin Gulf Resolution. And I think it's important that everybody know it. . . . We have made mistakes before, but I think this is the first time in our history that we have been deliberately deceived and lied to by our chief executives.

Lyndon Johnson also misled citizens during his campaign for the Presidency in 1964. He won the Presidency as "a man of peace," while behind the scenes, he prepared for war. After his inauguration as President in January 1965, he waged a bitter and futile war in Vietnam.

The power of the President to wage war, to deceive citizens, and to suppress dissent did not end with Lyndon Baines Johnson. Richard Nixon's deceptive tactics and cover-up were far more extensive and effective than Lyndon Johnson's. Nixon had at his side a diplomatic master in the art, his ever more powerful secretary of state, Henry Kissinger.

During Nixon's campaign for the Presidency, he claimed that he had a "plan to end the war." Americans hoped that at long last the blood-letting in Vietnam would cease. After becoming President, his actions disclosed that he had no intention of ending the war short of a total victory. As he said later, "There is no substitute for victory." During his Presidency, almost as many American youths died or were injured in Vietnam as during the Johnson administration, and millions of additional Southeast Asians were slaughtered.

Nixon also told the American people that he intended to withdraw American troops from Vietnam and turn the war back to the Vietnamese in a process that he called "Vietnamization." He gradually withdrew American soldiers, but replaced them with an all-out technological air war against both North and South Vietnam. He then began the most intensive air bombardment in the history of aerial warfare in an effort to force the Vietnamese peace negotiators to surrender.

When this failed, Nixon invaded Cambodia without the consent of Congress or the American people, devastating this country, destroying its people.

In 1971 Nixon also engineered an invasion of Laos. He did so, despite a Congressional prohibition against using any U.S. forces for such a purpose, by utilizing South Vietnamese ground troops. Despite massive aerial assistance by American bombers, the ARVN were soundly defeated and needed to be evacuated by their U.S. protectors or be annihilated.

What has been acclaimed as Nixon and Kissinger's greatest triumph was their summit conference in the People's Republic of China at Peking in February, 1972. There was an intensive discussion of the Vietnam problem in Peking, and the end result of this summit conference was sensational. The United States, which had fought a bitter Cold War against the Chinese since the inception of their Communist government in 1949 and which characterized them as their main enemy during the Vietnam War, now called off the Cold War against China. A rapprochement was affected—a result that the Chinese had always longed for. Few stopped to ask why Richard Nixon did not make this visit as soon as he became President, which, Chinese officials told the author, might have ended the Vietnam War much sooner.

The next Nixon-Kissinger "triumph" was the Moscow summit in May of 1972, which was not difficult to arrange. The Russians desperately wanted a rapprochement with the United States and the establishment of normal trading relationships.

But the Soviet Union had no success in achieving the same result as did China. Instead, its bitter enemy, China, perhaps gained an ally in the United States. Nixon retained the U.S.S.R. as an enemy and thus maintained all the "advantages" of the Cold War.

Even after the Peking and Moscow summits, the war did not come to an immediate end. President Nixon still wanted total victory, but he and Kissinger nevertheless continued to go through the charade of conducting peace negotiations and hammering out a peace treaty. 1972 was another Presidential election year, and Nixon felt he could not be reelected this time unless the people were convinced that the war was now about to end.

The monumental publicity and television coverage Nixon received during his Peking and Moscow summits helped insure his election. Many Americans overlooked the war in Vietnam as they witnessed their "new" statesmanlike President toasting their erstwhile Russian and Chinese enemies.

Richard Nixon was safely reelected as President in November 1972 but once again doublecrossed the Vietnamese negotiators and the American people in making a final desperate effort to win the war by launching the infamous Christmas Bombing of 1972, killing additional thousands of Vietnamese.

This effort also failed and Nixon ultimately signed the Paris Peace Agreement on January 13, 1973. The final agreement, another Nixon-Kissinger masterpiece, was little different from the one that might have been signed earlier, and it represents an historic achievement in the art of chicanery and cover-up.

It does not appear that any of the signators to the treaty intended to be bound by its terms. Once again, it was the American people, hoping that at long last the Vietnam disaster was over, who were deceived. The North Vietnamese, after a "decent interval" of about two years, marched into Saigon with little opposition ultimately to create a unified Communist Vietnam.

There is nothing affirmative about a disaster except the lessons learned that can prevent a similar happening. We now know what happens when the final discretion in matters of war and peace is left solely in the hands of political leaders. There has never been a better time for U.S. citizens to examine the facts and to exercise their democratic right to be heard. American citizens in this democracy will thus have the power to participate in the most important decision of our time: *How can we best save the United States from future wars that could lead to nuclear disaster?*

NOTES

Author's Note

1. "Nuclear War Is National Suicide," *Journal of the Federation of American Scientists (FAS)* 34, no. 2 (February 1981).
2. Richard Nixon, *The Real War*, pp. 244–45.
3. "Lyndon B. Reagan on Vietnam," *Newsweek*, March 1, 1982, p. 30.
4. Norman Podhoretz, *Why We Were in Vietnam* (New York: Simon & Schuster, 1982), pp. 106–7.

Chapter 1
Prelude to Vietnam: Origins of the Cold War

1. It was apparently composed of Paul Nitze and his colleagues on the Policy Planning Staff., Major General James Burnes, Major General Truman Landon, Najeeb Halaby, Robert LeBaron, and others.
2. Bohlen and Lovett, quoted in Fred M. Kaplan, "Our Cold-War Policy, Circa '50," *New York Times Magazine*, May 18, 1980, pp. 89–91.
3. Lawrence Wittner, *Cold War America: From Hiroshima to Watergate* (New York: Praeger, 1974), p. 87.
4. Ibid., p. 86.
5. Ibid., pp. 89–90.
6. Ibid., p. 91.
7. Ibid., pp. 91–92.
8. Ibid., p. 95.
9. Ibid., p. 101.
10. Lewis McCarroll Purifoy, *Harry Truman's China Policy: McCarthyism and the Diplomacy of Hysteria, 1947–1951 (New York: New Viewpoints, 1976), p. 191.
11. Ibid., p. 191.
12. Ibid., p. 192.
13. Dean Acheson, *Present at the Creation* (New York: Norton, 1969), pp. 408, 415; Purifoy, pp. 197–98.

Chapter 2
The First Eighteen Years

1. Memorandum by Roosevelt to Secretary of State Cordell Hull, January 24, 1944, in Gareth Porter, ed., *Vietnam: The Definitive Documentation of Human Decisions* (New York: E. M. Coleman, 1979), 1: 11.

2. Ho Chi Minh's letter to Truman, February 16, 1946, in Porter, *Vietnam,* 1: 95.

3. Department of State Policy Statement on Indochina, September 27, 1948, in Porter, *Vietnam,* 1:178.

4. Memorandum by the Department of State to the French Foreign Office, June 6, 1949, in Porter, *Vietnam,* 1: 201.

5. Memorandum by Raymond B. Fosdick for Ambassador at Large Philip Jessup, November 4, 1949, in Porter, *Vietnam,* 1: 214–15.

6. Report by the Bureau of Far Eastern Affairs, Department of State, On Military Assistance for Indochina, February 16, 1950, in Porter, *Vietnam,* 1: 239.

7. Donald Zagoria, *Vietnam Triangle: Moscow, Peking, Hanoi* (New York: Pegasus, 1967), pp. 37–41; Alexander Kendrick, *The Wound Within: America in the Vietnam Years 1945–1974* (Boston: Little, 1974), p. 51.

8. N. Khac Huyen, *Vision Accomplished: The Enigma of Ho Chi Minh* (New York: Macmillan, 1971), p. 275; George McTurnan Kahin and John W. Lewis, *The United States in Vietnam,* rev. ed. (New York: Dell, 1969), p. 271; Kendrick, pp. 51–53.

9. P. J. Honey, *Communism in North Vietnam* (Cambridge: MIT Press, 1963), p. 42.

10. Richard Nixon, quoted by Richard Barnet, *Intervention and Revolution: The United States in the Third World* (New York: World, 1968), p. 192.

11. Telegram from Dulles to the State Department, April 29, 1954, in Porter, *Vietnam,* 1: 545.

12. "Agreement on the Cessation of Hostilities in Vietnam (July 20, 1954)," otherwise known as the Geneva Accords, reprinted in Marvin Gettleman, ed., *Vietnam: History, Documents, and Opinions on a Major World Crisis* (New York: NAL, Mentor, 1970), pp. 164–78. Also, "Further Documents Relating to the Discussion of Indo-China at the Geneva Conference," June 16–July 21, 1954, Presented by the Secretary of State for Foreign Affairs to Parliament by Command of Her Majesty, August 1954.

13. *The Pentagon Papers: The Defense Department History of United States Decisionmaking on Vietnam,* Senator Gravel ed., 5 vols. (Boston: Beacon Press, 1971), p. 648. Hereafter referred to as *Pentagon Papers,* Gravel ed.

14. Letter from General Collins to Dulles, April 7, 1955, in Porter, *Vietnam,* 1: 695.

15. "Southeast Asia Treaty Organization: Response to the Communist Threat (September 1954)," otherwise known as the SEATO Treaty, reprinted in Gettleman, pp. 121–24.

16. President Suharto, quoted by William Winter in interview with author, fall 1979.

17. Bernard Fall, *The Two Vietnams: A Political and Military Analysis* (New York: Praeger, 1967), pp. 302–8; Kahin and Lewis, pp. 66–72.

18. Committee of Concerned Asian Scholars, *The Indochina Story* (New York: Bantam, 1970), pp. 31–32. Hereafter referred to as *Indochina Story.*

19. Joseph Buttinger, *Vietnam: A Political History* (New York: Praeger, 1968), pp. 447–48.

20. *Indochina Story,* pp. 29–31.

21. Richard West, *Sketches from Vietnam* (London: Jonathan Cape, 1968), p. 107.

22. *Pentagon Papers,* Gravel ed., 1: 254.

23. AID official as told to Charles Mohr, quoted in Howard Zinn, *Vietnam: The Logic of Withdrawal* (Boston: Beacon Press, 1967), p. 49.

24. Thich Nhat-Hanh, *Vietnam: Lotus in a Sea of Fire* (New York: Hill & Wang, 1967), p. 65.

25. Kahin and Lewis, pp. 99–100.

26. Bernard Fall, *Vietnam Witness 1953–1966* (New York: Praeger, 1966), p. 235; John Osborne, "The Tough Miracle Man of Vietnam," *Life,* May 13, 1957, p. 164.

27. Kahin and Lewis, pp. 101–2.

28. Vietnamese peasant, quoted in Staughton Lynd and Thomas Hayden, *The Other Side* (New York: New American Library, 1966), pp. 174–75. See also Joseph Alsop, "A Reporter at Large," *The New Yorker,* June 25, 1955, p. 48.

29. Kahin and Lewis, p. 103.

30. Fall, *Vietnam Witness,* p. 237; Kahin and Lewis, pp. 72–75, 103–4; John Montgomery, *The Politics of Foreign Aid* (New York: Praeger, 1962), p. 124.

31. Phillipe DeVillers, "The Struggle for the Unification of Vietnam," *The China Quarterly* 9 (January–March 1962), p. 13.

32. Vietminh peasant, quoted in Lynd and Hayden, p. 181.

33. Douglas Pike, *VietCong: The Organization and Techniques of the National Liberation Front of South Vietnam* (Cambridge: MIT Press, 1966), pp. 74–76; Kahin and Lewis, pp. 109–10, 142–44.

34. Fall, *Vietnam Witness,* p. 236.

35. Kahin and Lewis, p. 108.

36. Ibid., pp. 108–12.

37. Fall, *Vietnam Witness,* p. 237.

38. "Declaration of Former Resistance Fighters, March 1960," March 1960, in Kahin and Lewis, appendix 5, pp. 458–61; *Le Monde,* April 15, 1965, quoted in Kahin and Lewis, p. 114.

39. "The Ten Point Program of the NLF, December 20, 1960," December 20, 1960, in Kahin and Lewis, appendix 6-B, pp. 464–69; Kahin and Lewis, pp. 114–15.

40. Fall, *Vietnam Witness,* pp. 240–41; Kahin and Lewis, pp. 133–35.

41. Pike, p. 117.

42. Kahin and Lewis, pp. 129–32.

43. Pike, pp. 136–37; Fall, *Vietnam Witness,* pp. 240–41; Kahin and Lewis, pp. 133–35.

44. Kahin and Lewis, pp. 77–80, 127–29.

45. Secret message from American Embassy, Saigon, to Secretary of State Rusk #11782, May 18, 1961 (Declassified 12/3/74), in Declassified Documents Reference System (Washington, D.C.: Carrollton Press), located at the Air Force Academy Library, Colorado Springs, Colorado.

46. Vice-President Johnson, quoted in Arthur Schlesinger, Jr., *A Thousand Days* (Boston: Houghton-Mifflin, 1965), p. 542.

47. Secret message from Ambassador Nolting to Secretary of State Rusk #5237, October 9, 1961 (Declassified 12/16/74), in Declassified Documents Reference System.

48. Secret messages from Ambassador Nolting to Secretary of State Rusk #8379 and #13438, October 13 and October 21, 1961 (Declassified 12/6/74), in Declassified Documents Reference System.

49. Top secret memo from Roger Hilsman to McGeorge Bundy, November 16, 1961 (now declassified); secret message from Nolting to Rusk #12183, November 20, 1961 (now declassified), in Declassified Documents Reference System.

50. Top secret message from J. K. Galbraith for President Kennedy's eyes only #25879, November 21, 1961 (Declassified 2/27/74), in Declassified Documents Reference System.

51. Cablegram from Lodge to Rusk, August 29, 1963, in Porter, *Vietnam*, 2: 188.

52. Cablegram from CIA Station Chief Richardson to McCone, October 5, 1963, in Porter, *Vietnam*, 2: 506.

Chapter 3
President Johnson Plans Vietnam War

1. Doris Kearns, *Lyndon Johnson and the American Dream* (New York: Harper & Row, 1976), pp. 264–65.

2. "Report by Vice President Johnson on His Visit to Asian Countries," May 23, 1961, Neil Sheehan et al., *The Pentagon Papers: As Published by The New York Times*, Document #21 (New York: Bantam, 1971), pp. 127–30. Hereafter referred to as *Pentagon Papers*.

3. David Halberstam, *The Best and the Brightest* (New York: Harper & Row, 1972), p. 135.

4. LBJ, quoted in Tom Wicker, *JFK and LBJ* (New York: Morrow, 1968), p. 205.

5. LBJ, quoted in Halberstam, p. 434.

6. LBJ, quoted in Anthony Austin, *The President's War* (Philadelphia: Lippincott, 1971), p. 9.

7. Humphrey, quoted in *New York Times*, April 26, 1966.

7a. Austin, pp. 130–33.

8. Rusk, address to the American Society of International Law, April 23, 1965, quoted in Gettleman, p. 375.

9. Halberstam, p. 214.

10. Rostow, quoted in interview with General Milton, February 20, 1978.

11. "U.S. Order for Preparations for Some Retaliatory Action," March 17, 1964, *Pentagon Papers*, Document #64, p. 284; Kahin and Lewis, p. 324, note 45. Hearings before the U.S. Senate Foreign Relations Committee, 89th Congress, 2d Session.

12. *New York Times*, February 23 and March 9, 1965.

13. "McNamara Report to Johnson on the Situation in Saigon in 1964," December 21, 1963, *Pentagon Papers*, Document #61, pp. 271–74.

14. "McNamara Report, 1963" (see note 13 above), p. 273.

15. "1964 Memo by Joint Chiefs of Staff Discussing Widening of the War," January 22, 1964, *Pentagon Papers,* Document #62, pp. 274–75.

16. LBJ, quoted in *New York Times,* January 1 and 2, 1964.

17. "Cable from President to Lodge on Escalation Contingencies," March 20, 1964, *Pentagon Papers,* Document #65, pp. 285–86.

18. *Pentagon Papers,* pp. 235–40; "State Department Aide's Report on Actions Taken After Tonkin," November 7, 1964, ibid., Document #73, pp. 304–5.

19. LBJ, quoted in *Pentagon Papers,* p. 241; speech by Walt Rostow, Fort Bragg, N.C. (1961), paraphrased in *Pentagon Papers,* p. 241.

20. "1964 McNamara Report on Steps to Change the Trend of the War," March 16, 1964, *Pentagon Papers,* Document #63, pp. 277–83; "U.S. Order for Preparations" (see note 11 above), pp. 283–85.

21. Report from Saigon Strategy Session, April 1964, quoted and paraphrased in *Pentagon Papers,* p. 245.

22. Ibid.

23. Ibid., pp. 246–52.

24. Marshall Ky, quoted in *New York Times,* July 23, 1964.

25. U Thant, quoted in *New York Times,* July 9, 1964, and in Kahin and Lewis, p. 155.

26. Hanoi Radio, July 24, 28, and 29, 1964; Moscow Radio, July 26, 1964; Peking Radio, August 2, 1964; in *Documents Relating to British Involvement in the Indo-China Conflict 1945–65,* Command 2534, p. 239 (London: H. M. Stationery Office, 1965), paraphrased in Kahin and Lewis, p. 155.

27. LBJ, quoted in *New York Times,* July 25, 1964; *New York Times,* July 28, 1964; Kahin and Lewis, pp. 155–56.

Chapter 4
Tonkin Gulf: Incident and Resolution

1. Senator Ernest Gruening, Eleanor Roosevelt Peace Award acceptance (SANE), December 3, 1972.

2. Eugene Windchy, *Tonkin Gulf* (New York: Doubleday, 1971), pp. 78–80, 109–10, 152–53; L. Fletcher Prouty, *The Secret Team: The CIA and Its Allies in Control of the United States and the World* (Englewood Cliffs, N.J.: Prentice-Hall, 1973), pp. 23–30, 467.

3. Victor Marchetti and John Marks, *The CIA and the Cult of Intelligence* (New York: Knopf, 1974), p. 119; Windchy, p. 295.

4. Windchy, pp. 55, 128–30; *Pentagon Papers,* p. 259.

5. Windchy, pp. 2–3; original release made by USAF Colonel William Helmantoler in Hawaii at 10:15 A.M. EDT; LBJ and Rusk, quoted by Windchy, p. 5.

5a. Winchy, p. 196.

6. Ibid., pp. 196–210; DOD official "Chronology of Second Attack" cited in ibid.; Commander Ogier, quoted in ibid., p. 208.

7. TWX from Commodore John Herrick, August 4, 1964, which arrived at the Pentagon at 1:27 P.M. EDT, August 4, 1964, quoted in Windchy, p. 211.

8. Gruening, Eleanor Roosevelt Peace Award (see note 1 above).

9. DOD announcement, quoted in John Galloway, ed., *The Gulf of*

Tonkin Resolution (Rutherford, N.J.: Fairleigh Dickinson University Press, 1970), pp. 67–68.

10. Austin, pp. 39–43; *Pentagon Papers*, pp. 263–64.

11. LBJ, quoted in *Department of State Bulletin*, August 24, 1964, p. 259; *New York Times*, August 5, 1964.

12. *Department of State Bulletin*, August 24, 1964, pp. 260–63, 269, 272–74; Galloway, pp. 72–73.

13. "Joint Resolution, U.S. Congress," August 7, 1964, Kahin and Lewis, appendix 9, pp. 477–78.

14. "Joint Hearings Before the Committee on Foreign Relations and the Committee on Armed Services, United States Senate, Eighty-eighth Congress, Second Session," August 6, 1964, Galloway, appendix 6, pp. 188–91, 196–236, hereafter referred to as Joint Hearings; Austin, pp. 67–70, 80.

15. *Congressional Record*, August 6, 1964, p. 18400.

16. Ibid., pp. 18400–402.

17. Ibid., pp. 18402–8.

18. Ibid., p. 18415.

19. Ibid., pp. 18415–20; Humphrey quotation at p. 18420.

20. Ibid., p. 18411.

21. Ibid., pp. 18413–14.

22. Ibid., pp. 18423–25; see also Austin, pp. 101–2.

23. Gaylord Nelson, quoted in Austin, p. 102; Austin, p. 103.

24. Fulbright, quoted in Galloway, p. 75.

25. "President Johnson's Remarks of August 10, 1964, in Signing the Gulf of Tonkin Resolution," August 10, 1964, Galloway, appendix 5, pp. 178–79.

Chapter 5
LBJ, Peace Candidate/War Planner

1. LBJ, speech before the American Bar Association, August 12, 1964, quoted in *New York Times*, August 13, 1964.

2. Ibid.

3. Goldwater press release, *New York Times*, August 16, 1964.

4. LBJ press conference, August 15, 1964, quoted in *New York Times*, August 16, 1964.

5. Peter Grose, *New York Times*, September 4, 1964.

6. Halberstam, p. 487.

7. Rusk and Taylor, press conferences on September 10, 1964, quoted in *Department of State Bulletin* #1318, September 28, 1964. These statements actually reflect Ambassador Taylor's views.

8. "Top Secret Memo for the Record, Subj: The Gulf of Tonkin Incident, Sept. 18, 1964," by McGeorge Bundy, September 20, 1964 (Declassified 8/31/77); Max Frankel, *New York Times*, September 19, 1964; Jack Raymond, ibid., October 2, 1964. According to Bundy, "the evidence of actual hostile attack is 'thin to nonexistent.' "

9. LBJ, speech at Stonewall, Texas, August 29, 1964, quoted in *Pentagon Papers*, p. 311.

10. LBJ, speech at Manchester, New Hampshire, September 1964,

quoted in Herbert Schandler, *The Unmaking of a President: Lyndon Johnson and Vietnam* (Princeton: Princeton University Press, 1977), p. 7.

11. LBJ, speech at Belleville, Illinois, October 21, 1964, quoted in *New York Times*, October 22, 1964.

12. "William Bundy Memo on Actions Available to U.S. After Tonkin," August 11, 1964, *Pentagon Papers*, Document #70, pp. 294–98.

13. "U.S. Missions' Recommendations on Further Military Steps," August 18, 1964, ibid., Document #76, pp. 349–52.

14. "Joint Chiefs' Recommendations on Military Courses of Action," August 26, 1964, ibid., Document #78, pp. 354–55.

15. "Plan of Action Attributed to McNaughton at Pentagon," September 3, 1964, ibid., Document #79, pp. 355–57.

16. "Top Aide's Proposal to Johnson on Military Steps in Late 1964," September 8, 1964, ibid., Document #80, pp. 357–59; "Memo on Johnson's Approval of Renewed Naval Operations," September 10, 1964, ibid., Document #81, pp. 359–60.

17. *Pentagon Papers*, pp. 316–17; "Rusk Query to Vientiane Embassy on Desirability of Laos Cease-Fire," August 7, 1964, ibid., Document #74, pp. 345–46; "Report of Meeting of U.S. Envoys to Review Operations in Laos," September 19, 1964, ibid., Document #82, pp. 360–62.

18. *Pentagon Papers*, p. 320.

19. Joint Chiefs action report to Secretary McNamara, quoted in ibid., pp. 320–21.

20. *Pentagon Papers*, p. 322.

21. "William Bundy Draft on Handling World and Public Opinion," November 5, 1964, ibid., Document #84, pp. 363–64; Draft proposals forwarded to President Johnson by McGeorge Bundy via top security memo for the President, November 28, 1964 (Declassified 11/2/76), Declassified Documents Reference System; "McNaughton's November Draft on Vietnam Aims and Choices," November 6, 1964, *Pentagon Papers*, Document #85, pp. 365–68; *Pentagon Papers*, pp. 323–24.

22. "View of Chiefs' Representative on Options B and C," November 15, 1964, *Pentagon Papers*, Document #86, pp. 369–70.

23. *Pentagon Papers*, pp. 325–26, 330.

24. "Taylor's Briefing of Key Officials on Situation in November 1964," November 27, 1964, ibid., Document #87, pp. 370–73; "Final Draft Position Paper Produced by Working Group," November 29, 1964, ibid., Document #88, pp. 373–78.

25. LBJ, press conference November 28, 1964, quoted in *New York Times*, November 29, 1964.

26. *Pentagon Papers*, pp. 332–35.

27. National Security Council Memorandum, December 12, 1964, quoted in ibid., p. 336.

28. "Account of Taylor's Meeting with Saigon Generals on Unrest," December 24, 1964, ibid., Document #89, pp. 379–81.

29. *New York Times*, December 12 and 16, 1964.

30. Ibid., January 14 and 15, 1965.

31. Morse, speech in U.S. Senate, January 19, 1965, quoted in *Pentagon Papers*, p. 339.

32. LBJ inauguration speech, quoted in *New York Times*, January 21, 1965.

Chapter 6
The Air and Ground Wars

1. Halberstam, p. 377.
2. Ibid., pp. 513–14.
3. Kahin and Lewis, pp. 169–70.
4. Secret memo to President Johnson from McGeorge Bundy, subject: Vietnam Decisions, dated February 16, 1965 (Declassified 11/14/77), Declassified Documents Reference System; LBJ, quoted in Halberstam, p. 521.
5. Kahin and Lewis, pp. 168–70; Secretary General U Thant, quoted in ibid., p. 171.
6. *New York Times*, February 5 and 25, 1965.
7. J. William Fulbright, ed., *The Vietnam Hearings* (New York: Random, 1966), pp. 4–7.
8. Kahin and Lewis, pp. 164–68; *New York Times*, September 2 and 14, 1964.
9. *New York Times*, January 23, 24, and 31, February 10 and 16, 1965.
10. *Indochina Story*, pp. 41–43; Kahin and Lewis, pp. 350–58, note * on p. 241.
11. Alfred McCoy, *The Politics of Heroin in Southeast Asia* (New York: Harper & Row, 1972), pp. 175–80.
12. Ibid., chapter 5.
13. Statements made to the author by Chinese officials during his trip to China, September 1979.
14. For details on Flaming Dart I and II, see *Official History of the United States Air Force in Southeast Asia* (Washington: U.S. Government Printing Office, 1977), p. 69. Hereafter referred to as "USAF in SEA."
15. "USAF in SEA," pp. 69–72; interview with General T. R. Milton, Colorado Springs, Colorado; Associated Press Dispatch from Qui Nhon, reprinted in *Washington Post*, March 4, 1965.
16. Huyen, p. 295.
17. Kendrick, pp. 214–15.
18. Kahin and Lewis, pp. 189–90.
19. Huyen, pp. 299–300.
20. Gareth Porter, *A Peace Denied: The United States, Vietnam and the Paris Agreement* (Bloomington: Indiana University Press, 1975), p. 110.
21. "USAF in SEA," pp. 74–77.
22. Author's interview in China, September 1979, with Chinese officials.
23. President Johnson to General Johnson, March 4, 1965, quoted in Halberstam, p. 564.
24. General William Westmoreland, *A Soldier Reports* (Garden City, N.Y.: Doubleday, 1976), p. 68.
25. Schandler, pp. 18–21.
26. Halberstam, p. 566.
27. Ibid., p. 570.
28. Schandler, pp. 21–23.

29. General Maxwell Taylor, *Swords and Plowshares* (New York: Norton, 1972), pp. 341–42; Taylor, quoted in Schandler, p. 23.

30. Halberstam, pp. 571–78.

31. Westmoreland, *Soldier Reports*, p. 134.

32. Message from General Westmoreland to Admiral Sharp, MACV 19188 DTG 070335Z, June 1965, quoted in Schandler, p. 26.

33. Westmoreland, *Soldier Reports,* pp. 141–43.

34. Schandler, p. 31; Westmoreland, *Soldier Reports,* p. 144. See also LBJ quotations in Clyde Pettit, ed., *The Experts* (Secaucus, N.J.: Lyle Stuart, 1975), pp. 211–18.

35. "USAF in SEA," pp. 69–70.

36. Ibid., especially p. 70.

37. Westmoreland, *Soldier Reports*, p. 160.

38. "USAF in SEA," p. 79.

39. *New York Times,* February 22 and May 10, 1966.

40. Lyndon B. Johnson, *The Vantage Point: Perspectives of the Presidency* (New York: Cowles, 1970), pp. 246–47.

41. General William Westmoreland, *Report on Operations in South Vietnam* (Washington, D.C.: U.S. Government Printing Office, 1968), p. 127.

42. Ibid., pp. 124–30.

43. Theodore Draper, *Abuse of Power* (New York: Viking Press, 1967), pp. 107–8.

Chapter 7
The Fulbright Challenge

1. LBJ's message to Congress, May 4, 1965, text in *Congressional Quarterly Almanac,* 1965, p. 1372.

2. Austin, pp. 117–18; Senator Morse, quoted in ibid., p. 118.

3. Galloway, p. 99; Austin, pp. 116–22.

4. Austin, p. 111.

5. Ibid., pp. 122–23.

6. Secretary Rusk, quoted in Fulbright, *Vietnam Hearings*, pp. 4–7.

7. Senator Fulbright, quoted in ibid., p. 33.

8. Senators Morse, Gore, Clark, and McCarthy, quoted in ibid. pp. 14, 17, 22, 28.

9. Senator Fulbright, quoted in ibid., pp. 41, 47–48.

10. *New York Times,* February 6, 1966; Kahin and Lewis, pp. 241–43; Austin, pp. 125–26.

11. Fulbright, *Vietnam Hearings*, pp. 67–106, especially pp. 64–65, 70, 73.

12. Kennan, quoted in ibid., pp. 108–11, 114, 117–18, 125–26, 133–34.

13. Fulbright, *Vietnam Hearings,* pp. 167–79; General Taylor, quoted in ibid., p. 177.

14. Senator Morse and General Taylor, quoted in ibid., pp. 187–88.

15. Senator Fulbright and General Taylor, quoted in ibid., pp. 204, 223–24.

16. Fulbright, *Vietnam Hearings*, pp. 228–54; Secretary Rusk, quoted in ibid., pp. 228–29, 234–36, 240–41, 260–61; Austin, p. 141.

17. Secretary Rusk and Senators Morse, Church, Fulbright, and Symington, quoted in Fulbright, *Vietnam Hearings,* pp. 258, 260–61, 269, 274–75, 287–88, 294.

18. Senator Morse, quoted in Austin, pp. 151–52.

19. Senator Fulbright, quoted in Galloway, pp. 99–100.

20. Galloway, pp. 101–2; Tom Wicker, quoted in Austin, p. 16.

21. J. William Fulbright, *The Arrogance of Power* (New York: Random, 1966), pp. 130, 138.

22. "Associated Press Dispatch, July 16, 1967, 'Tonkin Gulf,' " July 16, 1967, Galloway, appendix, pp. 483–97. Hereafter referred to as AP Dispatch; Austin, p. 153; Admiral True, quoted in Galloway, p. 104.

23. AP Dispatch, pp. 484–87, 490–92; Austin, p. 157.

24. Austin, pp. 160, 168–72; Senator Fulbright, quoted in ibid., p. 168; Galloway, pp. 106–7.

25. Galloway, pp. 105–6; anonymous letter, quoted in ibid., p. 106.

26. Austin, pp. 182–90.

27. Senator Fulbright, quoted in Galloway, pp. 108–9; "The Gulf of Tonkin, The 1964 Incidents," February 20, 1968, Galloway, appendix 7, pp. 252–53, 256, 260–65. Hereafter referred to as 1968 Hearings.

28. 1968 Hearings, pp. 266, 269–74.

29. Ibid., pp. 292–93, 306–7, 314–15; Galloway, pp. 123, 126–30, 134.

Chapter 8
Citizen Protest

1. Thomas Powers, *The War at Home: Vietnam and the American People, 1964–1968* (New York: Grossman, 1973), pp. xi–xv, 43–49.

2. Kendrick, pp. 181–82.

3. Richard Walton, *The Remnants of Power* (New York: Coward, 1968), pp. 176–78.

4. Powers, pp. 54–61; Marcus G. Raskin and Bernard Fall, eds., *The Vietnam Reader: Articles and Documents on American Foreign Policy and the Vietnam Crisis,* rev. ed. (New York: Vintage Books, 1967), pp. 143–55.

5. Powers, pp. 64, 69–70.

6. Ibid., p. 71; Kendrick, p. 205; LBJ, quoted in *New York Times,* August 10, 1965.

7. Kendrick, p. 205; Powers, pp. 83–87.

8. *New York Times,* October 16–17, 1965; J. Edgar Hoover, quoted in ibid., November 2, 1965.

9. Powers, pp. 90–94.

10. Kendrick, p. 205; J. William Fulbright, quoted in *New York Times,* April 22, 1966.

11. Powers, pp. 119–37.

12. Kendrick, pp. 180, 198–99.

13. Ibid.; Powers, pp. 154–56; Martin Luther King, quoted in ibid., p. 154.

14. Kendrick, p. 219; Powers, p. 198.

15. Dr. King, quoted in William Miller, *Martin Luther King* (New York: McKay, Weybright, 1968), p. 236.

16. Powers, pp. 139, 145.

17. SNCC statement, quoted in Jon Neary, *Julian Bond* (New York: Morrow, 1971), pp. 90–91.

18. Stokely Carmichael, quoted in Powers, pp. 152–53.

19. Kendrick, pp. 181, 206–8, 238; Powers, pp. 160–66, 219.

20. Dr. King, quoted in Miller, p. 266; Dr. King, quoted in *New York Times*, April 5, 1967; *Washington Post*, April 6, 1967; Powers, p. 163.

21. Kendrick, p. 212.

22. Powers, p. 223.

23. Ibid., pp. 171, 222–28; Kendrick, p. 231.

24. Powers, p. 167.

25. Kendrick, p. 235, 246; Department of State Bulletin, April 10, 1967; Jerome Skolnick, *The Politics of Protest: A Report, Submitted by Jerome H. Skolnick* (New York: Simon and Schuster, 1969), pp. 35–65; Powers, pp. 192–93, 229–45.

26. Kendrick, p. 250.

27. Powers, p. 289.

28. Robert Kennedy, quoted in *New York Times*, March 25, 1968.

29. Powers, p. 294; Kendrick, pp. 257–75.

30. Robert Kennedy, quoted in Kendrick, p. 257.

31. See Thomas Powers's chapter on "Black Power"; *New York Times*, April 2, 1968; Jules Archer, *Riot! A History of Mob Action in the United States* (New York: Dutton, Hawthorn, 1974), pp. 9–10.

32. Kendrick, p. 262.

33. Ibid., pp. 260–61.

34. Ibid., pp. 264–68; Archer, pp. 147–48.

35. *New York Times*, June 5, 1968; Kendrick, pp. 265–68, 272–73.

36. Archer, pp. 10–13.

37. Kendrick, p. 263.

Chapter 9
The Embattled President

1. "Secretary McNamara's Position of May 19 on Bombing and Troops," May 19, 1967, *Pentagon Papers*, Document #129, pp. 577–85.

2. *Pentagon Papers*, pp. ix–xxv, 535–38.

3. Johnson, pp. 369–70.

4. Westmoreland, *Soldier Reports*, p. 227.

5. Schandler, pp. 52–56.

6. Westmoreland, *Soldier Reports*, p. 233.

7. Johnson, pp. 373–78, 600–601.

8. Schandler, p. 64; Westmoreland, *Report on Operations*, pp. 138–39.

9. Westmoreland, *Soldier Reports*, p. 315.

10. Ibid., pp. 316–17.

11. Schandler, p. 85.

12. JCSM 78–68, February 3, 1968, quoted in ibid., p. 92.

13. Westmoreland, *Soldier Reports*, p. 338.

14. JCS message 01272, DTG 030332Z February 1968, Wheeler to Westmoreland, subject: Khe Sanh, quoted in Schandler, p. 92; Johnson, pp. 370–80.

15. JCS message 01529, DTG 080448Z February 1968, Wheeler to

Westmoreland; MAC message 01858, DTG 091633Z February 1968, Westmoreland to Wheeler; quoted by Westmoreland, *Soldier Reports*, p. 352.

16. Westmoreland, quoted in Schandler, p. 97.

17. Schandler, p. 101; Westmoreland, *Soldier Reports*, p. 353; Report of the Chairman, JCS, Subj: Situation in Vietnam and MACV Force Requirements, February 27, 1968, quoted in Schandler, p. 110; Marvin Kalb and Elie Abel, *Roots of Involvement: The U.S. in Asia 1784–1971* (New York: Norton, 1971), pp. 216–17.

18. Kalb and Abel, pp. 220–22; Schandler, pp. 140–41.

19. Westmoreland, *Soldier Reports*, p. 359.

20. Taylor, p. 388.

21. Schandler, p. 174.

22. Ibid., pp. 179–80; Johnson, p. 399.

23. Rusk and Warnke, quoted in Schandler, pp. 183, 192, 192–93; Kalb and Abel, pp. 223–26.

24. Kalb and Abel, p. 236.

25. Ibid.

26. LBJ, quoted in ibid., p. 230.

27. LBJ, quoted in Pettit, p. 355.

28. Westmoreland, *Soldier Reports*, p. 361; Kalb and Abel, pp. 239–40; LBJ, quoted in Schandler, p. 264; Schandler, p. 265.

29. Schandler, pp. 270–72; Kalb and Abel, pp. 255–56.

30. LBJ, quoted in *New York Times*, April 1, 1968.

31. Ibid.

32. Kalb and Abel, pp. 255–56; Westmoreland, *Report on Operations*, pp. 165–66; Westmoreland, quoted in Pettit, p. 357.

33. Johnson, p. 497.

34. Westmoreland, quoted in Pettit, pp. 357–60.

35. Kahin and Lewis, pp. 161–66; *New York Times*, September 2 and 14, 1964.

36. *New York Times*, January 23, 24, and 31, February 10 and 16, 1965; Kahin and Lewis, pp. 246–49.

Chapter 10
President Nixon Assumes Command

1. Barbara W. Tuchman, "An Inquiry Into the Persistence of Unwisdom in Government," *Esquire*, May 1980, pp. 25, 29–30.

2. Richard M. Nixon, *RN: The Memoirs of Richard Nixon* (New York: Grosset & Dunlap, 1978), pp. 343–44. Hereafter referred to as *Memoirs*.

3. Ibid., p. 123.

4. Ibid., p. 271; William Shawcross, *Sideshow: Kissinger, Nixon and the Destruction of Cambodia* (New York: Simon & Schuster, 1979), p. 85.

5. Richard Nixon, quoted in Kendrick, p. 212; Kendrick, p. 190; Shawcross, pp. 85–86.

6. Nixon, April 17, 1967, quoted in Pettit, p. 322.

7. Nixon, March 5, 1968, quoted in Pettit, p. 355; Nixon, quoted in Theodore White, *The Making of the President 1968* (New York: Atheneum, 1969), p. 130.

8. Stephen C. Shadegg, *Winning's a Lot More Fun* (Toronto: Macmillan, 1969), p. 180; Richard Whalen, *Catch a Falling Flag* (Boston: Houghton-Mifflin, 1972), p. 125.

9. White, *1968*, pp. 245–46, 253–56; Nixon, acceptance speech, quoted in *New York Times*, August 10, 1968.

10. Lewis Chester, Godfrey Hodgson, and Bruce Page, *An American Melodrama* (New York: Viking Press, 1969), pp. 423–24.

11. Shadegg, p. 228; White, *1968*, pp. 275–313.

12. White, *1968*, pp. 324–25; Chester, Hodgson, Page, pp. 623–24.

13. Chester, Hodgson, Page, p. 418.

14. Humphrey, quoted in Shadegg, p. 254.

15. Nixon, quoted in Whalen, pp. 217–18.

16. White, *1968*, pp. 370–72; Shadegg, pp. 267–68.

17. White, *1968*, p. 382.

18. *Memoirs*, pp. 336–37.

19. Ibid., pp. 357–58.

20. Marvin Kalb and Bernard Kalb, *Kissinger* (New York: Dell, 1975), pp. 59–63; Henry Kissinger, *A World Restored: The Politics of Conservatism in a Revolutionary Age* (Grosset & Dunlap, 1964).

21. Henry Kissinger, *White House Years* (Boston: Little, 1979), p. 230. Hereafter referred to as *White House Years*.

22. Ibid., pp. 230–35.

23. Kalb and Kalb, pp. 147, 151–52; *White House Years*, pp. 237–39.

24. *Memoirs*, pp. 347–48.

25. Ibid., pp. 348–49.

26. Ibid., p. 348.

27. *White House Years*, pp. 38–48; *Memoirs*, pp. 340–41; Kalb and Kalb, pp. 98, 105–8; Kissinger, quoted in Shawcross, p. 84; Allen Drury and Fred Maroon, *Courage and Hesitation* (New York: Doubleday, 1971), pp. 74–77.

28. Henry Kissinger, "The Vietnam Negotiations," *Foreign Affairs* 47, no. 2 (January 1969): 211–34; *White House Years*, pp. 234–35; Kalb and Kalb, pp. 142–45.

29. *White House Years*, p. 228.

30. Kissinger, quoted in Kalb and Kalb, p. 142; Nixon, inaugural address, January 20, 1969, quoted in *Memoirs*, p. 366.

31. *New York Times*, June 9, 1969; *Memoirs*, pp. 392–93; Kalb and Kalb, pp. 158–60.

32. *Memoirs*, p. 392; *White House Years*, pp. 271–72; Donald Kirk, *Wider War: The Struggle for Cambodia, Thailand and Laos* (New York: Praeger, 1971), pp. 18–19.

33. *White House Years*, p. 271.

34. Ibid., pp. 274–75.

35. Ibid., p. 273.

36. Ibid., p. 274.

37. Official transcript of Nixon's Guam news conference, July 25, 1969, quoted in Kirk, p. 18; *White House Years*, pp. 222–25; *Public Papers of the United States: Richard Nixon: 1969* (Washington, D.C.: U.S. Government Printing Office, 1971), pp. 544–56.

38. *Memoirs*, pp. 394–95; Kendrick, p. 284; Shawcross, pp. 166–67.

39. Kalb and Abel, pp. 272–73; Kendrick, pp. 279–80; *Memoirs*, pp. 348–49.

40. Nixon to Ho Chi Minh, July 15, 1969, reprinted in *New York Times,* November 4, 1969, and in Gettleman, p. 484.

41. Ho Chi Minh to Nixon, August 25, 1969, reprinted in *New York Times,* November 4, 1969, and in Gettleman, p. 485.

42. Nixon, quoted in Noam Chomsky, *At War with Asia: Essays on Indochina* (New York: Pantheon, 1970), p. 107; Kalb and Lewis, p. 284.

43. *White House Years,* p. 283.

44. *Memoirs,* p. 400.

45. Kendrick, p. 280; Edgar O'Ballance, *The Wars in Vietnam, 1954–1973* (New York: Hippocrene Books, 1975), pp. 145–47; Chomsky, pp. 100–102; William Nighswonger, *Rural Pacification in Vietnam* (New York: Praeger, 1967), p. 116.

46. Kissinger, quoted in *Memoirs,* p. 396.

47. *Memoirs,* p. 402.

48. Ibid., pp. 408–9; *White House Years,* pp. 306–7; Kalb and Abel, p. 286; Kalb and Kalb, pp. 166–69.

49. *Memoirs,* p. 409.

50. Nixon's November 3, 1969, speech reprinted in *New York Times,* November 4, 1969. See also Gettleman, pp. 486–97; *Memoirs,* p. 409; *White House Years,* pp. 305–7; Kalb and Abel, pp. 287–88; Kendrick, pp. 293–94.

51. *Memoirs,* pp. 409–11; Kendrick, p. 294.

52. *Memoirs,* p. 410–11.

Chapter 11
Nixon's Secret End-the-War Plan: An Air War

1. Richard Nixon, *The Real War,* (New York: Warner, 1980), p. 315.

2. Paul Dickson and John Rothchild, "Electronic Battlefield: Strangelove's Answer to War Crimes," *Washington Monthly,* May 1971, pp. 6–14; Arthur Erikson, "Air Force Plans With Computers, Army Sees by Starlight," *Electronics,* October 26, 1970, pp. 70–77; Peter Dale Scott, *The War Conspiracy: The Secret Road to the Second Indochina War* (Indianapolis: Bobbs, 1972), p. 179.

3. Peter Dale Scott, "Cambodia: Why the Generals Won," in Marvin Gettleman et al., eds., *Conflict in Indochina: A Reader on the Widening War in Laos and Cambodia* (New York: Random, 1970), pp. 407–9; Scott, *War Conspiracy,* pp. 177–79; Townsend Hoopes, *The Limits of Intervention* (New York: McKay, 1969), p. 213.

4. Kendrick, p. 338; O'Ballance, p. 164; Cornell University Air War Study Group, *The Air War in Indochina,* ed. by Raphael Littauer and Norman Uphoff, rev. ed. (Boston: Beacon Press, 1972), pp. 155–56.

5. Bernard Brodie, *War and Politics* (New York: Macmillan, 1973), p. 171.

6. Kendrick, pp. 331, 338–39; O'Ballance, p. 164.

7. Kendrick, p. 315; Scott, *War Conspiracy,* pp. 174–75; Laird, quoted in ibid., p. 175; *New York Times,* March 15, 1971; *San Francisco Chronicle,* May 24, 1971.

8. Porter, *Peace Denied,* pp. 92–94; Cornell Study Group, p. 281.

9. Scott, "Cambodia," pp. 400–403; *New York Times,* April 21 and May 3, 1970.

10. Scott, "Cambodia," p. 404; Gavin, quoted in ibid.

11. Scott, "Cambodia," pp. 404–6; Joseph Goulden, "Talks With China: The Military Saboteurs," *The Nation*, March 2, 1970, pp. 231–33.

12. Kalb and Kalb, pp. 200–203; *New York Times*, September 18, 1970.

13. Porter, *Peace Denied*, pp. 88–91; Nixon, quoted in Weldon Brown, *The Last Chopper: The Denouement of the American Role in Vietnam 1963–1975* (Port Washington, N.Y.: Kennikat Press, 1976), p. 189.

14. Porter, *Peace Denied*, p. 91.

15. Kalb and Kalb, pp. 208–9; Porter, *Peace Denied*, pp. 91–92.

16. Porter, *Peace Denied*, pp. 97–98.

17. Ibid.; Kalb and Kalb, pp. 210–13.

18. Kendrick, p. 336; Porter, *Peace Denied*, p. 98; Kalb and Kalb, p. 212; O'Ballance, p. 164.

19. Bunker, quoted in Kendrick, p. 336; Brown, p. 198.

20. Porter, *Peace Denied*, pp. 98–100.

21. *New York Times*, July 2, 1970.

22. Kennedy, quoted in Kendrick, p. 302.

23. Louis Fanning, *Betrayal in Vietnam* (New Rochelle, N.Y.: Arlington House Publishers, 1976), pp. 65–69.

24. Kendrick, p. 308.

25. Gloria Emerson, *Winners and Losers: Battles, Retreats, Gains, Losses and Ruins from the Vietnam War* (New York: Harcourt Brace Jovanovich, 1976), pp. 343–48.

26. Kendrick, pp. 318–19.

27. Ibid., pp. 319–20.

28. Ibid., p. 339.

29. Muskie, quoted in Brown, p. 213.

Chapter 12
The Invasion of Cambodia

1. Nixon to Kissinger, January 8, 1969, *White House Years*, p. 241.

2. Shawcross, pp. 20, 91.

3. *White House Years*, p. 240.

4. Shawcross, pp. 36–45; Malcolm Caldwell and Lek Tan, *Cambodia in the Southeast Asian War* (New York: Monthly Review Press, 1973), pp. 1–52.

5. *White House Years*, pp. 250, 457–58; Shawcross, pp. 46–51.

6. Dulles's NSC study, quoted in Shawcross, p. 52.

7. Shawcross, pp. 52–60; *New York Times*, September 12, 1953; *Time*, March 16, 1959; Norodom Sihanouk, *My War With the CIA: The Memoirs of Prince Norodom Sihanouk* (New York: Pantheon, 1973), pp. 91–144.

8. Kalb and Kalb, pp. 178–79; Shawcross, pp. 24–26, 63–71; Sihanouk, p. 23; Sihanouk interview in *New York Times*, July 8, 1973; François Ponchaud, *Cambodia: Year Zero* (New York: Holt, Rinehart & Winston, 1977), p. 174.

9. *Memoirs*, p. 380.

10. Ibid., pp. 380–82; *White House Years*, pp. 243–47; Shawcross, pp. 19–23.

11. "Bombing in Cambodia," Hearings Before the Committee on Armed Services, U.S. Senate, 93rd Congress, First Session, July/August, 1973, pp. 158–60.

12. *Memoirs*, p. 384; *White House Years*, pp. 247–50; Shawcross, pp. 23, 28–30.

13. General Wheeler, quoted in Shawcross, pp. 22–23; Kalb and Kalb, pp. 154–55.

14. *White House Years*, p. 252.

15. *White House Years*, pp. 249–52; *Memoirs*, p. 382.

16. Kalb and Kalb, pp. 155–56; Shawcross, pp. 30–32; testimony of Hal Knight, "Bombing in Cambodia," pp. 2–70.

17. *White House Years*, p. 253; *Memoirs*, p. 382.

18. Shawcross, p. 94.

19. Robert Drinan, quoted in *White House Years*, p. 249 and in *Report of the Committee on the Judiciary on the Impeachment of Richard M. Nixon, President of the United States*, 93rd Congress, August 20, 1974, p. 308.

20. Kendrick, p. 298; Shawcross, pp. 94–95, 113; *White House Years*, pp. 253–54; testimony of General Abrams, "Bombing in Cambodia," pp. 357–59.

21. Secretary Rogers's statement to the House Appropriations Subcommittee, *New York Times*, May 5, 1975; Rogers, quoted in Kendrick, p. 298, and in Shawcross, p. 139.

22. *White House Years*, pp. 458–63; Kalb and Kalb, p. 178; Shawcross, pp. 114–21; Kirk, pp. 92–102. See also *New York Times*, March 9–10, 1970.

23. *Memoirs*, p. 447.

24. *White House Years*, p. 463.

25. Kalb and Kalb, p. 178; Caldwell and Lek Tan, p. 268; Scott, *War Conspiracy*, p. 163.

26. Frank Snepp, quoted in Shawcross, p. 123. See also I. F. Stone, "Only the Bums Can Save the Country Now," in Gettleman, *Conflict in Indochina*, p. 439.

27. Sihanouk, quoted in Shawcross, p. 125.

28. Shawcross, p. 131.

29. Ibid., pp. 239–56 passim.

30. *White House Years*, pp. 464–67; Scott, pp. 164–65; Kendrick, p. 299; Shawcross, pp. 135–39; "Bombing in Cambodia," p. 343; Westmoreland, *Soldier Reports*, p. 388.

31. Nixon, quoted in Roger Morris, *Uncertain Greatness: Henry Kissinger and American Foreign Policy* (New York: Harper & Row, 1977), p. 174, and in Shawcross, pp. 134–35.

32. Kalb and Kalb, pp. 179–81.

33. Nixon, quoted in Kalb and Abel, p. 296.

34. *Memoirs*, pp. 448–49; *White House Years*, p. 489 and note 9, p. 1484.

35. *White House Years*, p. 490.

36. Ibid., pp. 490–92; *Memoirs*, pp 449–50; Kalb and Kalb, p. 183.

37. *White House Years*, p. 486.

38. Kalb and Kalb, pp. 189–90; Kissinger and Haig, quoted in William Safire, *Before the Fall* (New York: Doubleday, 1975), pp. 186–87, and in Shawcross, pp. 145–46.

39. Nixon, quoted in Kalb and Kalb, p. 186.

40. *White House Years*, pp. 496, 499–502; *Memoirs*, p. 450.

41. Nixon, quoted in Safire, pp. 102–3, and in Shawcross, p. 144.

42. *White House Years*, p. 498.

43. *New York Times*, April 30–July 1, 1970; Kendrick, p. 299.

44. Nixon speech reprinted in Gettleman, *Vietnam,* pp. 538–45; *Memoirs,* pp. 451–52; *White House Years,* pp. 504–5; Kalb and Kalb, pp. 190–91; Kendrick, p. 299; Shawcross, pp. 146–48. See also Jonathan Schell, *The Time of Illusion* (New York: Knopf, 1976), pp. 90–100.

45. O'Ballance, p. 156.

46. *White House Years,* pp. 512–14.

47. Ibid., p. 517.

48. Shawcross, pp. 161–68.

49. Ibid., pp. 168–75.

50. Laird to Kissinger, September 11, 1970, quoted in ibid., p. 178.

51. Shawcross, pp. 178–81.

52. Ibid., pp. 192–95; *New York Times,* July 15, 1970, and September 20, 1971; *Newsweek,* October 18, 1971.

53. Shawcross, pp. 200–208, 227–35.

54. Ibid., pp. 213–19; Laird, quoted in ibid., p. 217.

55. Shawcross, pp. 218–19; Colby, quoted in ibid., p. 265.

56. Gareth Porter, "The Broken Promise to Hanoi," *The Nation,* April 30, 1977, pp. 520–21; Shawcross, pp. 259–64.

57. Shawcross, pp. 262–63.

58. Ibid., pp. 265–76; Morse-Lowenstein report for the Senate Foreign Relations Committee, April 1973, quoted in ibid., p. 275.

59. *Memoirs,* pp. 887–88 (Nixon veto message reprinted on p. 888). See also Shawcross, pp. 282–83.

60. Mansfield, quoted in Shawcross, p. 284.

61. Shawcross, pp. 284–85.

62. Ibid., pp. 296–97.

63. Ibid., pp. 182–86, 220–30, 316–19. See also George Hildebrand and Gareth Porter, *Cambodia: Starvation and Revolution* (New York: Monthly Review Press, 1976), p. 74.

64. Kissinger, quoted in Shawcross, p. 323.

65. Nixon, quoted in Shawcross, p. 325.

66. Shawcross, pp. 344–49; Hildebrand and Porter, pp. 23–26, 38.

67. McCloskey, *Hearings on Supplemental Assistance to Cambodia* before the Senate Foreign Relations Committee, February 24, 1975, p. 64.

68. Dean, quoted by Stewart Dalby, *Financial Times* (London), April 6, 1975.

69. Shawcross, pp. 357–64.

Chapter 13
The Devastation of Laos

1. Len E. Acklund, "No Place for Neutralism: The Eisenhower Administration and Laos," in *Laos: War and Revolution,* edited by Nina S. Adams and Alfred W. McCoy (New York: Harper & Row, 1970), p. 141. See also *Life,* January 16, 1956.

2. Ibid., p. 146.

3. Ibid., pp. 143–46.

4. "The Vientiane Agreements" (Joint Communiqué by Prince Souvannaphouma and Prince Souphanouvong, November 2, 1957), in Gettleman, *Conflict in Indochina,* pp. 157–71; Acklund, p. 148; Bernard S.

Fall, *Anatomy of a Crisis: The Laotian Crisis of 1960–61* (Garden City, N.Y.: Doubleday, 1969), p. 78.

5. Parsons testimony, House of Representatives Committee on Governmental Operations, "U.S. AID Operation in Laos," Hearing March 11–July 1, 1959 (Washington, D.C.: U.S. Government Printing Office, 1959), p. 195.

6. Acklund, p. 149; Hugh Toye, *Laos: Buffer State or Battleground* (London: Oxford University Press, 1968), pp. 119–37.

7. Scott, *War Conspiracy*, pp. 11–13; Arthur Dommen, *Conflict in Laos: The Politics of Neutralization* (New York: Praeger, 1964), p. 115; *Pentagon Papers*, p. 137; Bernard S. Fall, *Street Without Joy* (Harrisburg, Pa.: Stackpole, 1964), pp. 334–35.

8. Fall, *Anatomy of a Crisis*, p. 154.

9. Ibid., pp. 154–55.

10. Jonathan Mirsky and Stephen Stonefield, "The Nam Tha Crisis, Kennedy and the New Frontier on the Brink," in Adams and McCoy, pp. 163–68; Toye, pp. 182–83. See also Fall, *Anatomy of a Crisis*, pp. 173–213.

11. "Declaration on the Neutrality of Laos (1962)" in Gettleman, *Conflict in Indochina*, pp. 185–90; "Protocol to the Declaration on the Neutrality of Laos (1962)," in ibid., pp. 191–200.

12. Hilsman, quoted in Gareth Porter, "After Geneva: Subverting Laotian Neutrality," in Adams and McCoy, p. 179.

13. Charles Stevenson, *The End of Nowhere: American Policy Toward Laos Since 1965* (Boston: Beacon Press, 1972), pp. 184–85, 208–12.

14. Porter, "After Geneva," pp. 182–94; William Colby, *Honorable Men: My Life in the CIA* (New York: Simon & Schuster, 1978), pp. 195–201; Fred Branfman, "Presidential War in Laos, 1964–1970," in Adams and McCoy, pp. 251–55.

15. Colby, p. 195.

16. Porter, "After Geneva," p. 206; Branfman, pp. 219–21.

17. Colby, pp. 182–83.

18. Fulbright, quoted in Branfman, pp. 214–15.

19. Steams, deputy chief of mission, quoted in Branfman, p. 240.

20. Branfman, pp. 231–33.

21. U.S. diplomat in Vientiane, quoted in Jacques Decornoy, "Laos: The Forgotten War," *Bulletin of Concerned Asian Scholars*, July–August 1970, p. 27 and in *Indochina Story*, p. 44.

22. Decornoy, quoted in *Indochina Story*, p. 44.

23. Branfman, pp. 240–41.

24. *Memoirs*, p. 270.

25. *White House Years*, pp. 987–92; Kalb and Kalb, p. 204.

26. "The Situation in Laos: The Case for Escalation" (Nixon's March 6, 1970, speech), in Gettleman, *Conflict in Indochina*, pp. 259–68.

27. Chomsky, pp. 213–16; Kirk, p. 250; *White House Years*, pp. 991–1002.

28. Kalb and Kalb, p. 204.

29. O'Ballance, pp. 160–62.

30. Kalb and Kalb, pp. 204–5; Kendrick, p. 316; *White House Years*, pp. 1002–10.

31. *Memoirs*, p. 498.

32. Ibid.

33. Ibid., pp. 498–99.

34. *White House Years*, p. 992.
35. Scott, *War Conspiracy*, pp. 180–84; Stevenson, pp. 236–38; Chomsky, pp. 127–28.

Chapter 14
The Nixon War at Home

1. *White House Years*, pp. 288, 513–14.
2. Emerson, pp. 314–15.
3. *White House Years*, p. 288.
4. *New York Times*, January 19–21, 1969; Emerson, pp. 314–17; *Memoirs*, p. 366. See also Commission on the Causes and Prevention of Violence, *Rights in Concord: The Response to the Counter-Inaugural Protest Activities in Washington, D.C.* (Washington, D.C.: U.S. Government Printing Office, 1969).
5. "Mobilizing for Peace," *Newsweek*, February 17, 1969, pp. 68–69.
6. Hugh Sidney, "The Right of the Individual vs. The Right of the Group," *Life*, May 9, 1969, p. 4; Kissinger, quoted in ibid.
7. Chalmers Roberts, quoted in *White House Years*, p. 288.
8. *White House Years*, pp. 288–91; Kendrick, pp. 285–86.
9. *Memoirs*, p. 399; Nixon, quoted in *New York Times*, September 27, 1969.
10. *Memoirs*, pp. 400–401; "Nixon's Worst Week," *Time*, October 10, 1969, pp. 15–18; *Washington Post*, October 7, 1969.
11. "Antiwar Protests Confront Nixon Administration," Special Report, *1969 Congressional Quarterly Almanac*, p. 1017; *White House Years*, pp. 290–91; *New York Times*, September 25–October 16, 1969.
12. *Congressional Record—House*, October 14, 1969, p. 30011.
13. *1969 Congressional Quarterly Almanac*, p. 1019.
14. "Vietnam Policy Debated in Late House Session," Special Report, *1969 Congressional Quarterly Almanac*, pp. 1017–19; "Congress Debates Vietnam Issue, Resolutions Adopted," *1969 Congressional Quarterly Almanac*, p. 857; *New York Times*, October 15, 1969.
15. "Antiwar Protests," pp. 1017–18; Kendrick, p. 293; *White House Years*, pp. 291–92; *Memoirs*, pp. 402–3.
16. *Memoirs*, p. 403.
17. Ibid., pp. 410–11.
18. *Memoirs*, p. 411. Agnew delivered his attack on the news media in a speech at Des Moines, Iowa, on November 13, 1969. See also "Antiwar Protests," p. 1018; Kendrick, p. 294; Brown, pp. 176–80.
19. *Memoirs*, p. 412; Frank Stanton, George McGovern, and Gerald Ford, quoted in ibid.
20. "As War Protests Hit a Crest," *U.S. News and World Report*, November 24, 1969, p. 29; *Memoirs*, pp. 412–13.
21. "Reds in Antiwar March?" *U.S. News and World Report*, November 24, 1969, p. 28.
22. Kendrick, p. 297; Senator Stennis, quoted in ibid.
23. Eliot Asinof, "The Peace Suicides," *Seventeen Magazine*, March 1970, pp. 124, 231, 238; Eliot Asinof, *Craig and Joan: Two Lives for Peace* (New York: Viking Press, 1971), pp. 3–245.

24. Roger Neville Williams, *The New Exiles: American War Resisters in Canada* (New York: Liveright, 1971) (Williams wrote *The New Exiles* while living in Canada as a war resister); Renee G. Kasinsky, *Refugees from Militarism: Draft-Age Americans in Canada* (New Brunswick, N.J.: Transaction Books, 1976); Kendrick, p. 297.

25. For example, see C. D. B. Bryan, *Friendly Fire* (New York: Putnam, 1976), which inspired a made-for-TV movie in 1979.

26. Emerson, pp. 302–7; Douglas Allen, quoted in ibid., p. 307.

27. "Moratorium: The Radicals Move In," *Newsweek*, April 27, 1970, p. 33; *Memoirs*, p. 455.

28. "Nixon's Gamble: Operation Total Victory?" *Newsweek*, May 11, 1970, p. 22.

29. *Memoirs*, p. 454; *White House Years*, p. 511; "Nixon's Gamble," p. 33; Kendrick, pp. 299–300.

30. Author's personal observation at Princeton University, May 1970.

31. *White House Years*, pp. 511–15.

32. Thomas Schelling, quoted in Kalb and Kalb, p. 193.

33. James A. Michener, *Kent State: What Happened and Why* (New York: Random, 1971), see entire work; Kendrick, p. 302.

34. *Memoirs*, p. 457.

35. "May Day," *Newsweek*, May 11, 1970, p. 33; Peter Schrag, "After Kent State: The First Hundred Days," *Saturday Review*, August 29, 1970, p. 12.

36. *White House Years*, pp. 511–12.

37. Fulbright, quoted in Robert Johansen, "Of Politics and Prophecy: Student Activism Today," *Christian Century*, February 17, 1971.

38. Kendrick, pp. 306, 312–15, 322, 356.

39. *Memoirs*, p. 459; Nixon news conference, reported by *New York Times*, May 9, 1970.

40. Kent (Ohio) attorney, quoted in Michener, p. 442; Emerson, p. 296; Kendrick, pp. 309–11. See also "The Price of Campus Peace," *Life*, May 29, 1970, p. 38; and *Memoirs*, pp. 469–76.

41. *Indochina Story*, pp. 123–27.

42. "The Peace GI's," *Newsweek*, April 21, 1969, p. 36; David Cortright, *Soldiers in Revolt: The American Military Today* (Garden City, N.Y.: Doubleday, Anchor Press, 1975), pp. 59–60.

43. Joan Crowell, *Fort Dix Stockade* (New York: Links Books, 1974), pp. 1–46.

44. Cortright, pp. 53–57, 62–63; Kendrick, p. 311.

45. Cortright, pp. 66–68.

46. Ibid., pp. 70–74.

47. GI's United Against the War in Vietnam, "Statement of Aims," in Clyde Taylor, ed., *Vietnam and Black America: An Anthology of Protest and Resistance* (Garden City, N.Y.: Doubleday, Anchor Books, 1973), pp. 220–22.

48. John Kerry and the Vietnam Veterans Against the War, *The New Soldier* (New York: Macmillan, 1971), pp. 3–10; Emerson, p. 212.

49. *White House Years*, pp. 1010–11.

50. *Milwaukee Journal*, March 4, 1971, quoted in ibid., p. 1012.

51. *White House Years*, pp. 1010–11.

52. Senator Mansfield's resolution, quoted in *White House Years,* p. 1012; *New York Times,* June 23, 1971.

53. Senator Fulbright, spring 1971 speech, quoted by Elizabeth Drew, "Washington," *Atlantic,* April 1971, pp. 14ff.; also quoted in Brodie, p. 215.

54. Kerry and VVAW, pp. 26–31; Kendrick, pp. 318–20; Emerson, pp. 329–32; *White House Years,* p. 1013; *New York Times,* April 19–26, 1971.

55. John Kerry, testimony before the Senate Foreign Relations Committee, April 22, 1971, reprinted in Kerry and VVAW, pp. 12–24; Kerry, quoted in Emerson, pp. 331–32; *Congressional Record,* April 22, 1971.

56. Cortright, pp. 81–82; Kendrick, pp. 320–21.

57. *White House Years,* pp. 1013–16; Kendrick, p. 323.

58. *Pentagon Papers,* introduction and foreword; Kendrick, pp. 324–25.

59. Kalb and Kalb, pp. 276–77; *Memoirs,* pp. 508–15; Shawcross, pp. 206–7; *Pentagon Papers,* appendix 1: "Editorials from the *New York Times,* June 16–30, 1971" and appendix 2: "Supreme Court Decision, June 30, 1971."

60. *Memoirs,* pp. 508–15; Kendrick, pp. 323–25.

61. *White House Years,* pp. 1190–91, 1197–99; Kendrick, pp. 353–55. See also Ron Kovic, *Born on the Fourth of July* (New York: McGraw, 1976), pp. 168–69.

62. *White House Years,* pp. 1452–53; Gordon, quoted in ibid., p. 1453; *St. Louis Post-Dispatch,* December 19, 1972; *Boston Globe,* December 20, 1972; *Washington Post,* December 28, 1972; *Los Angeles Times,* December 28, 1972.

63. Emerson, p. 317; Kendrick, p. 388.

Chapter 15
The Peking Summit

1. *Memoirs,* p. 544; announcement also quoted in *White House Years,* pp. 759–60.

2. Lerner, quoted in *Memoirs,* p. 554.

3. Stennis, quoted in *Memoirs,* p. 555.

4. *Memoirs,* p. 270. See Shawcross, pp. 85–86.

5. Nixon inaugural address, January 20, 1969, quoted in *Memoirs,* p. 545; Nixon news conference, January 27, 1969, quoted in *White House Years,* p. 168.

6. Nixon statement, quoted in *White House Years,* p. 170.

7. *White House Years,* pp. 179–81; *Memoirs,* pp. 546–47.

8. *White House Years,* pp. 180–91.

9. Kissinger press briefing, December 18, 1969, quoted in ibid., p. 192.

10. Stoessel, quoted in *White House Years,* p. 687.

11. Chou En-lai, quoted in *White House Years,* p. 689.

12. *White House Years,* pp. 692–95.

13. Nixon, quoted in ibid., pp. 695–96.

14. "I Did Not Want the Hot Words of TV," *Time,* October 5, 1970; p. 12; Nixon quote also appears in Safire, p. 371, and in *Memoirs,* p. 546; *White House Years,* p. 699; Tad Szulc, *The Illusion of Peace* (New York: Viking Press, 1978), p. 347.

15. *Memoirs*, p. 546.
16. U.S. reply to Chou's message, December 16, 1970, quoted in *White House Years*, p. 702.
17. Mao Tse-tung, quoted in *White House Years*, p. 702.
18. *Memoirs*, p. 547; Safire, p. 372.
19. *People's Daily* (Peking), quoted in *Memoirs*, p. 548.
20. *Memoirs*, p. 548.
21. *White House Years*, pp. 708–13.
22. Chou En-lai, quoted in ibid., p. 714 and in *Memoirs*, p. 549.
23. *White House Years*, pp. 724–27, 736–45.
24. Ibid., p. 735; Szulc, *Illusion of Peace*, p. 414.
25. Kissinger report to Nixon, quoted in *White House Years*, pp. 754–55.
26. *White House Years*, pp. 770–74; Szulc, *Illusion of Peace*, p. 498; Nixon quote from *Memoirs*, p. 556.
27. Shanghai Communiqué, February 28, 1972, reprinted in *White House Years*, pp. 1490–92. See especially p. 1492.
28. *Memoirs*, p. 557.
29. Kissinger, quoted in Safire, p. 374.
30. Nixon, quoted in Safire, p. 377.
31. *White House Years*, pp. 1049–53; John Chancellor, "Who Produced the China Show?" *Foreign Policy*, Summer 1972, pp. 88–95; Stanley Karnow, "Playing Second Fiddle to the Tube," ibid., pp. 96–103.
32. *Memoirs*, pp. 559–61; Mao Tse-tung, quoted in ibid., p. 561.
33. Mao Tse-tung, quoted in *White House Years*, p. 1062, and in *Memoirs*, p. 563; Szulc, *Illusion of Peace*, p. 517.
34. *White House Years*, pp. 1070–74; *Memoirs*, pp. 564–68.
35. Chou En-lai, quoted in *Memoirs*, p. 568.
36. *Memoirs*, pp. 568–69.
37. Schell, p. 206; author's interview with Zhang Deuveir, under secretary of foreign affairs—Indochina, People's Republic of China, September 30, 1979.
38. *White House Years*, pp. 1087–96; Nixon toast, February 27, 1972, quoted in *Memoirs*, p. 580.
39. Nixon, *The Real War*, p. 139.
40. Ibid., pp. 139–40.
41. Ibid., p. 139.
42. Ibid., pp. 143–44.
43. Ibid., p. 302.
44. Ibid., pp. 148–49.

Chapter 16
The Moscow Summit

1. *White House Years*, pp. 837–41; *Memoirs*, pp. 522–25. See also *New York Times*, October 13, 1971.
2. *White House Years*, p. 143; *Memoirs*, pp. 369–70.
3. Kissinger memo, February 18, 1969, reprinted in *White House Years*, pp. 143–44.
4. *Memoirs*, pp. 391, 399; *White House Years*, p. 144.

5. *Memoirs,* pp. 405–7.

6. *White House Years,* pp. 552–57, 793–97; "Following our established policy . . ." quote appears on p. 552.

7. Ibid., pp. 810–40; *Memoirs,* pp. 522–25.

8. O'Ballance, pp. 163–65; Porter, *Peace Denied,* pp. 102–3; Kalb and Kalb, pp. 301–3, 324; Kendrick, p. 348.

9. Porter, *Peace Denied,* pp. 104–6.

10. Ibid., p. 105.

11. Ibid., pp. 105–8; O'Ballance, pp. 167–69.

12. *Memoirs,* p. 586.

13. Kalb and Kalb, pp. 324–27, 330.

14. Ibid., pp. 329–30.

15. Porter, *Peace Denied,* pp. 106–7.

16. Kalb and Kalb, pp. 339–44; Bob Woodward and Carl Bernstein, *The Final Days* (New York: Avon, 1976), p. 202, note *.

17. *Memoirs,* pp. 601–2.

18. Ibid., p. 602.

19. Ibid., pp. 603–4; *White House Years,* pp. 1184–86.

20. Kalb and Kalb, pp. 346–47; *Memoirs,* p. 605; *White House Years,* p. 1189.

21. O'Ballance, p. 169; Porter, *Peace Denied,* p. 108; Kalb and Kalb, pp. 330–31.

22. Kendrick, p. 348; Kalb and Kalb, pp. 331, 349–54.

23. O'Ballance, p. 171; Porter, *Peace Denied,* p. 110.

24. *Memoirs,* pp. 587–90.

25. Ibid., pp. 593–94.

26. Ibid., pp. 594–95. See also Kalb and Kalb, p. 340.

27. Kissinger, quoted in *Memoirs,* p. 609.

28. Ibid., p. 610; *White House Years,* pp. 1206–9.

29. Nixon toast, reprinted in *White House Years,* p. 1209.

30. *White House Years,* pp. 1211–12.

31. *Memoirs,* p. 611.

32. *White House Years,* pp. 1216–19; Kalb and Kalb, pp. 362–64.

33. *White House Years,* pp. 1222–27.

34. *Memoirs,* p. 613.

35. Ibid., p. 614.

36. *White House Years,* pp. 1229–44.

37. *Memoirs,* pp. 616–17.

Chapter 17
Bombing—Campaigning—Negotiating

1. Nixon, quoted in Szulc, *Illusion of Peace,* p. 588.

2. O'Ballance, pp. 171–72, 174; Kendrick, p. 355.

3. O'Ballance, pp. 169–70.

4. Nixon, quoted in Szulc, *Illusion of Peace,* p. 604.

5. Porter, *Peace Denied,* pp. 117–19, 297, note 63; Szulc, *Illusion of Peace,* p. 609.

6. Nixon, quoted in Brown, p. 240.

7. Ibid.
8. Ibid.
9. Kendrick, pp. 354–55.
10. Szulc, *Illusion of Peace*, p. 624.
11. Kendrick, p. 354.
12. For details on Watergate from the inside, see Nixon's *Memoirs*, p. 625 ff.; for details of the investigation from the outside, see Carl Bernstein and Bob Woodward, *All the President's Men* (New York: Simon & Schuster, 1974).
13. Szulc, *Illusion of Peace*, pp. 606–7.
14. Kalb and Kalb, pp. 385–86; Porter, *Peace Denied*, pp. 119–21.
15. Brodie, p. 173.
16. Szulc, *Illusion of Peace*, pp. 612–13; Kalb and Kalb, pp. 395–98.
17. Szulc, *Illusion of Peace*, pp. 609–10, 623.
18. Porter, *Peace Denied*, pp. 120–22.
19. Nixon, quoted in Szulc, *Illusion of Peace*, p. 625.
20. See Kissinger's statement: "[W]ithdrawal isn't the problem. The problem is they [the North Vietnamese] won't let us. They want us there right now; they don't want us out," quoted in Kalb and Kalb, p. 400.
21. Theodore White, *The Making of the President, 1972* (New York: Atheneum, 1973), p. 231.
22. *Memoirs*, p. 544.
23. White, *1972*, p. 116.
24. Ernest R. May and Janet Fraser, eds., *Campaign '72: The Managers Speak* (Cambridge: Harvard University Press, 1973), p. 23.
25. Ibid., p. 25.
26. Johnson, quoted in *Memoirs*, p. 674.
27. *White House Years*, pp. 1190–91; Kendrick, pp. 351–54.
28. Kovic, pp. 168–69.
29. Szulc, *Illusion of Peace*, pp. 625–26; Kalb and Kalb, pp. 402–4.
30. Porter, *Peace Denied*, p. 122.
31. Szulc, *Illusion of Peace*, pp. 626–27.
32. Porter, *Peace Denied*, pp. 124–25.
33. Ibid., p. 125.
34. Szulc, *Illusion of Peace*, p. 632; Kendrick, pp. 376–78.
35. *New York Times*, October 9, 1972.
36. Porter, *Peace Denied*, pp. 128–29.
37. Szulc, *Illusion of Peace*, p. 629.
38. Kalb and Kalb, pp. 416–27.
39. Porter, *Peace Denied*, pp. 127–28; Szulc, *Illusion of Peace*, pp. 629–30.
40. Porter, *Peace Denied*, p. 130.
41. Ibid., p. 127.
42. Ibid., p. 128.
43. Kalb and Kalb, p. 431.
44. Kissinger, quoted in ibid., pp. 433–34.
45. Kalb and Kalb, pp. 434–37.
46. Szulc, *Illusion of Peace*, p. 633.
47. Ibid., p. 634; Porter, *Peace Denied*, p. 135.
48. *Memoirs*, p. 707.

Chapter 18
The Paris Peace Agreement

1. Szulc, *Illusion of Peace,* pp. 635–36; Porter, *Peace Denied,* pp. 143–44; Kalb and Kalb, pp. 440–41.
2. Kalb and Kalb, p. 441.
3. Szulc, *Illusion of Peace,* p. 636; Kalb and Kalb, pp. 441–45; Porter, *Peace Denied,* p. 144.
4. Gregory F. Rose, "The Stolen Secrets of Vietnam," *New York,* November 27, 1978, p. 76.
5. Kalb and Kalb, p. 441.
6. Le Duc Tho, quoted in Porter, *Peace Denied,* p. 145.
7. Porter, *Peace Denied,* pp. 145–51.
8. *Memoirs,* p. 721.
9. Ibid., p. 718; Szulc, *Illusion of Peace,* p. 637.
10. Szulc, *Illusion of Peace,* pp. 637–38.
11. Ibid., pp. 638–40.
12. Kalb and Kalb, pp. 467–69; Porter, *Peace Denied,* pp. 153–56.
13. Kissinger, quoted in Porter, *Peace Denied,* pp. 156–57.
14. *Memoirs,* p. 727.
15. Haig, quoted in Bernstein and Woodward, *Final Days,* p. 212.
16. Szulc, *Illusion of Peace,* p. 654.
17. Kalb and Kalb, pp. 469–71.
18. Porter, *Peace Denied,* pp. 158–59; administration spokesman, quoted in ibid.
19. Szulc, *Illusion of Peace,* p. 654.
20. Porter, *Peace Denied,* pp. 159–60.
21. Nixon, quoted in ibid., p. 158.
22. Porter, pp. 160–62; Kalb and Kalb, p. 471.
23. Kalb and Kalb, pp. 471–72; Porter, *Peace Denied,* p. 162.
24. Porter, *Peace Denied,* p. 165.
25. Woodward and Bernstein, *Final Days,* p. 207.
26. Szulc, *Illusion of Peace,* p. 655.
27. Porter, *Peace Denied,* pp. 166–73.
28. Kalb and Kalb, p. 477.
29. Ibid., p. 478.
30. "The Vietnam Agreement and Protocols, signed January 27, 1973," reprinted in Porter, *Peace Denied,* pp. 319–49.
31. Porter, *Peace Denied,* pp. 186–87. See also *Washington Post,* December 9 and 11, 1972; Jack Anderson, *Washington Post,* March 20, 1973.
32. Charles Taylor, *Snow Job: Canada, the United States and Vietnam* (Toronto: Anasi, 1974), p. 148.
33. Porter, *Peace Denied,* p. 186.
34. Porter, *Peace Denied,* p. 183; quotations within quoted material from *Tin Song,* January 22, 1973.
35. Porter, *Peace Denied,* pp. 188–96, 206–32.
36. Ibid., p. 187. Copies of these letters were passed out at a press conference in Washington, D.C., on April 30, 1975, by Dr. Nguyin Tien Hung.
37. Frank Snepp, *Decent Interval* (New York: Random, 1977), p. 51. For

insight on the effect of Watergate on the President at this time, see Woodward and Bernstein, *Final Days*, p. 198.

38. Porter, *Peace Denied*, p. 199.
39. Tad Szulc, "Behind the Vietnam Cease-Fire Agreement," *Foreign Policy* (Summer 1974), p. 66.
40. Snepp, p. 52.
41. *Memoirs*, pp. 882–87.
42. Nixon, *The Real War*, pp. 244–45.

Chapter 19
Final Countdown

1. Porter, *Peace Denied*, p. 278.
2. Ibid., p. 259.
3. Snepp, p. 91.
4. Porter, *Peace Denied*, pp. 261–62.
5. Ibid., pp. 260–61.
6. Snepp, pp. 91–94.
7. Porter, *Peace Denied*, p. 262.
8. Ibid., pp. 262–63.
9. Ibid., p. 260; Snepp, pp. 91, 94.
9a. Snepp, p. 74.
10. Ibid., pp. 66–75; Martin's associates, quoted in ibid.
11. Snepp, pp. 77–81; Kendrick, p. 394.
12. Snepp, pp. 85–90.
13. Ibid., p. 96.
14. Porter, *Peace Denied*, pp. 263–64.
15. Thieu, quoted in ibid., p. 264.
16. Szulc, *Illusion of Peace*, p. 753.
17. Kalb and Kalb, pp. 491–92.
18. Le Duc Tho, quoted in ibid., p. 492.
19. State Department bulletin, reprinted in Szulc, *Illusion of Peace*, p. 754.
20. *Memoirs*, p. 977.
21. Kissinger, quoted in Snepp, p. 97.
21a. Sneep, pp. 101 and 102.
22. Martin, quoted in Snepp, p. 101.
23. Snepp, pp. 101–2; ibid., p. 102, note *.
24. Congressional Committee, quoted in Szulc, *Illusion of Peace*, p. 764. See also Szulc, *Illusion of Peace*, pp. 763–64 and Snepp, pp. 94–95, 102–5.
25. Nixon, quoted in Szulc, *Illusion of Peace*, p. 767.
26. Snepp, pp. 104–5.
27. Porter, *Peace Denied*, pp. 264–65.
28. Snepp, pp. 105–6.
29. Ibid.; Porter, *Peace Denied*, pp. 265–66.
30. Snepp, pp. 108–13.
31. Ford, quoted in ibid., p. 113.
32. Snepp, pp. 117–20, 123–24, 130–33, 154–57.
33. Porter, *Peace Denied*, pp. 266–68; ibid., p. 268, note *.
34. PRG statement, quoted in ibid., p. 269.

35. Snepp, pp. 129–35.
36. Alan Dawson, *55 Days: The Fall of South Vietnam* (Englewood Cliffs, N.J.: Prentice-Hall, 1977), p. 28.
37. Snepp, p. 137.
38. Ibid., pp. 139–48.
39. Dawson, pp. 102–3.
40. Snepp, pp. 159–69.
41. Ibid., pp. 177–84, 205–8; Dawson, pp. 33–82 passim.
42. Snepp, pp. 209–14, 223–24, 228–29; Dawson, pp. 83–150 passim.
43. Snepp, pp. 230–61 passim; Dawson, pp. 151–88 passim.
44. Snepp, p. 297.
45. Ibid., pp. 301–5; Dawson, pp. 156–57.
46. *New York Times*, April 2 and 3, 1975.
47. Snepp, pp. 283–87.
48. Ibid., p. 240.
49. Ibid., p. 302.
50. Ibid., p. 301.
51. Ibid., pp. 301–3; Dawson, pp. 213–16.
52. Snepp, pp. 306–7; Weyand, quoted in ibid., p. 307.
53. Porter, *Peace Denied*, p. 275.
54. Dawson, pp. 227–28.
55. Snepp, p. 416.
56. "Graham Martin: Our Man in Saigon," *Time*, April 21, 1975, p. 19.
57. Snepp, p. 368.
58. Ibid., p. 380; Porter, *Peace Denied*, pp. 275–76; Dawson, p. 279.
59. Wilfred Burchett, *Grasshoppers and Elephants: Why Vietnam Fell* (New York: Urizen Books, 1977), p. 37.
60. Dawson, pp. 241–50; McCoy, chapter 5.
61. Snepp, pp. 394–96.
62. Ibid., pp. 396–562 passim; Dawson, pp. 259–347 passim.
63. Tiziano Terzani, *Giai Phong! The Fall and Liberation of Saigon* (New York: St. Martin's Press, 1976), p. 86.
64. Ibid., p. 96.
65. Ibid., p. 97.

Chapter 20
Vietnam's Catastrophe

1. Corporal Campbell, testimony in *The Dellums Committee Hearings on War Crimes in Vietnam: An Inquiry into Command Responsibility in Southeast Asia* (New York: Vintage Books, 1972), p. 273. Hereafter referred to as *Dellums*.
2. Sergeant Henry, testimony in Vietnam Veterans Against the War, *The Winter Soldier Investigation: An Inquiry into American War Crimes* (Boston: Beacon Press, 1972), pp. 44–45. Hereafter referred to as *WSI*.
3. *Indochina Story*, p. 108.
4. Hammer, pp. 70–71, quoted by Telford Taylor, *Nuremberg and Vietnam: An American Tragedy* (Chicago: Quadrangle Books, 1970), p. 170.
5. Pitkin, quoted in Kerry and the VVAW, p. 84.
6. Sergeant Henry, quoted in *WSI*, pp. 43–44.

7. United Press International dispatch, August 3, 1965, quoted in Zinn, p. 53.

8. Heidtman, quoted in Kerry and the VVAW, p. 50.

9. Captain Johnson, quoted in *Dellums,* pp. 42–43.

10. Orville and Jonathan Schell, *New York Times,* November 26, 1969.

11. Sergeant Smith and Corporal Heidtman, quoted in *WSI,* pp. 36–37, 26–28, 29.

12. *The Nation,* April 21, 1969, pp. 484–85.

13. *Washington Post,* March 13, 1965; Reuters dispatch, March 18, 1965, quoted in Zinn, p. 52; Zinn, p. 59.

14. Charles Mohr, *New York Times,* September 5, 1965.

15. Sergeant McCusker, quoted in *WSI,* p. 31.

16. Caldwell, quoted in *WSI,* p. 75.

17. Sergeant Hunter, quoted in *WSI,* p. 52.

18. Secret message from American Embassy, Saigon, to secretary of state No. 4573 dated October 8, 1961 (Declassified 12/16/74); secret message from Rusk to American Embassy, Saigon No. 2963, dated November 7, 1961 (Declassified 5/27/75); secret memo from McNamara to Kennedy, subject: Defoliant Operations in Vietnam, dated February 2, 1962 (Declassified 4/17/73); top secret message from Chief, MAAG to CINCPAG, DTG 030405Z Feb 62 (Declassified 4/17/73); secret letter from Brown to McGeorge Bundy, April 11, 1962 (Declassified 4/23/73); secret memo from McNamara to Kennedy, subject: Herbicide operations in South Vietnam, August 1962 (Declassified 4/23/73); secret memo from McNamara to Kennedy, subject: Chemical crop destruction in South Vietnam, August 1962 (Declassified 4/23/73), Declassified Documents Reference System.

19. Charles A. Joiner, *The Politics of Massacre* (Philadelphia: Temple University Press, 1974), pp. 245–47; Major Warren Milberg, *The Future Applicability of the Phoenix Program* (Alexandria, Va./ Defense Documentation Center, Cameron Station, May 1974).

20. Colby, pp. 245–47, 266–88, 277; Milberg, p. 26.

21. *Indochina Story,* p. 129.

22. Sergeant Hunter, quoted in *WSI,* p. 54.

23. Kerry and VVAW, p. 54; Taylor, *Nuremberg,* p. 162.

24. Emerson, p. 357; Robert Warren Stevens, *Vain Hopes, Grim Realities: The Economic Consequences of the Vietnam War* (New York: New Viewpoints, 1976), pp. 3, 197, note 1.

25. Emerson, p. 357.

26. Ibid., p. 314; *Indochina Story,* p. 97.

27. Emerson, p. 314; Stevens, p. 4.

28. Cao Van Nguyen, M. D., quoted in *Indochina Story,* p. 111.

29. Buckley, quoted in *Indochina Story,* p. 98.

30. Young, quoted in Emerson, p. 225.

31. *Rocky Mountain News* wire service, Washington, November 11, 1981.

Chapter 21
America's Tragedy

1. "The Troubled Vietnam Vet," *Newsweek,* March 30, 1981, pp. 24, 29.

2. Emerson, pp. 58–59.

3. Paul Starr, writing in Nader study, quoted in ibid., pp. 254–55.

4. Emerson, p. 58.

5. This statistic compiled through research at the Air Force Academy Library, Colorado Springs, Colorado. See also Bryan, *Friendly Fire*.

6. Emerson, p. 59.

7. Robert Kennedy, quoted in *New York Times*, March 25, 1968.

8. Emerson, pp. 59, 335; Kendrick, p. 307.

9. Kendrick, p. 321.

10. Gorman, quoted in Emerson, pp. 378–79.

11. Mrs. Perrin, quoted in Emerson, p. 127.

12. ACLU spokesman, quoted in Emerson, pp. 132–33.

13. Emerson, pp. 133–34.

14. Tom Riddell, "The $676 Billion Quagmire," *The Progressive*, October 1973, p. 33.

15. Stevens, chapter 14, esp. p. 186.

16. Ibid., chapters 5–7, 11–12.

17. Emerson, p. 303; Stevens, table 1–3, p. 25; ibid., table 8–1, p. 83; ibid., figure 12–2, p. 140; ibid., p. 199, note 2. See also Stevens, p. 33.

18. Stevens, chapters 9–10.

BIBLIOGRAPHY

Acheson, Dean. *Present at the Creation*. New York: Norton, 1969.

Adams, Nina S., and McCoy, Alfred W., eds. *Laos: War and Revolution*. New York: Harper & Row, 1970.

Archer, Jules. *Riot! A History of Mob Action in the United States*. New York: Dutton, Hawthorn, 1974.

Asinoff, Eliot. *Craig and Joan: Two Lives for Peace*. New York: Viking Press, 1971.

———. "The Peace Suicides," *Seventeen Magazine*, March 1970.

Austin, Anthony. *The President's War*. Philadelphia: Lippincott, 1971.

Barnet, Richard. *Intervention and Revolution: The United States in the Third World*. New York: World, 1968.

Bernstein, Carl, and Woodward, Bob. *All the President's Men*. New York: Simon & Schuster, 1974.

———. *The Final Days*. New York: Avon, 1976.

"Bombing in Cambodia," Hearings Before the Committee on Armed Services, U.S. Senate, 93rd Congress, First Session, July/August 1973.

Boston Globe.

Braestrup, Peter. *Big Story: How the American Press and Television Reported and Interpreted the Crisis of Tet 1968 in Vietnam and Washington*. Boulder, Colo.: Westview Press, 1977.

Brodie, Bernard. *War and Politics*. New York: Macmillan, 1973.

Brown, Weldon. *The Last Chopper: The Denouement of the American Role in Vietnam 1963–1975*. Port Washington, N.Y.: Kennikat Press, 1976.

Bryan, C. D. B. *Friendly Fire*. New York: Putnam, 1976.

Burchett, Wilfred. *Grasshoppers and Elephants: Why Vietnam Fell*. New York: Urizen Books, 1977.

Buttinger, Joseph. *Vietnam: A Political History*. New York: Praeger, 1968.

Caldwell, Malcolm, and Tan, Lek. *Cambodia in the Southeast Asian War*. New York: Monthly Review Press, 1973.

Chancellor, John. "Who Produced the China Show?" *Foreign Policy*, Summer 1972.

Chester, Lewis; Hodgson, Godfrey; and Page, Bruce. *An American Melodrama*. New York: Viking Press, 1969.

Chomsky, Noam. *At War with Asia: Essays on Indochina*. New York: Pantheon, 1970.

Colby, William. *Honorable Men: My Life in the CIA*. New York: Simon & Schuster, 1978.

Commission on the Causes and Prevention of Violence. *Rights in Concord: The Response to the Counter-Inaugural Protest Activities in Washington, D.C.* Washington, D.C.: U.S. Government Printing Office, 1969.

Committee of Concerned Asian Scholars. *The Indochina Story.* New York: Bantam, 1970.

Congressional Quarterly Almanac, 1965, 1969.

Congressional Record.

Cornell University Air War Study Group. *The Air War in Indochina.* Edited by Raphael Littauer and Norman Uphoff. Rev. ed. Boston: Beacon Press, 1972.

Cortright, David. *Soldiers in Revolt: The American Military Today.* Garden City, N.Y.: Doubleday, Anchor Press, 1975.

Crowell, Joan. *Fort Dix Stockade: Riot and Demonstration.* New York: Links Books, 1974.

Dalby, Stewart. *Financial Times* (London), April 6, 1975.

Dawson, Alan. *55 Days: The Fall of South Vietnam.* Englewood Cliffs, N.J.: Prentice-Hall, 1977.

Declassified Documents Reference System. Washington, D.C.: Carrollton Press, located at Air Force Academy Library, Colorado Springs, Colo.

Decornoy, Jacques. "Laos: The Forgotten War." *Bulletin of Concerned Asian Scholars,* July–August 1970.

The Dellums Committee Hearings on War Crimes in Vietnam: An Inquiry into Command Responsibility in Southeast Asia. Edited by the Citizens Committee of Inquiry. New York: Vintage Books, 1972.

Denver Post.

Deuveir, Zhang. Under Secretary of Foreign Affairs, Indochina; Peking, China. Interview with author, September 30, 1979.

DeVillers, Phillipe. "The Struggle for the Unification of Vietnam." *The China Quarterly* 9 (January–March 1962).

Dickson, Paul, and Rothchild, John. "Electronic Battlefield: Strangelove's Answer to War Crimes." *Washington Monthly,* May 1971.

Dommen, Arthur J. *Conflict in Laos: The Politics of Neutralization.* New York: Praeger, 1964.

Draper, Theodore. *Abuse of Power.* New York: Viking Press, 1967.

Drew, Elizabeth. "Washington." *Atlantic,* April 1971.

Drury, Allen, and Maroon, Fred. *Courage and Hesitation.* New York: Doubleday, 1971.

Ellsberg, Daniel. *Papers on the War.* New York: Simon & Schuster, 1972.

Emerson, Gloria. *Winners and Losers: Battles, Retreats, Gains, Losses and Ruins from the Vietnam War.* New York: Harcourt Brace Jovanovich, 1976.

Erickson, Arthur. "Air Force Plans With Computers, Army Sees by Starlight." *Electronics,* October 26, 1970.

Fall, Bernard. *Anatomy of a Crisis: The Laotian Crisis of 1960–61.* Garden City, N.Y.: Doubleday, 1969.

———. *Hell in a Very Small Place.* Philadelphia: Lippincott, 1966.

———. *Street Without Joy.* Harrisburg, Pa.: Stackpole, 1964.

———. *The Two Vietnams: A Political and Military Analysis.* New York: Praeger, 1967.

_____. *Vietnam Witness, 1953–1966.* New York: Praeger, 1966.
Fanning, Louis. *Betrayal in Vietnam.* New Rochelle, N.Y.: Arlington House, 1976.
Fitzgerald, Frances. *Fire in the Lake.* Boston: Little, 1972.
Foreign Affairs.
Friend, Robert C. Journalist, Peking, China. Interview with the author, September 30, 1979.
Fulbright, J. William. *The Arrogance of Power.* New York: Random, 1966.
_____, ed. *Vietnam Hearings.* New York: Random, 1966.
"Further Documents Relating to the Discussion of Indo-China at the Geneva Conference," June 16–July 21, 1954, Presented by the Secretary of State for Foreign Affairs to Parliament by Command of Her Majesty, August 1954.
Galloway, John, ed. *The Gulf of Tonkin Resolution.* Rutherford, N.J.: Fairleigh Dickinson University Press, 1970.
Gallucci, Robert. *Neither Peace Nor Honor: The Politics of American Military Policy in Viet-Nam.* Baltimore: Johns Hopkins University Press, 1975.
Geld, Leslie H. and Betts, Richard K. *The Irony of Vietnam: The System Worked.* Washington, D.C.: Brookings Institute, 1979.
Gettleman, Marvin, ed. *Vietnam: History, Documents, and Opinions on a Major World Crisis.* New York: NAL, Mentor, 1970.
Gettleman, Marvin; Gettleman, Susan; Kaplan, Lawrence; and Kaplan, Carol, eds. *Conflict in Indochina: A Reader on the Widening War in Laos and Cambodia.* New York: Random, 1970.
Goulden, Joseph. "Talks with China: The Military Saboteurs." *The Nation,* March 2, 1970.
Gruening, Senator Ernest. Eleanor Roosevelt Peace Award acceptance (SANE). December 3, 1972.
Halberstam, David. *The Best and the Brightest.* New York: Harper & Row, 1972.
_____. *The Making of a Quagmire.* New York: Harper & Row, 1972.
Hammer, Richard. *One Morning in the War: The Tragedy at Son My.* New York: Coward, 1970.
Hearings on Supplemental Assistance to Cambodia before the Senate Foreign Relations Committee, February 24, 1975.
Herr, Michael. *Dispatches.* New York: Knopf, 1978.
Hildebrand, George, and Porter, Gareth. *Cambodia: Starvation and Revolution.* New York: Monthly Review Press, 1976.
Honey, P. J. *Communism in North Vietnam.* Cambridge: MIT Press, 1963.
Hoopes, Townsend. *The Limits of Intervention.* New York: McKay, 1969.
Huyen, N. Khac. *Vision Accomplished: The Enigma of Ho Chi Minh.* New York: Macmillan, 1971.
Johansen, Robert. "Of Politics and Prophecy: Student Activism Today." *Christian Century,* February 17, 1971.
Johnson, Lyndon B. *The Vantage Point: Perspectives of the Presidency.* New York: Cowles, 1970.
Joiner, Charles A. *The Politics of Massacre: Political Processes in South Vietnam.* Philadelphia: Temple University Press, 1974.

Joint Hearings Before the Committee on Foreign Relations and the Committee on Armed Services, U.S. Senate, Eighty-eighth Congress, Second Session, August 6, 1964.

Kahin, George McTurnan, and Lewis, John W. *The United States in Vietnam.* Rev. ed. New York: Dell, 1969.

Kalb, Bernard, and Abel, Elie. *Roots of Involvement: The U.S. in Asia 1784–1971.* New York: Norton, 1971.

Kalb, Marvin, and Kalb, Bernard. *Kissinger.* New York: Dell, 1975.

Kaplan, Fred M. "Our Cold War Policy, Circa '50." *New York Times Magazine,* May 18, 1980.

Karnow, Stanley. "Playing Second Fiddle to the Tube." *Foreign Policy,* Summer 1972.

Kasinsky, Renee. *Refugees from Militarism: Draft-Age Americans in Canada.* New Brunswick, N.J.: Transaction Books, 1976.

Kearns, Doris. *Lyndon Johnson and the American Dream.* New York: Harper & Row, 1976.

Kendrick, Alexander. *The Wound Within: America in the Vietnam Years 1945–1974.* Boston: Little, 1974.

Kerry, John, and the Vietnam Veterans Against the War. *The New Soldier.* New York: Macmillan, 1971.

Kirk, Donald. *Wider War: The Struggle for Cambodia, Thailand and Laos.* New York: Praeger, 1971.

Kissinger, Henry A. *A World Restored: The Politics of Conservatism in a Revolutionary Age.* New York: Grosset & Dunlap, 1964.

———. *White House Years.* Boston: Little, 1979.

Kovic, Ron. *Born on the Fourth of July.* New York: McGraw, 1976.

Lacouture, Jean. *Ho Chi Minh.* New York: Random, 1968.

———. *Vietnam: Between Two Truces.* New York: Vintage, 1966.

Lewy, Gunther. *America in Vietnam.* New York: Oxford University Press, 1978.

Life.

Lifton, Robert J. *Home From the War: Vietnam Veterans, Neither Victims Nor Executioners.* New York: Simon & Schuster, 1973.

Los Angeles Times.

Lynd, Staughton, and Hayden, Thomas. *The Other Side.* New York: New American Library, 1966.

Marchetti, Victor, and Marks, John D. *The CIA and the Cult of Intelligence.* New York: Knopf, 1974.

May, Ernest, and Fraser, Janet, eds. *Campaign '72: The Managers Speak.* Cambridge: Harvard University Press, 1973.

McCoy, Alfred W. *The Politics of Heroin in Southeast Asia.* New York: Harper & Row, 1972.

Michener, James. *Kent State: What Happened and Why.* New York: Random, 1971.

Milberg, Major Warren H. *The Future Applicability of the Phoenix Program.* Alexandria, Va.: Defense Documentation Center, Cameron Station, May 1974.

Miller, William. *Martin Luther King.* New York: McKay, Weybright, 1968.

Milton, General T. R. United States Air Force, Retired, Colorado Springs, Colorado. Interview, February 20, 1978.

Montgomery, John. *The Politics of Foreign Aid.* New York: Praeger, 1962.
Morris, Roger. *Uncertain Greatness: Henry Kissinger and American Foreign Policy.* New York: Harper & Row, 1977.
Nation.
Neary, Jon. *Julian Bond.* New York: Morrow, 1971.
New York Times.
Newsweek.
Nhat-Hanh, Thich. *Vietnam: Lotus in a Sea of Fire.* New York: Hill & Wang, 1967.
Nighswonger, William. *Rural Pacification in Vietnam.* New York: Praeger, 1967.
Nixon, Richard. *RN: The Memoirs of Richard Nixon.* New York: Grosset & Dunlap, 1978.
———. *The Real War.* New York: Warner Books, 1980.
"Nuclear War Is National Suicide." *Journal of the Federation of American Scientists (FAS)* 34 (February 1981).
O'Ballance, Edgar. *The Wars in Vietnam 1954–1973.* New York: Hippocrene Books, 1975.
Official History of the United States Air Force in Southeast Asia. Washington, D.C.: U.S. Government Printing Office, 1977.
The Pentagon Papers: The Defense Department History of United States Decisionmaking on Vietnam. Senator Gravel ed. Boston: Beacon Press, 1971.
Pettit, Clyde E. *The Experts.* Secaucus, N.J.: Lyle Stuart, 1975.
Pike, Douglas. *VietCong: The Organization and Techniques of the National Liberation Front of South Vietnam.* Cambridge: MIT Press, 1966.
Podhoretz, Norman. *Why We Were in Vietnam.* New York: Simon & Schuster, 1982.
Ponchaud, François. *Cambodia: Year Zero.* New York: Holt, Rinehart & Winston, 1977.
Porter, Gareth. *A Peace Denied: The United States, Vietnam, and the Paris Agreement.* Bloomington: Indiana University Press, 1975.
———. "The Broken Promise to Hanoi." *The Nation,* April 30, 1977.
———, ed. *Vietnam: The Definitive Documentation of Human Decisions.* 2 vols. Stanfordville, N.Y.: E. M. Coleman Enterprises, 1979.
Powers, Thomas. *The War at Home: Vietnam and the American People, 1964–1968.* New York: Grossman, 1973.
Prouty, Fletcher. *The Secret Team: The CIA and Its Allies in Control of the United States and the World.* New York: Ballentine Books, 1972.
Public Papers of the Presidents of the United States: Richard Nixon: 1969. Washington, D.C.: U.S. Government Printing Office, 1971.
Purifoy, Lewis McCarroll. *Harry Truman's China Policy: McCarthyism and the Diplomacy of Hysteria, 1947–1951.* New York: New Viewpoints, 1976.
Raskin, Marcus G. and Fall, Bernard, eds. *The Vietnam Reader: Articles and Documents on American Foreign Policy and the Vietnam Crisis.* Rev. ed. New York: Vintage Books, 1967.
Report of the Committee on the Judiciary on the Impeachment of Richard M. Nixon, President of the United States, 93rd Congress, August 20, 1974.

Riddell, Tom. "The $676 Billion Quagmire." *The Progressive*, October 1973.
Roberts, Chalmer M. "The Day We Didn't Go to War." *Reporter*, September 14, 1954.
Rocky Mountain News.
Rose, Gregory F. "The Stolen Secrets of Vietnam." *New York*, November 27, 1978.
Safire, William. *Before the Fall*. New York: Doubleday, 1975.
Salisbury, Harrison E. *Behind the Lines: Hanoi, December 23, 1966—January 7, 1967*. New York: Harper & Row, 1967.
San Francisco Chronicle.
Schandler, Herbert. *The Unmaking of the President: Lyndon Johnson and Vietnam*. Princeton: Princeton University Press, 1977.
Schell, Jonathan. *The Time of Illusion*. New York: Knopf, 1976.
Schlesinger, Arthur, Jr. *A Thousand Days*. Boston: Houghton-Mifflin, 1965.
———. *The Imperial Presidency*. Boston: Houghton Mifflin, 1966.
Schrag, Peter. "After Kent State: The First Hundred Days." *Saturday Review*, August 29, 1970.
Scott, Peter Dale. *The War Conspiracy: The Secret Road to the Second Indochina War*. Indianapolis: Bobbs, 1972.
Shadegg, Stephen C. *Winning's a Lot More Fun*. Toronto: Macmillan, 1969.
Shawcross, William. *Sideshow: Kissinger, Nixon and the Destruction of Cambodia*. New York: Simon & Schuster, 1979.
Sheehan, Neil; Smith, H.; Kenworthy, E. W.; and Butterfield, F. *The Pentagon Papers: As published by the New York Times*. New York: Bantam, 1971.
Sihanouk, Norodom. *My War With the CIA: The Memoirs of Prince Norodom Sihanouk*. New York: Pantheon, 1973.
Skolnick, Jerome H. *The Politics of Protest: A Report, Submitted by Jerome H. Skolnick*. New York: Simon & Schuster, 1969.
Snepp, Frank. *Decent Interval*. New York: Random, 1977.
Stevens, Robert Warren. *Vain Hopes, Grim Realities: The Economic Consequences of the Vietnam War*. New York: New Viewpoints, 1976.
Stevenson, Charles. *The End of Nowhere: American Policy toward Laos since 1965*. Boston: Beacon Press, 1972.
Szulc, Tad. "Behind the Vietnam Cease-Fire Agreement." *Foreign Policy 15* (Summer 1974).
———. *The Illusion of Peace: Foreign Policy in the Nixon Years*. New York: Viking Press, 1978.
Taylor, Charles. *Snow Job: Canada, the United States and Vietnam*. Toronto: Anasi, 1974.
Taylor, Clyde, ed. *Vietnam and Black America: An Anthology of Protest and Resistance*. Garden City. N.Y.: Doubleday, Anchor, 1973.
Taylor, General Maxwell. *Swords and Plowshares*. New York: Norton, 1972.
Taylor, Telford, *Nuremberg and Vietnam: An American Tragedy*. Chicago: Quadrangle Books, 1970.
Terzani, Tiziano. *Giai Phong! The Fall and Liberation of Saigon*. New York: St. Martin's, 1976.
Time.
Times (London).

Toye, Hugh. *Laos: Buffer State or Battleground?* London: Oxford University Press, 1968.

Tuchman, Barbara W. "An Inquiry Into the Persistence of Unwisdom in Government." *Esquire*, May 1980.

United States Department of Defense. *A Pocket Guide to Vietnam.* Washington, D.C.: U.S. Government Printing Office, 1966.

United States Department of State. *Aggression From the North: The Record of North Vietnam's Campaign to Conquer South Vietnam.* Washington: U.S. Government Printing Office, 1965.

――――. *Department of State Bulletin.*

――――. *Joint Declaration by Vice President Johnson and Ngo Dinh Diem* (Department of State Bulletin). Washington, D.C.: U.S. Government Printing Office, June 19, 1961.

United States House of Representatives Committee on Governmental Operations. "U.S. AID Operation in Laos," Hearing March 11–July 1, 1959. Washington, D.C.: U.S. Government Printing Office, 1959.

United States Senate, Committee on Foreign Relations. *Background Information Relating to Southeast Asia and Vietnam.* Rev. ed. Washington, D.C.: U.S. Government Printing Office, 1969.

U.S. News and World Report.

Vietnam Veterans Against the War. *The Winter Soldier Investigation: An Inquiry into American War Crimes.* Boston: Beacon Press, 1972.

Walton, Richard. *The Remnants of Power.* New York: Coward, 1968.

Warner, Denis. *Certain Victory: How Hanoi Won the War.* Kansas City: Andrews and McMeel, 1978.

Washington Post.

Watson, Thomas J. "Issues and Answers," February 8, 1981.

West, Richard. *Sketches from Vietnam.* London: Jonathan Cape, 1968.

Westmoreland, General William. *A Soldier Reports.* Garden City, N.Y.: Doubleday, 1976.

――――. *Report on Operations in South Vietnam.* Washington, D.C.: U.S. Government Printing Office, 1968.

Whalen, Richard J. *Catch a Falling Flag.* Boston: Houghton-Mifflin, 1972.

White, Theodore, *The Making of the President 1964.* New York: Atheneum, 1965.

――――. *The Making of the President 1968.* New York: Atheneum, 1969.

――――. *The Making of the President 1972.* New York: Atheneum, 1973.

Wicker, Tom. *JFK and LBJ.* New York: Morrow, 1968.

Williams, Roger Neville. *The New Exiles: American War Resisters in Canada.* New York: Liveright, 1971.

Windchy, Eugene G. *Tonkin Gulf.* New York: Doubleday, 1971.

Wittner, Lawrence. *Cold War America: From Hiroshima to Watergate.* New York: Praeger, 1974.

Zagoria, Donald S. *Vietnam Triangle: Moscow, Peking, Hanoi.* New York: Pegasus, 1967.

Zinn, Howard. *Vietnam: The Logic of Withdrawal.* Boston: Beacon Press, 1967.

INDEX